D0623281

On Thrones of Gold

Durjudana, Sangkuni, Durna, and Burisrawa

On Thrones of Gold

Three Javanese Shadow Plays

Edited with an introduction by James R. Brandon

Harvard University Press   Cambridge, Massachusetts   1970

Distributed in Great Britain by Oxford University Press, London

Library of Congress Catalog Card Number 73-88802
SBN 674-63775-5
Printed in the United States of America

This book was produced with assistance from the Asian Literature Program of The Asia Society.

Book design by David Ford

To Ann and Jack,
whose idea this first was,
and to Wendy

Preface

Among the traditional theater arts of Asia, Indonesia's *wajang kulit* shadow theater has long been one of the most admired. For information about it the Western theater artist has turned to scholarly research by Dutch and, more recently American, ethnologists, anthropologists, archeologists, and musicologists, who wrote about wajang kulit primarily as it relates to the other arts (especially music) or as an ethnographic phenomenon through which the culture of Java or Bali might be elucidated. To date no general study has been written in English of wajang kulit as a theater art. Within this decade a number of new Javanese sources have appeared in print, especially play texts and analyses of theatrical form. The purpose of this book is to make use of these new materials and to present English versions of three plays from the standard Javanese wajang kulit repertory. The plays have been approached in a creative spirit and it is hoped the general play reader will find them enjoyable and theater artists will be stimulated to perform them on the stage.

There are well over two hundred plays in the wajang kulit repertory, and three cannot "represent" this great wealth of dramatic literature. But I have tried to select plays which dramatize different periods in the lives of wajang's Pandawa heroes and illustrate some of the wide range of wajang's subject matter, thematic content, mood, and theatrical techniques. Beyond this, they were chosen because they appealed to my dramatic imagination. *The Reincarnation of Rama* is based on the published script *Wahju Purba Sedjati* and *Irawan's Wedding* on *Irawan Rabi* (see the Bibliography for these and other texts). There is no published script for *The Death of Karna,* but the play is well known and this version follows the detailed synopsis of *Karna Tanding* which appears in *Serat Baratajuda.*

Preface

The translations show the plays as they might be performed. Except where indicated, performance notation follows Surakarta-style wajang traditions as found in *Serat Tuntunan Padalangan,* the standard textbook for Surakarta wajang. Each play is substantially complete though abbreviated in detail. The three parts of a play, names of standard scenes, and the type of narration being spoken are indicated in the left margin. The reader who wishes to concentrate on content may ignore these marginal notes; one interested in the dramaturgy of wajang kulit should find them helpful. The names of songs and of instrumental melodies and music cues appear in the text of a play as they occur. The number of musical selections in each play (about a hundred) is typical. Fighting movements and important physical movements of the puppets are briefly described in stage directions. Photographs illustrate the plays, scene-by-scene.

The translations are the result of a group effort. They were written mainly during 1965–66 by Mr. Pandam Guritno Siswoharsojo, Mr. Stephen Alkire, and myself at Michigan State University. Each play was written in three major drafts. The first was a literal translation into English. Mr. Guritno wrote a Javanese version and a first English draft of *The Death of Karna;* first draft translations of the other two plays had been prepared by friends in Indonesia the previous year. Mr. Alkire wrote a second draft of each script. This was an exploratory draft. After consulting with Mr. Guritno on the meaning of scenes, characters, and difficult or vague passages, the attempt was made to totally recast these dramatic images into the English language. Clown scenes were written and rewritten, for example, searching for comic expressions, puns, and actions that would be as funny in English as the originals were in Javanese. Two of the plays were then studied in a class on Wajang Kulit Drama, taught by Mr. Guritno and myself. As part of course work students suggested alternative ways of approaching scenes. Performance techniques were also learned, and this experience produced ideas for modifying traditional Javanese ways of describing performance techniques so they would be more understandable to a non-Javanese. Many of these ideas are incorporated in the Introduction. In May 1966, five outdoor performances of a two-hour English version of *The Death of Karna* were presented on campus by the Performing Arts Company of Michigan State University, and in July two more performances

Preface

were given. We learned much about the remarkable theatrical possibilities of this classical shadow theater form at that time. A final version of each script was written by myself, in consultation with Mr. Guritno, incorporating song lyrics, stage movement, music cues, and photographs. This draft represented a return toward the original. I describe our procedure in some detail because I believe group projects, in which the knowledge and abilities of several people are pooled, offer unusual prospects for the study of other complex Asian theater forms.

The Introduction provides information which will allow the plays to be read with greater understanding and pleasure. It is hoped the reader will come to appreciate some of the quite remarkable structural features of wajang kulit drama and some of the richness of the performing technique. At this time we still know very little about the great bulk of wajang kulit drama. Further study of more plays, especially as they are performed, would help us reach a fuller understanding of wajang kulit's meaning—as art, as entertainment, and as a manifestation of Javanese culture. Mr. Guritno generously contributed to the ideas and data found in the Introduction; for errors of fact or of interpretation I assume responsibility.

Terminology is generally that used in Surakarta, though there are exceptions. Wajang abounds in terms which are synonymous, overlapping to some extent, or vague. When a term is first introduced common synonyms are given. Current Javanese spelling is used. The letter "j" is pronounced as "y" in "yet," and "dj" as "j" in "judge."

Photographs for Figures 8, 9, 10, and 11, of puppets in my own collection, were taken by Michigan State University Information Services. I took the photograph used as frontispiece during a performance in Indonesia. All other photographs are of puppets in a palace set, owned and most graciously lent for the purpose by Prince G. P. H. Tedjakusuma, of Jogjakarta. I took the color photographs of these puppets, but the black and white ones were posed and taken by Roger Long; it is a measure of his friendship that he took the pictures five times until, after countless difficulties, they met his exacting standards. The *dalang* who appears in the photographs is Wisnoe Wardhana.

To Ibrahim Alfian, Hadian Soekarno, Achmad Wirono, Hardja Sumitra, and Edward Daniel Johannes I am deeply indebted for preliminary translations of two of the scripts as well as translations of a number of other works. It was my good fortune to have been able to consult with P. J. Zoetmulder, S. J. Poedjo Semadi, and Pak Hadisumarta, experts in wajang literature and performance. My deepest gratitude goes to Mr. Indrosoegondho, former Director of the Cultural Office, Ministry of Education, Republic of Indonesia, for his help in obtaining puppets, music, and translation materials, and for his deep personal interest in this project. My thanks to Mrs. K. R. T. Kusumubroto and Miss Elisabet Lind for their friendship and encouragement of my study of wajang during a difficult time, and to my endlessly patient dalang teacher, M. B. Radyomardowo. Professor Koen de Heer gave helpful advice on translation of some terms, and Farley Richmond was an indefatigable editorial assistant. Roger Long generously read the translations in their final versions; his comments on descriptions of puppet actions proved invaluable and many have been incorporated.

The support of several people and institutions made a group project of this kind possible. I am greatly indebted to my colleagues at Michigan State University, Professors John Dietrich, William Ross, and Jack Bain, who encouraged my research in Indonesia in 1963–64 out of which this project grew. Mrs. Bonnie R. Crown, Director of the Asian Literature Program, The Asia Society, has been a constant friend and a sympathetic supporter of the work for five years. A subsidy from The Asia Society made possible the inclusion of color illustrations; grant funds for the collection of materials, translation, research, and preparation of the manuscript during 1965–66 and for further research in Indonesia in the summer of 1967 were provided by The JDR 3rd Fund and Michigan State University–International Programs/Ford Foundation. For their generous assistance I am most grateful.

J. R. B

Honolulu, Hawaii
1969

Contents

Illustrations

Illustrations

Illustrations

Illustrations

On Thrones of Gold

Introduction

On festival nights, especially during the dry monsoon, *wajang kulit* is performed in hundreds of cities and villages in Java. From area to area, from performance to performance, one or another aspect of this complex art form is emphasized, but wherever seen its basic pattern is the same. A *dalang*, or puppeteer, relates a familiar story from the island's mythological past while manipulating flat leather puppets. In the flickering light of a lamp, kings on thrones of gold and jewels, court ladies, generals, scheming advisers, gods, and ogres cast against a white screen shadows that tremble with life. Forty, fifty, sixty stylized figures move through scene after scene of a play which seems episodic but actually is highly structured. With only the help of his accompanying *gamelan* musicians and female singers the dalang performs the entire play. He speaks the dialogue of the characters. He narrates sections of exposition and description. He directs and cues the gamelan ensemble. He sings transitional mood songs. He extemporizes intricate battles. Sometimes following tradition, sometimes setting new precedents, he weaves for his audience a theatrical fabric of great variety and richness for eight to nine hours, without pause or intermission, from early evening, through the night, until dawn of the following morning.

This is wajang kulit as it is performed today. Though a "shadow play," it is one of the world's most complex and refined dramatic and theatrical forms, having developed through an unbroken succession of artists, generation by generation, for more than a thousand years. Its classic dramatic repertory of more than two hundred plays constitutes the fullest artistic expression we possess of traditional Javanese culture. In the mid-twentieth century wajang kulit is performed by perhaps five-thousand dalang, making it not only Java's most revered performing art but its most popular one as well.

[1]

On Thrones of Gold

In Javanese, the word *wajang* means "shadow" and *kulit,* "leather." The literal meaning of wajang kulit is "shadow-made-by-leather," that is, shadows made by puppets cut out of leather, and hence a theatrical performance by shadow puppets.* By extension it also has come to mean not only the technique of shadow-play performance but the plays themselves. For at least ten centuries, the most popular and the most important shadow plays have been those in four related cycles, known collectively as *wajang purwa,* or "original" wajang plays.† The *purwa* plays dramatize episodes in the lives of Java's oldest mythological figures, most especially the heroes of the final cycle—the five Pandawa brothers. Other play cycles have been performed in the past as shadow drama, and other theatrical media may be used to present purwa plays in Indonesia (most notably doll-puppets and live actor-dancers); but no other combination of performance technique with play cycle has even remotely challenged the supreme position of the original combination of shadow-play technique with purwa stories. When Javanese refer to "wajang kulit" today, this combination is almost always meant, and in such a sense I use wajang kulit here.

The existence of shadow puppets in Java is first hinted at in two royal charters, establishing freeholds, inscribed on copper plates. The first, dated 840, mentions the names of six kinds of officials who were performers or who supervised musicians, clowns, and possibly wajang performers (the precise meaning of the terms cannot be determined, unfortunately).‡ The second, from 907, describes dances, epic recitations, and *mawajang,* a performance which may have been a shadow play. Wajang is mentioned several times in the copious and elegant court literature written between the eleventh and fifteenth centuries

---

* Some scholars hold the puppets are of greater significance than the shadows produced by them. Mellema flatly says, "Wayang is not a shadow play" (*Wayang Puppets* [Amsterdam, 1954], p. 5). From its beginnings, however, the art of wajang kulit has been characterized by the combination of lamp, puppet, screen, and resulting shadow, and the English term which best describes this is "shadow play."

† Purwa may be related to Sanskrit *parva,* the chapters or books into which Indian and Javanese epics are divided (Moebirman, *Wayang Purwa* [The Hague, 1960], p. 21).

‡ For the source of these and other references, and of quotations see A Note On Sources at the back of this book.

Introduction

at various kingdoms in east Java. A famous reference appears in The Meditation of Ardjuna (*Ardjuna Wiwaha*), composed by a court poet of King Airlangga (1035–1049): "There are people who weep, are sad and aroused watching the puppets, though they know they are merely carved pieces of leather manipulated and made to speak. These people are like men who, thirsting for sensuous pleasures, live in a world of illusion; they do not realize the magic hallucinations they see are not real." In 1157 the court poet Mpu Sedah wrote in the Great War (*Bratajuda*): "The booming of frogs in the river sounds like xylophones [*saron*] accompanying the wajang play. When wind blows over empty bamboo cylinders it is like flutes playing for the performance." The fifteenth-century Treatise on Poetic Composition (*Wrtta Sancaja*) contains the poetic comparison that "trees against the clouds in the sky give the impression of being like wajang figures passing before the white playing screen." The fact that poets chose wajang shadows as poetic metaphor and that audiences were deeply moved by performances points to an art of considerable sophistication. Clearly, wajang kulit was a well-established form of theatrical expression at the courts of east Javanese princes as early as one thousand years ago, suggesting that shadow theater must have been known in Java many hundreds of years before this.

Hazeu suggests that shadow theater in Java grew out of native animistic ancestor worship, in which the souls of ancestors were brought to life as shadows in order to gain from them advice and magical assistance. He believes that Javanese in prehistoric times carved puppet figures depicting the ancestors of their chiefs and used them to enact stories of the tribe's mythological origin. Rassers thinks it probable that knowledge of some form of Indian shadow play impelled the Javanese to develop the indigenous ancestor worship rituals described by Hazeu into the high art which wajang kulit eventually became.

The Indian origin of wajang theory has been widely debated, with inconclusive results. The main reason for believing that Indian theater influenced Javanese theater is that the Javanese borrowed and assimilated so many other Indian cultural elements in the centuries following the birth of Christ. Most wajang characters originated in Indian epics, and the *vidusaka* clown figure of Indian Sanskrit drama is similar to the wajang clown Semar. Yet, as far as we know, Indian Sanskrit drama has never been known in Java. (In the scores of old Hindu-Javanese writings there is no scrap of translation of an Indian play or of any Indian dramatic treatise.) India may have had a shadow theater in ancient times, but none is described in the famous *Natya Sastra;* the usual Sanskrit term for shadow play, *chaya nataka,* does not occur in this or any other Indian dramaturgical work. The word *rupparupakam,* which appears in an Indian Buddhist text of around the first century b.c., and *rupopajivana,* from the twelfth book of the *Mahabharata* epic, are believed by Pischel to refer to shadow plays, but the words are only used in passing and it is impossible to be sure of their meaning. Not until a full century after the first reference to wajang in Java is positive evidence of a shadow theater found in India. Show-men of leather puppets (*camma rupa*) are described as being employed as spies in Ceylon in the twelfth century. In 1243 a full-fledged shadow drama, Angada the Envoy (*Dutangada*), was written and performed in Gujarat. And the seventeenth-century commentator Nilikhanta tells that in southern India leather puppets enact stories of kings and ministers before a cloth screen. Hazeu notes that all technical terms for wajang kulit equipment and performance techniques, save one (*tjem-pala*) are ancient Javanese and not derived from an Indian language—which would seem improbable if shadow theater had been brought from India.

A further possibility is that a rudimentary shadow play was known to prehistoric peoples in central Asia and that it spread from there—before the Christian era and over a period of thousands of years—into India, China, and Southeast Asia, accounting for the existence of shadow theater in these areas. Because of the lack of evidence it is unlikely that we will ever know with certainty the genesis of the shadow play in any part of Asia. What is clear is that, whatever its origin, wajang kulit in its maturity represents a unique Javanese form of artistic expression.

By the time the first written accounts of wajang kulit appear, around the eleventh century in the east Javanese courts, the basic technique of one man telling a story while manipulating puppets before a screen has been set. There is every reason to think dalang were performing wajang kulit both at court and in villages and that there was regular interchange between court

Introduction

and folk performers. We do not know just what the puppets looked like, but they may not have had movable arms. One indication of an emerging puppet style comes from reliefs carved on the fourteenth-century temple at Panataran in east Java. Figures stand in profile position and wear curling head-dress; these distinctive features of today's wajang kulit shadow puppets are not found on any earlier temple carvings. Presumably the reliefs reflect a developing "wajang style" of representing mythological figures.

Two other forms of theater, *wajang beber* and *wajang topeng*, competed for court favor at the successive east Javanese kingdoms of Mataram-Kediri (929–1222), Singosari (1222–1292), and Madjapahit (1293–ca. 1520). Like wajang kulit, both probably originated in prehistoric times. In wajang beber, or "paper-scroll play," scrolls illustrating the story are unrolled as the dalang narrates the play. One of the simplest forms of theater known (an indication of its antiquity), it seems to have been closely connected with animistic rites of ancestor worship and at one time may have been more important religiously than wajang kulit. Wajang topeng, or "masked dance-play," probably grew out of indigenous dance. Masked dances are still found in many isolated areas of Indonesia, and masks have long been noted as a common artistic property of peoples throughout the Pacific area. Performing masked plays was very popular at east Javanese courts, but when political power shifted to central Java, several centuries later, wajang topeng lost its previous strong court support and became less important. Wajang beber, too, gradually lost out to an increasingly sophisticated shadow play form. For example, traditional accounts say that in 1630 the King of Mataram, in central Java, ruled that wajang beber might no longer be used as a medium of performance for the magically powerful play The Birth of Kala (*Murwakala* or *Purwakala*). Monopoly rights to its performance passed to wajang kulit.

For perhaps a thousand years prior to this, Indian political systems, religion, literature, and arts became known and, to varying degree, were borrowed and assimilated into Javanese culture. In wajang kulit, as in virtually every Javanese performing art of the period, new plays were composed, drawing on figures and events from Javanese epics, which in turn were based, at least in part, on borrowed Indian sources—most importantly the *Ramayana* and the *Mahabharata*. Three of wajang kulit's four play cycles grew up around borrowed characters: the Ardjuna Sasra Bau cycle, the Rama cycle, and the Pandawa cycle. Although some of the plays of these cycles directly put on stage incidents taken from Javanese epics, the bulk of wajang drama cannot be considered "dramatizations of the epics." Reliefs of the bathing-place at Djalatunda, built in east Java in 977, depict events in the lives of the last nine or ten generations of the Pandawas; studying them, Bosch has concluded that the sculptor was following neither Indian nor Javanese epics, but wajang dramatic episodes. If his analysis is correct, the special wajang world that was to crystalize in later centuries, distinct from the epics and Javanese mythology, was beginning to be formed in the plays of this period.

Traditional Javanese accounts claim that numerous changes took place in wajang kulit during the sixteenth century as a result of the conversion of Java to Islam. As these accounts were written several hundred years after the events they purport to describe, their accuracy is open to question. According to them, the present-day highly stylized shape of wajang kulit puppets dates from the sixteenth century. The Moslem Sunan of Giri is supposed to have ordered a nonrealistic puppet set made in order to circumvent the Islamic proscription against the portrayal of the human form in art, a proscription which for a time had led to the Islamic authorities' banning of wajang kulit. The same Sunan of Giri is said to have determined the order in which puppet figures are set up on either side of the screen prior to performance and to have added more figures, especially animals. He is also credited with creating, in 1553, a new form of shadow play, *wajang gedog,* to enact stories about Java's legendary Prince Pandji. Supposedly, in 1555, designs were first incised in the previously solid shape of the leather puppets, and eyes, ears, mouth, and other facial features were cut out to make the shadow more detailed and pleasing. And in 1584 the Sunan of Kudus is supposed to have created *wajang golek,* three-dimensional "doll-puppet wajang," to perform plays of the Menak cycle about the great Islamic hero Amir Hamzah.*

---

* *Wajang Menak* (or *wajang tengul*), in which the cycle is enacted by leather shadow puppets, is a minor, later creation.

Introduction

These accounts of early Islamic leaders personally guiding the development of wajang may or may not be historically valid. Yet it is notable that nowhere do they describe Islamic stories or characters supplanting or even entering the traditional purwa repertory. Some changes in puppet configurations may be due to Islamic influence, and the new Islamic Menak play cycle was created to capitalize on wajang kulit's popularity, but if the intention of Java's new religious leaders was to reform wajang kulit into a Moslem art form, as it is commonly held, this intention was not realized. Menak plays never remotely challenged the appeal of purwa plays with the popular audience and the essentially Hindu-Javanese nature of wajang kulit drama was too firmly set by this time to be penetrated, except occasionally, by Islamic thought.

Two highly significant developments in wajang kulit are traditionally ascribed to the following century. Puppet arms are said to have been made movable in 1630 at the central Javanese court of Mataram. In the wake of this startling innovation must have come a virtual revolution in the art of puppet manipulation, particularly in the many fighting movements. That same year a new ogre (*raseksa*) puppet, nicknamed Tjakil, or "Fang," because of his grotesquely protruding tusks, is said to have been created; and, some years later, companion ogres named Terong, Pragalba, and Galijuk. Tjakil and his cohorts introduced a new group of antagonists into wajang drama and several important new scenes came into being around them. The "classic" or textbook wajang dramatic structure, considered typical and learned by student dalang as the model for performance, apparently dates from this time, for in the classic play Tjakil and his companions play fixed vital roles.

During the eighteenth century the kingdom of Mataram was divided into four smaller states in Surakarta and Jogjakarta. For the next two centuries, until World War II, the rulers of the Principalities, as the states were collectively called, lavished patronage on wajang kulit and other arts. Major changes in wajang kulit are not recorded, but the art was polished and refined into a unique Javanese form of cultural expression. The plays' view of life is one in which local and borrowed elements have been fused: the great heroes like Ardjuna are Javanese-born; places such as the Kurusetra battlefield in the Great War and even the home of the gods, Mahameru, are placed in Java; the first four scenes of a play reveal the precise layout of a nineteenth-century Javanese *keraton,* or palace; and so on. Superb puppet sets were carved with exquisite attention to detail and were lavishly covered with pure gold leaf. Thirty to forty beautiful keraton puppet sets, made for rulers of the Principalities, are still in existence in the palaces of Surakarta and Jogjakarta. Some minor performance innovations were: the use of metal plates to mark time during battles, apparently introduced about a hundred years ago; soldiers dressed in European uniforms and using rifles and cannon carved on the Marching Army puppet (*ampjak*) as a result of contact with the Dutch; and the substitution of electric lights or gas-pressure lamps for oil lamps.

Though the Principalities bordered each other and the ruling families were closely related, with the passage of years dalang at the courts of Surakarta and Jogjakarta developed somewhat different styles of wajang performance. Jogjakarta-style wajang is considered more vigorous, direct, and simple; Surakarta-style wajang more delicate, refined, and complex in structure. Jogjakarta wajang is considered the more orthodox, the more conservative; there is more innovation, more interest in keeping up-to-date in Surakarta style. Jogjakarta battles are livelier and contain more kinds of puppet movements; Surakarta music is richer in nuance and broader in range, with more melodies to choose from. The proportions of Surakarta puppets are smaller than those of Jogjakarta. The types of scenes performed differ. Differences between the two styles are not great, but the usual wajang devotee is passionately fond of one and disdainful of the other because of them.

Several other forms of wajang play evolved from wajang kulit at the Principalities. Wajang kulit's purwa plays were taken over by court dancers and performed in classic dance style. The resulting dance-drama, *wajang orang* (or *wajang wong*), literally, "human wajang," became extremely popular at court. In the late nineteenth century professional troupes were formed; today some thirty troupes perform wajang orang in commercial theaters. The Surakarta court poet Ranggawarsita wrote *Pustaka Radja Madya,* a genealogy of Javanese kings said to be the descendants of the Pandawas, thus linking the Pan-

Introduction

dawa cycle and the later Pandji cycle of plays. The lives of these kings were dramatized and performed by leather shadow puppets and called *wajang madya,* literally "middle wajang," referring to the middle position of the stories. Another set of shadow puppets was created to play incidents from the Java War of 1825–1830, with Prince Diponegoro as their hero, in a form called *wajang Djawa.* At least another half-dozen cycles of plays were created, with sets of puppet figures carved to perform them. The plays are no longer performed, however; and most of the puppet sets reside, dustily, in museums.

Two new forms of shadow play have been created within recent years. In 1947 *wajang suluh* ("torch" or "information" wajang) was created by Indonesian guerrillas during their war of independence. Puppets depicting contemporary figures— soldiers, politicians, peasants—carved and painted realistically, acted out stories about the struggle against the Dutch. Wajang suluh was crude as an art and after the war it was rarely performed. *Wajang Pantja Sila,* "Five Principles wajang," was an attempt to modernize traditional wajang kulit content while maintaining its outward artistic form. In it the five Pandawa brothers appear virtually unchanged in appearance but are given the symbolic interpretation of being the five Pantja Sila principles: Belief in God, Nationalism, Humanity, Sovereignity of the People (or Democracy), and Social Justice. In these and in the other earlier spin-off wajang forms performance techniques and the basic dramatic structure of wajang kulit plays were taken over almost intact.

When Javanese migrated to areas outside their island they carried wajang kulit with them. It may be that as far back as the ninth century, King Djajavarman II, raised at a Javanese court, took wajang kulit along when he moved with a Javanese retinue to what is now Cambodia and established the Khmer dynasty in the vicinity of Angkor, and that the great, nonjointed *nang sebek* puppets of Cambodia are descendants of wajang kulit puppets of that time, which had not as yet acquired movable arms.* Wajang kulit became known in Bali, just when is not

---

* Sheppard suggests that Cambodian *nang sebek* shadow puppets were borrowed directly from shadow puppets of the Andhra region of India (Dato Haji Mubin Sheppard, "The Khmer Shadow Play and its Links with Ancient India," *Journal of the Malaysian Branch Royal Asiatic Society,* 41:199–204 [part 1, 1968]).

known, but peak periods of Javanese cultural influence there were the eleventh and the fifteenth centuries.* The simpler, less stylized shapes of Balinese puppets are believed to reflect the style of Javanese puppets four or five centuries ago. Wajang kulit also was taken to the Malay Peninsula by Javanese merchants and settlers. Plays were translated and adapted into Malay, and the shadow play became, as in Java, the classic theater form. And, finally, wajang kulit's repertory of purwa plays was adapted into the wajang golek doll-puppet medium to become the most important type of theater in Sundanese-speaking west Java.

THE PLAYS

CYCLES

The several hundred plays, or *lakon,* of wajang kulit can be divided into four cycles, each revolving around a different group of characters. Taken together, these cycles comprise the purwa dramatic repertory. The Dutch scholar Kats compiled from Javanese court records a comprehensive list of purwa lakon. In his list of 179 standard plays, 7 belong to the first, or animistic cycle, of prehistoric legend. Of these, 3 concern attacks on the dwelling of the gods by giants; 3 describe the origins of plants, and feature the local animistic Goddess of Rice, Dewi Sri; and 1 is The Birth of Kala, performed as an exorcism ritual in a special performance called *ruwatan.* The action of the last-named play shows the god Guru (Siwah) and his fellow gods descending to earth where they perform gamelan music and the wajang shadow play in order to exorcise, through a particular prayer spoken during performance, the bloodthirsty god Kala and thereby prevent magically vulnerable children from being eaten by him. Although Kala and some of the other gods are borrowed from the Hindu pantheon, the ruwatan ceremony, which is the heart of the play and the purpose even today for giving a performance, is a local animistic ritual.

---

* Shadow plays may have been indigenous to Bali, as well as to Java, in pre-historic times. In any case, Javanese-style puppets and wajang stories later were taken to Bali.

Introduction: The Plays

The second cycle of plays, the Ardjuna Sasra Bau cycle, consists of 5 lakon which show: the conquests of Dasamuka (King
Rawana in a former life); Ardjuna Sasra Bau's meditation to
achieve magical power; accession to kingship by Ardjuna Sasra
Bau; the slaying of Dasamuka; and Ardjuna Sasra Bau's death.
The third cycle, of 18 plays, the Rama cycle, chronicles: the birth
of Sinta and her marriage to Rama (4); Rama's banishment to
the forest and Sinta's kidnaping by Rawana (2); Rama's grief
and his meeting with the monkey warriors Anoman and
Sugriwa (2); and the many battles through which Rama and his
allies conquer Rawana's kingdom of Alengka (Ceylon), slay
Rawana, and rescue Sinta (10). Most of the plays in the Ardjuna
Sasra Bau and Rama cycles are based on events in the *Ramayana*
epic. The three cycles account for 30 lakon; the remaining five-
sixths listed by Kats—almost 150—belong to the final cycle, the
Pandawa cycle. Not only are Pandawa plays more numerous,
they are preferred in performance over any others, and the
major developments in dramaturgy and performance techniques have taken place within them. They form the core of
wajang kulit's dramatic repertory.*

The Pandawa cycle covers a span of twelve generations,
beginning with the god Wisnu, the Pandawas' ancestor, and
ending with Parikesit, who supposedly was the father of the
first "historic" king of Java, Jadajana. It focuses on the generation of the sons of Pandu, or Pandawas, from whom the cycle
takes its name: Judistira, Bima, Ardjuna, Nakula, and Sadewa.
The opponents of the Pandawas, in the epics and in Javanese
mythology, are their cousins, the ninety-nine Kurawa brothers,
the most important of whom are Durjudana, the eldest, and
Dursasana, Kartamarma, Durgandasena, Tjitraksa, and Tjitraksi. The nuclear story of the generation of the Pandawas tells
how the young Pandawas and Kurawas are raised together at
the court of Astina and how the Pandawas always emerge
victorious in their many competitions; how Durjudana attempts

* Although interest in the Rama cycle seems to have increased recently in Java,
the Pandawa cycle has always been far and away more important. To cite two
examples from the early nineteenth century: puppets of Rama and Leksmana
came to be patterned after those of Kresna and Ardjuna (see illustrations of
these figures in B. R. O'G. Anderson, *Mythology and the Tolerance of the Javanese*
[Ithaca, N.Y., 1965], pp. 13, 14, 66) in 1803, and in the same year the god-clown-
servants of the Pandawa cycle joined the cast of the Rama cycle (L. Serrurier,
De wajang poerwa [Leiden, 1896], pp. 48–70).

to burn the Pandawas to death in a house of lac, but fails; how the Pandawas wander in the forest until they receive the protection of Matswapati, King of Wirata; how the Pandawas build in the midst of the forest the splendid Kingdom of Amarta; how Durjudana, jealous of the Pandawas' glory, wins the Kingdom of Amarta from Judistira in a dice game and with it all the Pandawas' possessions, including their freedom; how the Pandawas are exiled for twelve years and in the thirteenth return once more to the protection of King Matswapati of Wirata; how the Pandawas' adviser Kresna attempts to negotiate with the Kurawas return of at least part of Astina as agreed upon at the time of the Pandawas' exile, and how he fails; how the Great War ensues and in it the sons of the Pandawas are slain as well as all the Kurawas, including Durjudana; how Judistira assumes rule over Astina and, after a period of years, passes the kingship of Astina on to Ardjuna's grandson, Parikesit.

This nuclear story of the Pandawas' conflict with their Kurawa cousins, however, is *not* the main concern of wajang drama. Only 32 of the 149 Pandawa cycle plays on Kats's list dramatize these events,* while 94 lakon, about two-thirds of the Pandawa cycle, are set during the brief period the Pandawas ruled the Kingdom of Amarta, which in the epics is but an interlude and given scant attention.

Where did all these lakon come from? Most were invented by dalang; their stories are original to wajang kulit. The picture they paint of the Amarta period is a glorious one. It was the Golden Age of the Pandawas, a time of youthful self-confidence, when they lived exuberantly, reveling in excitement and in adventure. From the wilderness the Pandawas had created in Amarta a kingdom surpassing all others in splendor and greatness. Favored of the gods, they were invincible in everything undertaken. They lived, Kats says, "a life of power and recklessness, giving rise to ceaseless battle with ogres who threatened man and the gods, and to an almost unbroken succession of

---

* Seven dramatize the time of the Pandawas' youth and their wandering in the forest before the Amarta period; 13 the loss of Amarta by dice, their exile, and preparations for the Great War; and the final 12 plays the terrible slaughter of the Great War and the brief period of Pandawa rule of the Kingdom of Astina which follows. The remaining 23 plays listed by Kats dramatize the births and marriages of the nine generations of the Pandawas' ancestors: Wisnu, Sri Unon, Parikenan, Manumajasa, Sakutrem, Sakri, Palasara, Abijasa, and Pandu. (See J. Kats, *Het Javaansche tooneel* [Weltevreden, 1923], chart following p. 446.)

Introduction: The Plays

bridal abductions and bridal contests, through which the most beautiful princesses and daughters of holy seers were brought into the royal palaces of the Pandawas." The loss of the kingdom, their fall from power, and the terrible war in which so many would be slain lay in the future. But for a few brief years the world was dazzled by their grace and their power.

The plays themselves are lofty in sentiment, aristocratic in mien. They abound in romantic episodes, royal audience scenes, fearful battles, and philosophic and mystical observations. Their mythological heroes, ancestors of the Javanese and demigods themselves, commune with the highest gods. Chief figure is Ardjuna, third Pandawa brother, refined and modest, yet a supernaturally endowed warrior of such exquisite physical beauty that he has served as the model of *alus*—refined— behavior to the Javanese for centuries. The beau ideal of wajang, Ardjuna, with his almost equally attractive sons, Abimanju and Irawan, are central figures in more than 40 lakon set in the Amarta period. He is alluded to as the bridegroom of "100,000-minus-one" brides, and the plays recount many of his marriages, the marriages of his sons, and other romantic adventures of these ravishingly handsome heroes. Bima, the second Pandawa brother, as crudely powerful and blunt as Ardjuna is delicate and controlled, and his favorite son, Gatutkatja, are major figures in 10 plays set in Amarta. Five are about the fourth and fifth Pandawa brothers, Nakula and Sadewa. Another 4 concern the very special adventures of the *punakawan,* the Pandawas' god-clown-servants, Semar and his two sons, Gareng and Petruk. Semar, actually the god Ismaja, cursed and transformed into a misshapen dwarf, saves the kingdom of the gods from the fury of the goddess Durga in one play; in others, he and his sons become for a time kings.

While some Amarta lakon were adapted from plays set in earlier or later periods, most were new plays with invented plots. Kats's list contains only those recognized by court officials as standard works; unquestionably more invented plays existed which he did not record. New plays are being composed constantly. There is no way of knowing how many invented plays there are in the repertory now, but certainly there are more than Kats's list suggests.

The Javanese make a clear distinction between lakon based on epic or other court literature and those which were created by dalang. The former are called, fittingly, *pokok,* or "trunk" lakon,* the latter *tjarangan,* or "branch" lakon.† In this collection, *The Death of Karna,* one of the last plays in the group about the Great War, is a trunk lakon for it uses as dramatic material events which comprise a whole chapter in the epic. *Irawan's Wedding* and *The Reincarnation of Rama* are branch lakon. The former owes only the basic idea of its plot to the epic. *The Reincarnation of Rama* is totally invented, not even hinted at in the epic. It is not surprising that the true essence of wajang lies in the invented tjarangan plays. The very special world of wajang, centering on the glorious and adventurous period of Amarta, was created in them. And from them the "classic" form of wajang play, with its conventionalized structure and highly systematized techniques of performance, gradually evolved.‡

TYPES

Wajang kulit is performed when some group or person hires a dalang to celebrate a specific occasion. It is not performed as a commercial entertainment in theater buildings, nor is the audience charged admission (except for special performances, such as those sponsored by Radio Republic Indonesia). The host normally requests a specific lakon, one suited to the occasion. He may even compose a play scenario himself.

Historically, wajang kulit has always been performed this way; as a consequence, play types are linked to definite performance occasions. Following rice harvest a village may sponsor an animistic "village cleansing" (*bersih desa*) performance as part of a purification ceremony of the village and its inhabitants. A play of the animistic cycle, such as *Sri Mantuk,* in which Dewi Sri, Goddess of Rice, brings rich harvests to mankind would be suitable. The animistic ruwatan ceremony to

* Also *lakon dapur, lakon djedjer, lakon ladjer,* or *lakon lugu.* The word pokok also can be used in the sense of "standard" to identify any play, regardless of its origin, which has become a part of the standard repertory. Used this way, the three plays in this book—and most on Kats's list—would be called pokok, a meaning not intended here.

† A wholly invented play also may be called *lakon sempalan* (Kats, p. 86), but Hazeu suggests this is not usual (*Bijdrage tot de kennis van het Javaansche tooneel* [Leiden, 1897], pp. 123–124).

‡ Kats noted the significance of the Amarta period plays almost half a century ago. Yet wajang drama continues to be described, with embarrassing regularity, as "taken from the Hindu epics" or "derived from the . . . epics" or "drawn from the *Mahabarata*" by almost all writers on wajang.

Introduction: The Plays

exorcise the dread Kala requires a special, and magically sacred, wajang performance: only one play, The Birth of Kala of the animistic cycle, may be performed, and it takes place during the day with screen and lamp, although a shadow cannot be seen in the daytime. Only an old, experienced, and spiritually pure dalang is considered capable of carrying out the ritual act of performance.

Celebrations of birth are held in Java during the seventh month of pregnancy (*tingkeb*), and when the infant's navel cord drops away (*pupak-puser*). There is a birth play for each major wajang figure and it is considered highly auspicious to have performed, on either of the two occasions, the birth play of the figure whom the family hopes the infant will grow up to emulate: The Birth of Ardjuna (*Ardjuna Lahir*) if they wish a refined son; The Birth of Bima (*Bima Bungkus*) for a strong, masculine son; The Birth of Sumbadra (*Lahirpun Lara Ireng*) for a modest, beautiful daughter; and so on. Lakon featuring the abduction of brides or bridal contests are appropriate to celebrate a boy's introduction to manhood as part of his rites of circumcision. A number of them are set during the Amarta period. They are lively and good-humored, with plots of complicated intrigue. But weddings are perhaps the most popular of all occasions for wajang performance. Major wajang figures have several wives, hence there are numerous wedding lakon to choose from (Kats lists 41). Like plays for circumcision, they are light and good-natured. Pokok wedding plays often begin with a marriage and end with the birth of a child, stressing the continuation of generations. But in most tjarangan wedding plays set in Amarta, scenes showing the lovers' courtship and obstacles to the marriage—such as the kidnaping of the intended bride by an ogre—lead to a marriage, or promise of marriage, at the play's conclusion. *Irawan's Wedding* is both a marriage play and an abduction play.

The two remaining major types of lakon are serious in tone. One depicts a hero receiving a gift or boon (*wahju*) from the gods. Such a play is ideally suited for a "vow" or "thanksgiving" (*kaul*) performance, in which a sponsor, whose requested favor the gods have granted, fullfils his vow to present an offering to them in the form of a play performance. *The Reincarnation of Rama* is one of the most famous of these plays. The plot may hinge on a contest over who will receive the gods' favor; in the end the hero most noble, most dedicated to meditation, is favored. The gift or boon often is some form of supernatural knowledge or power; scenes may contain considerable philosophic discussion; and the gods normally appear, imparting to the plays a strongly religious character.

The final play type concerns affairs of state. The fate of a kingdom is decided or the death of some great wajang figure occurs. Many are pokok plays, handling Pandawa-Kurawa conflicts taken directly from the epics. Their tone is somber; they contain numerous battle scenes, often of great pathos. *The Death of Karna,* from the Great War which concludes the Pandawa cycle, is a major play of this type. Normally a private person would not sponsor a performance, except perhaps to honor the anniversary of the death of an important member of the family. A more likely host would be a noble of the palace, an organization, or a village.

WAJANG KULIT'S MEANING

The plays of wajang kulit and later cycles of shadow plays can be viewed as linked series, dramatizing the legitimate descent of Javanese kingship from the earliest gods, through some sixty generations of Javanese kings, down to rulers of the twentieth century. The three last purwa cycles are linked by successive reincarnations of the god Wisnu—from Ardjuna Sasra Bau to Rama, and from Rama to Kresna and Ardjuna. In *The Reincarnation of Rama* the god Guru explicitly commands the incarnation of Wisnu's Authority and Truth to Kresna and Ardjuna, thus passing on to the Pandawas the rights of kingship previously held by Rama and Leksmana (an idea not found in the Indian epics). In the Pandawa cycle, twelve generations of Java's rulers are shown to descend directly from Wisnu, including the generation of the Pandawas, ending with Parikesit, the son of Abimanju and grandson of Ardjuna, who inherits the kingship of Astina from Judistira after the Great War. The Pandawa cycle, in turn, is linked to later historical periods by other play cycles, beginning with wajang madya, in which Jadajana is the descendent of Parikesit and hence the legitimate successor of the Pandawas' divine rights of Javanese kingship. Table 1 gives a condensed version of this genealogy and some of the play cycles. Of course, the later cycles of lakon are rarely, if ever, performed, and among performances of purwa lakon

Table 1. Javanese dynastic genealogy and wajang play cycles.

WAJANG FORM	DRAMATIC CYCLE	WAJANG HERO	HISTORIC PERIOD
WAJANG KULIT (or wajang purwa)	Animistic Ardjuna Sasra Bau Rama	Dewi Sri, etc. Ardjuna Sasra Bau Rama (six generations) ｜ Palasara ｜ Abijasa ｜ Pandu ｜ ARDJUNA and brothers ｜ Abimanju ｜ Parikesit	Ancient mythology
	PANDAWA		
wajang madya	Djajabaja	｜ Jadajana ｜ (one generation) ｜ Djajabaja ｜ (ten generations) ｜ Lembuamiluhur	Legendary Javanese kings
wajang gedog	Pandji	｜ Pandji ｜ (eleven generations)	Kediri-Singosari (c.1000–1293)
wajang klitik	Damarwulan	｜ Damarwulan (Brawidjaja) ｜ (four generations)	Madjapahit (c. 1293–1520)
wajang dupara	Surakarta history	｜ Pamanahan ｜ (eleven generations)	Mataram (c. 1550)
wajang Djawa	Diponegoro	｜ Diponegoro ｜ (three generations)	Java War (1825–1830)
wajang wahana	——	｜ Pakubuwana X	Dutch rule (c. 1920)

CAPITAL LETTERS indicate most important wajang form, dramatic cycle, and wajang hero.

｜ Lines connecting heroes indicate direct descendent; intervening generations are also directly descended.

only a small minority directly dramatize the succession of kings within this theoretical genealogy. Still, it can be argued that the concept of legitimate kingship has had considerable bearing on the creation of wajang kulit and later derivative shadow theater forms.

In another view, the historical process whereby local Javanese gods were demoted to lesser status by new Hindu-derived gods can be seen in certain character relationships. Semar, the clown-servant of the Pandawas, was originally Ismaja, the most powerful native Javanese god. But with the arrival of Hinduism, the god Guru (Siwah) comes to reign in Suralaja as the highest of the manifested wajang gods. Ismaja is cursed, transformed into a ludicrous dwarf, and sent to earth as servant to the heroes. Yet, though a servant, his status as a god of supernatural powers is acknowledged by the Pandawas.

On a mystic level, the screen in wajang kulit may be said to symbolize heaven; the banana-log stage, earth; the puppets, man; and the dalang, god, who through his knowledge and spiritual power brings man to life. A lakon can be interpreted as a three-part parable of the life-cycle, showing man in his youth, when he acts immaturely and irresponsibly; in middle age, attempting to find the right path of conduct as he meets and conquers external evils (represented by killing Tjakil and his ogre companions); and in old age, having defeated his enemies and achieved inner spiritual harmony.

In another view, the puppets are not enacting a drama of Pandawa versus Kurawa at all. They and their actions are merely the external, symbolic representation of the conflict which takes place within every man's spirit, with the puppets standing for different aspects of a single personality: Judistira is selflessness; Ardjuna, introspection; Bima, pure will; and so on. Mysticism is important in Javanese religious experience, and the number of mystical interpretations one can make of plays, characters, and actions is countless.

Wajang kulit drama presents no easily described ethical world view. The simplest and most common interpretation is that the plays enact a conflict between good and evil. A good many aspects of wajang support this: puppets are called wajang of the left (*wajang kiwa*) and wajang of the right (*wajang tengen*); the Pandawas are of the right and the Kurawas are of the left; and, in all except a few unusual plays, the Pandawas are shown

Introduction: The Plays

defeating their opponents. By and large, the Pandawas are pictured as more righteous, more spiritual, more refined than their opponents, and in the final convulsive conflict of the Great War they destroy their Kurawa cousins utterly. The Kurawas are pictured as motivated by greed, lust, chicanery.

At the same time, it is also apparent that the ethical cleavage between Pandawas and Kurawas is not absolute but contains many ambiguities. For example, most important wajang figures of the two camps have both good and bad traits. Kresna, a god, assists the Pandawas, yet he lies and tricks the Kurawas constantly. Ardjuna, "shining warrior" and perhaps the most admired wajang figure, is fickle and lacking in human sympathy. Bima is half ogre; overbearing in his self-pride, he refuses to speak, even to the gods, in respectful Javanese. Karna, overproud, is still the noble son of the god Surja; he is slain by Ardjuna only because his own father-in-law, Salja, betrays him in the Great War. Durjudana, the Pandawas' chief opponent, is a generous ruler, his chief fault being that he cannot refuse the basely motivated requests of his younger brothers. The ethical ambivalence of his nature is sharply evident in his name: he may be addressed either as Durjudana—*dur* meaning "evil" —or Sujudana—*su* meaning "good." And when the Kurawas are killed in the great War the mood is somber and fearful, for great figures, though flawed, have fallen.

We are probably closer to the truth if we think of the Pandawas only as the "better" and the Kurawas as the "less good" sides of the conflict. The Pandawas and Kurawas are cousins, the offspring of brothers. Because both are Javanese and descended from the gods, even the lesser of the two groups —the Kurawas— cannot properly represent pure evil.* If there is a purely "bad" side in wajang it is the ogres, non-Javanese who reside "overseas" in foreign lands and who embody every trait detestable in Javanese eyes. Their coarse bodies bulge obscenely, they are smelly and bad-mannered, they shout and

---

* It is Rasser's belief that the original animistic wajang plays were a dramatization of the conflict between two divisions of a clan: the older, left division and the younger, right division. Though in conflict, and though eventually the right division subsumes the left, audience feelings toward them are "ambivalent" because they are also "equal and equivalent," complementary halves of the same clan sharing a feeling of "affinity and higher unity" (W. H. Rassers, *Panji, the Culture Hero* [The Hague, 1959], p. 58). The Pandawa-Kurawa conflict fits this construct remarkably well.

leap about unthinkingly, they stare with open eyes and gaping mouths. Their kings may be described as brave and powerful, and the enormous Kumbakarna, from the Rama cycle, is admired as exemplifying the virtue of loyalty more fully than any other wajang character. But the typical ogre, like Tjakil, has no redeeming feature. In a conflict between Pandawa and Kurawa, as in the conflict between Ardjuna and Karna in *The Death of Karna,* there is indeed ambiguity as to where moral right lies; in the standard conflict between Pandawa prince and ogre, as in the other two plays, there is none: the conflict is unequivocally between good and evil.

DRAMATIC STRUCTURE

A wajang kulit play is conceived of and performed in three parts: *patet nem,* which theoretically lasts from nine in the evening until midnight; *patet sanga,* which lasts from midnight until three in the morning; and *patet manjura,* which lasts from three until the gray of dawn around six. There is no break between patet; the play continues without interruption until it is completed. *Patet* refers to a "key" or "mode" of music; *nem, sanga,* and *manjura* are the specific keys used during the three parts of the drama. Because these music keys are irrevocably associated with the progress of the play, patet has come to be applied both to the music and to the section of the play in which it is played.

In the type and arrangement of scenes, wajang kulit lakon are unlike any other plays (except those of other wajang forms which copy wajang kulit). A spectator can easily identify the several *djedjer,* or "major audience scenes," which occur in a play. A djedjer is an impressive scene set in the main audience hall *(siti hinggil)* of a palace; it introduces, in all its glory, a kingdom, its ruler, and his retinue. Scenes which follow in the same kingdom or short scenes along the road or in the forest can be called *adegan,* simply "scene."* *Perang,* "battle scenes," occur with increasing frequency as a play progresses:

---

* A wajang play in Jogjakarta has seven major audience scenes called djedjer and other scenes are adegan or have no special designation. In Surakarta only the first scene of a play is a djedjer while other scenes, including audience scenes, are adegan. The distinction made in Jogjakarta is useful, and in the translations major audience scenes are identified as djedjer and other scenes as adegan.

Introduction: The Plays

two in Part One, two or three in Part Two, and as many as four or more in Part Three. Place, characters, or action may be specified in a scene, for example, *djedjer Pandawa*, "Pandawa audience scene," *adegan wana*, "forest scene," or *perang ageng*, "great battle."

One of the characteristic features of wajang drama is that certain standard scenes, identified by fixed names, appear in a regular order. Half of a play may consist of these standard scenes. Some must occur; others may be included or left out at the discretion of the dalang. We can identify at least eighteen standard scenes; if all occurred in one play, they would appear in the order which follows.

Part One (patet nem)

1: First Audience scene (*djedjer*). This, the longest and most elaborate scene in a play, opens with a king, or prince, entering the main audience hall of his palace. He receives in audience relatives, allies, ministers, and officials. The kingdom may be the Kurawas' Astina (as in *The Death of Karna*) or one belonging to an ally of the Pandawas (such as Dwarawati, Kresna's kingdom, as in *The Reincarnation of Rama* and *Irawan's Wedding*). (Rarely is it the Kingdom of Amarta, ruled by the Pandawas, for their entrance is usually delayed until a third to half of the play is over, following a common playwriting principle that the longer you can delay the entrance of the hero, the more impressive will be his eventual appearance.) The audience proper is preceded by an extended and impressive description of the kingdom and the king, which may take twenty minutes or more. Then the king inquires about the state of the land, leading to a statement of the problem of the play: a marriage is to be arranged; a diplomatic mission is to be sent to another country; an envoy of another king makes an unacceptable request; the gods' omen has been received and requires action. The scene concludes with the king issuing his orders—one of which is that the army should be assembled and sent off to guard the border, escort an envoy, or attack the enemy—after which he ends the audience and enters the inner palace.

2 and 3: Gate scene (*gapuran*) and Inner Palace scene (*kedatonan*). The king walks from the outer audience hall through the great inner gate, pausing to admire its beauty, and then

proceeds to the inner chambers of the palace. There he meets his queen or queens, informs them of what has occurred, and enters the palace temple to pray. The dramatic function of the Gate scene is slight. As the king gazes on the beauty of the magnificent gate his heart, unsettled by the news he has received in the audience hall, is quieted with restful thoughts. The Inner Palace scene also serves little dramatic function, for the queens seldom add anything new to the plot, but it has a delicate mood which serves as an interlude between the formal audience scene just ended and the boisterous one which follows. Unlike the First Audience scene, which can never be omitted from a play, both of these may be.

4: Outer Audience scene (*paseban djawi*). This picks up the plot again as the king's son or minister enters the outer audience hall to give lesser officials and warriors the king's command that the army is to march. The order is given; the troops assemble to clanging gamelan music; the army marches in review and off on its mission. Ministers and generals may cross the screen on prancing horses, in a technique called *budalan kapalan.*

5: Chariot scene (*adegan kereta*). If the plot of the play requires a king or prince of the First Audience scene to travel in state to another kingdom, at this point in the play he enters his chariot and, after a lengthy description of the magic powers of the chariot and its mounts, drives away.

6: Road-clearing scene (*perang ampjak*). The dispatched army, marching boisterously through the countryside, is halted by an overgrown section of the road in a dense forest. After a few traditional exchanges between griping and dedicated soldiers, the army clears the forest of trees and brush in a *perang,* or battle scene. The forest is symbolized by the large puppet, the Kajon, which is struck by the Marching Army puppet (*ampjak, prampogan, rampogan*) in rhythm to the music, as if the soldiers were chopping trees. The road is cleared and the army passes on, triumphant.

7: Foreign Audience scene (*djedjer sabrangan*). This second major audience scene introduces the second kingdom that will be involved in the plot. In plays of the classic mold it normally is set in a non-Javanese kingdom of ogres (overseas kingdoms only occasionally are inhabited by humans)—hence its name *sabrangan* or "overseas" scene. But if the kingdom is on Java, by convention it is still called a Foreign Audience scene. It follows the same plan as the First Audience scene, though in condensed form: the king welcomes his ministers, allies, relatives, or officials and either states his desires or is informed of a problem which needs attention. The scene concludes as did the First Audience scene—with the king issuing orders, including one to dispatch the army. This scene must appear in a play.

8: Foreign Outer Audience scene (*paseban djawi denawa*). This can be included or not as the dalang sees fit. It follows the pattern of the first Outer Audience scene: an official issues the king's orders for the army to assemble, after which the army departs.

9: Opening Skirmish scene (*perang gagal*). In this second battle scene, the armies dispatched by the two kingdoms meet, challenge each other, and fight. Rarely is anyone killed, but one side is routed and flees the field. Technically speaking the scene is perang gagal ("inconclusive battle") only when battle is sought by the army of the first kingdom, usually following presentation by an envoy of the ogre king of an unacceptable demand in the First Audience scene. In the three plays of this book the meetings between armies occur accidentally, and the more precise term for this type of battle is *perang simpangan*, "battle on crossing paths." Normally, however, this distinction is not made, and any battle between the first two kingdoms at this juncture in the plot is called perang gagal.

10: Second Foreign scene (*djedjer sabrang rangkep*). In the majority of plays Part One concludes with the Opening Skirmish scene. If the plot requires it, however, a third kingdom can be introduced at this point and the scene is called, literally, the "repeat foreign scene," or, more understandably, the Second Foreign scene. The scene is seldom laid outside Java; if a foreign kingdom is involved in the play it would have been introduced in the preceding Foreign Audience scene so that its army could participate in the Opening Skirmish scene. The structure of this scene is similar to the first two audience scenes, but even more condensed.

Part Two (patet sanga)

11: Nature's Turmoil and Clown scene (*gara-gara*). In a narrow sense gara-gara refers just to the narration describing natural disturbances on earth which may open Part Two; as

generally used, however, it also includes a long scene in which
god-clown-servant Semar and his two sons, Gareng and Petruk
sing, dance, quarrel, fight, and joke.* The ostensible reason the
earth is being racked with earthquakes, tidal waves, plagues,
and famine is that the hero of the play, who has not yet appeared, has upset the balance of the world by intense meditation. In animist and Hindu belief a human, through his own
powers of meditation, can obtain great magical and spiritual
powers which even the gods may be unable to control or limit.
That is how King Dasamuka, or Rawana as he is more commonly known, obtained immortal life. That is how Ardjuna has
become the invincible warrior he is. Only in some plays is
this connection made obvious. Ardjuna meditates in *The
Reincarnation of Rama,* but not in *The Death of Karna.*

The self-contained joking scene of the clowns, which normally occurs within the gara-gara, follows a general pattern.
First, Semar's two sons enter, quarreling. They may sing or
dance or act out some scene in which they play their masters,
poking fun at the noble class. They end up bickering over some
problem, the mischievous younger son, Petruk, getting the
better of Gareng. The quarrel degenerates into a scuffle and
they exit. Next, Semar appears looking for his sons. To attract
them he sings the risque song Kagok Ketanon. Gareng reenters
to hush his father, and goes on to complain of a practical joke
Petruk has just played on him. After hearing him out, Semar
calls Petruk to listen to his side of the story, which is, as can be
expected, quite different. The two are about to quarrel again,
when Semar reminds them they "must serve their master,"
usually Ardjuna or one of his sons. Semar, who knows what
needs to be done through his godlike omniscience, says, "we
must go to such-and-such a place and help so-and-so." They
exit singing and dancing. This is a fairly standard sequence,
but the clown scenes are the most flexible in a play and it is up
to the dalang to develop the scene as he wishes. Clown scenes
lasting one, and even two hours, are not unusual. The full
gara-gara appears in every Jogjakarta-style play; often it is
excluded in Surakarta.

* This is in Surakarta-style wajang. In Jogjakarta wajang a third son, Bagong,
also appears. Another variant has just Semar and Bagong. The Surakarta tradition of three clowns is followed in the translations.

Introduction: The Plays

12: Hermitage scene (*djedjer pandita*).* The scene's name derives from the fact that usually a *pandita*, a religious teacher or seer, receives in audience Ardjuna or one of his sons at his hermitage in the depths of the mountains. A different type of scene may occur at this point, if the play requires it, but it is still called the Hermitage scene. In both *The Reincarnation of Rama* and *Irawan's Wedding*, the scene is a true Hermitage scene: in the former Ardjuna visits the seer Abijasa, and in the latter Irawan visits the seer Kanwa. (In *The Death of Karna*, the scene which appears in this part of the play is set in the women's quarters of a battle camp; it could also be referred to as *adegan putri*, or "women's quarter scene.") In Jogjakarta-style wajang the refined hero normally makes his first entrance here. He comes to ask the advice or blessing of the seer, who is often his grandfather (as in *The Reincarnation of Rama* and *Irawan's Wedding*). After receiving advice the hero takes his leave, accompanied by the three punakawan. But in Surakarta-style, if the gara-gara scene is excluded, as it often is, this scene opens Part Two. The clowns then make their first entrance here and, having no special scene to themselves, must work their jokes into the fabric of this and succeeding scenes (as in *Irawan's Wedding*).

13: Forest scene (*adegan wana*). The hero's descent from the mountain through the forest (*wana*) occurs next. This brief scene ends with the hero and the clown-servants entering a dangerous ogre-infested forest, often the one into which the routed ogre army fled after its defeat in the Opening Skirmish scene of Part One (as in *The Reincarnation of Rama* and *Irawan's Wedding*).

14: Flower Battle scene (*perang kembang*).† It is called a "flower" battle because the fighting movements of the refined hero are especially beautiful, requiring of the dalang the utmost skill in manipulation and timing. Or this may be thought of as an unfolding scene, in which the hero engages in his first battle and the play's crisis begins to flower. A refined hero, usually Ardjuna or one of his sons, meets and kills three, or occasionally four, ogre antagonists. These ogres may first appear in a play in the Flower Battle, but more commonly they are

---

* In Jogjakarta, *djedjer pertapan,* or "meditation scene."
† In Jogjakarta, often *perang gendiran,* or "flicking-arms battle."

officials of the overseas king, who have already appeared in Part One (as in *The Reincarnation of Rama* and *Irawan's Wedding*). The chief ogre figure is Tjakil, who is slain when the refined hero turns Tajkil's dagger against him and plunges it into his breast. Pragalba is killed with an arrow because the ogre's breath is so foul it is dangerous to approach too closely. If the refined hero kills Terong, he does so with an arrow; other times Gatutkatja enters the battle and kills Terong by snapping the ogre's neck with his bare hands (*Irawan's Wedding*) or he may be killed by Semar's clown-servant sons. A fourth ogre, Galijuk, may appear and be killed (*The Reincarnation of Rama*).* If the ogres are from the Part One foreign kingdom, Togog and Saraita, the clown-servants of the foreign king, usually are present during the Flower Battle; supposedly Javanese, their traditional role is that of guide for the invading foreign army. In this scene, they rush away to tell their king of the ogre's deaths.

15: Battle of Part Two (*perang sampak sanga*).† If necessary another major battle scene may occur in Part Two after the Flower Battle. Ardjuna and Karna begin their extended sequence of combats in this scene in *The Death of Karna,* but in *Irawan's Wedding* it is not called for and none is included in *The Reincarnation of Rama.* (A Battle of Part Two could be inserted in *The Reincarnation of Rama* by having Bima meet an opponent as he journeys through the countryside.) After the Battle of Part Two, the requirements of each play determine which scenes will follow until around the middle of Part Three. This is the most unstructured section of a lakon. Approaching the conclusion, once again we find standard scenes.

Part Three (patet manjura)

16: Battle of Part Three (*perang sampak manjura*).‡ In the middle of Part Three a major battle scene occurs without fail. In it the mission of the opposing king is foiled. In *The Reincarnation of Rama*, Sumbadra is rescued; in *The Death of Karna,*

---

*Alternatively, the refined hero may fight forest giants (*raseksa hutan*), or animal spirits instead of Tjakil and his friends; then called *perang begal,* "Highwayman battle," in Jogjakarta.

† Also *perang tanggung,* or "middle battle," in both Surakarta and Jogjakarta.

‡ *Perang tandang* in Jogjakarta.

Ardjuna kills Karna with his magic arrow; in *Irawan's Wedding*, Gatutkatja slays the ogre official Mingkalpa. Other scenes may intervene, but when news of this defeat reaches the opponents of the Pandawas the next scene inevitably follows.

17: Great Battle scene (*perang amuk-amukan* or *perang ageng*).* *Amuk* is the source of "running amok" and *ageng* means "great;" this perang is the fastest and loudest, and normally involves the most combatants of any in the play. Usually the king of the opposing kingdom himself fights and is defeated. This battle occurs in *The Reincarnation of Rama* when King Dasasuksma leads his ogre army to avenge the trick Ardjuna played on his son Begasuksma; in *Irawan's Wedding* it occurs when King Barandjana leads his ogre army in one last attempt to capture his beloved Titisari; and in *The Death of Karna,* when King Durjudana hears of Karna's death in the Great War, he leads the Kurawa forces in an attack on the Pandawas. Although Ardjuna may take part in the fighting, traditionally Bima has the major role. After the enemy is routed, Bima performs a brief, exultant victory dance (*tajungan*).

18: Final Audience scene (*djedjer tantjeb kajon*). Literally this is "planting the Kajon scene," in which the Pandawas gather to celebrate and to offer thanks to the gods for their victory. It is brief, and at the end the Kajon is placed in the center of the screen ending the performance. A brief dance by a wajang golek doll-puppet may precede the planting of the Kajon.

Standard scenes account for perhaps half of a play, but only the beginning of the plot and its resolution are covered in them. In other words, the standard scenes reveal the structure of a typical play more than its content. The twists and turns of the often complicated plot call for other scenes as well: short audience scenes, chance meetings while traveling, and other battles. For example, *Irawan's Wedding* has ten other scenes in addition to twelve of the eighteen standard ones.

If the "classic" structure just described is remarkable, as indeed it is, we must consider still more remarkable one of its major consequences: that the conflict of the typical play is not between Pandawas and Kurawas, but either between Pandawas,

* Perang ageng is the usual term in Jogjakarta.

Kurawas, and an ogre kingdom—or between Pandawas and an ogre kingdom. Not all plays follow the classic form, but most tjarangan plays do and, as we have seen, the largest number of plays are precisely of this type. Regardless of minor variations within the classic, textbook form just described, an overseas kingdom appears and the net effect is that the Kurawa-Pandawa conflict is reduced in importance, and, in some plays, replaced completely. Both *Irawan's Wedding* and *The Reincarnation of Rama* are tjarangan plays and the importance of their ogre antagonists is typical. In the former the conflict is three-sided, between Pandawas, Kurawas, and an ogre kingdom; yet, although the Kurawas play a substantial role in the plot, three of the four major battle scenes are between Pandawas and traditional ogre figures. In *The Reincarnation of Rama* a typical ogre kingdom has completely replaced the Pandawas' opponents of mythology; the Kurawas do not appear at all.

Unfortunately not enough is known of the history of wajang drama to describe how this development came about. It may be that dalang purposely created a group of new antagonists for their Pandawa heroes to fight, that as they invented more and more new episodes set in the brief Amarta period, they found it difficult to put both Kurawas and Pandawas into these new situations without seriously disturbing the established relationships already set forth in the epics (imagine how complicated it would be to write *The Reincarnation of Rama* using the Kurawas as the Pandawas' opponents, instead of the convenient ogre kingdom!). Or it may be that the ogres Tjakil, Pragalba, Terong, and Galijuk—the most important of the overseas figures—were intended at first to be incidental figures, introduced to add variety, but that, proving popular and useful, they unintentionally, and gradually became stock figures of major importance. Whatever the original intent of their creators, in time Tjakil and his ogre companions came to play required roles in wajang's classic form, to the point where now they appear in almost every play whether they have any plot function or not (the Flower Battle of *The Reincarnation of Rama,* for instance, does not contribute to the play's forward action, but is merely a beautiful set-piece).

Foreign ogres appear in plays of the animistic cycle and in the Rama and Ardjuna Sasra Bau cycles, derived from earlier myths and epics. The interesting thing about these figures is that they

were created in wajang.* They have no names, no kingdoms, no
genealogies. (Tjakil takes the name Maritja and is a minister of
King Dasasuksma in *The Reincarnation of Rama,* but in *Irawan's
Wedding* he is Bantjuring, minister to King Barandjana, for
example.) Though Tjakil has personal characteristics, he can
best be described as the "ogre whom the refined hero kills with
a dagger in the Flower Battle in Part Two." His function, and
that of his friends, is to provide "scenes" within a set play
form. They appear in play after play, doing the same things.
They have no place in the literature, nor in the mythology of the
Javanese. They cannot be imagined to exist outside of their
simple dramatic function; they could not exist, for example, in
an epic or narrative piece because it is not in the nature of the
narrative to require a figure which reoccurs, chapter after chapter, doing the same things. The evolution of the new ogres into
figures indispensable to the classic play form is a fascinating
example of the triumph of theatrical art over literature and
shows how independent of the epics wajang plays had become.

The Death of Karna is an example of a play which does not
follow the classic pattern. Very likely, it was created before
Tjakil was invented. Its structure might be called "preclassic."
Though similar in most ways to the classic form; the lakon does
not contain an overseas, foreign kingdom (Bima's scene in Part
One is called a Foreign Audience scene only by convention);
Tjakil does not appear; there is no Flower Battle.

A high degree of structuring of wajang plays is apparent on
several levels. As noted, a play consists of three parts, and
certain standard scenes occur in each. In turn, a scene is made
up of certain standard dramatic elements, or building blocks:
two types of narration, dialogue, and songs (in addition to puppet movements, which will be discussed later). The two kinds of
narration, *djanturan* and *tjarijos,* differ in characteristics and
use. Djanturan, "to tell," introduces major scenes, djedjer. The
new kingdom, the palace, the ruler, and his ministers are
described in eloquent phrases as instrumental music plays in
the background to create an appropriate mood. Tjarijos, "to
narrate," describes action rather than places; it is the form of

---

* In Rassers' theory of early wajang, an ogre was the necessary "demon of
initiation" (p. 21) whom the hero of the right division overcame in the course
of the play. Rassers does not discuss Tjakil, but presumably he would see in this
puppet a new manifestation of the older dramatic element.

narration which usually introduces an adegan, or minor scene. Offstage and between-scenes events are described in tjarijos, as well as the entrance of a new character in the midst of a djedjer. It is shorter than djanturan—the tjarijos in the gara-gara normally being the longest in a lakon—and normally it is spoken without background music. On rare occasions when music is employed, it is called *tjarijos kadjantur,* or "djanturan-like tjarijos." A special type of tjarijos describes actions of characters within a room, but without that scene being shown on the screen, in what is called *tjarijos pagedongan,* literally "description within-a-building."

Ginem is the spoken dialogue of the play, the words each puppet character speaks in the first person to some other puppet character. In wajang kulit, ginem is straightforward dialogue; no asides or soliloquies are needed, as the dalang can express in the third person a character's unspoken thoughts through narration or songs. Formal gamelan melodies usually are not played during dialogue. *Suluk* are songs which the dalang sings. Some suluk are sung after a djanturan has introduced a new scene, establishing a sad or lively or romantic mood for the dialogue which follows. Or it can express the state of mind of a king or prince, prior to discussion of a matter which concerns him. If a character receives shocking news during a scene the dalang can sing a suluk which expresses surging emotions. Or a suluk can cover a character's hurried exit or, less often, entrance. There are three types of suluk, each with its particular expressive range, *patet (an), ada-ada,* and *sendon,* which will be described in more detail later.

Here is the way a dalang might put together djanturan, tjarijos, ginem, and suluk to create an audience scene:

> djanturan—the kingdom, its king, officials in audience, time, and occasion are introduced;
> suluk—the king's state of mind is described and the atmosphere of the audience scene is established through song;
> ginem—the king speaks with his ministers and officials about the subject at hand;
> suluk—informed of terrible news, the king's turbulent emotions are expressed through song;
> ginem—the king continues his conversation, asking that a certain official be summoned;
> suluk—a minister departs to summon the official as the

Introduction: The Plays

general emotion of the minister is expressed through song;

tjarijos—the offstage action of the minister summoning the official is briefly described;

suluk—the action of the minister and the official returning is described in song;

ginem—there is further dialogue ending with the king's concluding the audience and all depart to instrumental music.

The richness of wajang's theatrical effect in performance is indicated by the proportions of these elements within a play. In Western drama, plot action and characterization are achieved almost entirely through the single medium of dialogue, and dialogue accounts for most of the playing time in performance. But in wajang kulit, only about one-third of a play's performance time is given over to ginem, and hence to plot development and direct characterization. Another third of performance time is given over to djanturan, tjarijos, and suluk combined, and their function is to amplify and elaborate on the action of a play. Narration provides exposition of past events, interprets characters' feelings and thoughts, and comments on events. Suluk establish moods and emotional states and vary the tempo of performance. Puppet movements—the visually delightful entrances, exits, parades, and battle sequences—account for the final third of a play's performance time. So that, in all, the wajang kulit spectator watches and listens to gamelan music, singing, narration, and puppet actions twice as long during the evening as he does to dialogue.

LANGUAGE

The form of Javanese language used in wajang kulit is a blend of Sanskrit, Old-Javanese (*Kawi*), special forms of palace address, and colloquial language. It has been described as "the language of wajang" because no other form of Javanese is quite like it. It is sophisticated and complex. As many as seven levels of politeness can be spoken by wajang characters, determined by the relative status of the character speaking and the one being spoken to. The most esoteric of these levels are spoken to the gods, and to the highest kings. The two levels most commonly spoken are high-Javanese (*krama*), and low-Javanese (*ngoko*). The general rule of usage is: a high character speaks low to a low character; a low character speaks high to a high character; and characters of equal status speak the same level. Thus, Samba speaks high-Javanese to his father, Kresna, and Kresna speaks low-Javanese to him. Baladewa speaks low-Javanese to Kresna, his younger brother. Bima is an exception. Because of his unyielding nature he speaks ngoko to everyone, to Judistira (his king and elder brother) and even to the gods; only to the figure of his divine essence, Dewa Rutji, does he humble himself and speak krama.

Although the gods' scene in Suralaja contains extremely formal language, the unusual words are mainly special forms of address; the average person has little difficulty understanding the scene because only personal pronouns are altered. Archaic forms of Javanese pose a more serious barrier. The opening djanturan, which contains the ritual eulogy of the first king-dom, is filled with Sanskrit and Kawi words of obscure meaning. The description of Dwarawati's Gate of the World and the listings of characteristics and titles of major wajang figures also contain esoteric and difficult words. Like litanies in any ancient language, these are not fully understood. Traditional lyrics for suluk, many taken verbatim from Old-Javanese literature, pose the greatest problem. Not only are they difficult to decipher; even when understood they may lack relevance. For example, the traditional lyric for Ada-ada Girisa, which follows a play's opening djanturan, goes like this:

> Remembering the importance
> Of his mission to Astina,
> Kresna reaches the Plain of Kuru.
> He meets the gods: Parasu Rama,
> Kanwa, Djanaka, and Narada.
> They meet King Kresna on the plain,
> Wishing to join his mission.

The verse comes from Book II of the Great War epic, written in Old-Javanese in 1157. Unchanged, it will fit no other play than that dramatizing the event referred to in the epic. Modern-minded dalang tend to revise suluk lyrics to make them more understandable. Conservative dalang say the mood of the music is what counts, whether or not the lyrics are understood.

One of the traditions of dalang art is that foreign or con-temporary words may not be inserted except in clown scenes. The clown-servant of the ogres, Saraita, may speak Indonesian rather than Javanese and Gareng and Petruk when joking may go so far as to use English for a phrase or two; otherwise the rule against the intrusion of untraditional language is closely observed in wajang. Even Arabic words are found only in scattered places: the opening prayers (*mantra*) of the dalang mention Allah; the name of Judistira's secret heirloom, the Kalimasada, is thought to be a Javanization of the Islamic profession of faith "Kalimat Sjahadah"; Bima's mystical explanation in *The Reincarnation of Rama* contains some Arabic words.

WAJANG IN PERFORMANCE

PLAY SCRIPTS AND SCENARIOS

I have translated lakon as "play," but the word does not mean the written script implied by its English equivalent. Originally, narratives of the Pandawas and other mythological figures were known in Java through both oral and written traditions. Those in the oral tradition may go back as far as the beginning of the Christian era. The first epic written in Javanese was the *Ramayana,* adapted from a famous Indian Sanskrit version of the epic in the ninth century.* Scores of epics written in prose and poetry (*kakawin*) followed. Famous court poets of the eighteenth and nineteenth centuries wrote dynastic accounts of Javanese kings, incorporating into them epic stories, history, myth, and Islamic views of the origins of the Javanese.† But this literature was narrative or epic; although it may have served as material for some plays, it was not drama. Plays were being composed by dalang, however, and performed, and passed on to following generations within the oral tradition; and some became well-known. The plots they related and the scenes which occurred in them became traditional. They became part of the repertory. Though not written, they were "plays," and their stories are what is meant by lakon.

* The *Bhatti-Kavya.*
† Among them, *Pustaka Radja Purwa, Paramajoga,* and *Purwa Kanda.*

On Thrones of Gold

A dalang could remember scores of lakon because they were structured according to standard scenes. As in oral literature everywhere in the world, there were stock expressions and formula phrases which, once learned, were used again and again. The extent of formula phrases in wajang kulit has not been examined in detail, but it appears to be very considerable indeed. Descriptions of characters and of kingdoms are replete with standard expressions, and the long opening section of the first djanturan is repeated by a dalang almost verbatim (as the translations show). There are set patterns of greeting in audience scenes and fixed forms of insult which a warrior hurls at his opponent prior to combat.

Eventually the stories of well-known lakon were written down, scene by scene, in *pakem*, or "performance guides." The first known pakem date from only a few hundred years ago. In recent years a number have been published (see Bibliography). The written form of a wajang play, therefore, is not an original work intended for the stage, as is a play script in the West. Rather, it is shorthand record of the way a lakon already has been performed, perhaps for decades or centuries. The briefest form of pakem, called *pakem balungan* or "bone guide," contains only the barest plot outline. A nine-hour play takes up one or two printed pages in a book of pakem balungan, each scene being described in two or three sentences. A *pakem gantjaran*, literally "prose guide," runs ten to fifteen printed pages and contains the important plot action of a play. The third type of pakem is the very complete *pakem padalangan*, or "guide-for-the-dalang," in which most narration and some dialogue is written out and action, music, songs, and sound effects indicated. Dalang may read this longest form, but in spite of its name it is not intended for use in performance; for the most part, pakem padalangan are written for the general public.

Normally when a dalang performs he works from one of the shorter forms of pakem. It may be published, but more likely is handwritten, handed down from father to son or copied from the notebook of one's teacher (*guru*). In a few minutes time a skilled dalang can glance at a brief pakem and refresh his memory on the sequence of scenes required for a lakon. In addition to knowing the characters, stories, and typical structure of wajang plays, he also has at his command an impressive

Introduction: Wajang in Performance

repertory of performance techniques with which he fleshes out the bare bones of the plot indicated in the pakem of the play.

There may be several versions of a lakon, often varying considerably in detail. For example, *Kartapijoga* is published in two versions by different dalang. The lakon concerns the daughter of King Salja, who is kidnaped by the young ogre Kartapijoga; both Kurawas and Pandawas try to rescue her; Ardjuna succeeds and delivers her to the young ascetic, Djaladara, whom she loves. Most scenes are similar in the two versions, but in one, three kingdoms appear in Part One, the Opening Skirmish is between the armies of Salja and the ogre king, and the Pandawas are attacked by Durjudana and the Kurawa army in the final Great Battle scene; in the other version, two kingdoms appear in Part One, the Opening Skirmish is between the armies of the Kurawas and the ogre king, and the Pandawas are attacked by an ogre army, not the Kurawas, in the Great Battle scene.* Smaller differences abound as well.

STAGE EQUIPMENT

The stage equipment used for a wajang kulit performance is simple. A large white screen (*kelir*) of cotton cloth is stretched tightly inside a frame to make the background against which the cast of puppets is moved. It is made of thin cloth which shows a clear, dark shadow when a light shines on puppets held against it. The kelir is bordered with red cloth at the top and bottom, the bottom strip serving to mark the ground or floor level on which the puppets walk or sit. The traditional light source is a coconut-oil lamp (*blentjong*) made of heavy bronze, often in the shape of a *garuda,* or eagle, with its wings partially outstretched. A thick wick, inserted into a spout in the front of the lamp, burns with a waving yellow flame four to six inches high. The shadow cast is distinct for a relatively short distance only, but because of the moving and waving flame it seems infused with life (Fig. 1). In recent years gas pressure lamps and electric bulbs have almost completely replaced the blentjong. The shadow produced by an electric light or pressure lamp is more distinct and can be seen farther,

---

* An English synopsis of one version, by Ki Reditanaja, *Kartawiyoga,* can be found in Claire Holt, *Art in Indonesia* (Ithaca, N.Y., 1967), pp. 293–296. The other version, by Ki Wignjawirjanta, *Kartapijoga Tjidra,* is listed in the Bibliography.

but because of the constant light source it lacks the living quality of a blentjong shadow.

The light source, whatever it may be, is hung about sixteen inches away from the screen and just above the dalang's head. A sharply defined shadow, the normal ideal, is produced only when a puppet is pressed tightly against the screen. When a puppet walks or runs, the full length of its figure cannot be pressed against the screen; in this case care is taken at least to keep the face, the most important part of the shadow figure, pressed to the kelir. The finest puppets are carved in intricate detail, so that the lacy shadow patterns produced on the kelir contain every shade of gray between pure black and pure white. Supernatural characters can be made to grow in size by bringing the puppet closer to the lamp. An extremely beautiful effect is created by moving a puppet slowly to the edge of the playing area while withdrawing it from the screen, then bringing it back on again. The shadow dissolves and vanishes in the air, then rematerializes. Because puppets are two-dimensional, a special effect is produced when a figure is turned to face in the opposite direction: it looks as if the character compresses into a thin line, then expands outward again. Normally a puppet is turned by pivoting it on its nose so that the face of the figure is seen for the longest possible time. A figure can be made to pant with exertion by slightly bending the main stick of the puppet in and out. Magical happenings, such as flying, entering a ring (*Irawan's Wedding*), or incarnating a spirit in another body (*The Reincarnation of Rama*), which are almost impossible to stage satisfactorily with live actors, are astonishingly effective in wajang shadow plays.

Spectators who sit on the dalang's side of the screen watch a puppet play, and only occasionally see shadows (when a puppet is momentarily lifted away from the cloth). Those who sit on the opposite side of the screen see only shadows; they see neither dalang, puppets, or orchestra. Observers a hundred years ago described audiences segregated by sex, with the women seated on the shadow side, the men on the dalang's side. Whether this was the traditional seating arrangement, or whether it was a recent development brought about by an Islamic insistence on the separation of men and women in public, is not known. Today it is usual to see the largest number of spectators—men and women—watching a performance from the dalang's side (partly because the hall is arranged this way?), but the true connoisseurs of wajang art generally prefer the other side of the screen, where they can serenely view the passing world of wajang shadows undistracted by the glamor and bustle of performance.

The red strip along the bottom of the kelir serves as the stage floor for the puppets as far as the spectators are concerned. But for the dalang, the stage is made of the trunks of banana trees, called *debog* (or *gedebog*), which are fastened at two levels beneath the screen on his side. The higher trunk touches the frame around the screen; the lower projects eight to ten inches forward. The upper debog extends far beyond the width of the screen, as much as fifteen feet in either direction. The soft pulp of the banana trunk, peeled to a gleaming yellow-green, makes an ideal stage floor into which the sharp ends of the puppets' sticks can be stuck during performance.

Behind the dalang as he faces the screen, musicians (*nijaga*), who play the twelve to twenty instruments of the gamelan ensemble, sit in a horseshoe shape around him. A female singer or two, *pesinden,* sit behind the dalang in the center of this arrangement. In important performances, such as those sponsored by the Sultan of Jogjakarta on the festival of *grebeg,* as many as half-a-dozen pesinden join the nijaga, singing alternately or in unison with them. Additional male singers may also join in for certain scenes.

The dalang uses three important sound-effect implements: two wooden tappers, *tjempala,* and a set of four or five hanging metal plates, *kepjak* (also *keprak* or *ketjrek*). The larger tjempala is held in the left hand, and the dalang taps out signals and sound effects with it against the wooden puppet chest which is always at his left side. He may strike the inside wall to produce a deep "tun-tun-tun" sound; by tapping on the top edge he can produce a higher-pitched, less resonant "tuk-tuk-tuk." Sitting cross-legged he holds the smaller tjempala between the large and index toes of his right foot. With it he taps out sound effects or signals on the wooden chest if his hands are busy with the puppets at the moment. Or, either with the tjempala or his bare foot, he beats out a clangorous rhythm on the kepjak, which hangs on the outside of the chest.

On Thrones of Gold

PUPPETS

A wajang puppet is made of well-cured water-buffalo hide. The leather is pressed flat, the outline of the figure cut out, and costume designs, facial features, and purely decorative carvings are carefully incised. Both sides of the figure are then painted, or, if an expensive puppet, covered with pure gold leaf. In painting, the previously transluscent leather becomes opaque, so its shadow is virtually colorless. Three sticks of transluscent buffalo horn, collectively called *tjempurit,* are attached to the leather figure (Figs. 12, 13). The main stick, *gapit,* is split down the middle, so one half extends up each side of the figure. At half a dozen points along the gapit the two pieces are tied together with thread, tightly securing the leather figure. The gapit is sharply pointed so it easily sticks into the banana log. Both arms of most wajang puppets are hinged at the elbow and at the shoulder, and *tuding,* short sticks of buffalo horn, are attached to the hands so the dalang can move the arms. Large, one-armed ogre puppets have one tuding. Guru may have no movable hands and hence no tuding.* The human figure is presented in profile so that just one eye is seen; some ogre and monkey figures face three-quarter front, showing both eyes (Fig. 83).

An ordinary village puppet set contains from one hundred to one hundred and fifty pieces. A better set may contain up to three hundred pieces, and the finest sets, owned by keraton aristocrats, five hundred or more. A set of puppets is kept in a large chest (*kotak*). In performance this is placed to the left of where the dalang sits, cross-legged, before the screen; its lid is removed and placed to the right. Between one hundred and fifty and two hundred puppets are taken out of the chest and divided into two groups. One is stuck in the left and right debog in long rows extending ten or fifteen feet. In each row the figures are arranged facing outward according to height, with the smallest puppets—perhaps only six inches high—near the center, and the largest figures—as high as four feet—at the outsides. This decorative arrangement, framing the five-foot-wide playing area in the middle of the screen, is known as the *simpingan* (literally, "tapered ornament"). Most of the figures

---

* Or two of Guru's four arms may be jointed, especially in Jogjakarta wajang (see Fig. 135).

Introduction: Wajang in Performance

placed in it—and called *wajang simpingan*—are kings, princes, and court ladies. Generally speaking, Pandawa figures are placed in the right simpingan, with Kurawa and ogre figures in the left. However, this division is not absolute: on the left also are placed the Pandawa twins Nakula and Sadewa, Kresna's son Samba and his minister Setyaki, Ardjuna's two sons Abimanju and Irawan, and even the Pandawa's great ally King Matswapati; while on the right are Karna as a youth and all women of nobility, including Karna's wife Surtikanti, the sister of the ogre king Rawana, the mother of the Kurawas, and Durjudana's sister. The identity of the puppets and the order in which they are arranged in the simpingan is fixed by tradition.

The second group of puppets contains less exalted figures which appear in the performance. They are known as *wajang dudahan* (literally, "taken-out-wajang") and are placed either inside the puppet chest or on its lid. On the lid to the dalang's right go clown figures, seers or ascetics, female attendants, and other minor puppets. Ministers and officials of various kingdoms, the Kurawa brothers, and ogre figures are placed in the chest, in layers as the dalang will use them in performance. Some puppets standing in the simpingan may also appear in a play—Karna, Dasasuksma, Sumbadra, and Irawan in these translations, for example. They are removed by an assistant and handed to the dalang as needed. Wajang neither placed in the simpingan for decoration nor laid out for use are kept in the bottom of the puppet chest out of the way. Between forty and sixty puppets may be used in performance. Forty-five appear in *The Reincarnation of Rama*, forty-four in *Irawan's Wedding*, and forty-two in *The Death of Karna*.

In addition to puppets of human, god, and ogre figures, there are special puppets for horses, elephants, serpents, apes, the Marching Army of soldiers, and inanimate objects such as chariots, daggers, arrows, and clubs. Magically endowed weapons, usually gifts of the gods, are attributed to a number of characters. Each is of a special shape, requiring individual wajang: Kresna threatens Bima at the end of *Irawan's Wedding* with his divine disc-tipped weapon, Tjakra; in *The Death of Karna*, Karna shoots the arrow Widjajandanu that passes over Ardjuna's head, while Ardjuna kills Karna with the invincible arrow, Pasopati.

The most important wajang figure of all is the Kajon, or mystical "tree of life" (also called *gunungan*—"mountain"). The derivation of the word is obscure; perhaps it came from Old-Javanese *kajun*, "living," or from *kaju*, "wood." In any case, the interior of the Kajon puppet is carved to represent a tree, swelling outward at the base and tapering to a point at the top. No two Kajon are identical in their carving, but a typical design shows serpents in the tree and a gate flanked by a pair of garuda birds and ogres and with an ox and a tiger or lion over it (Fig. 28). This design is painted on one side of the puppet, but the reverse side is usually painted with leaping flames of red. The Kajon is placed vertically in the center of the screen to open a play and again at its conclusion. It is also planted in the center, either vertically or inclined to the right or left,* to signify the end of a scene. To indicate the close of a minor scene the Kajon is fluttered across the screen, and when a scene is about to begin it is placed in the banana log on the right side of the screen (except before the gara-gara, when it is placed on the left side). Before the gara-gara it is twirled and fluttered violently to portray nature's turmoil. The Kajon may also represent places within a scene: the forest in the Forest-clearing scene, the palace gate in the Gate scene, a crypt *(The Reincarnation of Rama),* or the mountain descended by the refined hero in the Forest scene. If the dalang wishes, he may use two Kajon, framing the playing area of the screen with one planted on either edge. Except for brief moments the Kajon is visible throughout performance.

The several hundred human, god, and ogre figures in the wajang cast can be classified and identified through some twenty-five physical features. Body build, foot stance, nose shape, eye shape, and the slant of the head are five of the most crucial. According to the most detailed Javanese texts, there are thirteen different eye shapes, thirteen nose shapes, and two or three types each of body build, foot stance, and slant of head. These different types of features can be combined into dozens

---

* The general rule is: inclined to the right indicates Part One; vertical, Part Two; and to the left, Part Three. *The Reincarnation of Rama* illustrates how the Kajon may be positioned this way each time it is placed center to conclude a scene; *Irawan's Wedding* and *The Death of Karna* illustrate how it may be positioned this way once in each part of the play and thereafter be placed center, inclined to the right.

Introduction: Wajang in Performance

of identifiable puppet types; here only a few of the chief ones can be mentioned.*

Javanese art is often discussed in terms of its *alus*, "refined," and *kasar*, "coarse," qualities. Wajang puppets may be so described. Judistira, of the Pandawas, is one of the most alus of wajang figures (Fig. 2). His body build is delicate, his foot stance is narrow, his nose is thin and sharply pointed; his eyes are almondlike slits, and he looks modestly almost straight at the ground. These are all very alus features to the Javanese. On the other hand, the ogre king, Barandjana, whose body is fat and bulging and covered with mats of repulsive hair, whose foot stance is broad and aggressive, whose nose is bulbous (like the "inside of a mango," the Javanese say), whose eyes are large, round, and staring, and who haughtily looks straight out, is kasar in almost every possible way (Fig. 83).

Alus characteristics are highly admired by the Javanese, while kasar qualities are shunned. The temptation is therefore great to assume that ethical qualities of a puppet can be determined by noting its alus-ness or kasar-ness. In the extreme cases of Judistira and Barandjana, physical features and ethical qualities do match closely—Judistira is "good" and Barandjana is "bad"—and over-all the Pandawa figures are more alus than either the Kurawa or the ogre figures, but for any given puppet, physical features are no certain guide to that figure's ethical qualities. Physical features very clearly identify a general personality type or emotional cast, but only by watching a character's actions in the plays can we know his moral qualities.

The way in which body build, stance, nose shape, eye shape, and head inclination help distinguish personality types can be seen in the following illustrations of six human puppet figures, arranged in descending order of alus-ness, from extremely alus to around the midpoint between alus and kasar (only ogres are wholly kasar). Judistira and Karna (Figs. 2, 3) are extremely refined or alus. The small and delicate body shape and the restrained, narrow foot stance are alus (or *luruh*). The nose is thin and pointed (*mbangir*) and the eyes are delicately almond-shaped with a small pupil shaped like a rice-grain

* There is no agreement among Javanese writers on terminology for the large number of different puppet features. The puppet types identified here and the terminology for their features were kindly suggested by Mr. Guritno.

Fig. 2   Judistira

Fig. 3   Karna

Fig. 4   Salja

Fig. 5   Baladewa

Fig. 6   Bima

Fig. 7   Durjudana

On Thrones of Gold

(*gabahan*). The major difference between them is the inclination of the head. The modestly downcast face of Judistira, called *lijepan,* shows he is the more restrained, the more refined, while Karna's gaze, boldly straightforward, called *lanjapan,* expresses his assertiveness. So important is this distinction that lijepan and lanjapan are recognized as clearly distinct puppet types.*

Salja and Baladewa (Figs. 4, 5) are moderately refined character types, which the Javanese usually identify as *kedelen* figures, referring to the puppets' kedelen, or "soy-bean," eyes. Both figures share the same general physical characteristics of medium-sized body build (*pideksa*), medium-sized and pointed nose (*sembada*), and large, oval-shaped eye (*kedelen*). This type of puppet indicates a noble figure, often a king, who has a violent temper or bold and vigorous ways. The straightout gaze of Baladewa, his broad stance, and his slightly larger size mark him as the more aggressive of the two. His domineering attitude in *The Reincarnation of Rama* and *Irawan's Wedding* are in keeping with his visual characteristics. Salja's downcast look and narrow stance indicate a character considerably less assertive than Baladewa, yet twice in *The Death of Karna* we see his quick temper and pride burst out, in a manner characteristic of kedelen figures.

The largest human puppet figures are called *gagah,* "muscular," after their large body size, or *telengan,* after their round eye shape (Figs. 6, 7). They are easily distinguishable from both the very refined and the moderately refined puppet types: the eye, which was first a narrow slit and then partially rounded, is now round and staring (telengan) and the nose shape, which changed from thin and pointed to moderately thick and pointed, is now rather large and has a rounded bump at the end (*dempak*). Most gagah figures stand with feet planted wide apart (*djangkahan*). Gagah figures are the strongest warriors in wajang, with thick, muscular bodies. Some ogres are equally strong, but lacking human intelligence they regularly lose to gagah figures in battle. Bima is described as blunt, almost crude, he speaks low-Javanese, and does not bow or make the *sembah* gesture of obeisance. His body is larger than Durjudana's and his foot stance more broad, but Durjudana looks out somewhat more aggressively. The two puppets basically

* *Luruh* (downcast), *longok* (intermediate), and *langak* (up-turned) are other terms indicating direction of gaze in puppets in general.

are very similar, though one is a Pandawa and one a Kurawa. In addition, some of the more crude and villainous figures among both the moderately refined and muscular types have exposed gums (*gusen*), as if laughing foolishly or sneering. And further, among nonhuman figures, the large ogre, or raseksa, puppet is an identifiable type.

Most major characters in the translations can be assigned to these broad categories of puppet configuration:

lijepan—a small, extremely refined, controlled character, whose manner is modest (Judistira, Ardjuna, Irawan, Sumbadra, Surtikanti);

lanjapan—a small, extremely refined, but active and aggressive character (Karna, Srikandi, Kresna);

kedelen—a dignified, medium-build character of great temper and impetuosity (Baladewa, Salja, Setyaki);

gagah—a large, muscular character straightforward in manner (Bima, Durjudana, Baju, Gatutkatja);

gusen—a medium or large character with exposed gums, of rough manners and violent behavior (Dursasana, Kartamarma, Tjakil);

raseksa—a gross-featured, nonhuman ogre who acts unthinkingly and whose actions are extremely rough (Barandjana, Terong, Pragalba).

Other features can further identify a puppet figure. A king wears a three-tiered crown or a thronelike ornament (*praba*) over his shoulders (Figs. 3–5). Gods, seers like Abijasa and Kanwa and Durna wear shoes, jacket, and scarf (*slendang*) over the shoulder (Fig. 32). There are various types of hair arrangements. To give just a few illustrations, a young person's hair often falls loosely to the shoulders (Fig. 119), a refined person's hair is done up in a conservative bun (*gelung keling*) (Fig. 2), Ardjuna's hair usually curls up behind him in a style called "shrimp's tong" (*supit urang*) (Fig. 40). The skirt of a refined character may be rounded (Fig. 2) while a more vigorous figure wears silken trousers beneath a tucked-up skirt (Fig. 5). Most figures wear armbands, necklaces, ankle bracelets, earrings; refined figures wear few or none. Bima can be recognized not only by his large size and curling headdress but by a huge talon on each hand with which he rips apart his enemies (Fig. 57). Anoman and Baju, too, have these talons (Fig. 47). Some patterns on a puppet are decorative and do not serve to identify it; the open-mouthed garuda, peacock feathers, serpents, and flower motifs are common designs (Fig. 11).

On Thrones of Gold

Minor figures are represented by puppets of a general type. Sandjaja, in *The Death of Karna,* is portrayed by a general lijepan puppet (one of several in a set) which identifies him as being refined and modest, but not specifically as Sandjaja; little-known Suwega in the same play can be represented by any of several general kedelen puppets (by way of illustration, two different puppets, varying only in hair style, are used for him in the translations, Figs. 113, 119). A major wajang hero will be represented by two, three, four, or more puppets of varied configurations which characterize age, status, and even momentary emotional state or mood (*wanda*). There are puppets of Bima as a youth, as an adult, and as a king; eight all together. Semar is made in four, sometimes five, wanda; Gatutkatja and Baladewa in four. Wajang's chief hero, Ardjuna, has no less than thirteen standard puppet shapes: as a youth, when he is known as Pamade, he wears stylish arm bracelets and a long neck ornament in three wanda; as an ascetic, wearing a scarf over the shoulder, in four; and as an adult, who has outgrown adolescent ornaments, in six.* Because there can be several puppets for a figure, "doubling," an effect so difficult to achieve with live actors, is simple in wajang kulit. Even in these three plays the technique is used three times: two Ardjuna puppets, and later two Karna puppets, appear simultaneously on the screen in *The Death of Karna* (when the two warriors dress like each other); and in *The Reincarnation of Rama* Leksmana's spirit is shown to divide into two when two overlapped Leksmana puppets slowly separate.

Color is an important indication of mood or emotional state. A puppet with gold wanda (face or face and body) indicates dignity and calmness, while black can mean anger or strength (Figs. 8 and 10). Thus, Bima may be represented by a completely black puppet during a furious battle late in the play, or an all gold puppet for the calm final scene. Red indicates tempestuousness or fury; the usual wanda for Salja, an aggressive kedelen figure, shows him with a brilliant red face (Fig. 9). Youth or innocence may be shown by a white face. The expression of a wanda is created in part by color, and in part by

* Ardjuna is portrayed by puppets without ornamentation in the photographs. Since he is still unmarried in *The Reincarnation of Rama,* in that play he could be represented by ornamented puppets of Pamade.

Fig. 8   Ardjuna

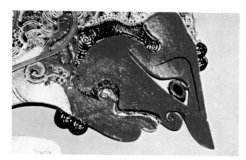

Fig. 9   Salja

Fig. 10   Bima

Fig. 11   Flower motif on Ardjuna's skirt

Fig. 12   Semar: gold wanda

Fig. 13   Semar: black wanda

Introduction: Wajang in Performance

varying the size and thickness of the puppet's limbs and body, the tilt of the shoulders, the slant of the head, and, very important, the incised facial features. When Kresna is angry the wanda of that emotion shows his head higher, his chin smaller, his shoulders slanted back, his body slightly smaller, than wanda for a more relaxed mood. Two of Semar's wanda, in Figures 12 and 13, illustrate easily seen differences of body size, facial configuration, and coloring. The gold wanda, called *dunuk* ("plump"), which shows a pot-bellied Semar, smiling and pleasant, would be used in quiet scenes; the black wanda, called *mega* ("cloud"), has a much more severe face (jutting jaw, narrowed eyes) and a smaller body, and would portray Semar in an angry mood. Taken all together, the iconography of wajang puppets is exceptionally varied and complex. The large cast of characters, the wide range of physical and personality types, coupled with the several ages, and possible moods for each major figure, make for a remarkably rich and subtle visual expression, even within the technically restricted medium of a shadow play.

MUSIC

Gamelan music is essential to the performance of wajang kulit. It provides the cadence to which puppets move across the screen, take their places in the banana-log stage, and fight. It establishes or alters mood. It provides respite between major actions. Except for brief moments, some instruments play continuously throughout the eight or nine hours of a performance. Several extensive studies of Javanese gamelan music have been made; here I shall discuss music only as it relates to wajang performance.

The Gamelan. A typical gamelan ensemble for wajang kulit consists of several large hanging gongs (*gong*), a set of five medium-sized hanging gongs (*kempul*), a set of five inverted bronze bowls (*kenong*), a single inverted bronze bowl (*ketuk*), one or two tuned sets of inverted bronze bowls (*bonang*), three or more xylophones of heavy bronze bars (*saron*), two or three xylophones of thinner bronze keys suspended over resonating tubes (*gender*), a xylophone with wooden keys (*gambang*), one, two, or three double-faced drums beat with the fingers (*ken-*

dang), a flute (*suling*), a plucked zither (*tjelempung*), and a two-stringed fiddle (*rebab*). When there are two or more instruments of a single type they are tuned in connecting (or overlapping) octaves, giving the total ensemble a wide melodic range (usually six or seven octaves); normally only the saron, which plays the nuclear gamelan melody, has doubled instruments for any one octave.

Gamelan music is extremely beautiful even to the unaccustomed ear. The preponderance of bronze percussion instruments gives it a brilliant, lingering sound, and the size and variety of the ensemble make its texture richer than that of most other Asian music. There are melodies expressive of many moods, ranging from clangorous Sampak fighting music to delicate laments like Tlutur.

Gamelan ensembles in Java may be made in one of two scales: *slendro*, in which the octave is divided into five notes, or *pelog*, in which it is divided into seven notes. (In the wajang kulit ensemble just described there are five kenong, one for each note of the slendro scale; in a pelog ensemble there would be seven kenong, one for each note of the pelog scale.) Because notes of the two scales are of different intervals most instruments of either ensemble are incompatible with the other. The slendro-tuned gamelan accompanies wajang kulit, as well as wajang orang dance-drama and wajang golek doll-puppet plays. Pelog-tuned ensembles are intended primarily for concert listening and for court dances. They also accompany wajang gedog, on the rare occasions it is performed. Slendro melodies are the more dignified in character; pelog melodies are lighter and gayer. Nowadays pelog melodies may be played for certain scenes in wajang kulit if the dalang and the sponsor of the performance wish, and if pelog-tuned instruments are available. Wajang kilit would never be performed solely to pelog music, however. The census of 1930 counted 9040 slendro-tuned gamelan sets in Java which could be used for wajang kulit.

Slendro melodies are composed in one of three *patet*, keys or modes, which correspond to the three parts of the play. Thus, melodies in the key of patet nem are played during the first part of the play; melodies in the key of patet sanga are played in the second part of the play; and melodies in the key of patet manjura are played in the third part of the play. The pitch of each patet is progressively higher. The tonic, or first gong tone, in patet nem is two, on the Javanese scale; in patet sanga, five; and in patet manjura, six. The rise in the musical pitch at these major dividing points creates a growing sense of tension and excitement. Selections are played with ever greater liveliness. Also typical melodic patterns are different in each patet and induce feelings of increasing tension. Occasionally a melody will be moved forward, that is, played earlier than its key indicates. A melody in the key of patet manjura might be played during the patet sanga part of a play, thus increasing the tension level sooner than usual. However, an earlier, hence quieter and more relaxed, melody will not be played later than its normal part of the play, for that would be operating against the general principle that there be a continual increase in dramatic tension and excitement throughout a play.

The drummer who plays the kendang and the lead gender player, who plays the *gender barung,* are the most important musicians in an ensemble. They work with the dalang as a team. When a dalang travels and cannot take a full group of musicians with him, he relies on them to lead an ensemble of unknown, local musicians in his particular style of performance. The kendang player sets tempos which the others follow. Especially during battle scenes he beats out intricate patterns of rhythm which must coincide exactly with the dalang's swift movements of the puppets as they flash across the screen. The gender barung sets the pitch for the dalang when he sings suluk or speaks dialogue or narration. Usually the gender barung starts a melody (although the rebab may) and cues the other players.

Instrumental Melodies. Two major kinds of music are heard in wajang kulit: *gending* and *suluk.* Gending are instrumental melodies, and a useful way of describing them is in terms of their rhythmic structure, for puppets are moved according to their rhythm, and the structure of a gending helps determine its emotional quality and hence its appropriateness for certain types of scenes. In the broadest sense, a gending can be classified according to the number of saron beats within a major musical phrase, punctuated at the end by the boom of one of the great gongs (and so called a "gong phrase"). In wajang kulit most gending have gong phrases of 16, 32, 64, or 128 saron beats. The saron plays the nuclear melody of the gending, in regular rhythm, usually one note per beat. Within

a gong phrase the saron's nuclear melody is divided and sub-
divided into smaller phrases by other instruments: a gong
phrase is marked off by kenong beats into two or four "kenong
phrases" of equal length; in turn, these are divided in half by
a kempul beat into "kempul phrases"; which further may be
divided in two by a ketuk beat. For example, a gending with
sixteen saron beats in a gong phrase might be structured like
this (with each saron beat indicated by a dot):

·   ·   ·   ·   ·   ·   ·   ·

ketuk   kempul   ketuk   kenong

·   ·   ·   ·   ·   ·   ·   ·

ketuk   kempul   ketuk   gong

The gender, gambang, and bonang paraphrase and elaborate
upon the nuclear melody of the saron; the gender, especially,
weaves intricate patterns of rippling sound around this
melody. Drums, flute, and rebab add counterpoint and tone
color. But it is the four-square rhythm of the saron and the
mathematically regular punctuation by the gong, kenong,
kempul, and ketuk which give gamelan music the distinctively
clear rhythm so important to the dalang in timing his performance.

Gending have several functions in a wajang kulit play.
Each djedjer opens with one. The cast of the scene is brought
out and placed in position as the music is played. When puppets are in place, the gending softens and continues in the
background as the dalang recites the djanturan description
of the kingdom and of the figures before the screen. This quiet
playing of a gending under djanturan is called *sirepan*. A
gending accompanies the exit of the characters at the conclusion
of a scene. A gending plays during most major movement of
the puppet figures across the screen, and always during battle
scenes.

One or more female singers, *pesinden,* and the musicians may
sing during a gending. Female singing is known as *sinden,*
male singing as *gerong.* Sinden is heard when the puppets are
being brought out for a new scene, after the dalang finishes
djanturan, for exits, and sometimes during battles. Because she
usually sings solo, a pesinden may choose any lyric she wishes,

Introduction: Wajang in Performance

traditional or modern, and she is free to improvise around the nuclear gamelan melody. Because gerong is group singing, usually traditional lyrics are sung in unison and the nuclear gamelan melody is followed closely. The unison singing of many male voices during stately gending is singularly impressive.

Occasionally a character in a play—most often a clown—sings. Most such songs are *tembang matjapat,* the lyrics of which may be composed in one of several rhyme schemes. Irawan's love song to Titisari in *Irawan's Wedding* is a tembang matjapat in the Kinanti rhyme scheme of six lines of eight syllables each, with successive lines ending in u, i, a, i, a, and i (this form is maintained in the translation).

Mood Songs. Suluk are mood songs sung with great emotional power and in a slow tempo by the dalang. They establish mood at the beginning of a scene, bridge widely variant moods of contiguous scenes, or provide in the midst of action brief pauses for reflection or elaboration on emotions. The three types of suluk are patet(an) (normally abbreviated to patet in the title of a song, adding one more meaning to the word), sendon, and ada-ada.* Patetan are used in descriptive situations or where emotive content is slight. They are accompanied by four instruments of the gamelan ensemble—rebab, gender, gambang, and suling—and are sung to slow and stately tempo. So we find patetan sung after the djanturan in the opening scene of a play, and as a bridge between the first and second, and between the second and third parts of the play. The emotion-laden sendon are accompanied by the same musical ensemble, minus the rebab. (The rebab is considered to sound like the human voice, so it does not play during sendon in order to allow the human voice to come out clearly, without distraction.) Surakarta-style wajang identifies fifteen traditional patetan, but only eight sendon—an indication of the latter's more specialized nature. The most beautiful of all suluk, Sendon Tlutur, is reserved for scenes of intense pathos—such as Karna's death in *The Death of Karna.* The music for ada-ada is the simplest of the three types of suluk. The singing of one is

---

* This follows Surakarta usage. Jogjakarta terminology differs somewhat, but the concepts of usage are similar (see Jaap Kunst, *Music in Java* [The Hague, 1949], I, 322–329).

accompanied by a single gender, plus either steady tapping (*angganter*) of the tjempala against the side of the puppet chest or beating of the hanging metal plates.* The dalang varies the speed and the loudness of his tapping or beating to suit the mood of the scene.

Normally no action occurs during patetan because it is largely descriptive of a static situation. Like an aria in Western opera, it elaborates on a set mood. In general, this is also true of sendon, though in *The Death of Karna* during the singing of Sendon Tlutur Princess Srikandi enters and finds Sandjaja's corpse. Because sendon occur in the most highly emotional moments of a play, it is unusual for them to be sung in patet nem, where the play's over-all emotional level is at its lowest. The only sendon regularly sung in patet nem is Sendon Pananggalan, which follows the entrance of a guest in the first scene of *The Reincarnation of Rama.* The faster tempo of singing ada-ada and the loud accompanying sound effects make them ideally suited to emphasize violent emotions. The term *gregetsaut* may or may not be included in the title of an ada-ada, but its meaning of anger and exasperation is central to that suluk's function in a play. When the dalang sings ada-ada to tense rapping, expressing the violent emotion of a stationary character, the dalang makes the puppet's arm tremble with excitement. In other cases, an ada-ada is used alternatively in place of a gending to move an aroused character offstage, or to bring one onstage. Numerous examples are seen in each part of the plays translated.

As mentioned, the dalang may sing traditional lyrics of a suluk or else he may alter them to suit the needs of the play he is performing. Traditional suluk melodies do not vary to any appreciable degree from performance to performance. Musical notation for them indicates the pitch of each sung note. The singing, however, is done in a free rhythm. When a dalang substitutes new lyrics for traditional ones they may be composed of a different number of syllables than in the original lyric—though theoretically they are not supposed to be—in which case the contour of the singing is somewhat altered from the original. In singing the dalang follows the pitch given him by the gender barung. He may, for a phrase or an entire suluk,

---

* In addition, gong, kenong, kempul, and ketuk normally punctuate the singing of all three types of suluk.

Introduction: Wajang in Performance

sing "oooooo" or another syllable rather than the lyrics, in a technique called *gombangan* or *ombak*. (If the dalang sings this way during a gending, as he may, it is called *njuluki* or *gerong*.)

Dramatic Function. In all, between one hundred and one hundred and fifty gending and thirty to forty suluk traditionally may be used for wajang kulit. Through long-established custom, certain of the selections are considered appropriate for certain uses and not for others. A gending normally occurs within the part of the play matching its patet or musical key; this is true also of suluk. The rhythmic structure of a gending partially determines where and for what purpose it may be used. Gending with short gong phrases tend to be played at a fast tempo and are suitable for lively moments, such as the bright-sounding Gangsaran, which concludes a play, or Kebogiro, played for the marching of the troops in Part One. Bouyant yet dignified gending of medium-length gong phrases are suitable for major audience scenes—for example, Krawitan, of 64 beats to a gong phrase, for the opening scene of a play. Gending of long gong phrases—128 or 256 beats—in which a delicate web of melody is woven over a long span of time, are excellent in concert or to accompany dances, but they are so long they are not easily used in wajang. One of the longest gending in these translations is Laler Mengeng, with 128 beats to a gong phrase, used for the majestic and stately audience scene late in Part Two of *The Death of Karna*, in which the saddened Pandawas first appear.

It is apparent that some gending and suluk have one and only one use, while others can be used often and in several ways, although Javanese do not classify them in this manner. Selections of the first type might be termed "specific," and of the second "general" in use. If the appropriate situation for a specific gending or suluk does not arise in a play, it will not be played. And, since situations seldom are repeated within a play, a specific gending or suluk would normally occur but once in a performance. Textbooks match specific gending and suluk with location, scene type, action, and character. Here are a few examples, following Surakarta textbook usage and taken from the translations. In the opening scene, when King Durjudana is the major character, Kabor is the appropriate gending (*The Death of Karna*), but when King Kresna is the major character,

Krawitan is more suitable (*The Reincarnation of Rama* and *Irawan's Wedding*). In the Outer Audience scene, Kembangtiba should accompany the entrance of Minister Sangkuni (*The Death of Karna*), but Kadaton Bentar is needed for Prince Samba or Minister Setyaki (*The Reincarnation of Rama* and *Irawan's Wedding*), and Ada-ada Astakuswala Alit should be sung for whoever exits to assemble the troops (all translations). The gending Langengita may only accompany a refined hero in his Part Two forest journey (*The Reincarnation of Rama*), and Ada-ada Gregetsaut Gatutkatja is sung only for Gatutkatja's appearance flying (*The Reincarnation of Rama* and *Irawan's Wedding*).

In some cases the dalang can choose from among several appropriate specific gending. Either Babad or Parianom may accompany the ogre King Dasasuksma's entrance in the Foreign Audience scene in Part One (Babad is used in *The Reincarnation of Rama*), though neither is appropriate in Part Two for an ogre king. (Galagotang would be used, as in *Irawan's Wedding*.) There are five possible gending for reviewing the troops in Part One—Wrahatbala (*The Reincarnation of Rama* and *Irawan's Wedding*), Kebogiro (*The Death of Karna*), and Manjarsewu, Bubarannjutra, and Singanebah which are not used; four for Judistira's entrance in Part Three—Bangbangwetan (*Irawan's Wedding*), and Budjangganom, Lagudempel, and Ramjang which are not used; and so on.

The elaborate system of matching specific gending and suluk to certain scenes, characters, and actions in Surakarta-style wajang is outlined in Appendixes A and B. It is the rare dalang who knows all, or even most, of the almost two hundred musical selections listed in textbooks. The dalang is also limited by the number of musical selections his musicians know. And no single play requires the use of more than a fraction of the total, perhaps fifteen gending and twenty or more suluk. Gending and suluk are fewer in number in Jogjakarta-style wajang and the system of matching is less complex.*

Three gending, played many times in a play, can be considered general purpose gending: Ajak-ajakan, Srepegan, and Sampak. Each has different, though overlapping, uses. Ajak-ajakan accompanies entrances (often substituting for a specific

---

* Differences in how gending are used in Surakarta and Jogjakarta are discussed in Kunst, I, 336–343.

Introduction: Wajang in Performance

gending), and is the gending which most commonly accompanies the exit of characters at the conclusion of a scene. Srepegan, lively and faster than Ajak-ajakan, is played for faster exits and entrances, and for the slower, more showy battles in the early or middle sections of a play. Sampak, fastest and loudest of the three, is standard for excited entrances and exits in the later sections of a play and for battle scenes. As tension in a scene rises, the music may shift from a quieter to one of the stronger of these gending. Here are two examples from *The Reincarnation of Rama:* the warriors enter to Ajak-ajakan Nem prior to the Opening Skirmish scene, but as the battle begins the music shifts to Sampak Nem; and Ardjuna begins to fight the ogre Tjakil in Part Two to lively but light Srepegan Sanga, which changes to louder, stronger Sampak Sanga when Gututkatja, a more vigorous character, joins the battle.

General purpose suluk are suitable for a range of use within a particular patet. The suluk Patet Nem may be sung after any gending in the first part of the play where there is no other suluk specified; Ada-ada Gregetsaut Manjura may be sung for any tense emotional moment within the third part of the play; the suluk Patet Sanga may be sung, according to wajang texts, "wherever needed" within scenes in Part Two; and so on.* General purpose patetan and ada-ada may have short *(djugag),* long *(ageng),* and normal length *(wantah)* versions; the dalang can pick the length which best fits the timing of the scene.

Cues. With instrumental and vocal music of such great importance in a wajang kulit performance, some system of signaling the gamelan is necessary. Even within the somewhat abbreviated translations in this book, more than one hundred separate musical selections are indicated in the stage directions of each play. Counting times when music starts, stops, changes melody, softens, or becomes louder, between one hundred and fifty and two hundred music cues would be made by a dalang during the performance of one of these translations. A dalang has four different ways of signaling his intentions to the musicians during a performance: *wangsalan,* or word cues;

---

* The ways in which general purpose suluk can be used are outlined in Appendix B.

On Thrones of Gold

tapping of the wooden tjempala or the metal kepjak; singing a melodic phrase of the desired music; through movements of the puppets.

Each gending in Appendix A has a traditional wangsalan associated with it; these are listed in wajang textbooks. To cue the gamelan, a dalang works the required wangsalan into his preceding tjarijos. A wangsalan may be a synonym or a homonym. That for the gending Remeng (*The Death of Karna*) is a synonym. Remeng means "dim" and the wangsalan *kadi surja kalingan mega* means "like the sun covered by the clouds." The connection in meaning can be made by one familiar with wajang, but most people probably could not. Homonymous wangsalan are easier to grasp, because they rely on similarity of sounds, not meaning. The wangsalan for the gending Galagotang, in *Irawan's Wedding,* is *tan gotang,* and as long as a person knows there is such a melody as Galagotang, the cue is clear. In some cases a dalang is able to have a character simply say the name of the gending, as Petruk says in *Irawan's Wedding,* "Come on, 'Reng, let's go. I'll sing Langengita for you."

A dalang can signal his musicians with a variety of tapping cues, only a few of the more common of which are given here. If Ajak-ajakan is the gending desired, the Surakarta dalang signals by making five spaced taps of the tjempala against the side of the puppet chest. This is known as *banju tumetes,* or "dripping water," because of its slow, steady rhythm. Srepegan is signaled by double taps (textbooks say seven) during the last sentence of dialogue or narration in a configuration called *geter,* because it resembles the double-beat of the human heart. Sampak is started by five quick, sharp raps, followed by loud beating of the kepjak. The usual way to begin a specific gending is to rap three times in a signal called *dero dug,* the onomato-poetic sound for the Morse code · — —. In performance these three raps would be preceded by the appropriate wangsalan, to tell the musicians *which* gending to play.

A dalang raps three times, dero dug, to soften the gending (sirepan) after the puppets are in place. Then he begins his djanturan description. The djanturan finished, he raps loudly; the gending resumes normal level and the female singer and the musicians often sing along with the melody. If the dalang wishes to sing a suluk after this he can sing "oooo . . . ," or a phrase of lyrics, in the melody of the suluk he wishes. If he does not want to sing he raps as the gending ends and goes immediately into dialogue. Because a specific gending has a fixed length, determined by the length of the gong phrase, the musicians automatically cease playing when it concludes; the dalang's signal, therefore, is not a signal to end the gending but to tell the musicians what he intends to do next. Since the dalang cannot alter the length of these important gending, he must carefully time his speaking and the entrance of the puppets to match precisely the internal punctuation of the gong phrase and the final gong beat.

Unlike specific gending, Ajak-ajakan, Srepegan, and Sampak have no fixed length and therefore no automatic stopping place. They are made up of short musical phrases, repeated as many times as the needs of the scene dictate. To stop one of them the dalang raps sharply, the musicians play a concluding phrase, and the music ends.

In battle scenes and in shorter dialogue scenes in the later sections of a play, the entrance of a puppet or some specific gesture or movement of a puppet may be taken as a cue to end a gending. It is very apparent when a battle is ending. Often the music slows down, and the major character moves in precise rhythm to it, so that when he is firmly planted in the banana log on a gong beat, this is a clear signal for the music (often Sampak) to stop on that note. In the Flower Battle in *The Reincarnation of Rama*, the cue for the gamelan to end Srepegan Sanga and to begin Sampak Sanga is the action of the arrow's striking Pragalba.

The kepjak metal plates are beat in time to mark the entrance of some puppets (such as Durna) but their major use is in battle scenes. Throughout a perang the dalang maintains a rather constant beating and then each time a puppet lands a blow or strikes the ground, he smashes the plates making a great crashing sound to reinforce the action. In delicate perang, such as the Karna-Srikandi fight, the kepjak are not used.

SPEAKING TECHNIQUES

Different vocal techniques are associated with the dalang's delivery of djanturan, tjarijos, and ginem. The ritual descriptive passages of djanturan are delivered in deliberate stylized phrases. Sentences may be separated by a sharp rap or two on the puppet chest. A specific gending plays in the background, and the pitch of the dalang's voice during djanturan as well as the tempo of his delivery are determined largely by its melodic and rhythmic pattern. Since the over-all pitch level of the gending rises in each successive patet, so does the pitch of the dalang's voice—lowest during the first part of the play, higher during the second, highest during the third.

Passages of dialogue, ginem, are also pitched one or more notes higher in each successive part of the play. Also, pitch and vocal quality are varied to distinguish puppet types. The higher the puppet's gaze, the higher the vocal pitch and intensity. Karna, with straight-out gaze, speaks in a high, tense, rapid voice; Ardjuna, with downcast gaze, speaks slowly, without tension, in a relatively low pitch. As between puppets of different body shapes, larger figures have lower and more resonant voices, while the voices of smaller figures are higher pitched and, more noticeable, are thinner in quality. Bima's voice booms and rumbles, while both Karna's and Ardjuna's voices are higher than his and less resonant. Figures like Durjudana, Bima, and Ardjuna speak on a single tone most of the time, and the pitch of the dalang's voice is quite precise during their speeches. The speaking voices of more excitable figures like Karna, or Dursasana rise and fall over a range of a octave or more. It might be wondered how the dalang can keep his pitch during dialogue, for neither gending nor suluk are playing then. Throughout a scene, the gender barung player quietly improvises around the basic notes of the patet. The audience is scarcely aware of it, but it provides the dalang with a constant musical frame of reference for the dialogue.

A dalang must be highly skilled in vocal impersonation to be able to distinguish vocally forty to sixty characters in performance. Unquestionably, the systematic assignment of certain pitches and qualities to certain types of puppets makes his job easier. A dalang may at his discretion rap, usually three times, between major speeches of conversing figures. The rapping punctuates the end of a character's line and calls attention to the next speaker. It also gives the dalang a second or two to change his voice. He often separates with one or more raps important phrases within a character's speech.

Tjarijos is delivered in a less stylized manner than djanturan; still it is far from normal speech. Because it is matter-of-fact narration and without musical accompaniment, few special techniques are associated with it. The dalang's voice pitch is supposed to conform to the pitch of the patet, and during gara-gara and other exciting tjarijos he will emphasize the scene's tension with steady angganter tapping during his delivery.

MOVEMENT TECHNIQUES

The dalang is concerned with five aspects of movement techniques, which, together, are called *sabetan*. They are; holding the puppet (*penjepenging*), lifting the puppet from the debog or banana trunk (*bedolan*), placing the puppet in the debog (*tantjeban*), basic movements (*lampahan*), and battles (*perang*).

A puppet is held in one hand. It is grasped on the main stick, or gapit, just below the feet, the exact place and method depending upon the type of puppet. The larger the puppet, the higher it is held. The smallest figures—females and alus males (lijepan and lanjapan)—are gently held at the tips of the fingers, three to four inches below the feet of the puppet. These puppets are light in weight, and the dalang uses a delicate grip to execute the graceful movements expected of them. Intermediate-sized puppets—kedelen up through Gatutkatja, smallest of the important gagah figures—are grasped in the fist about two inches below the feet, with the tip of the thumb resting against the feet of the puppet for support. Large gagah figures like Bima and ogres are grasped as high on the stick as possible while the whole length of the thumb is placed along the feet for the greatest possible support. The largest puppets weigh several pounds; hence considerable strength is required to manipulate them smoothly. The dalang may hold only one puppet at a time or he may hold one in each hand. Rarely he holds three or more at once. (In *The Death of Karna,* the dalang holds three puppets as Gareng and Petruk carry off the corpse of Sandjaja.)

When the dalang sets up a scene he brings the puppets on one at a time and places them in the debog; except for exits and the entrance of an additional character or two, they remain in their places throughout the scene. There is no "blocking," or movement between characters, to speak of. Hence, the original composition of the figures is of the utmost importance. The general rule is that the figures should be placed half way between the center and outer edges of the playing area. When there are an equal number of puppets on either side of the stage this rule works out in practice (Figs. 35, 140). But in many scenes, especially djedjer, the major figure is on the right of the screen alone, or with one or two minor figures beside him, while facing him from the left may be as many as four (Fig. 71), five (Fig. 50), or even six (Fig. 97), figures. For proper visual balance of the scene, the dalang moves the major figure further right and some of the left figures may even cross the center line (Fig. 43). Actually, the dalang usually sits slightly left of center to bring his hands near the largest number of puppets. If more than two puppets are called for on either side of the screen, they must overlap, as can be seen in the pictures of each play. The forearm of each puppet is left free, so it can be moved, and the silhouette of the face should be as unobstructed as possible.

To indicate that a character is standing, a dalang places the main stick of the puppet in the upper trunk of the debog, with its feet parallel to and resting on top of the red border. Though a king is conventionally described in djanturan as "sitting" on his throne of gold and jewels, the legs of a puppet do not bend nor are properties such as a throne used, so the king is placed in standing position. The relative rank of those facing the king in audience can be determined by their placement in the debog. Puppets of dependent rank are stuck into the lower debog, at an angle, as if they were sitting on the floor with heads bowed low out of respect. Samba, for instance, is seen in this position before Kresna (Fig. 17). Kings in their own right—for example, Baladewa—stand on the upper debog, even when they appear on the left attending another king (Fig. 17). Bima is a special case. He is merely a prince, like Ardjuna, but he is so strong-willed he stands straight in the upper debog even in the presence of a king (Fig. 44).

Good dalang technique requires that a puppet be placed in the debog firmly, in a single movement. Though this may sound simple, it requires strength and delicacy of control. The placing must be timed to occur at the end of a musical phrase, usually on a gong or kenong beat. Entrance, the pace of walking, making the sembah, and placing the puppet are all precisely timed to the length and tempo of gending phrases. To describe fully all movements and their coordination with music during the entrance of puppets for a major scene would require several pages, but perhaps something can be gathered from a few examples taken from textbook instructions for performing the Inner Palace scene:

Lift the Kajon on the third kenong beat and place it to the right in the lower debog.

Limbuk enters on a gong beat, moving from right to left, swaying her arms, regulated by the kendang rhythm.

Limbuk is placed in the lower debog on the left, facing to the right, on the second kenong beat.

Tjangik enters on a gong beat, moves from right to left as if laughing, and is placed before Limbuk.

Setyaboma enters on the third kenong beat of the third gong phrase.

To bring a puppet figure alive before the screen, a dalang may, immediately on his entrance, have him tie his sash, fix his headgear, or stroke his moustache. If the dalang is holding a puppet in each hand, he puts the right puppet in first, mainly because his right arm is stronger and he can use it alone more easily than his left. If he is holding only one puppet, he is advised to use both hands to place it properly. Once placed, the dalang arranges the arms in positions appropriate to the type of puppet. The technique of removing a puppet from the debog is not complicated, but it too must be accomplished in one decisive movement, without false starts. To remove large puppets smoothly requires both hands. If two puppets are to be removed simultaneously, as in a battle sequence, both hands are used to gather up the arm sticks of the left puppet first and then the right hand alone prepares the right puppet for lifting.

There are basic movements of walking and standard gestures. A lijepan puppet like Ardjuna walks smoothly across the screen, with no vertical movement. Both arms hang straight down or one swings back and forth gently. A lanjapan figure like Karna walks smoothly, with no vertical movement, but more briskly than the lijepan character; the rear arm is akimbo and the forearm may be held out at a thirty-degree angle to illustrate his forcefulness. A dignified gagah figure like King Durjudana walks with his rear hand on his hip, moving slowly up and down, like the swell of the sea. A rough gagah figure like Bima, bounds across the screen in two or three great leaps, rear arm cocked behind him and forearm raised high in a strong gesture. Ogres walk with a rolling, dancelike gait if comic—like Terong —or with precipitous and violent motions. The sembah is a gesture of respect, most commonly occurring in audience scenes. The two hands are brought together, lifted to the face, and then in one motion—either sharp or gentle, as the situation demands—the arms are lowered (Fig. 15). If a dalang is holding the puppet in the air at the time, he may bow the figure during the sembah. Every dalang is skillful enough to execute the sembah by moving the two arm sticks with just the thumb of the hand which is holding the main stick, if his other hand is not free. Shock is expressed by stroking the chest or striking it with one hand (Fig. 141). Sorrow is illustrated by draping the forearm over the shoulder, normally during suluk. As a greeting, Bima or Karna or Sangkuni salute by bringing the rear arm sharply forward from the face (Fig. 100). Puppet figures may embrace (as do Kresna and Judistira—Fig. 97), hold hands (Fig. 110), carry a small object (like the mirror Sangkuni holds up to show Karna that his moustache has been shaved off, Fig. 121), and in battles weapons are carried and used. The number of specific gestures is not large, and most are conventionalized. Compared to *bunraku* doll-puppet theater in Japan, whose puppets are famed for recreating every conceivable human activity—eating, changing clothes, smoking pipes, sobbing realistically—wajang movements are restricted. In aristocratic wajang no value is placed on displays of middle-class domesticity. It is concerned with courts, love scenes, mystic philosophy, and battles—all removed from the pettiness of daily life. The virtual absence of domestic actions taken together with the vast array of battle movements, is a clear reflection of wajang's world-view.

Battle movements as sharply defined and executed as the movements of classic ballet are wajang's most intricately conceived and spectacular performance technique. In Jogjakarta-style wajang kulit, one hundred and nineteen separate attacking, chasing, striking, biting, kicking, blowing, fleeing, holding, rising, fainting, choking, climbing, falling, lifting, wrestling, avoiding and blocking movements are used in hand-to-hand combat. Still other movements are used for fighting with weapons: lijepan and lanjapan puppets fight with arrows (Figs. 40, 41, 42) or daggers (Fig. 128); Tjakil's weapon is a dagger (Fig. 37); gagah and large ogres fight with clubs.

Combat is a personal contest. Two characters of equal rank meet; they attack each other; one either flees or is thrown off screen; and the other pursues. Every perang—regardless of length, complexity, or type of puppet fighting—is a linked series of meet-attack-flee-pursue confrontations. Within succeeding confrontations, fighting movements become more difficult, more interesting, and faster, building to a climax in which one combatant is either driven off or killed. As a play progresses, battle scenes become longer and more complex. While each confrontation is between two opponents, the hero may be challenged successively by several foes (as Ardjuna is in *The Reincarnation of Rama*), or a battle may be made up of a sequence of combats between different sets of opponents (as in the Great Battle scene).

It would be too complicated to describe in detail a complete perang, which would consist of several hundred separate movements. The basic movements used in one section of the Flower Battle—the killing of Terong by Ardjuna—are given in Appendix C. In this battle the alus Ardjuna moves slowly and with great control. He shows his utter contempt for his roaring, charging opponent by calmly turning his back to the ogre. When Terong charges, Ardjuna reaches out behind, and without looking, holds and strikes the ogre a stunning blow to the head. In battle scenes the large ogre typically goes into a fit of rage, in which he turns somersaults, whirls around, eats the earth, and throws rocks at his alus foe.

A typical sequence showing two alus figures fighting (Figs. 124, 125, 126, 127) has the opponents first leaping past each other. After several feints, one puppet strikes the other swiftly (Ardjuna holds his opponent's head and strikes), lifts him, and hurls him off left. A gagah figure like Bima absorbs blows, rather than avoiding them like an alus figure. One of Bima's favorite fighting techniques is to smash his foe against a rock, crushing him to death (Fig. 109). There are nine different ways a puppet, hurled off, may fly across the screen and fall to the ground. Depending upon the type of puppet and the situation, the fall may be on the face, on the back, horizontally and backward, after making a somersault in the air, arrested by the arms, or, for a hapless ogre, flat on the face after flipping over twice in the air.

On the basis of puppet type and location of the battle in the play, thirty-two distinct battles are identified in Jogjakarta-style wajang. One is "alus versus alus" in Part Two; another, the same puppet types in Part Three; a third, "gagah versus alus" in Part Two. Other battles are special for gods, women, or monkeys, and Bima and Gatutkatja each star in two. A student dalang practices a skeletal, standard battle of each type. When he has mastered them, he also has learned the complete repertory of battle movements and can, in performance, improvise from them complex and extended fighting scenes of many hundreds of linked movements.

THE DALANG'S ABILITIES

A good dalang is one who knows the basic requirements of his art. Texts prescribe the abilities and knowledge he should possess. He should know sufficiently proper court etiquette (*unggah-ungguh*) to make his puppet figures act like the gods and demigods they are. He should not allow hesitations (*remben*) to break the smooth flow of music, action, and dialogue. He should know the pakem, or traditional play scenarios, well and clearly present the major story line (*tutuk*) while avoiding audience-pleasing material not pertinent to the action of the play. In spite of the ethical and religious nature of much of the drama he performs, the dalang is enjoined not to have favorites among his characters but to allow each to perform his allotted deeds without taking sides (though the audience undoubtedly will take sides). He should have a flexible voice (*antawatjana*) that can distinctly characterize the various figures, and he should be able to manipulate the puppets adroitly (*trampil*) in battle scenes. His performance is deemed faulty if it continues into daylight (*karahinan*), if it is cut short (*kabogelan*), or if the three patet are not equal in length. No rule is more constantly mentioned than the injunction that a play must last precisely until dawn and that each part should be three hours long (Part Two beginning at midnight, Part Three at 3 A.M.). In actual fact, though, it is the rare performance that lasts precisely nine hours—eight or eight-and-a-half is nearer average—and seldom does a patet last just three hours. Patet of four-two-two or even four-three-one hours are more typical than the textbook division.* These may be recent

* For example, a performance of the final play of the *Bratajuda,* given in 1964 in the palace of the Sultan of Jogjakarta, lasted eight hours and fifteen minutes: patet nem lasted three hours and forty-five minutes; patet sanga, four hours; and patet manjura, just twenty-seven minutes.

changes in performance patterns, or it may be that this neat theoretical division of a lakon into three equal parts has never been consistently reflected in performance.

The truly excellent dalang not only follows the technical requirements of wajang tradition but also infuses his performance with a living vitality which one unfamiliar with the possibilities of a "shadow play" may find difficult to imagine. No theatrical experience in the world is as hypnotically fascinating as watching the ephemeral, yet strangely super-real, figures of wajang's shadow world live, suspended in space against the screen. The truly superior dalang is the one who can, as the Javanese say, move his audience to tears (nges), as in the Karna-Surtikanti scene in *The Death of Karna*, make them laugh uproariously at the jokes of the clowns (lutju), arouse their erotic sensibilities (sem), as in *Irawan's Wedding*, and grip them in the awful suspense of the outcome of the play (greget), as the audience is gripped by the terrible beauty of Karna's death-battle, knowing and waiting for the moment he will die, his throat pierced by Ardjuna's arrow.

THE TRANSLATIONS

The Reincarnation of Rama occurs early in the Amarta period. The Pandawas are young: Ardjuna is beginning to court Sumbadra, who will become his first wife; Baladewa is on good terms with the Pandawas, and has not as yet become their adversary; Anoman, from the earlier Rama cycle, is alive, though a very old and weary ape. The main plot tells how the gods offer the generation of the Pandawas, as divine gifts, reincarnations of the spirits of the gods Wisnu and Basuki, thus linking the Rama and Pandawa cycles. Wisnu's spirit passes to Kresna and to Ardjuna from its previous incarnation in Rama and Leksmana. Released by this act from their last mortal obligations, Rama and Leksmana take their leave of earth. The ogre king in the play is the spirit of the dead King Rawana, Rama's demon enemy of the Rama cycle; the subplot of the lakon concerns his abduction of Sumbadra, a reincarnation of Sinta, Rama's wife. When Anoman finds that the spirit of Rama, his old master, has been reincarnated in Kresna, he offers him his loyalty. Not only does the lakon link the Rama and the Pandawa cycles, and in so doing demonstrate the continuity of kingship so important in Javanese cosmology, but the lakon would seem to mark the real beginning of the Pandawas' glorious days at Amarta. Authority and Truth have passed to Kresna and Ardjuna, setting the seal of the gods' approval on the Pandawas.

Conflict and high passion are largely absent in this lakon. The abduction of Sumbadra precipitates what little conflict there is, and this seems scarcely more than a mechanical following out of classic play structure. The abduction has no effect on the main plot, which concerns the receipt of the divine gifts. It is notable that this action proceeds without serious obstacle. The mood of *The Reincarnation of Rama* is dignified, speculative, and almost casual. The play can be faulted for poor construction, but its importance lies in its philosophic content.

Irawan's Wedding takes place at the height of Pandawa splendor and power. Ardjuna has married countless times. Sumbadra, his first wife, has borne him a son, Abimanju, who has grown up and is on his honeymoon as the lakon begins. Irawan is the son of another wife, Ulupi. Baladewa is firmly allied with the Kurawas; it is he who precipitates the conflict of the lakon, by demanding Titisari, already engaged to Irawan, as a bride for Durjudana's son Lesmana Mandrakumara. In the intrigue that follows, the Kurawas are outwitted, tricked, and humiliated. At the very time Lesmana is journeying to meet his expected bride, she is discovering the joys of love with Irawan in the garden. At the end of the play Baladewa challenges Bima to admit that the Pandawas have deceived him. Bima cheerfully agrees they have—because they are in the right.

Irawan's Wedding is considered one of the most difficult lakon to perform because of its intricate plot. The three-sided conflict between the Pandawas, the Kurawas, and the ogre kingdom is well integrated: complication after complication arise naturally to keep in motion the pell-mell sequence of events. The plot involves many people (more than either of the other plays): Kresna, Ardjuna, Bima, Baladewa, Siti Sendari, Samba, Sangkuni, Barandjana, Lajarmega, and Gatutkatja all have a hand in the palace intrigue. The young lovers, Titisari and Irawan, are not movers in the drama, but spectators. This is in part a reflection of the custom of arranged marriages, but also Irawan is

Introduction: The Translations

manipulated because he is by nature an unassertive young man. This type of hero is not usual in Western drama, but in many Southeast Asian countries the handsome young prince, retiring to the point of ineffectuality, is a common dramatic figure. Princess Siti Sendari is the one who schemes and even lies to Kresna, her father, to bring the young couple together and, by so doing, save her own marriage to Abimanju. The separation of the newly married Siti Sendari and Abimanju is a genuinely touching moment, but it passes quickly. Other than this, the mood of *Irawan's Wedding* is light, romantic, and at times frenetically comic. No one appears to be taking very seriously the problem of whom Titisari will marry. Audience scenes spoof the pompous greetings and ritual expressions of fealty which the usual lakon present with the greatest seriousness (here wajang's conventionalized dramaturgy offers delightful opportunities for satire). In all, it is a smiling play.

The Death of Karna is one of the lakon portraying the Great War which brings to an end the lives of the Pandawas and the Pandawa cycle. The time is fifteen to twenty years after *Irawan's Wedding*. Gone are the easy and glorious days when the Pandawas sported at Amarta. Amarta has been lost to the Kurawas in a game of dice, and for twelve years the Pandawas have lived in poverty in the forest. They have been befriended once more by King Matswapati of Wirata, and with the help of their adviser, Kresna, have tried to negotiate the return of at least some of their lands. But Durjudana has refused to listen. Remembering all the humiliation he and the Kurawas suffered at the hands of the Pandawas from the time they were children, he has refused to give them any land, "not even the dust that can cover the head of a pin." Reconciliation between the cousins is impossible, and the Great War, which all know must end in almost total destruction, begins.

In *The Death of Karna* many of the characters from the earlier plays are gone. Anoman, presumably, is still guarding the mountain cave where the spirit of Rawana is entombed (in some interpretations, Durjudana is a reincarnation of Rawana). Baladewa is not aware of the conflict (were he, the Kurawas probably could not be defeated), for Kresna has tricked him into meditating far from the battlefield. Abimanju has been slain in the war, and Siti Sendari, true to the vow she made in *Irawan's Wedding*, has thrown herself on his funeral pyre and burned to death. Gatutkatja and Irawan have been killed in battle. On the Kurawa side, of King Durjudana's ninety-eight brothers, ninety-four have been slain. The slaughter is so great and so terrible, lakon of the Great War were seldom performed in Java before World War II, because it was believed an error in performance of lakon as important as these would bring on calamity. *The Death of Karna* begins on the seventh day of the Great War and continues through to the ninth (the count of days varies in different versions). It is the lakon which immediately precedes King Durjudana's death and is considered one of the most beautiful and moving of wajang kulit plays.

Although he is slain by Ardjuna, the play's nominal "hero," Karna is the play's central figure. He is a demigod, the son of Surja, God of the Sun. Karna is also Ardjuna's elder half-brother, but because he was rebuffed by the Pandawas in his youth and because Durjudana generously befriended him, he lends his great military strength to the Kurawas in the Great War. Kresna has appealed to him to join the Pandawas, as has Kunti, his and Ardjuna's mother, but he nobly remains faithful to his Kurawa benefactors. The play focuses directly on the conflict between Karna and Ardjuna, the two "shining" warriors. The battle between them, which lasts almost a third of the play, is so noble a sight the gods and nymphs gather in the heavens to watch. A strong mood of pathos prevails, for it is intimated that Karna knows he is fated to be slain. Except for the jokes of the punakawan—and these limited to the gara-gara scene—the lakon is consistently serious.

STRUCTURE

The Reincarnation of Rama and *Irawan's Wedding* are tjarangan plays which follow classic dramatic structure. An ogre kingdom, Tjakil and his ogre companions, and the Flower Battle are important in each. In *Irawan's Wedding* the sabrangan, or ogre, element is well integrated into the plot; in *The Reincarnation of Rama,* the main plot moves independently of the ogre subplot. But both plays, from the beginning of the Foreign Audience scene in Part One until the end of the Flower Battle in Part Two, rely heavily on subplot scenes. In *Irawan's Wedding* the main plot begins when Baladewa forces Kresna to send a message canceling Irawan's marriage, yet it is not until the middle of Part Two that we hear of the message again, when Samba arrives before Ardjuna. This great gap in the main plot line is filled largely by ogre-related incidents.

While *The Death of Karna* is a pokok play, its structure has numerous parallels with the classic structure of the other plays. The scene of Bima in the battle camp in Part One fulfills the ogre function of providing the army of the first kingdom with opposition so that there can be an Opening Skirmish scene. The three linked battles in Part Two—Suwega versus Drestaketu, Karna versus Sandjaja, and Karna versus Srikandi—are the equivalent in dramatic function of the linked combats of the Flower Battle. A departure from the usual form is that the major battle between Ardjuna and Karna begins early, in Part Two, and continues through many variations throughout most of Part Three. But the main difference is that, without a third—ogre—kingdom in the plot, the dramatic conflict between Karna and Ardjuna can be focused upon much more strongly than can the conflict in the other two plays. From a dramatic standpoint, *The Death of Karna* is probably the most satisfying of the plays for the Western reader..

There is no gara-gara scene in *Irawan's Wedding,* though a dalang could include one if he wished to. But the lakon is long and does not require the scene to flesh it out. Also, the violent mood of the gara-gara opening seems inconsistent with the light, romantic quality of this lakon. Gate scene and Inner Palace scene are included in *The Reincarnation of Rama,* for the play's subdued tone and philosophic mood are enhanced by the description of the splendors of Dwarawati's Gate of the World and by the grace and charm of the women's scene. Again, a dalang could include almost identical scenes in *Irawan's Wedding* if he wished. Here they are not in order to maintain the forward movement of what is already an intricately plotted play. Neither Gate scene nor Inner Palace scene would be appropriate in *The Death of Karna.*

CHARACTERS

Characters in drama are revealed by what is said about them and by what they do. Major characters in wajang kulit are introduced in long djanturan passages which describe their many virtues: Ardjuna is praised as "Paragon of Men" and "Invincible

Warrior," Judistira is "He Whose Blood Flows White," Ardjuna's first wife is the "lovely and delicate Sumbadra who inspires peace of mind," and so on. These traditional formula descriptions of character are well known (often deriving from epic literature) and it is tempting to take them at face value. Characters, however, do things in the plays not hinted at in djanturan. The Sumbadra who is so vain and coquettish in *The Reincarnation of Rama* that she prefers being abducted by an ogre rather than let Ardjuna rescue her, is different from the one described in the djanturan. Kresna, the all-wise "divine king" is lied to and tricked by his own daughter in *Irawan's Wedding*; he doesn't have a single bright idea on how to cope with the dilemmas of his two daughters, leaving the problem to Siti Sendari to solve. Only at the end of the play, when he defends the honor of his elder brother Baladewa, does he assume the qualities traditionally associated with him.

What could be more contrary to the ritual description of Ardjuna as an "Invincible Warrior" than for him to send his young son Abimanju to plead with Kresna for the father's life? Within the lightly humorous context of the play, we do not object to his action, knowing nothing serious will come of it. Still, this is not the way djanturan describes him. According to the standard description it would be expected that Ardjuna would subordinate his grief over the death of his son Abimanju, in *The Death of Karna,* in order to carry out his duty as commander of the Pandawa army; instead he is listless and moping, and it is only when Srikandi bitterly recounts how Karna humiliated her by shooting off her dress (forgetting to explain that she forced him to fight her) that Ardjuna is roused to anger and wants to storm off to fight Karna. This action is very human, but it is a different side of his personality than that described traditionally. (It is the ritual description of Ardjuna, always in control of his emotions, regardless of the hatred or despair he feels, which makes Samba's scene before him in *Irawan's Wedding* so funny: the audience knows Ardjuna is masking his anger; Samba does not.) Bima's accusation in *The Reincarnation of Rama*—that Judistira always pretends to be about to burn or drown himself if he doesn't get his way—is a far cry from the formula description of Judistira as "Purest of the Pure," who cannot think a devious thought. The ritual, set-piece description of character which appears in djanturan may

Introduction: The Translations

serve to sketch in the general personality of a character, but it is idealized and thus misleading. For a true picture of the figures in wajang kulit drama there is only one reliable source— the action of the lakon themselves.

Within the three lakon Ardjuna emerges as the central wajang figure; he is the single most important character in *The Reincarnation of Rama* and a major figure in the other two. He is reputed to have some seventy names or titles, more than any other figure in wajang (more than any king). No other figure is given seven possible gending to accommodate variations of a single scene, as he is in the Hermitage scene. (He even has a special gending just for loosing his arrow in the Flower Battle.) Bima is probably the second most important character. He too has many names, and, like a king, his dress is described in minute detail (*The Reincarnation of Rama*). A special suluk is sung when he leaps off on one of his prodigious journeys (only Gatutkatja also has a special suluk for himself). It is he who turns back the enemy during the final battle of a play, and normally it is his right to execute the victory dance. In *Irawan's Wedding* it is Bima who boldly lies to the Kurawas and then confronts Baladewa to win the day for the Pandawas. And, for all of his roughness, he—not a god, a seer, or other mortal— explains to Anoman the mystic meaning of the five forces, the five colors, and the five brothers. Bima's role is not as large as Ardjuna's, but it is crucial. Irawan, ostensibly the hero of *Irawan's Wedding,* actually is a minor figure in the play. Karna, as the central figure in *The Death of Karna,* has the largest single role in any of these translations, but, as he is a major figure in only two other standard lakon, over-all he is of less importance than, say, Kresna or Baladewa, who appear in lakon after lakon. Semar is traditionally spoken of and thought of by audiences as being the greatest god of all, Ismaja, who could, "if he so desired, rule the world." His great powers are mentioned in these three lakon, but they are not demonstrated as they are in some other plays. Most subsidiary characters are shown in a typical light. The Kurawa minister, Sangkuni, renowned for his craftiness, uncovers Siti Sendari's abduction plot. Kresna's empty-headed and idle son, Samba, unknowingly, hilariously botches his mission to Ardjuna. Lesmana Mandrakumara is foolish, vain, a laughing-stock, even to his own relatives. Judistira rules but does not act; Nakula and Sadewa fill in the stage picture and do nothing at all. Rawana is treated with respect, as befits a great ogre king, while Barandjana, who is a younger ogre king of no particular standing, is outrageously ridiculed.

A major characteristic of the language used in wajang is its formality. There are fixed patterns of formal salutation. In the First Audience scene, four lines of dialogue traditionally are spoken in greeting: welcome by the king; thanks by the guest for the welcome and a greeting; acceptance by the king of the greeting and a blessing to the guest; acceptance of the blessing by the guest. This four-part salutation is seen in full in *The Reincarnation of Rama* and *Irawan's Wedding*; in *The Death of Karna* it is slightly abbreviated for dramatic effect. In the course of a lakon the formality of salutation diminishes; this is reflected by salutations of three or even two lines of dialogue. The lakon with the most formal language is *The Death of Karna,* because of the high seriousness of the piece. Special forms of address are used in the gods' scene in Suralaja in *The Reincarnation of Rama.*

Wajang characters address each other using honorifics and titles except in the most informal situations. A warrior addresses his king as "noble King" or "honored Majesty," or speaks to a seer as "divine Teacher." These formal salutations often include the speaker's blood relationship to the person being addressed: Kresna calls his elder brother Baladewa, "brother King"; Irawan addresses his grandfather Kanwa as "holy Grandfather." But "uncle," "son," "father," and other such terms are also used in Javanese even when a blood relationship is not implied. Karna's wife Surtikanti speaks to their chief minister Adimenggala as "Uncle Adimenggala" and Sumbadra calls Semar "Father" to show respect for the age and wisdom of the two men; Sangkuni speaks to Durgandasena as "my Son" because he is Durgandasena's elder. In most situations it should be apparent from the context which relationship is intended.

Formula phrases and even what must be called, for lack of a better term, formula paragraphs occur in all the plays. The most important are the ritual titles of kings and princes, the oath of fealty to the king, the descriptions of kingdoms and of

Introduction: The Translations

major wajang figures, the gara-gara, the hero's forest journey, and in particular the opening section of each play. Wherever formula expressions occur they have been given the same translation, although in performance there might be variation.

One of the most tragic events in the plays, Surtikanti's suicide in *The Death of Karna*, hinges on a pun in the original text. Karna dispatches Adimenggala for *sedah*, "betel nut," which Surtikanti hears as *seda*, "death"; thinking her husband slain, she kills herself. No convincing English equivalents could be found for these words which have almost identical sounds in Javanese (and a literal translation into "betel nut" and "death" would have been meaningless), so the situation is transposed in the translations to one in which actions, rather than words, are misunderstood. Karna dispatches Adimenggala to return to Surtikanti a ring she had given him; when he tells her Ardjuna still lives and thrusts the ring into her hands she thinks Karna has been slain and so kills herself. The dramatic point of the scene is that Surtikanti dies through a misunderstanding and this is kept in the translation.

In translating suluk, original lyrics have been followed whenever the meaning of the suluk is appropriate to the lakon. Where the meaning of a traditional lyric is not appropriate, suitable lyrics have been created—just as a dalang would create new lyrics in Java today. About a third of the lyrics approximate the originals, a third are variations on the originals, and a third are new.

ETHICS

The actions of some characters in the plays present interesting ethical issues. Because the society depicted is aristocratic, it is not surprising to find that the moral principle of absolute loyalty to one's king is often expressed. Samba's pledge of fealty to Kresna—his king and his father—in *The Reincarnation of Rama* and in *Irawan's Wedding,* as well as minister Pragalba's to his king, the ogre Barandjana, are examples. Karna's great nobility lies in his refusal to be swayed by the arguments of Kresna and his mother to join the Pandawas in the Great War; his loyalty is to his king, Durjudana. But other characters act against their king, following a "higher ethic" which demands that each weigh the moral issues and act according to the greater good. King Dasasuksma's servant Togog says that because the king is in the wrong he can not actively support him; though he does not desert his king, he sulks and withdraws from contact with him. In the Great War, Sandjaja leaves the Kurawas and joins the Pandawas, saying the Pandawas represent justice and virtue. Karna, following the ethic of loyalty, hotly calls Sandjaja a traitor. Sandjaja, true to his belief that virtue lies in supporting the good and the true, says Karna fights merely for prestige and honor, not out of virtue. Both Karna and Sandjaja are killed defending opposite ethical principles. There are many ramifications to the conflict between these two moral positions, but the action of the play seems tacitly to support Sandjaja, for the Pandawas, who above all people should not accept unethical support on their behalf, never suggest that Sandjaja has acted improperly in leaving the Kurawas. They accept his sacrifice, implying that he, not Karna, was right. (Contrast, for example, how, in his struggle with Ardjuna, Karna refuses help from the serpent Ardawalika because it would be improper.)

Some actions of the Pandawas clearly are contrary to the ethical norms established in the plays, yet are not explained or justified. An elder brother's word must be obeyed, as Kresna makes abundantly clear in *Irawan's Wedding,* yet Siti Sendari interferes with the wishes of Kresna's elder brother Baladewa and arranges for Titisari to be spirited away from her bridegroom-to-be, Lesmana Mandrakumara. Siti Sendari not only is not punished for her deception, but because of it her marriage is happily restored. This is hardly an example of the immutable law of *karma,* which is supposed to underly wajang morality, in which each act receives its just reward or punishment. Bima lies to Baladewa, and teaches Gatutkatja and the gentle Irawan to lie as well. We can accept as some justification Bima's argument that Baladewa, after agreeing to the marriage of Titisari and Irawan, broke his word. Yet, does Baladewa's single improper act justify the succession of deliberate deceits which the Pandawas then perpetrate?

Combat is supposed to be between two individuals who first announce themselves and their rank; interference by a third person is considered foul play. Yet, in the midst of the Flower Battle in *The Reincarnation of Rama* and *Irawan's Wedding,* Gatutkatja intervenes: unheralded, he swoops down from the

Introduction: The Translations

sky to strike the unsuspecting ogre a stunning blow; Terong is so surprised he exclaims, "The sky is clear, yet lightning strikes!" (In the Great War when Abimanju is killed, not by a single opponent but by the arrows of scores of Kurawa warriors striking him simultaneously, the Pandawas loudly protest that *this* is foul play.)

It is not easy to draw conclusions from only three plays, and issues raised in one may be settled in others. Yet it does seem as if the Pandawas, because they are in the right to begin with, are granted a certain license in achieving their goals which is not permitted the Kurawas or the ogres.

HUMOR

Humor is largely the province of the punakawan characters: Semar and his sons, and Togog and Saraita. The latter normally appear in the Foreign Audience scene of Part One, but the servants of the Pandawas, the most important clown figures, do not appear until Part Two, as in the translations. They joke in colloquial Javanese and often make contemporary, hence anachronistic, remarks. They may, in Java, speak of the high price of rice or criticize some recent government action. In the translations, they act anachronistically when they shake hands, take up a boxing stance, speak of the "rules of heredity," advertise the "ass on this donkey," and when Petruk goes out to buy cigarettes.

Puns are basic to punakawan humor, but unfortunately they are difficult to translate. Some puns have been retained and others created, to at least give the flavor of their word-play. Semar's "non-a-meat-all forest," and Petruk's "your Washer" for "your Worship" are examples. But the clowns' zany antics, storytelling, physical humor, and ribaldy are not so different in spirit from that of Western vaudevillians and present no special problems in translation. In the Hermitage scene the clowns are more subdued than when they are by themselves in the gara-gara for the very good reason that their master and a holy seer are present. The punakawan also delight in parodying the manners and actions of their noble masters, as when, in *The Death of Karna,* Gareng and Petruk marvelously mangle the ritual confrontation of Ardjuna and Tjakil in the Flower Battle.

Tjakil and his friends are also a source of humor in the two plays in which they appear. Their gait and uncouth actions provoke laughter. They are superb foils to the Pandawas' clowns when the two groups meet and trade insults prior to the Flower Battle, as in *Irawan's Wedding*. Situation humor is an important element of the less serious plays. The plot of *Irawan's Wedding* is almost an extended practical joke, and scene after scene is framed in a humorous context: the Kresna-Baladewa encounter in the first scene, Samba's report back to his father, the repeated dagger-sheath references, Irawan's courting of Titisari, Bima's lying scene and the subsequent throwing off of Baladewa, and the sudden turning coward of both the vaunted warriors Ardjuna and Bima before Kresna's wrath. Wajang humor is often ribald and uninhibited; wherever this type of humor occurs we have tried to maintain its spirit in translation.

The translations follow textbook rules for structure and performance techniques, perhaps suggesting that wajang possesses a rigidity that does not in fact exist. In shaping a performance, a dalang has wide latitude to depart from the standard rules and traditions. Will there be a gara-gara? Shall the play be lightened with a scene set in the inner palace? What topics of the day will the clowns joke about, and should they be on stage half an hour, an hour, two hours? Should the second, third, and fourth scenes of Part One be dropped and a special battle inserted in their place? Should traditional or modern melodies be used? How long should major battles last? Which wanda, or expression, of puppets should be used? How will major characters be interpreted? In making these and scores of other decisions a dalang considers the occasion of performance, his host's requests, the mood of the audience, and, in the end, his personal inclinations. In part he follows past traditions; in part he innovates, improvising and experimenting as much as he wishes. Born of the stage, not the poet's pen, wajang kulit is still—in spite of its cultural and literary significance—a performer's art par excellence and no rules can fully encompass its creation. The translations, then, though standard, are only one way each play might be done. There could be as many versions of each as there are dalang to perform them.

The Reincarnation of Rama   Wahju Purba Sedjati

Translated by Pandam Guritno Siswoharsojo
and Stephen R. Alkire

English version by James R. Brandon

Cast of Characters

KINGDOM OF DWARAWATI

King Kresna, ally of the Pandawas
Prince Samba, Kresna's son, crown prince of Dwarawati
Prince Setyaki, Kresna's brother-in-law
Udawa, chief minister of Dwarawati
Queen Djembawati, Kresna's first wife
Queen Rukmini, Kresna's second wife
Queen Setyaboma, Kresna's youngest wife
Princess Sumbadra, Kresna's younger sister
Limbuk, attendant to the queens, Tjangik's daughter
Tjangik, attendant to the queens
Maidservants

KINGDOM OF MANDURA

King Baladewa, Kresna's elder brother
Pragota, chief minister of Mandura
Prabawa, chief minister of Mandura

KINGDOM OF TAWANGGANTUNGAN

King Dasasuksma, spirit of slain ogre king Rawana (of Rama cycle)
Prince Begasuksma, Dasasuksma's son, spirit of slain Indradjit (Rawana's
    son in Rama cycle)
Togog, clown-servant of Dasasuksma, brother of Semar
Saraita, clown-servant of Dasasuksma
Maritja, commander of the ogre army (portrayed by puppet of Tjakil)
Lodra, an ogre warrior (portrayed by puppet of Terong)
Pragalba, an ogre warrior
Galijuk, an ogre warrior
Saksadewa, an ogre warrior

HERMITAGE OF SAPTAARGA

Abijasa, religious ascetic, former king of Astina
Disciple

KINGDOM OF AMARTA

King Judistira, eldest Pandawa brother
Prince Bima, second Pandawa brother
Prince Ardjuna, third Pandawa brother
Prince Nakula and Prince Sadewa, fourth and fifth Pandawa brothers,
    twins
Prince Gatutkatja, Bima's son
Semar, clown-servant to the Pandawas, in reality the god Ismaja
Gareng, eldest son of Semar
Petruk, second son of Semar

KINGDOM OF SURALAJA

Guru, highest manifested god, ruler of the world
Narada, Guru's elder cousin, messenger of the gods
Basuki, god formerly in serpent's shape
Baju, god of wind

FROM RAMA CYCLE

Spirit of Rama, former king of Ajodya
Spirit of Leksmana, Rama's younger brother
Anoman, white monkey, ally of Rama

The Reincarnation of Rama

Before leaving home the dalang begins to concentrate his senses upon the performance. He silently prays, "Om. May nothing give hindrance, O Spirits of this house, flying over the earth, Mother of Generations. Allah, assist me, fulfill my wish, gratify my intentions. Creatures, male and female, look at my work, be pleased, and love by God's will. Oh, Allah! Oh, Allah! Oh, Allah!" Holding his breath, he stamps three times with his right foot.

On arriving at his host's home the dalang repeats the same prayer, requesting the help of the spirits of the host's dwelling. At about eight-thirty the fifteen to twenty musicians who make up the gamelan begin to play the Talu, or introductory music. As the Talu draws to a close, the dalang takes his place before the center of the screen praying. "O Great Serpent who supports the earth, O Spirits all here, I ask your help. Let not the onlookers disperse before I have finished performing my art."

The dalang inspects the performance equipment which is set up on the veranda of the host's home. He checks to see that the screen has been fastened tightly, that the banana-log "stage" which holds the puppets is properly installed, that the puppets not being used for this performance have been set up on either side of the screen or put away in the big puppet chest on his left, that those which will first appear in the evening's drama are beside him, within easy reach, and that the KAJON, the "Tree of Life," is firmly planted vertically in the center of the screen.

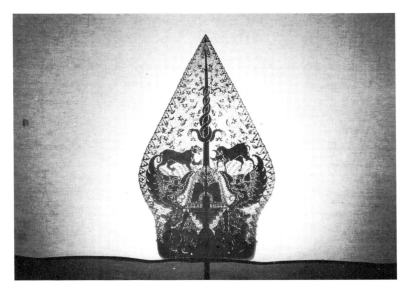

Fig. 14
Kajon

On Thrones of Gold

Most of the audience has gathered. The host and his guests are seated on chairs set up on either side of the screen. Casual passersby sit on the ground or stand crowding around the performance area. Spectators on the dalang's side of the screen will see a "puppet" performance; those on the opposite side will see a "shadow" performance. It is now nine o'clock. As the introductory music concludes, the dalang raps sharply five times against the puppet chest on his left to signal the gamelan ensemble to play Ajak-ajakan Nem, the opening melody of the play, quietly saying as he does, "The hills and mountains are my abode, may the strength of the wind and storm be mine." He reaches above his head to the coconut-oil lamp which casts the shadows on the screen. Adjusting its flaming wick, he prays silently, saying, "Om. O God of the Soul, Essence of the One, O God of Light, may the flame of the lamp shine over the world. May those who come be silent, show pity and love, and may they stay to look at me." The dalang reaches for the KAJON, raises it carefully out of the banana trunk, then slowly lowers it.

He holds the KAJON in his lap so that the tip rests on the puppet chest. Gently, with his left hand, he bends its tip several times, quietly speaking his final prayer before the performance begins: "May my body be large and strong like the mountains. May those who come be silent. May they show pity and love as is God's will." The dalang moves the KAJON from the lower left to the upper right corner of the screen, twirls it three times, and places it at the right of the screen, indicating that the play is about to begin.

The Reincarnation of Rama

PART ONE

Scene 1

(The dalang takes up the puppets of the two MAIDSERVANTS. *One in each hand, he presses them against the screen to make a clear shadow. They enter right and move gracefully to the center of the screen.* They look about them and see the king, their master, approaching from the right. They sit cross-legged on the floor, their faces cast down, honoring the king with the sembah—the traditional gesture of obeisance in which the hands, palms pressed together, are brought before the face. The imperious figure of* KRESNA *enters from the right. He is refined in appearance, but his head is proudly held high and he walks with his hand authoritatively on his hip.*

Fig. 15
Kresna and
Maidservants

With a slight gesture he acknowledges the MAIDSERVANTS, *who sembah again, rise, and move deferentially to assigned places to the rear of the king. The three chief members of the king's retinue enter from the left, greet their lord, and take their traditional places in audience before the king. First to enter is* SAMBA, *the king's son and crown prince. His figure is delicate, refined. He enters crawling, honors* KRESNA *with the sembah, and sits respectfully before him.* SETYAKI, *the king's brother-in-law and commander of the kingdom's*

---

* Right and left as seen from the dalang's point of view. Pictures of the shadows show puppets reversed.

armies enters crawling, makes the sembah, and moves behind
SAMBA. *He is followed by* UDAWA, *the king's chief minister. The*
characters remain in tableau as the dalang signals the gamelan to
end the melody Ajak-ajakan Nem and begin Krawitan by a steady
tapping on the side of the puppet chest. The tapping speeds up, end-
ing with three loud raps; Krawitan softens and the dalang begins
the story of the kingdom.)

djanturan NARRATION *(intoned, following pitch and rhythmic patterns of*
Krawitan): May silence prevail. Numerous are God's creatures
that roam the earth, fly in the sky, and swim the seas. Countless
are the world's beautiful women. Yet none can equal those to
be found in the Kingdom of Dwarawati—Gate of the World.
Search one hundred countries, you will not find two, nor among
a thousand, ten, to match it. Thus, do I introduce this Kingdom
as our story's beginning!

Long, high, sands, mountains, fertile, prosperous, trade,
peace, foreigners. Long is Dwarawati's reputation and the telling of it. High is its prestige. Ocean's sands border it; mountains guard its rear. On its right lie fields of rice, to the left a
great river leading to a harbor on its shore. Fertile is its soil;
prosperity abounds. Merchants trade by day and night, unceasingly in perfect safety while peasants' flocks and herds
freely roam. Never has rebellion stirred the peacefulness of
this land. Foreigners throng to make Dwarawati their home.
The roofs of their dwellings touch in friendship, crowding the
largest places and making them seem small. All state officials
are united in a single aim—to increase the glory of the Kingdom
of Dwarawati. The Kingdom stands firm over the earth. Its
torch is high, illuminating all the world with its radiance.
Many are its colonies. Not only on Java do countries submit
themselves to its rule, but kings from afar proffer allegiance,
so great is their love for the perfection of the Kingdom of
Dwarawati. Near, they bow to the earth before its perfectness;
farther afield they incline to show their respect. Annual tribute
of maidens and precious gifts is offered by all as token of their
submission.

Who is the King who rules this Kingdom? He is King Kresna
—"Kresna the Black," whose skin, blood, and bones are black
as the color of ebony. Many are his titles: "Guardian of the
Pandawas," for he loves and advises the five virtuous brothers,
"Bridge Between Man and God," "Giver of Life," "Kresna the
Charitable," "Kresna the Seer," "Deterrent to Disaster," and

The Reincarnation of Rama

"Incarnation of Wisnu." Among the god Wisnu's several incarnations, it is said that two are King Kresna and the Pandawa Prince, Ardjuna. As a flower and its scent, or a fire and its flame, the flower is Kresna, the scent Ardjuna, the fire is Kresna, the flame Ardjuna. Like the front and the back sides of a leaf, their appearance is different, their taste the same. The King of Dwarawati is endowed with the characteristics of sage, judge, warrior, and noble. The most excellent of kings, he is powerful yet humble, wise yet shares his wisdom. He cares for his subjects; he clothes the naked and feeds the hungry, aids the infirm and offers shelter from the sun and rain, cheers the mournful and heals the sick. To recount all the King's virtues and the greatness of his Kingdom would consume the long night. What has been said must be sufficient.

It is on a Wednesday that the King appears in the audience hall. He seats himself upon his throne of gold and precious jewels. A lush carpet of fresh-cut flowers, fragrant with the scent of exotic perfumes, cushions his feet. Maidservants, dancers, and concubines in elegant costume attend him. They bear golden, gem-incrusted figures of state—swan, serpent, cock, and elephant. Servants on either side of the King stir cooling breezes with fans of peacock plumes until his fragrance reaches to the outermost quarters of the palace. In the midst of such spectacle, the King appears no longer human, but the image of the god Wisnu descended to earth and accompanied by heavenly nymphs. In reverence to the King even the breeze ceases to whisper. Still are the leaves on the trees. Only the soft music of the gamelan, the tinkling rhythm of the goldsmith's hammer, and the call of the kolik bird perched in the banyan tree in the square are heard from afar, enhancing the dignity of the occasion.

Who are those who sit respectfully before the King? Directly in front of the King is his son, Crown Prince Samba. He is a handsome young man of great virtue and integrity. Considerate of others before himself, his understanding of human nature is both wise and compassionate. The Prince's energetic actions always accord with his father's desires. Behind the Prince sits the King's cousin and brother-in-law, the warrior Setyaki, adviser to the King and Commander of Dwarawati's armies, and chief minister of the Kingdom, Udawa. To the rear, the great audience hall is filled to overflowing with Dwarawati ministers and officials of all ranks, seeking places even in the outer courtyard to attend the King.

On Thrones of Gold

SONG (*The dalang raps once on the gong beat; the gamelan ends Krawitan melody and begins accompaniment for song Patet Nem Ageng which the dalang sings*):

> Oh Ruler of the Universe,
> > My prayers to thee.
> On your favor
> > We depend for our well-being
> > In this world and after.
> Oh I pray have pity on me
> > And my followers,
> > Night and day worshiping thee.
> Shower your blessings on Dwarawati
> > Oooooo . . . oooooo . . .
> So the King prays in his heart.

SONG (*The dalang continues with the song Ada-ada Girisa, his singing accompanied by gentle tapping and the soft sound of the xylophone*):

> Silent is all in the great hall,
> > Even the wind ceases blowing
> > In reverence to the King.
> Sitting in wordless wonder
> > At the divine secret
> > To him alone just revealed.
> Far away he will travel
> > Across plains and mountains
> > To the stillness
> Of his ancestors' tombs
> > Oooooo . . . oooooo . . .

(*Since the king and his court have taken their places there has been no movement before the screen. Now the dalang raises* KRESNA'S *forearm and the king speaks.*)

*Fig. 16
Maidservants,
Kresna, Samba,
Setyaki, and
Udawa*

The Reincarnation of Rama

KRESNA *(speaking in a tense, strong voice of medium-pitch):* Samba, my Son, you are welcome in my presence.

(A triple rap on the side of the puppet chest punctuates the end of KRESNA'S *speech.)*

SAMBA *(strong, but light voice):* Majesty, my Father, I accept your welcome with both hands. Allow me to present my reverent greetings.

(The dalang makes a triple rap on the chest as SAMBA *bows deeply before his father, raising his hands before his face and making the sembah of respect.)*

KRESNA: May your greetings delight me, my Son. I extend to you my blessings. *(Triple rap.)*

SAMBA: I accept them in the warmth of my heart, kingly Father. *(Makes the sembah.)*

KRESNA *(gesturing to* SETYAKI*):* Cousin Setyaki, I hope you arrive well? *(Triple rap.)*

SETYAKI: In the presence of Your Majesty, I lack nothing. Please accept my homage, oh King. *(Triple rap as* SETYAKI *makes the sembah of respect.)*

KRESNA: Thank you, Cousin. Accept my blessings. Rest comfortably while I speak with my son. *(Triple rap.)*

SETYAKI: Thank you, Your Majesty. *(Triple rap while he makes the sembah.)*

KRESNA *(gesturing to* SAMBA *with forearm):* Samba, were you not surprised when you received the summons of your King?

SAMBA: Majesty, when I received the royal command, I felt as though my spirit had been shattered, crushed against a rock, as though lightning bolts had struck me, but, as if by a miracle, I was unhurt. My heart trembled like grass blown by the wind in the great square; it fluttered like a leaf caught in the eye of a storm. But when I arrived in Your Majesty's presence, my heart grew peaceful again, as if cooled and cleansed of fear by the sprinkling of holy water. *(Makes deep sembah of obeisance.)*

KRESNA: How is it, my Son, that your anxiety so quickly passed? *(Triple rap.)*

SAMBA: Seeing Your Majesty, I realized that if I were guilty of some sin, it would be Your Majesty who would punish me, that were I to be condemned to death, it would be Your Majesty who would command it. My only wish is to do Your Majesty's will, though it mean my life. Remembering this, I felt content, my King. *(Makes the sembah.)*

KRESNA: My Son, your loyalty greatly pleases me, but you allow imagination to overcome you. There is a saying that however fierce the tiger, he will not devour his own young. Should he be judged guilty and sentenced to death, the King's forgiveness is always there. He who sits upon the throne of Dwarawati may cut the grass where it blocks the light and give solace to the suffering as he chooses. But do not misinterpret my meaning. Expect neither reward nor punishment. Gifts are as far from my mind as a star in the sky, my Son. *(Three raps.)*

SAMBA: My Father, gifts are not in my thoughts, nor even in my dreams. Your generosity flows like the surge of a mighty river, so that being near you your kindness overwhelms me. I expect nothing, but live only to fulfill your commands. Your smallest word I shall obey. *(Makes the sembah.)*

KRESNA: Your replies greatly please me. What is the state of the Kingdom, my Son? Tell me frankly what you observe.

SAMBA: All is in order, Majesty, because of your beneficence. Every subject performs his duties properly and in your name. The army stands ready, the people enjoy good health. Farmers live peacefully and happily, there is food and clothing for all. *(Makes the sembah.)*

KRESNA *(gesturing):* Excellent. You have discharged your duties well, my Son. You may take your ease, for I anticipate the arrival of an honored guest.

SAMBA: Yes, Your Majesty. *(Makes the sembah.)*

SONG *(The dalang sings Sendon Pananggalan):*
>All sit in silent amazement
>>Of their King's powers.
>An unknown guest will be arriving
>>To visit their Lord.

tjarijos NARRATION *(spoken in normal voice):* The audience hall is tense with silence. All wonder who their Lord's guest will be. Suddenly, before the high walls of the palace, speeding with the force of an elephant on the rampage, there appears the figure of the King of Mandura riding in his chariot. Called King Baladewa, he is the brother of the divine Kresna. He is famous for his blunt and forceful ways. With great strides, looking neither left nor right, he mounts the palace stairs and enters the presence of the King of Dwarawati.

(The dalang raps three times, signaling the gamelan to play the melody Diradameta for BALADEWA'S *entrance.* SAMBA *moves to*

KRESNA'S *side.* BALADEWA *enters from the left, his rear arm set pugnaciously on his hip. He approaches* KRESNA, *and the two kings briskly salute one another with their rear arms. As they stand in tableau the melody Diradameta ends.)*

KRESNA: My royal Brother, Baladewa, welcome.

BALADEWA *(impulsive, somewhat domineering):* Kingly Brother, I thank you! I am honored to be in your presence. I give you hearty greetings.

*Fig. 17
Maidservants,
Kresna, Samba,
Baladewa,
Setyaki, and
Udawa*

KRESNA: May your kind greetings extend throughout my kingdom, my Brother.

SAMBA: Honored Uncle, I offer my deepest respects. *(Makes the sembah.)*

BALADEWA: My blessings, Nephew.

SETYAKI: I offer you my greetings, noble King Baladewa.

BALADEWA: I accept them with thanks and offer you mine, Setyaki. *(Three raps.)*

KRESNA: Brother, you arrive unescorted and unannounced. Make yourself comfortable, I pray, and tell us the purpose of your sudden visit.

BALADEWA: I come on a mission of grave importance and divine mystery! As my kingdom is yours and your kingdom is mine, brothers should not stand on formality but rather should act directly out of mutual regard and in good will. And so I come before you as I do.

KRESNA: As you are my elder brother, your desires are mine. Yet do not forget, Brother, that we are kings, and kings are obliged to observe rules of decorum that they may maintain their dignity in the eyes of the world. What is it you wish to tell me?

BALADEWA *(gesturing):* Yes, yes, Brother. That is true. Of course it is. And if, in the haste of my mission I have broken precedence, I apologize. It was out of fraternal love, Brother. *(He considers.)* Tell me, Brother. Had you known of my intended visit what would you have done?

KRESNA: I would have commanded the royal chariot be sent for you and a guard of honor accompany you, my Brother.

BALADEWA *(laughing delightedly):* Ho-ho! Why, Brother, that would swell my pride to the mountain tops! It is good to have kings for brothers, is it not, Brother! Do not despair, there will be other opportunities for you to honor me. Ha-ha-ha! *(Becoming serious.)* But, now, Brother, hear me. I want your opinion on a wondrous event that has occurred.

KRESNA: Your brother listens attentively.

BALADEWA *(gestures strongly):* I have received a sign from the Gods, Brother! A divine gift is about to be granted. The divinely inspired kingly traits of Authority and Truth are to be bestowed upon a nobleman of exemplary character and deeds!

SONG *(The dalang sings Patet Nem Djugag):*
> The fragrance of flowers
>> Strewn by the breeze,
> Divine wisdom
>> Sets the King's heart at ease.

KRESNA *(arm trembling slightly, showing his emotion):* I, too, royal Brother, have received omens from the Gods of the same event. We have been chosen by the Almighty to carry out his desires. We must not reveal to any other these divine portents, for until a prophesy is fulfilled, it must remain a secret of the Gods guarded by those to whom it has been entrusted.

BALADEWA: You are correct, my Brother. I have spoken of this portent to no one but your royal self. I have asked no one's advice but yours. What should we do, Brother Kresna?

KRESNA *(slight gesture):* Desire must be followed by effort, knowledge by action, faith by total surrender. Our goals are the same. I intend to devote myself to meditation at the tombs of our ancestors. However, I can neither advise you nor speak for you, my elder Brother. Each must follow his own path to reach enlightenment.

BALADEWA: Brother, allow me to accompany you!

KRESNA: If that is my royal Brother's wish, let us leave this day for the burial ground at Gadamadana.

BALADEWA (*strong gesture*): Brother, I agree!

KRESNA: Samba, my Son. Command the army in my name.

SAMBA: Yes, my royal Father. (*Makes the sembah.*)

KRESNA: Cousin Setyaki, during my absence I entrust to your care the welfare of our Kingdom.

SETYAKI: Reverent Majesty, with trembling hand I accept your trust. (*Makes deep sembah.*)

KRESNA: Come, kingly Brother, let us enter the palace and inform my Queens of our departure.

NARRATION (*normal voice*): And so the King ends his audience. All he has said must be strictly noted, for a king speaks his desires but once. The regal King Kresna and his royal brother, King Baladewa, depart for the palace. Striding side by side they appear to be the gods Wisnu and Brama surveying the world. **tjarijos**

(*The dalang raps five times signaling the gamelan to play Ajak-ajakan Nem.* KRESNA *and* BALADEWA *rise and move off right together. The two* MAIDSERVANTS *sembah and follow.* SAMBA *and then* SETYAKI *and* UDAWA *sembah and exit to the left. The* KAJON *is placed right of center, representing the palace gate.* KRESNA *and* BALADEWA *approach the gate from the left, followed by the two* MAIDSERVANTS. *They stop. Three raps; music softens.*)

Scene 2 adegan gapuran

NARRATION (*intoned, following pitch and rhythm of the music Ajak-ajakan Nem which continues in the background*): The divine King Kresna retires from the audience hall and returns to the inner palace. He steps from his throne and walks between rows of dancers chosen for their beauty. Their clothes stylish, their faces bright, their temples set with dark curls, they are indeed provoking. The King is clad in magnificently jeweled garments. Precious gems sparkle in abundance, from the golden bracelets encircling his ankles to the rings on his fingers and the elegant three-tiered crown atop his head. Like a hungry tiger, the King strides toward the Great Gate of Dwarawati, called the most **djanturan** splendid in the world. For a moment the King pauses to admire it. Built not by human hands, but by the magical powers of the god Wisnu, the gate surmounts the rooftops. High as a mountain peak, a giant ruby the size of an elephant's head is set in its arch, where it reflects with dazzling brilliance the rays of the sun. Stairs approaching and receding from it are inlayed with multicolored precious stones and guarded by railings of burnished brass. Carved upon the immense span of the entrance doors are likenesses of the God and Goddess of Love. Through the archway a formal garden stretches toward the palace, the pathway strewn with gems and precious stones. A bubbling spring may be heard—its waters, perfumed with rose petals, flow through the palace cooling and scenting the air. In the distance the palace rises majestically, its jewel-adorned walls shining day and night, bathed in the glow of the sun and the moon. King Kresna gazes upon the imposing gate before him, and orders servants to inform his Queens of his arrival.

(On the gong beat three raps; the gamelan melody Ajak-ajakan Nem resumes normal volume for three gong phrases during which KRESNA *and* BALADEWA *move right, walk up the side of the* KAJON, *indicating they are climbing the steps of the palace gate, and exit right followed by the* MAIDSERVANTS. *As the* KAJON *is placed center, inclined slightly to the right, the gamelan melody stops.)*

tjarijos NARRATION *(normal speaking voice):* The Maidservants hurry toward the palace bearing the King's summons to his Queens.

adegan kedatonan Scene 3

(The dalang raps three times; the gamelan begins the melody Titipati. The KAJON *moves to the right of the screen.* LIMBUK, *a comic maidservant with the face of a bulldog, enters from the right and moves in time to the music to the far side of the screen. She turns and looks back to see if her mistress is coming, but instead* TJANGIK, LIMBUK'S *mother, enters, crosses the screen, and takes her place beside* LIMBUK. *The younger queens* RUKMINI *and* SETYABOMA *enter quietly from the right and gracefully stand facing the two servants. The elder queen,* DJEMBAWATI, *takes her place in front of her sisters. The* MAIDSERVANTS *bow low and make the sembah. Three sharp raps; music softens.)*

djanturan NARRATION *(intoned, following the pitch and rhythm of the melody Titipati):* And so our story moves to the Ladies' Chamber of the

The Reincarnation of Rama

palace, where the three favorite Queens of King Kresna are instructing the court dancers. Special favorite of the King is Lady Djembawati—gentle and patient, sincere in the practice of asceticism, loved and respected by the King's other wives. Three sons has she borne the King. The Lady Rukmini is King Kresna's second wife. She is first-cousin to the King, and, like a royal pet, a trifle spoiled. Youngest is the lovely Lady Setyaboma, first-cousin both to the King and to the Lady Rukmini. Gamelan music sounds softly in the background, while hands clap in rhythm and voices sing harmoniously, accompanying the movements of the royal dancers. Word comes that the King is on his way, and the Queens prepare to greet their Lord.

(A single rap on a gong beat; gamelan melody Titipati is played at normal volume for one gong phrase, then ends. During the music, the queens exit left, followed by LIMBUK *and* TJANGIK, *then re-enter right in time to greet the two kings entering from the left.)*

Fig. 18
Limbuk, Tjangik,
Setyaboma,
Rukmini,
Djembawati,
Kresna, and
Baladewa

SONG *(The dalang sings Patet Nem):*
> High in the heavens
>> Stars shine like pearls
>> On the palace.
> Radiant sunbeams
>> Glow upon it
>> Oooooo . . . oooooo . . .
> Gentle blossoms,
>> Fragrant dewdrops,
> The King's consorts
>> Await his pleasure
>> Oooooo . . . oooooo . . .

DJEMBAWATI: My noble Lord, I honor your arrival. *(Makes the sembah.)*

RUKMINI: Allow me to greet your royal presence, my Lord. *(Makes the sembah.)*

SETYABOMA: My King, I offer the warmest welcome of my heart. *(Makes the sembah.)*

KRESNA: I accept your greetings with all my might. My blessings on you all.

DJEMBAWATI: Thank you, my Lord. *(Makes the sembah.)* And to your royal Brother of Mandura, we present our reverent greetings.

RUKMINI: Our greetings, oh King. *(Makes the sembah.)*

SETYABOMA: Yes, your Majesty. *(Makes the sembah.)*

BALADEWA: Thank you, Sisters. Accept my blessings.

SETYABOMA: May they spread to all who are near us. *(Gesturing to KRESNA.)* My Lord, the audience in the inner hall seemed of lengthy import today.

KRESNA: Yes, my dear. Overriding matters of state were concerns of the divine Gods.

DJEMBAWATI: How may we serve you, my Lord? Tell us, so we may obey.

KRESNA: What may be spoken of you shall know, my dear consort. I shall accompany my royal Brother to the sacred tombs of our ancestors at Gadamadana. We prepare ourselves for departure now. Order servants to prepare a place for meditation. More than this I cannot say.

DJEMBAWATI: Yes, Majesty. It shall be done as you command. *(Makes the sembah.)*

SONG *(The dalang sings Sendon Kloloran):*
>Oooooo . . . oooooo . . .
>Stars shine like pearls
>>On the palace.
>Radiant sunbeams
>>Glow upon it.
>Gentle blossoms,
>>Fragrant dewdrops.
>The King's consorts
>>Obey his order
>>Oooooo . . . oooooo . . .

(During the singing, all exit right in procession. The KAJON is placed center, slightly inclined to the right.)

The Reincarnation of Rama

NARRATION (*spoken in normal voice*): Now it is told how the two great Kings, accompanied by the three Queens, and their servants retire to the dining hall for the midday meal. Then the two Kings enter a dressing chamber where they don ceremonial dress for meditation. Retiring to a private chamber which has been prepared with the sacred implements, the Kings begin their meditation. The fragrance of incense impregnates the air of the chamber, issues forth, and sweetens the breezes outside.

tjarijos pagedongan

SONG (*The dalang sings Ada-ada Mataraman Djugag to steady tapping and the accompaniment of a xylophone*):
> Fire and incense
>> Reach to the sky,
> Carrying prayers
>> To the heavens
> Oooooo . . .

NARRATION: King Kresna, the Divine, sits motionless, arms folded across his chest. His eyes focus upon the tip of his nose. He strives to concentrate his mind, to empty his heart, to control his five senses. Expert in the control of the will, King Kresna appears a manifestation of the god Wisnu. He enters the realm of the supernatural. His soul seems to leave his body. What was unclear to him is now revealed. The great King slowly unfolds his arms. Elated, he worships all of nature. The Brother-Kings withdraw from the place of meditation, enter the court, and exchange their priestly garments for the warrior's dress required for their journey to Gadamadana.

tjarijos pagedongan

Scene 4

adegan paseban djawi

(*The dalang strikes the puppet chest sharply three times; the gamelan plays Kadaton Bentar as the* KAJON *is moved from the center to the right side of the screen, marking the beginning of a new scene.* SAMBA, UDAWA, *and* SETYAKI *enter from the right, immediately followed by* PRAGOTA *and* PRABAWA *from the left, who honor them with the sembah, and sit on the floor respectfully in front of them. Three sharp raps on the chest; Kadaton Bentar softens.*)

NARRATION (*intoned, following pitch and rhythm of the music*): Meanwhile, the Crown Prince Samba and his uncle, Setyaki, have arrived in the outer audience hall where Chief Minister of the Kingdom, Udawa, and numerous officials and warriors are gathered to hear the King's commands. Courageous in

djanturan

On Thrones of Gold

battle, responsible in leadership, Minister Udawa is greatly loved by the people of Dwarawati. Remaining respectfully to the rear of Udawa are Pragota and Prabawa, Chief Ministers of Mandura, who have journeyed with King Baladewa to this Kingdom. Officials and warriors press in from all sides, as if to crush the pillars of the buildings. Flags wave blown by the winds look like waves of the ocean, ebbing and flowing. Seeing the Crown Prince Minister Udawa thinks, "Oh, God, what is the King's message?" Respectfully they face the King's envoy.

(Three sharp raps; the melody Kadaton Bentar comes up to normal level for several gong phrases, then ends.)

UDAWA: My Prince, I am at your service. *(Makes the sembah.)*

SAMBA: Thank you, Prime Minister Udawa.

Fig. 19
Setyaki, Samba,
Udawa, Pragota,
and Prabawa

UDAWA: And to our Uncle Setyaki, may I offer my respects?

SETYAKI: They are welcome, Udawa. I extend my greetings in return.

UDAWA: I am pleased to receive them.

PRAGOTA *(direct and unsophisticated)*: Ah-ha-ha! It's you, my young Master? I present you my warmest greetings. *(Makes brisk sembah.)*

SAMBA: Thank you, Uncle.

PRABAWA: My greetings, Prince. *(Makes the sembah.)*

The Reincarnation of Rama

SAMBA: You are welcome here. I trust your long journey has not tired you, Uncles.

PRAGOTA (*with a delighted gesture*): Heh, heeeh! For old men, we are spry, my Prince!

UDAWA (*interrupting*): Forgive me, Prince Samba. May we know the King's wishes? (*Makes the sembah.*)

SAMBA: Uncle Udawa, the King and his brother intend to visit the burial place of the ancestors of our Kingdom, at Gadamadana.

PRAGOTA (*excited gesture*): Splendid! At last something important is happening. And I'm to be part of it. Delightful! Yes, yes, I shall accompany their Majesties. I shall bring flowers to my father's grave. (*Pause.*) It's been so long since last I saw it.

SAMBA (*quiets him with a gesture*): Uncle, their journey is to be a pilgrimage of meditation. No retinue may accompany them nor enter the sacred grounds. In fact they are to travel in secret. We are commanded to remain at our posts and to defend the order of the Kingdom.

PRAGOTA: Ah, how disappointing. But if it is the King's will, I shall obey. (*Makes the sembah.*)

SAMBA: The King wishes the army to stand at alert. Uncle Udawa, the troops shall be under your command during our Majesty's absence. Go now, Uncle, and issue the army its orders.

UDAWA: At once, my Prince!

SONG (UDAWA *makes a sembah and backs off left as the dalang sings the song Ada-ada Astakuswala Alit to steady tapping, underscoring the excitement of the offstage scene*):
> Thunderous is the sound
>> Of trumpet and drum
>> And beating gong.
> Flags and banners wave
>> Like the ocean's tide,
> Beautiful is the sight
>> Oooooo . . .

UDAWA (*off*): Attention! Soldiers of Dwarawati! In the name of King Kresna, Giver of Life, hear my orders! Assemble in three divisions: the first will guard the capital city, the second defend our borders, and the third patrol the seacoast!

SOLDIERS (*off*): Yes, Sir! We obey, Minister Udawa!

UDAWA *(off)*: Arm yourselves and assemble in the great square at the sound of the first gong! Ready on the second! We march on the third!

SOLDIERS *(off)*: Yes, Sir! We obey! We are ready!

UDAWA *(off)*: Excellent! Each man must be alert! Stand ready and await the King's command!

SOLDIERS *(off)*: Yes, Sir!

SONG (UDAWA *re-enters and takes his place before* SAMBA *during the singing of Ada-ada Astakuswala Ageng, which the dalang accompanies by steady tapping)*:
> Horses wildly whinny
>> As their riders mount.
> Sharp bits cut their mouths
>> And springs of blood gush forth.
> Clamorous signals mix with their cries
>> As horses plunge and rear
>> Oooooo . . . warrior's strong hands guide them.

UDAWA: The troops stand ready, my Prince. *(Makes the sembah.)*

SAMBA: Then sound the gong, Uncle.

UDAWA: Yes, my Prince.

SONG *(The dalang sings Ada-ada Budalan Mataraman to steady tapping as* UDAWA, *followed by* PRAGOTA *and* PRABAWA, *make the sembah and exit left)*:
> Numerous are the troops
>> Their uniforms bright,
> Like the sun rising
>> From the horizon
> To cast its golden
>> Rays on the world,
> Partly visible behind the mountain
>> Illuminating the clouds
>> Oooooo . . .

tjarijos   NARRATION: Minister Udawa strikes the gong as if to break it. Three times its booming voice pierces the air. Drums, trumpets, flutes, and bells thunder in response as the mighty Dwarawati army marches from the city.

(Three raps on the puppet chest by the dalang and the marching music Wrahatbala is played. All exit left. UDAWA *re-enters from the right, turns, and gestures to the massed troops off-right to pass in review. The* MARCHING ARMY *enters, and halts before the Prime Minister, who salutes it.*

The Reincarnation of Rama

Fig. 20
Marching Army
and Udawa

The MARCHING ARMY *moves past* UDAWA, *and marches off left.* UDAWA *turns and exits left. Now* PRAGOTA *enters, reviews the* MARCHING ARMY, *and exits.* SAMBA *mounts his horse and marches across the screen.* SETYAKI *follows on a prancing white steed, then* UDAWA. *The* MARCHING ARMY *follows them off.* KRESNA *and* BALADEWA *appear upon a chariot from the right. As the dalang raps three times on a gong beat, the music rises to normal volume for one gong phrase, and, as the music ends, the chariot halts in the center of the screen.)*

Scene 5

adegan kereta

SONG *(Ada-ada Mataraman is sung, to steady tapping):*
> Soon the magic carriage
>> Will take the brother-kings
> Speeding like the lightning
>> To distant Gadamadana
>> Oooooo . . .

NARRATION *(in a normal speaking voice):* The divine King Kresna and his elder brother, King Baladewa, travel in a resplendent chariot drawn by twin white stallions of magical powers. The one possesses the ability to fly; the other can avert all weapons. Covered with precious gems, and shaped like a small house, the King's chariot was a gift from the Gods. Its roof is composed

tjarijos

of tinted sea shells. Four golden eagles, their tails joined with a steel band, protect it. From above they seem to swoop and strike when the carriage is in motion. The doors are made of fragrant wood into which are carved delicate designs painted with gold. Yellow silk curtains bordered with lace cover the windows; the wheels are of gold and crimson. The horses are decorated with ornaments of rhinoceros horn and with fresh flowers and their reins are of pure pink silk. Tinkling bells on their harnesses make the sound of the moving chariot resemble that of the music of the Gods. Thus do the two Kings depart for Gadamadana. The driver, dressed like a God, urges the horses forward. The wheels spin, striking sparks in every direction. The carriage speeds so swiftly, indeed, its wheels soon seem not to touch the ground at all.

(Seven double raps signal the gamelan musicians to play the lively melody Srepegan Nem. The chariot crosses the screen three times and exits to the left. The KAJON *is placed left of the center of the screen, representing trees in the forest. The* MARCHING ARMY *enters from the right and stops facing the* KAJON. *The dalang raps, the coda of Srepegan Nem is played, the music ends.)*

*Fig. 21
Marching Army
and Kajon:
meeting*

Scene 6

adegan perang
ampjak

ginem wadya

FIRST SOLDIER: Hey! What's up? What are we stopping for?

SECOND SOLDIER: Yiii! Halt back there! Put those damned spears down! If I'm going to get stabbed to death it ought to be in the line of duty and not because some jackass is too stupid to stop with the rest.

THIRD SOLDIER: Hold it! At ease, there! The road's overgrown up ahead.

SECOND SOLDIER: Whew, now that we're stopped, where are we going? Anybody know?

FIRST SOLDIER: Ha, did you leave your brains behind in the kitchen? You're marching in an army loaded to the teeth with sword and spears and lances, and you don't know where we're going?

SECOND SOLDIER: Don't make it sound so strange. I was feeding my new fighting cock when I heard the alarm gongs ring. I know my duty as a volunteer as well as the next man. I just dropped him, grabbed my spear and uniform, and ran. I even dressed along the way.

FIRST SOLDIER: You volunteers are all alike.

SECOND SOLDIER: Well, I'm here. And I'd like to know where I'm going. If that's not too much to ask.

THIRD SOLDIER: Listen, soldier! Your duty is to go where you're told and not to ask questions. But if you really want to know, we are marching to the border by the King's command to guard against enemy attack.

SECOND SOLDIER: Hm. Is that all? There's no invasion?

THIRD SOLDIER: Our orders are to prevent any hostile troops from crossing the border into the Kingdom. Now, you up there, let's clear out the road. The Prince's chariot will pass this way soon. You with swords and axes, to the front. Cut down the trees. Clean out the underbrush.

SECOND SOLDIER: Join the army and learn to chop wood!

FIRST SOLDIER: It's clear you're not a professional soldier! Stop griping and do what you're told.

SECOND SOLDIER: And on a volunteer's pay, too. Well, it's the King's command. I obey.

FIRST SOLDIER: Let's go then, Friend. Make room up front! Make room!

(Seven double raps; the gamelan plays Srepegan Nem. In time to the music, the MARCHING ARMY *strikes the* KAJON *several times as if cutting a tree.*

Fig. 22
Marching Army
and Kajon:
striking

The KAJON *is thrown off left.*

Fig. 23
Marching Army
and Kajon:
throwing off

The MARCHING ARMY *exits after it. This happens three times. Then the* MARCHING ARMY *crosses the screen unhindered, marching*

The Reincarnation of Rama

away. The KAJON *flutters across the screen from right to left, symbolizing the cleared forest, and, after several passes, is planted in the center of the screen, inclined to the right, the music stops.)*

NARRATION *(spoken in normal voice):* Dwarawati's marching soldiers travel far. Column after column passes by. A unit dressed all in black looks like a flock of ravens, a green one like parrots swooping to feed on grain. One in red is a blazing forest, one in white herons on the marsh. The afternoon sun glints from thousands of burnished and bobbing weapons, so they look like the gleaming scales of fish darting in a pool. The thudding of footsteps, the sounds of drums and gongs, and the whinny of stamping horses blend into a muffled roar, like the fall of rain on a teakwood forest. Thunderclouds of dust rise in the skies. So do the troops of Dwarawati march. Arriving at the border they halt, to rest and to stand guard with watchful eyes through the night.

tjarijos

SONG *(The dalang sings Patet Kedu):*
> Looking at the countryside
>> Dimly lit by stars,
> Like fireflies
>> Pale in the sky,
> Paler than the full moon
>> Whose rising beauty
>> Fills men's hearts
> And casts a glow upon the forest's trees.

Scene 7

djedjer sabrangan

(Three raps; the gamelan plays Babad as the KAJON *is moved from the center to the right.* DASASUKSMA, *a large and impressive ogre king in human form, strides on from the right. His son,* BEGASUKSMA, *enters from the left. The king's clown-servants,* TOGOG *and* SARAITA, *enter and sit at his feet. Three sharp raps; Babad softens.)*

Fig. 24
Saraita,
Dasasuksma,
Togog, and
Begasuksma

djanturan   NARRATION (*intoned, following the pitch and rhythm of the music*): Our story now moves to the foreign Kingdom of Tawanggantungan, inhabited by a race of ogres. Its ruler is the mighty King Dasasuksma—a spirit-king. Before assuming his present form, the King was known as Rawana, ruler of Alengka. Brave and victorious in battle, he was endowed with magic powers. Not only did men and ogres fear him, but even the Gods trembled, for through the practice of intense asceticism he had obtained almost invincible power of warfare and the gift of eternal life. Such was his greed and his arrogance that the Almighty implanted in King Rawana's breast an unquenchable lust for the Princess Widawati, so as to cause his downfall. The Princess, incarnated on earth as the lovely Sinta, was abducted by Rawana and carried off to his palace in Alengka, rousing to revenge the only person capable of defeating him—the divine Prince Rama, Sinta's husband.

Prince Rama, with the help of the monkey-warrior Anoman and an army of monkeys, stormed King Rawana's island fortress, annihilated his armies, and struck down the body of the King. Though Rawana's body was destroyed, his spirit lived on in the form of Dasasuksma, the ogre-king. Even now, as a spirit, Dasasuksma burns with the fever of lust for the Princess Widawati, presently incarnated as the Princess Sumbadra.

The King is in audience with his retinue of ghosts and spirits of former times. Nearest the King, bowing as if to touch his nose to the floor, is his eldest son, Prince Begasuksma, known as Indradjit in his former life. Behind the Prince sit King Dasasuksma's favorite advisers and servants to the throne, Togog and Saraita.

(*A single rap on the gong beat, the music comes up to normal volume for one gong phrase, then ends.*)

SONG (*The dalang sings Patet Lasem*):
> Oooooo . . . the King,
>> Generous is he
>> Oooooo . . .
> Endlessly to his subjects
>> His gifts pour forth
>> Honoring his word
> Oooooo . . .

DASASUKSMA (*speaking roughly, in a deep voice*): Son! Welcome before me, handsome boy! Are you well?

The Reincarnation of Rama

BEGASUKSMA: I am, Father, if you will it. *(Salutes.)*

DASASUKSMA: Why, have you done something you shouldn't, charming Son?

BEGASUKSMA: Nothing. Majesty-Father!

DASASUKSMA: Well, then! You remain in the gentle glow of my favor! *(Gesturing to* TOGOG.*)* And how are you, 'Gog?

TOGOG: Fine, my King. Greetings to you, Majesty. *(Makes the sembah.)*

DASASUKSMA: Accepted. *(Gestures to* SARAITA.*)* Saraita?

SARAITA: In the presence of your divine grace I am always content, your noble Majesty. *(Makes the sembah.)*

DASASUKSMA: Yes. Blessings on you both. *(To* BEGASUKSMA.*)* Now, Son, report to me on the welfare of my subjects. Speak frankly, my handsome Begasuksma. I know things are well, but it pleases me to hear you say it.

BEGASUKSMA: Majesty, Father, Sire, the people are healthy and all is in order.

DASASUKSMA: Splendid. Now, I must speak to you of a matter that weighs on my heart. You know of my passion for the incomparable Princess Widawati. Since I first beheld her, I have desired her uncontrollably. I approached her like the great king I am; she preferred to leap into a flaming pyre and burn to ashes! Through three reincarnations as the wives of Wisnu's three reincarnations—follow me, handsome Son—I pursued her. To what avail? She has eluded me generation after generation! First, as Princess Tjitrawati she spurned me. Next, as Princess Sukasalja she repulsed me. Then, as Princess Sinta she not only turned me away from the inner chamber of my own palace, but brought on the destruction of our great Kingdom of Alengka. But now I have received word that she has been reincarnated a fourth time! This time she is Princess Sumbadra of the Kingdom of Dwarawati! And this time she shall be mine!!

BEGASUKSMA: Father, I am delighted to hear this good news. *(Salutes.)*

DASASUKSMA: Yes! 'Gog, what do you advise your King to do?

TOGOG: Majesty, the past tells its own story. You should send an emissary this time, my gracious King, formally to request permission of the King of Dwarawati for her hand. *(Makes the sembah.)*

DASASUKSMA: I should, perhaps, 'Gog, but that I won't do! She's humiliated me in the past. And the problems are so tiresome. Her older brother, King Kresna, would never allow the marriage, no matter how much the Princess desired it. No, 'Gog, let us be clever and snatch her out of the palace while no one is looking. But we must be careful! King Kresna's a favorite of the Gods and he's no fool. Who can accomplish this delicate mission, I wonder?

SONG (*The dalang sings Ada-ada Mataraman Djugag*):
> By his father's words
>> A brave Prince
> Is stirred
>> To duty
>> Oooooo . . . oooooo . . .

BEGASUKSMA: Exalted Majesty, allow this unworthy son, Begasuksma, to kidnap for you your future wife—Princess Sumbadra of Dwarawati! (*Salutes.*)

DASASUKSMA: Heh-heh! Ho-ho! I'm pleased. If you succeed, my Son, I will give you my throne and my Kingdom. I'll live in seclusion with your new stepmother. Content, you may be sure.

BEGASUKSMA: With your permission, I will leave at once for Dwarawati, honored Father. (*Salutes.*)

DASASUKSMA: Go with speed, Son! I eagerly await your return with my bride!

BEGASUKSMA: Yes, Father.

DASASUKSMA: Togog! Summon our army! Let them accompany my son on his secret mission!

TOGOG: Yes, Majesty. (*Makes the sembah.*)

(*Five raps; the gamelan plays the lively and strong melody Sampak Nem.* DASASUKSMA *goes off right.* BEGASUKSMA *exits left, followed by* TOGOG *and* SARAITA.)

Fig. 25 Begasuksma, Togog, and Saraita

The Reincarnation of Rama

Scene 8

(BEGASUKSMA *re-enters from the right.* TOGOG *and* SARAITA *re-enter from the right, pass* BEGASUKSMA, *turn, and sit respectfully before him. The music stops as they sit.*)

SONG (*The dalang sings Ada-ada Mataraman Djugag to steady tapping*):

> By his servant's silence
>> A young Prince
> Is stirred
>> To anger
>> Oooooo . . . oooooo . . .

BEGASUKSMA: 'Gog, what's wrong? You just sit here, and before my Father you said scarcely anything.

TOGOG: Things change in this world, Master.

BEGASUKSMA: Well, I know that.

TOGOG: I feel the way I feel. And maybe I've changed.

BEGASUKSMA: 'Gog, I can't follow your riddles today. There's a change in your usual changeableness.

TOGOG: If you detect it, Master, it must be so.

BEGASUKSMA: 'Gog, your answers displease me! I don't understand them.

TOGOG: Pleasing you is not my concern. My duty to the Kingdom requires I advise frankly, and if that displeases you or his Majesty, I prefer to speak only when commanded.

BEGASUKSMA (*beginning to comprehend*): Oh? You mean you don't want to talk?

TOGOG: Yes.

BEGASUKSMA: You do?

TOGOG: I do not.

BEGASUKSMA: 'Gog, you're Father's oldest and best-loved adviser. It's your duty to speak to the King.

TOGOG: When I do he doesn't listen.

BEGASUKSMA: That shouldn't matter, 'Gog.

TOGOG: But it does. I can't help it. His Majesty is greedy, and always has been. I advised against kidnaping Princess Sinta, but he didn't listen. The Kingdom was razed and thousands of subjects slain. Now he's about to do the same thing all over again. I know it's wrong and I should insist he give up his scheme. But I'm a coward, Master, and I know how easy it is for your father to arrange a beheading. So I speak once, then remain silent.

BEGASUKSMA: 'Gog, you go too far! The King asks your advice, but he's not required to take it. Your duty is to obey!

TOGOG: Hmph. I obey. I spoke. I'm here. But, though I'm a servant, I still have my ideals.

BEGASUKSMA: Ho-ho! What ideals can a servant have, old 'Gog?

TOGOG: The same as any man: to hope for a perfect life on earth and after death. I'd be content with one, but I'm to be denied even that. During my earthly life I was a servant. Here I am, in the afterlife, still a servant, and to the same greedy king. Little by little, I must strengthen my will. Some day maybe I'll be able to free myself from my past sins and perfect my soul.

BEGASUKSMA: That's enough, 'Gog! Don't talk like that. Go now, and give the King's orders to the army!

SONG (TOGOG *makes the sembah and exits to the left as the dalang sings Ada-ada Mataraman Djugag to steady tapping*):

> The servant leaves
> To give the order
> To prepare
> The army to march
> Oooooo . . .

tjarijos NARRATION (*a normal speaking voice*): And now it happens that the soldiers of the ogre army are summoned. Their commanders order them into formation, but they rage about unheeding, like bloodthirsty tigers. Some throw boulders as big as buffalo. Some wear live snakes as belts, others ride astride lions, tigers, and rhinoceroses. Ogres roar, beasts roar. Both eat human flesh. Ogre upon ogre demonstrates a new ferocity to make the others quake. Again and again commanders call without answer, until they leap to the towers, striking enormous alarm gongs whose clamorous tones ring through the air. Then the ogre warriors gather to receive their orders. Near and far they shout, "Ho-ho, grab your knives and clubs! Bring buckets for blood! We're going to Java!" They are given their King's command, as Togog hurries back to report to Prince Begasuksma.

SONG (TOGOG *re-enters and faces* BEGASUKSMA *as the dalang sings Ada-ada Mataraman Djugag to steady tapping on the side of the puppet chest*):

> The servant returns
> To make his report
> That the army
> Is ready to march
> Oooooo . . .

The Reincarnation of Rama

TOGOG: The troops have received your orders, my Prince. (*Makes the sembah.*)

BEGASUKSMA: Order them out! I'll fly ahead to Java; have the troops follow.

TOGOG: Yes, my Prince. (*Makes the sembah.*)

(*Five spaced raps; the gamelan plays the spirited melody Ajak-ajakan Nem.* TOGOG *and* SARAITA *exit left.* BEGASUKSMA *rises into the sky, turns, and flies off right.*)

Scene 9

adegan perang gagal

(*Enter left the ogre warriors* MARITJA, *whose nickname is Tjakil, or "Fang," the huge* PRAGALBA, GALIJUK, *and the lumbering* LODRA, *whose nickname is Terong or "Eggplant-nose." From the right enter* UDAWA, SETYAKI, *and* PRAGOTA. *Suspiciously they look each other over. The music stops.*)

SONG (*The dalang sings Ada-ada Mataraman Djugag to steady tapping*):
>   Two thundering
>   Hostile armies meet
>   Oooooo . . . oooooo . . .
>   As if to beat their foe
>   Into the ground
>   Oooooo . . . oooooo . . .

MARITJA (*shaking his forearm furiously*): What the hell! What's going on here? We just get to Java and meet a column of soldiers? Move aside! Move aside, I say! (*No one moves.* MARITJA *shakes and trembles with fury.*) Ohhhh! Who's in command here? Tell me, tell me!!

UDAWA: Great God! We're not a day at the border and here's a whole regiment of foreign giants. You there. (*Pointing to* MARITJA.) Where are you coming from and where are you going? Speak, Ogre, for you soon will die.

MARITJA (*jumping up and down*): Haw-haw! You! Who do you think you are? I ask a question and you ask one back. Answer me first. Answer me!

UDAWA: Among civilized people it is common enough to exchange questions.

MARITJA: Haw! Is that so? Well, let me tell you then, so you can tremble and run when you hear my name! I am a minister of the Kingdom of Tawanggantungan, Commander-in-Chief of the great King Dasasuksma's army! I'm called the Super-Giant!

But Maritja is my name! Now, what do they call you before I tear you into tiny bits? Heh-heh!

UDAWA (*completely composed*): Udawa is my name. I am protector of the Kingdom of Dwarawati. You have reached the border of the Kingdom and you will turn back or die in your tracks.

MARITJA (*surprised and delighted*): Ho-ho! So this is Dwarawati! And you are its puny soldiers! Haw-haw-haw! Wait till Prince Begasuksma sees you! We'll chew up your bones and spit out the pieces!

UDAWA: What business has your Prince in the Kingdom of Dwarawati?

MARITJA: Haw! I don't make orders; I pass them on to others. I don't know his mission and you won't be alive to find out. Stand aside!

UDAWA: Ogre! Don't brave my anger. The borders of Dwarawati are closed to animals like you!

MARITJA (*leaping up and down in anger*): Animals? Animals!!

UDAWA: Turn back, Giant, while you still see peace in my eyes.

MARITJA: You sound like a hollow log, all noise and no fight! You dare fight the Super-Giant?

UDAWA: If you were four, I would not hesitate. Prepare to die, Ogre!

MARITJA: Haw! So you want to fight? I'll show you! Protector of Dwarawati, you die!

(*Five sharp raps signal the gamelan to play the fast fighting music, Sampak Nem.* MARITJA *and* UDAWA *rush at each other. The others withdraw.* MARITJA *slashes at* UDAWA *recklessly, but with little effect.* MARITJA *strikes;* UDAWA *deftly moves past him.*

*Fig. 26
Maritja and
Udawa*

The Reincarnation of Rama

UDAWA *forces* MARITJA *to flee off left, and follows in pursuit. The ogre* GALIJUK *rushes forward to take up the fight with* SETYAKI. *They strike, pass each other, squeeze each other in a bear-hug.* SETYAKI *kicks the ogre to the ground.*

Fig. 27
Setyaki and
Galijuk

GALIJUK *runs off left, pursued by* SETYAKI. *Old* PRAGOTA *comes forward and battles the lumbering ogre* LODRA. PRAGOTA *outwits and outmaneuvers his stupid and clumsy opponent, chasing him off the screen left. The melody changes from fast Sampak Nem to slower and quieter Ajak-ajakan Nem, as* SETYAKI *rushes on from the right, followed by* SAMBA, *who stops him.* UDAWA *and* PRAGOTA *enter from the left and face them.)*

SAMBA *(as the music ends):* Honored Uncle, stop. Calm yourself. The giant army has fled.

SETYAKI: If you hadn't stopped me, Prince, I would have slain them.

SAMBA: They are gone and that is enough, Uncle. Conserve your strength in case they return.

SETYAKI: Yes, my Prince, you are right.

PRAGOTA: Oh, my Prince, these ogres could not withstand our wrath. They will not soon be back. *(Makes the sembah.)*

SAMBA: Signal the troops to withdraw.

SETYAKI: Yes, my Prince. *(Makes the sembah and exits.)*

SONG *(The dalang sings Patet Nem Djugag):*
    The stricken ogre army
        Retires to the forest
        Fleeing in disorder
        Oooooo . . . oooooo!
SAMBA: Come, Friends, let us retire to rest for the night.

SONG *(All exit and the* KAJON *is placed vertically in the center of the screen, while the dalang sings Patet Lindur, marking the transition between Part One of the play, patet nem, and Part Two, patet sanga):*

Fig. 28
Kajon

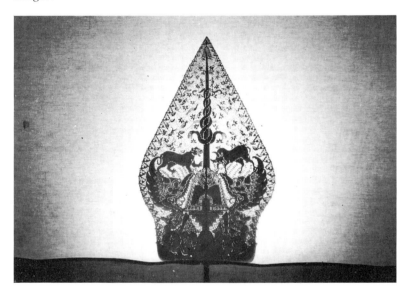

    Commanders and soldiers
        Take their rest
        Oooooo . . .
    Weapons glint
        In the light of the moon,
    To soldiers on guard
        Serene and beautiful
        Is the night
        Oooooo . . .

tjarijos NARRATION: And so the Dwarawati troups rejoice in their defeat of the enemy. Nevertheless, vigilance is maintained throughout the night in the event of future disturbance arising.

PART TWO

SONG (*The dalang sings Patet Sanga Wantah*):
>Late at night
>>Stars light the sky
>>Oooooo . . .
>The scent of flowers
>>Supports the seers' prayers
>>Like the murmur of bees.

Scene 1

NARRATION (*accompanied by continuous, tense rapping*): One, two, three, four, five, six, seven, eight, nine, ten! One: the land, enclosed by water. Two: the rice, planted in the land. Three: the mountain, the earth's axis. Four: the sea, encircling the land. Five: the forest, leaves covering all. Six: the plain, where cattle graze. Seven: the seers, blessed by the Gods. Eight: the sky, over the earth. Nine: the Gods, model for man. Ten! The King! Jewel among men! Nature's upheaval affects them all.

The world erupts! The earth shakes and volcanoes spew out fire. The oceans' waters boil and tidal waves inundate the land as if to drown the world. Crops cannot grow. Animals starve. Wild beasts, reptiles, and poisonous insects invade men's homes. On earth, men flee in panic, seeking shelter. Plague sweeps thousands away. They appeal to their seers but their seers cannot meditate and are helpless. They turn to their Kings but their Kings have no power. The world is dark as dust-clouded night. Lightning streaks and dragons roar. The violence reaches as high as the chambers of the Gods themselves, breaking the horns of the sacred cow Andini, fluttering Anantaboga's dragon-tail, and cracking the gates of Heaven askew. Boiling mud and molten lava vomit from the cauldron of Hell. The nymphs take flight, seeking the protection of the Supreme One. In the midst of nature's upheaval, there appear two funny creatures, seemingly unconcerned, the followers of the Prince Ardjuna. One is Gareng; one is Petruk. The two begin to quarrel, thereby intensifying the natural chaos.

(*The dalang raps five times in quick succession; medium tempo Sampak Sanga is played by the gamelan. To indicate the violence of the scene, the dalang raps steadily against the side of the puppet chest with his wooden tapper and beats time against hanging metal*

On Thrones of Gold

plates with his right foot. The KAJON *trembles furiously, symbolizing the quaking world; it flutters and twirls first to one side of the screen, then the other before stopping left.* PETRUK *dances across the screen, shouting "Ooy, ooy, ooy!" while pointing with his forehand.* GARENG *dances across the screen in the same direction. They re-enter and meet center. Quick raps; Sampak Sanga melody ends.)*

PETRUK *(poking with his long ungainly arms):* Ho! Brother Gareng! Welcome into the audience hall.

GARENG *(slower than his clever brother):* Heh? *(Looking out at the spectators.)* I see an audience. But where's the hall?

PETRUK: Stupid!

GARENG: We're outdoors, aren't we?

PETRUK: Of course, but . . .

GARENG *(very deliberately):* Then why did you say I was welcome in the hall, 'Truk? If we aren't in a hall. And we aren't. *(Pause.)* Are you sick?

*Fig. 29
Gareng and
Petruk*

PETRUK: Oh, for God's sake, 'Reng! I was trying to act refined, like our Pandawa masters, and you don't even recognize it.

GARENG: Oh. Is that what you were doing 'Truk? I wouldn't have guessed.

PETRUK *(thunks him on the head):* You have to *practice* being dignified. Don't you want to better yourself?

The Reincarnation of Rama

GARENG: I suppose so.

PETRUK: Then let's *practice!* Take it from the top. *(They turn their backs on one another, walk to the far edges of the screen, and turn back to face each other.)* Ready?

GARENG: Ready.

PETRUK: Remember! Be refined, stupid! *(They move toward each other.)* Ahem! Welcome into the audience hall, honorable Brother. *(They bow to each other, cracking their heads.)* Ouch!

GARENG: What'd you do that for, 'Truk?

PETRUK: It was you, shorty, not me.

GARENG: No, it was you, because you bent way down and hit me on the top of the head.

PETRUK: Well, never mind! Let's go on. Ahem. I extend to you my exalted prayers, elder Brother.

GARENG *(beginning to like it):* Hah! Er . . . revered Brother . . . I revel . . . ha, ha, ha . . . in Your Majesty's glowing presence, bask in your Kingship's glorious glory, and extend to your Deliriousness this humbleship's exquisite delight and anticipa–cipita–anticipica–

PETRUK: Anticipation!

GARENG: Hehh! 'Truk, this is fun. Let's do another one!

PETRUK: All right. Ho ho! What a surprise, elder Brother, to see you arrive behind me unannounced. *(Turns his back on GARENG and farts.)* Welcome into my presence, honored Brother.

GARENG *(holding his bulging nose in both hands and gasping for breath):* Gaah!

PETRUK *(hopping about, laughing):* Heh-heh-heh! Do you look funny!

GARENG: You did that on purpose, 'Truk. You know I have a sensitive nose! *(Pouting.)* I'm not going to play any more.

PETRUK: Can't you take a joke? Come on, let's do the scene properly this time without you interrupting it.

GARENG: *Me* interrupting . . .

PETRUK: You stopped the scene, 'Reng, not me. *(They walk to the outer edges of the screen, turn back, and approach each other.)* Ahem, ahem. Tell me, Brother, why is it you arrive before me unannounced and unescorted?

GARENG: Ah, ah . . . what do I say, 'Truk?

PETRUK *(whispering):* "Formalities," stupid!

GARENG: Oh. I came because of my brotherly feeling. We should set aside these formalities, stupid.

PETRUK (*doubling up with laughter*): Oh, oh, oh! Ha, ha, ha!

GARENG (*trying again*): We should set aside these stupid formalities?

PETRUK (*laughs all the harder*): Ho, ho, ho! Now you say, "We should set an example for our subjects."

GARENG: Oh. Why?

PETRUK: Because we're kings, you clown! That's why!

GARENG: Well, you're my kingly brother and I'm your kingly brother, and what's mine is yours and what's yours is mine, because we're kingly brothers. Which reminds me, 'Truk, you haven't paid me for your half of the donkey yet.

PETRUK (*quickly serious*): Kings don't touch money, 'Reng, and they don't discuss it. It's beneath our dignity.

GARENG: I don't care. It's time we settled this.

PETRUK: I don't know what you're talking about, 'Reng.

GARENG: You haven't held up your end of the bargain.

PETRUK: What's mine is yours and what's yours is mine.

GARENG: That's just it. We agreed to share that donkey fifty-fifty.

PETRUK: And we have.

GARENG: Fifty-fifty means 50 percent of everything. Not only riding it, but taking care of it, too. You haven't done that.

PETRUK: I ride it and you take care of it. Fifty-fifty. What could be fairer?

GARENG (*scratching his head thinking*): I'm not sure, but something's wrong. You're trying to cheat me again, Long Nose!

PETRUK: If I were, it'd be easy enough, Gimpy. (*Turns away and pretends to cry.*) You don't trust your own dear brother. Boo, hoo!

GARENG: Awww, 'Truk. Sure I do. Don't cry. (*Touches him gently on the shoulder.*)

PETRUK (*turning*): To show you how fair I want to be about our donkey, let's divide him equally between us. You take care of your half, 'Reng, and I'll take care of mine.

GARENG: You'll want the better half, I know you.

PETRUK: Dear Brother, I want you to be perfectly happy. You may have the front half, and I'll take the donkey's . . . ah, rear half. Now, isn't that more than fair?

The Reincarnation of Rama

GARENG: It's a deal, 'Truk! Now, remember, we've promised! Shake!

PETRUK: Shake! *(They shake hands.)*

GARENG: Now c'mon, 'Truk, we've got to go buy some hay before our donkey starves to death.

PETRUK: We? We, Gareng? The front half's yours—*you* buy the hay.

GARENG: Ohhh! I knew it! You tricked me again! *(He suddenly brightens and points over* PETRUK's *shoulder.)* Ha, ha, ha! Get the shovel, 'Truk! *You* clean up the stall! Your half of the donkey just dirtied it!

PETRUK *(unperturbed):* Oh, no. Sorry, 'Reng. That's your job.

GARENG: *My* job?

PETRUK: Of course. You made him do it. If you didn't feed him he wouldn't have to go.

GARENG: You . . . you . . .

PETRUK: An agreement is an agreement.

GARENG: There's only one way to settle this! Put 'em up, Flapper Mouth!

PETRUK: They'll scoop up your brains with a thimble, when I finish with you, Pea Head!

(Five sharp raps on the puppet chest; lively Sampak Sanga is played by the gamelan to accompany the clowns' slapstick fight. They charge at each other, miss, back off, then run each other down. GARENG *gets up first and stands on* PETRUK's *stomach. Then the two of them flail away ineffectually at each other for a few minutes until, almost by accident,* PETRUK *lands* GARENG *a terrific blow to the jaw, knocking him unconscious.* PETRUK *picks* GARENG *up and carries him off, dancing jubilantly. Enter* SEMAR, *an enormously fat old man with a gnarled but kindly face. He waddles across the screen, shaking from side to side, in a kind of gross dance step. He looks about, trying to locate his sons as the music ends.)*

*Fig. 30
Semar*

On Thrones of Gold

SONG *(The dalang sings Patet Sanga Djugag):*
  Nature's turmoil quiets
    Oooooo . . .
  In the east appears
    An odd creature
  Oooooo . . .

tjarijos NARRATION: As nature's turmoil subsides, a bright shaft of light pierces the sky in the east, and just as swiftly as it appeared it vanishes. In its place we see one of God's funnier creatures. Plump as a pumpkin quietly he sits like a mound of earth. He is called Clown Semar and people think of him as the father of the two quarreling brothers. One can hardly call him a man for his breasts are long, but one can't call him a woman for he is, in fact, a man. Though extremely ugly, he is in reality the ancient god Ismaja, protector of Java, descended to earth. He acts as servant to the Prince Ardjuna. But in truth he could rule the world if he so desired, and the highest Gods could not prevent it. Just now Semar is in a fretful mood and he mumbles to himself.

SEMAR *(in a voice cracked with age):* Well, well, they're gone again, those two handsome sons of mine. Hm, hm. I heard them just a minute ago, having a good time, but as soon as their old papa comes along there's a sudden suspicious silence—like a chirping cricket that's been stepped on. Hm. *(Looks around.)* I wonder where they are. *(Waddles forward a few steps, lifts his hand, and shouts off in a tremulous voice.)* Hiiii! Gareng-son! Hiiii! Petruk-boy! It's your dear daddy, boys! *(Exhausted by the effort he listens, but there is no reply.)* Heh, no answer. What is it they call each other? Such terrible names. *(Calling off.)* Gareng! Ah . . . Lump Head! Crooked Elbow! Pea Brain! Hm, Petruk is more excitable. *(Calling.)* Adorable . . . oh, my . . . Flappy Yappy! Bean Pole! Schnoz Nozzle! *(Cocks a hand to his ear.)* Not a sound. Hm. *(Sees someone off left.)* Say, noodle man! Have you seen my pretty little sons?

NOODLE MAN *(off):* Yes, Uncle Semar, I saw them just a few minutes ago.

SEMAR: Where were they? What were the darlings doing?

NOODLE MAN *(off):* They were having a grand time, going down the main street, at the head of a long procession.

SEMAR: A procession? What kind of procession?

NOODLE MAN *(off):* Oh, they were riding in great style, stretched out on a cart and covered with white flowers. Ha, ha!

The Reincarnation of Rama

SEMAR: What? You make it sound as if they're in a funeral procession! What kind of nonsense is that? Don't tease your elders. It's not right. Useless fellow! *(Shaking his finger at him.)* Oh, my, my. Shouting doesn't become an old man like me. Singing is more my style. *(Hums a few tentative notes.)* Yes, that's it. I'll sing to them. When they were young, when they heard their father's glorious voice raised in song, just like that, they'd stop what they were doing and dance all the way home. Besides, someone might hear me and treat me to something good to eat. Let's see, they always liked, "When It's Springtime in the Volcano." Hem, hem. *(Finds his key.)*

> The groom was anxious
>   The bride was not
> He said to her, "Darling
>   I wish you'd get . . ."

GARENG *(loudly off):* Papaaaaa!

SEMAR *(delighted with himself):* Heh, heh, heh.

GARENG *(rushing in from left):* What a crazy old man! Paw! You'll get us all arrested! *(Remembering the song,* SEMAR *chuckles to himself.)* I don't know what you're laughing about. Your sons desert you, but instead of feeling sad you jump around like an overweight grasshopper singing a song about newlyweds.

SEMAR: And what's wrong with that, Son?

GARENG: It's indecent for an old man like you, Paw. Besides you were off key.

SEMAR: You know the song that well, Gareng? Heh, heh!

GARENG: That wasn't what I meant. *(He looks down, silent.)*

SEMAR: What a tribulation to a father his sons are. I'm cheerful, loving. I sing without pay. But my sons either stay away or scold. Ah, me! *(Notices* GARENG *is unusually quiet.)* Gareng? *(*GARENG *sniffs and dabs at his eyes with the handkerchief in his left hand.)* Have you been quarreling with your brother?

GARENG: No, Paw.

SEMAR: Tell the truth.

GARENG: He was quarreling with me. I'll never speak to him again, Paw.

SEMAR: Now, now. He's your brother.

GARENG: I don't care. He went too far this time with his practical jokes. *(Pause.)* He embarrassed me.

SEMAR: What happened? Tell me all about it.

GARENG: Well, it's like this, Paw. We were playing around . . .

On Thrones of Gold

SEMAR: Yes, I heard.

GARENG: . . . and we were arguing about our donkey. Petruk hit me and knocked me out cold! While I was unconscious, he hung a sign around my neck, put me on our donkey, and led the donkey right through the middle of town.

SEMAR: What did the sign say?

GARENG: "Look at the ass on this donkey!"

SEMAR *(suppressing a laugh):* My, my, that was too bad.

GARENG: I was so embarrassed. *(Sniffs.)*

SEMAR: Call your brother and we'll see what he has to say.

GARENG *(mumbling):* I'll never speak to him again.

SEMAR: Come now, you're the elder. Don't pout.

GARENG: Hmph. *(Turns left to call.)* Heh, Schnoz No . . .

SEMAR *(interrupting):* Speak nicely to him and he'll speak nicely to you.

GARENG: Attention, younger Brother! Revered Father requests your presence! *(Turning back to* SEMAR.) Like that, Paw?

SEMAR: Ho, ho! That's nice Gareng.

PETRUK *(off):* Attention, thing over there!

GARENG *(reacts):* You see, Paw!

SEMAR *(calling off):* Come, adorable child! I hear you!

PETRUK *(off):* I obey my exalted Father's command! I come! *(Singing the popular melody Dangdanggula,* PETRUK *dances on from the left and stands behind* GARENG.)

Fig. 31
Semar, Gareng,
and Petruk

The Reincarnation of Rama

SEMAR: Gareng tells me you made a fool of him, Son.

GARENG (*protesting*): I didn't say *that*, Paw!

SEMAR: That's what you meant. Ha, ha!

PETRUK (*hops up and down laughing*): Ha, ha, ha' Oh, that's good, Papa.

SEMAR: Well, delightful boy, tell me what happened that made Gareng so upset.

PETRUK: I don't know, Papa. We were just fighting good-naturedly like we usually do. Suddenly, Gareng was gone.

GARENG: Gone? Paw, I . . .

PETRUK: I looked down and there he was. Did you faint, 'Reng?

GARENG: You hit me.

PETRUK (*mock surprise*): I did? Why, I don't know my own strength! Anyway, when I saw poor little crumpled-up knocked-down 'Reng, my heart was touched, Papa. I brought him home on my donkey.

GARENG: *Your* donkey? Why, why . . .

SEMAR: It seems I heard something about a sign . . .

GARENG: The one that read, "Look at the ass on this donkey!" Ask him about that, Paw.

PETRUK: Gareng, we agreed. That's *my* half of the donkey. I'm proud of it. Ha, ha, ha'

GARENG: What? Why, you . . .

PETRUK: I wanted people to look at it. Hee, hee, hee!

GARENG: You, you . . .

PETRUK: I was advertising!! Hahahahahaha! (*Hopping about and waving his arms.*)

GARENG: You . . .

SEMAR: Now, let's leave it at that. It's all settled. I called you here to tell you we must help our master, Prince Ardjuna. The Prince is going to visit his grandfather, the holy seer Abijasa. We must guard him from harm during his journey. Come along, now.

GARENG: Yes, Paw.

PETRUK: Okay, Papa. Let's go!

(*The dalang raps three times; the melody Lunta accompanies the three clowns as they exit, dancing.*)

On Thrones of Gold

djedjer pandita

Scene 2

(The gamelan continues the melody Lunta, introducing the scene of the distant hermitage of the holy teacher ABIJASA. *The* KAJON *flutters across the screen, and is placed on the right. A* DISCIPLE *enters from the right, crosses the screen, and turns and stands in a position of respect, looking off right. The holy seer,* ABIJASA, *quietly entering from the right, welcomes the* DISCIPLE *with a gesture. The* DISCIPLE *comes forward, greets his teacher with the sembah, and moves behind him.* ARDJUNA *enters from the left, followed by* SEMAR, GARENG, *and* PETRUK. *He bows with humility while making the sembah before* ABIJASA. ABIJASA *gently touches* ARDJUNA'S *forehead as a sign of affection.*

Fig. 32
Disciple, Abijasa,
Ardjuna, Semar,
Gareng, and
Petruk

ARDJUNA *bows low, makes the sembah, moves back, and sits respectfully before his grandfather. One after the other* SEMAR, GARENG, *and* PETRUK *greet the seer with the sembah and take their usual places behind their master,* ARDJUNA. *The dalang raps three times; the music softens.)*

djanturan   NARRATION *(intoned, pitch and rhythm following music):* Now our story moves to Saptaarga the famous Mount of Seven Peaks, the abode of the most holy of religious men, Abijasa. It is the place of the Bubbling Springs, where pure waters scent the cool air. A mystic force pervades the holy mountain, so that no

The Reincarnation of Rama

human nor ogre, animal nor bird, dares disturb its perfect tranquillity. The seer residing in the depth of this secluded holy place was once a divine king, former ruler of the jeweled Kingdom of Astina, and grandfather of the five Pandawa brothers. Choosing to leave worldly affairs, this former great ruler renounced his throne and kingdom for a life of stern meditation. Now he desires only to promote the well-being of the world and to advance his disciples' understanding.

This most holy seer is Abijasa, "Attainer of Perfection," "Light of the World," "Divine Teacher," "He Who Banishes Darkness," and "Golden Seeker of Virtue." He is revered by sages and the Gods themselves, seeking his counsel, descend from their mountain abode to speak with him on holy nights. Even the greatest of the Gods in Suralaja, Guru, on occasion descends to earth to bless him.

Now, as the seer is imparting to one of his young disciples the depth of his wisdom, there arrives the third of the Pandawa princes, Ardjuna. Humbly the genteel Ardjuna greets his grandfather, bowing his head as if to touch the ground. In attendance are the three servants, Semar, Gareng, and Petruk.

SONG (*The melody Lunta ends and the dalang sings Patet Sanga Ngelik*):

> Oh my teacher
>> Reveal to me
>> The will of the Almighty,
> Why do colors spread
>> Over the earth
>> Oooooo . . .
> Enlightening words
>> Of the holy seer's reply
>> Are interrupted
> Oooooo . . .

ABIJASA (*with quiet dignity*): Welcome, Ardjuna, my dear Grandson. May you find peace of mind in this humble place.

ARDJUNA (*modest, yet composed*): The words of my revered Grandfather fill my heart with joy. May I offer my honored greetings, oh most holy of Seers. (*Makes the sembah.*)

ABIJASA: My grandson's greetings warm my soul. I accept them with pleasure, and thank you, my child, for them. (*Quiet gesture to* SEMAR.) Brother Semar, I pray your journey finds you well?

SEMAR: Oh yes, your priestly Excellence. May I offer my prayers for your health, Holy One. (*Makes the sembah.*)

ABIJASA: I welcome them and offer you my blessing in return.

SEMAR: May it rest on my old head like a peacock's plume. *(Makes the sembah.)*

GARENG *(hand up to his face, stifling a laugh; he whispers to* SEMAR, *but loud enough for the others to hear):* Paw, you've been out in the sun too long. His Excellency welcomes you, and you say you've got a bird's nest in your hair. He, he'

ABIJASA *(smiling):* Ah, Gareng. You are welcome here.

GARENG: Thank you, your Holiness. I place my greetings in my nest and pray they may become eggs for your Divinityship *(Makes deep sembah.)*

ABIJASA: Why, thank you, Gareng.

PETRUK: Papa, Gareng makes fun of you, but it sounds like he's going to start a hatchery! *(Stifling his laughter.)* He, he!

ABIJASA *(quietly smiling):* Petruk, your arrival pleases me.

PETRUK: Ohhh, I thank thee, and present my reverent greetings, your Washer. *(Makes elaborate sembah.)*

SEMAR: Heh! *(Clucking disapprovingly.)* Your Washer!

GARENG *(turns to face* PETRUK*):* Why, 'Truk! You've insulted his Holiness! You said, "your Washer" when you meant to say, "your Worship." *(Turns back.)* He didn't even know it, Paw.

PETRUK: Gareng, you're ignorant of the subtleties of education, or you'd recognize a literary allusion when you hear one.

GARENG: Oh, no you don't, 'Truk. You're not going to talk your way out of this.

PETRUK: But if you listen carefully, I'll explain slowly and simply, so even you can understand.

GARENG: Hmph. I'm listening.

PETRUK: Those who strive to attain purity through meditation are said to wash themselves in clear water, so when I said the words, "your Washer," I meant no ordinary washtub, but referred to his honored Excellence. My thoughts were lofty. Heh, heh! Any fool can tell that.

SEMAR: Well, well, Petruk, you are very learned today. But, my Son, consider this: the word "Worship" is traditional. It means to serve and to honor. We all know that at the heart of worship is the Almighty. The sage whose meditation is accepted by the Almighty becomes one with Him. Whatever word he utters is God's word, even his most casual greeting. Thus, in holy affairs, Son, it is best to observe traditional forms. *(Chuckles.)* You'll get into less trouble that way.

ABIJASA: Whatever your words of greeting, you are all welcome. *(Pause.)* Ardjuna, my Grandson, you have not spoken since you arrived. Your face is solemn. Be at your ease and tell me the purpose of your visit.

ARDJUNA *(with serene composure):* My noble Grandfather, you are the most learned of the holy sages. The world's knowledge is yours. I do not speak my thoughts for they are known to you and there is no purpose in their utterance. *(Makes the sembah.)*

ABIJASA: You please me greatly, Ardjuna. For one so young your perception of God's will is clear. God has revealed to you an omen, whose secret nature you are obliged to speak of to no one, even myself. This I know.

ARDJUNA: Holy Grandfather, it is as you say. I come to seek your advice. *(Makes the sembah.)*

ABIJASA: The object of your search is not to be found here, Ardjuna. At this moment, your cousins, King Kresna and King Baladewa, hasten toward your ancestors' tombs at Gadamadana. More than this I cannot say.

ARDJUNA: I understand, Grandfather. I will go at once to Gadamadana. Allow me to have your blessing in my endeavor. *(Makes the sembah.)*

ABIJASA: My prayers accompany you, dear Grandson. May the God's prophecy be fulfilled.

SONG (ARDJUNA *makes the sembah and goes off left as the dalang sings Patet Sanga Djugag):*
> Peace in his heart
>> The Prince takes his leave,
> The sage's holy blessing
>> Goes with him
>> Oooooo . . . oooooo . . .

ABIJASA: Brother Semar, accompany your young master. Advise him well.

SEMAR: Yes, your Worship. I will hurry. Come, Sons.

PETRUK: Come on, 'Reng, let's go. I'll sing Langengita for you.

(On PETRUK'S *word cue, the gamelan begins the melody Langengita. In time to the music,* SEMAR *dances off left, then* GARENG *and*

PETRUK, *each making the sembah as he goes.* ABIJASA *and the* DIS-CIPLE *exit right. The* KAJON *is placed on the right side of the screen, slanted to the right, representing the "mountain."* ARDJUNA *appears at the top of the* KAJON, *descends it, and exits left. One by one the three servants move jerkily down the mountainside and off left. The* KAJON *is lifted, fluttered across the screen, and placed vertically in the center of it.)*

tjarijos
kadjantur

NARRATION *(music softens and continues under spoken narration):* Descending from the Mount of Seven Peaks, the radiant young Prince enters the lush plains. He passes villages and fields. Everywhere the news of his coming brings fresh maidens, handsome widows, and even wrinkled grandmothers to his path to gaze upon his unparalleled beauty. Many are the invitations that he rest and refresh himself in their company. But not for an instant does he tarry. Passing now into the dark forest, animals take care not to disturb him. Had they the gift of speech, they would say, "Take care. Do not dare hinder the passage of the one who walks swiftly here."

(The music quickens; the KAJON *is placed left of the center of the screen, where it represents the forest.* ARDJUNA *enters and stands right, facing the "forest." As the music softens, the three servants enter from the right and sit respectfully around their master.)*

Aware of Ardjuna's power, lions and elephants rage through the forest, seeking to avoid his path. Only the birds in the tree-tops sing gaily at his passing. One drops a piece of fruit at his feet as an offering. Ardjuna looks upward, pleased to see the winged creature and to hear its song.

(The dalang raps once; the melody Langangita resumes normal level for a gong phrase, then ends.)

adegan
wana

Scene 3

ARDJUNA: Father Semar, there is a foreboding quality to this forest. What place is this?

SEMAR: We are in the Forest of the Giants, my Lord. It is next to the Forest of Darkness.

ARDJUNA: It seems unhuman. Who rules the forest?

SEMAR: Pringgadani in the past. Once, a cruel ogre named Arimba lived here, brother of Prince Bima's bride, Arimbi. Even today fierce ogres make this their home.

The Reincarnation of Rama

PETRUK: Papa, you sound like a government forester. (*Turns to* GARENG.) Notice, 'Reng, how Papa knows the name and history of every dark forest we're in?

GARENG: That's what's good about traveling with your elders. They know just about everything about . . . just about everything.

PETRUK: I hope he knows enough to keep us out of trouble. This place gives me the creeps.

SEMAR: My Lord, pardon my asking, but where are you bound? We have come far. Perhaps it would be best to return home and tell your brothers of your plans.

ARDJUNA: Father Semar, we have no time. I must overtake my royal cousins on the way to Gadamadana.

SEMAR: I am at your service, my Lord (*Makes the sembah.*) May I say, my Prince, that I know something of your divine mission and that of your cousins from Dwarawati and Mandura. Do not be suspicious of them. The world is in order. To each of us has been assigned a particular duty and not another.

ARDJUNA: Your words comfort me, Father Semar. Let us continue through the forest. Take care, it is dark and mysterious.

SONG (*As* ARDJUNA *and the three clowns exit left, the dalang sings Ada-ada Gregetsaut Sanga to steady tapping and the accompaniment of a xylophone*):

> The ogre forest
>   Is deep and dark,
> The Pandawa heart
>   Is shining.

Scene 4

adegan perang
kembang

tjarijos

NARRATION: Straight through the forest strides the handsome Ardjuna and his three faithful companions, hurrying to reach Gadamadana. Meanwhile, the routed ogre army reforms its ranks in the center of the wood, directly in the Prince's path.

(*Three raps; the gamelan plays Djangkrik Genggong as* MARITJA *enters and stands right, and* GALIJUK, PRAGALBA, *and* LODRA *enter and stand left. A single rap; the music ends.*)

MARITJA (*gesturing continuously*): Haw! What do you think of those puny Dwarawati forces, Pragalba?

Fig. 33
Maritja, Galijuk,
Lodra, and
Pragalba

PRAGALBA: They were powerful, but you outsmarted them, running away! Ho, ho! They didn't expect that. Let's stay here, Brother. When we hear the Dwarawati people crying out, "Kidnaper! Kidnaper!"—or even "Princessnaper!"—that's the time to attack and divert their attention, while the Prince carries off the Princess.

MARITJA: Diversionary maneuvers! Good! We'll outwit them! Haw, haw' Until then we rest. There's nothing to worry about. Togog and Saraita are out scouting. I sent them. Ha, ha, ha' Better than us going out! Haw! Haw'

tjarijos NARRATION: Boisterous is the ogres' talk, when suddenly Togog and Saraita charge through the ranks, scattering soldiers in their path.

(Seven double raps; gamelan plays Srepegan Sanga as TOGOG *and* SARAITA *enter from the left and fall at the feet of* MARITJA. *Srepegan ends.)*

SONG *(The dalang sings Ada-ada Gregetsaut Sanga):*
> Growling ogres
>> Prowl aimlessly
> Enraged by the failure
>> Of their mission
>> Oooooo . . .

MARITJA: Hey, hey! 'Gog! What's the matter? Tell me, tell me' Something's happened! I knew it, I knew it' Well, 'Gog, what is it? Well? Well?

The Reincarnation of Rama

TOGOG: If you'll stop shouting a minute, I'll tell you, Master. Prepare to see a dead ogre.

MARITJA: *(hopping up and down):* Whaaaat? Who's been killed? Who? Who?

TOGOG: No one yet, Master, but soon there will be. I saw a knight in the forest.

MARITJA: Night? Night? It's daytime, 'Gog' How could you see a forest in the night?

TOGOG: *Knight,* Master. A warrior, a noble. A prince, in fact. In the forest, coming this way.

MARITJA: How many, 'Gog?

TOGOG: One.

GALIJUK *(ponderously):* Hoooo? Just one?

Fig. 34
Togog, Maritja, Saraita, Galijuk, Lodra, and Pragalba

MARITJA: Haw' Glorious! I'll rip him to shreds. Where is he?

TOGOG: Take care, Master. I know him. Two like him could conquer the world.

MARITJA *(frightened):* Ehh? Why didn't you turn him back? You're sure he's alone?

TOGOG: Except for three servants.

MARITJA *(brave again):* Haw, haw' I'll pick my teeth with his bones!!

TOGOG *(laughing ruefully):* I wouldn't fool even with his servants, Master. They're my brother and his sons. Watch out for them.

On Thrones of Gold

Why, I greeted them in a friendly way just now, and they knocked the dagger right out of my hand.

MARITJA: Haw, haw! Show me that puny knight. Where is he? I'll annihilate him! Grrrrh!

(Seven double raps on the wooden chest and loud beating of the metal plates signals the gamelan to play Srepegan Sanga. The ogres exit right. ARDJUNA *enters from the right and stands quietly. Cautiously* MARITJA *enters from the left. Seeing* ARDJUNA, *he leaps with surprise. He circles* ARDJUNA, *jumping up in the air and waving his arms, growling, and roaring, trying to frighten his opponent.* MARITJA *creeps up behind* ARDJUNA, *but hastily retreats when the prince, without turning around, calmly rests his hand on the hilt of his dagger. After growling and making tentative feints at* ARDJUNA, MARITJA *turns and calls on* TOGOG *and* SARAITA *for moral support.* GARENG *and* PETRUK *enter from the right. Srepegan Sanga ends.)*

SONG *(The dalang sings Ada-ada Gregetsaut Sanga to steady tapping):*

> As if struck by lightning
>> Filled with fear and fury
> Eager to fight
>> Is the ogre warrior.

MARITJA: Hey, 'Gog, what the hell, is this the knight?

TOGOG: That's him, Master.

MARITJA: Weakling! Eggshell! I'll crush you under my feet!

PETRUK *(waving his arm):* Impudent ogre!

Fig. 35
Petruk, Ardjuna,
Gareng, Saraita,
Maritja, and
Togog

The Reincarnation of Rama

TOGOG: Because he looks delicate, don't think he's harmless.

MARITJA: Haw, haw' Him?

TOGOG: You'll believe me when he splits your skull, Master.

MARITJA: Watch your manners, fool! Haw! I'll handle him. (To ARDJUNA.) Hey, you! Little Knight' What's your name before I kill you? Where are you from? Where are you going? Tell me, tell me' Are you dumb? Answer me' (Turns to TOGOG.) What's wrong with him? He won't answer me.

TOGOG: Why should he, Master? You're rude. You shout. You wave your arms. He'll stand there and look at you until dooms-day. He's a noble. If you want him to speak, you've got to speak politely first. Do as he does, Master.

MARITJA: It's my nature to shout. I like to shout. I'll shout all I please I'm not going to change my ways for this piece of straw! (To ARDJUNA.) I demand to know your name' (Leaping up and down in fury.) Answer me, answer meeeeee

ARDJUNA (quietly): Gods, has this ogre begun again? You annoy me, Ogre. Hear me, Ogre. What do others call you? Where is the hole you call your home?

MARITJA: Ohhhhhh! I asked first! And what do you mean, "the hole you call your home"?

ARDJUNA: Is this not so, that the noble has his country and the ogre, like a stray cur, his hole?

MARITJA: Grrrrh! (Jumps about, infuriated.) I may be an ogre, but I happen to be a minister of the mighty King Dasasuksma'

ARDJUNA: Cover yourself with pure gold, you will remain an ogre at heart.

MARITJA: All right, you win, Knight' (Proudly.) Tremble as I speak! I come from the land Tawanggantungan across the seas! My name is Maritja I am called Tjakil! "Fang," the Super-Giant' Now, it's your turn. Tell me, tell me, tell me' What's your name?

ARDJUNA: I have none.

MARITJA (thinking he's been tricked): Aarrhhh! What?

ARDJUNA: If you wish to address me, ask my title.

MARITJA: Damn! What do you think you are, talking that way? A prince?

ARDJUNA: Are you blind? Can you not see that I am?

MARITJA: A prince? Hah! All right, what's your title, then?

ARDJUNA: I am named: "Champion in Battle," "Invincible

On Thrones of Gold

Warrior," "Star Among the Excellent," "Paragon of Virtue," "Beloved of the Gods."

MARITJA (*impressed in spite of himself*): Heeeeh! You could cover the world with those titles, Prince. Now, where are you going? How dare you travel through our forest and without an escort?

ARDJUNA: I follow the sight of my eyes and the will of my heart.

MARITJA: You talk riddles! You are rude, Knight, and shall not cross my boundaries.

ARDJUNA: I see no barriers.

MARITJA: Haw, haw! No barriers? Don't you see my army of ogres? Ho, ho, ho'

ARDJUNA (*anger rising, but controlled*): Ogres? I can crack their heads with my feet. Out of my way, Ogre'

MARITJA: Ha! You have the courage to fight me, little man? Haw, haw, haw!

ARDJUNA: Should I fear you, foolish Giant?

MARITJA: I am taller than you.

ARDJUNA: I have not far to reach to detach your head from your body.

MARITJA: I have magic powers.

ARDJUNA: The sight of your corpse will not disturb my rest.

MARITJA: Gnat' Louse! Flea' No bigger than my fist' I'll catch you, crush you, suck your flesh dry before licking on your bones! Haw, haw, haw' Fight! Fight! Fight!

(*Seven quick double raps; the gamelan plays Srepegan Sanga to accompany the fight between* ARDJUNA *and the ogres.* TOGOG *and* SARAITA *withdraw left;* GARENG *and* PETRUK *exit right.* MARITJA *creeps stealthily toward* ARDJUNA, *then drops to the ground to survey his foe.*

Fig. 36
Ardjuna and
Maritja

The Reincarnation of Rama

MARITJA *rushes at* ARDJUNA, *striking at him and passing, again and again. With cool indifference,* ARDJUNA *avoids his charges. Then in a lightning attack,* ARDJUNA *stuns* MARITJA *with a rain of blows on the head. He hurls him offstage and pursues left.* MARITJA *falls on from the right, rises groggily, fixes his headdress, shakes his fist in challenge. He draws his dagger and rushes off right after* ARDJUNA. *The ogre leaps at the prince with a roar of anger.* ARDJUNA *feints and, without looking, seizes* MARITJA'S *dagger and plunges it into* MARITJA'S *body.*

Fig. 37
Ardjuna and
Maritja

The ogre trembles and falls to the ground dead. ARDJUNA *withdraws, serenely, to the right. The huge ogre,* PRAGALBA, *enters from the left and embraces his friend. Music ends.)*

SONG *(The dalang sings Ada-ada Gregetsaut Sanga):*

> As if struck by lightning
> > Filled with fury
> Eager to fight
> > Is the ogre warrior.

PRAGALBA: Oh, Maritja' Never have I seen spilled one drop of your blood and now your corpse lies quivering before me' Do not despair, Brother! I'll crush your murderer or follow you myself. *(Shouts at* ARDJUNA, *jumping up and down and roaring with rage.)* Grrrh! You, toothpick of a knight! You did this? Grrrh! Speak your name before you die'

ARDJUNA *(off):* I am Prince Ardjuna. And who are you, restless Ogre?

PRAGALBA *(shaking his fist at* ARDJUNA*):* I am Pragalba! Haaaa! When you cut bamboo, Knight, you can't pick just the short stalks! Come cut them all, if you dare'

ARDJUNA (*off*): If you wish to die alongside your brother, Ogre, step closer.

PRAGALBA: Ohhhh!

(PRAGALBA *goes into a paroxysm of rage. He rolls on his back, roaring and growling like a wounded beast. He eats earth, flails the air, and even throws rocks at* ARDJUNA.)

PRAGALBA: Agggh! Grrrh! I'll rip off your skin and roast you! Now die, shadow!

(*Five quick raps; fast Sampak Sanga begins.* PRAGALBA *hurries off right. He re-enters from the left, meeting* ARDJUNA *center.* PRAGALBA *rushes in time and again to crush* ARDJUNA. *Cooly* ARDJUNA *avoids his huge opponent, then strikes him stunning blows to the head and body.* PRAGALBA *rises groggily, and once again goes into a fit of rage in which he rolls on the ground, eats rocks, and runs about distractedly. Furiously he throws himself on* ARDJUNA, *and, wrapping his arms around the prince's body, tries to crush him to death. Failing in this,* PRAGALBA *blows* ARDJUNA *off the screen.*

Fig. 38
Ardjuna and
Pragalba

Roaring with delight, the ogre rushes off in pursuit. ARDJUNA *is seen flying across the screen. As the prince falls toward the ground,* PETRUK *rushes in from the right and catches him in midair. Music softens.*)

The Reincarnation of Rama

Fig. 39
Petruk and
Ardjuna

PETRUK: My Lord, are you all right? Oooh, what a dirty fighter! *(Taking boxing position.)* Want me to show him?

ARDJUNA: It is not his strength that I fear. For a moment his foul breath made me dizzy and I could not defend myself. Give me my bow and arrows, Petruk. It is only safe to kill him at a distance.

PETRUK: Yes, Master. *(Smelling PRAGALBA's breath from off left.)* Ohhh! Kill him quickly, Master, before we all die.

ARDJUNA *(calling off left)*: Ogre! Cease your laughing and look upon your fate. (ARDJUNA *holds up the arrow.*)

PRAGALBA *(off)*: You fly better than you fight, skinny one! Ho, ho, ho! Are you still alive? Don't run away. I'll come get you!

ARDJUNA: Fear instead that I shall stay. Open your eyes, Ogre, and tell me what you see.

PRAGALBA *(off)*: Ho! Do you think that flimsy arrow can hurt me? It'll splinter like a twig!

ARDJUNA: Excellent, Friend. Then do not attempt to evade it.

SONG (ARDJUNA *and* PETRUK *exit left;* ARDJUNA *alone re-enters from the .right carrying an arrow as the dalang sings Ada-ada Astakuswala Sanga)*:
> With quiet composure
>   A gleaming arrow
> With golden feathers
>   Is lifted . . . oooooo
> Soon to seek
>   Its blood-red home
> Oooooo . . .

On Thrones of Gold

*Fig. 40
Ardjuna and
arrow*

(ARDJUNA *deliberately lifts the arrow and aims at the ogre off left to the melody Srimartana.*

*Fig. 41
Arrow*

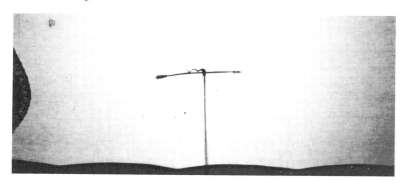

He looses the arrow and exits after it. It flies across the screen twice to the melody Srepegan Sanga.

*Fig. 42
Arrow and
Pragalba*

The arrow strikes PRAGALBA *full in the face as the ogre rushes in from the left.*

The Reincarnation of Rama

The music changes to loud Sampak Sanga. The ogre staggers, surprised, then falls dead. Enter LODRA, *from the left. He rushes to his fallen friend and takes him off, re-entering as the music softens.)*

LODRA: Ohhh! Two of my friends killed! Grrh! *(Shouting off right to* ARDJUNA.*)* Come, little Knight! Your job isn't done. See how well you do against me

ARDJUNA *(off):* Do not waste your breath. If you are bored with life, approach me.

LODRA: Hah! You're no bigger than a pea! I'll swallow you whole! You won't even tickle going down!

(Music Sampak Sanga is played loudly. LODRA *growls and rolls on the ground; just as he is about to rush off to attack the prince,* GATUTKATJA *appears from the right, flying high across the screen. He swoops down and strikes* LODRA *unconscious. Music stops.* LODRA *staggers to his feet.)*

LODRA: Good God! The sky is clear, yet lightning strikes! *(Trembles with fear.)* Yaaaiii!

GATUTKATJA *(looking down from above):* You are wrong, Ogre It is I, a noble, Gatutkatja, son of the Pandawa Prince, Bima Announce yourself, so I may kill you!

LODRA *(looking up, amazed):* Aaaaggh! A human, flying in the air! I am Lodra. Do you know this little fellow I'm fighting?

GATUTKATJA: It is no concern of yours whether I do or not, but I shall not witness his death.

LODRA: Hoooo! Devil! I can't fly! Come down here, and fight like a man'

GATUTKATJA: Fight where you wish. I shall separate your head from your body, Ogre'

(Sampak Sanga is played loudly. GATUTKATJA *swoops down and the two engage in furious battle. In a flash,* GATUTKATJA *twists the ogre's head, snapping his neck.* LODRA *falls dead.* GATUTKATJA *stands exulting over his dead foe, then rises into the sky, turns, and flies off right.* TOGOG *and* SARAITA *rush on from the left; music ends.)*

TOGOG *(seeing* LODRA'S *corpse):* Ohh! Master Lodra is dead too The army has been felled like so many trees!

SARAITA: 'Gog' Let's run. Quick!

TOGOG: All right. Straighten your clothes—you're a mess—and let's run. *(To* ARDJUNA *off right.)* Heh, Ardjuna' Don't think you've won yet I'll report to King Dasasuksma a dove for a

On Thrones of Gold

raven and a raven for a dove! You'll soon see his vengeance! *(Five spaced raps; the gamelan plays Ajak-ajakan Sanga as* TOGOG *and* SARAITA *run off left and* ARDJUNA *and the three clowns appear from the right.* GATUTKATJA *enters from the left, honors* ARDJUNA *by making the sembah, and sits before him. The music ends.)*

*Fig. 43
Ardjuna,
Gatutkatja,
Semar, Gareng,
and Petruk*

ARDJUNA: Your arrival is welcome, Nephew.

GATUTKATJA: I offer my respects, Uncle. *(Makes the sembah.)* Please accept my apologies for entering the combat. It was not proper, but I could not control my desire to help you, Uncle.

ARDJUNA: I am grateful, Gatutkatja.

GATUTKATJA: I was returning home to Amarta, Uncle, when I saw the dust of combat rising above the treetops. I stopped to investigate and saw you. May I ask, honored Uncle, why you are traveling through this deep forest?

ARDJUNA: At the command of our holy grandfather, Abijasa, I hasten to Gadamadana.

GATUTKATJA: Allow me to accompany you from above, oh Uncle. My father would wish it, I know. *(Makes the sembah.)*

ARDJUNA: If that is your desire.

SONG *(The dalang sings Patet Djingking):*
  Flowers in the field
   Sway in the wind
   Oooooo . . .
  Calmness and sweetness
   Follow their way
   Oooooo . . .oooooo . . .

The Reincarnation of Rama

(Five spaced raps; Ajak-ajakan Sanga is played. ARDJUNA *and the three clowns go off leaving* GUTUTKATJA *alone. Raps signal the music to end.)*

NARRATION: And now, the young warrior, Gatutkatja, arranges his clothing for flight. His hair is bound up and held with a ring of sparkling jewels made in the shape of an eagle. On his head rests a three-tiered diadem of solid gold. His earrings ward off death; pendant necklace, armbands, and ankle bracelets are fashioned in a dragon motif. His waistbelt is of gold cloth; silken sashes drape the dagger on his hip. Quickly Gatutkatja dons his divine apparel: the shield giving power of flight; the helmet that wards off sun and storm; and the sandals, made of the skin shed by the Dragon God, which protect him while in flight. Thus, does the flashing warrior Gatutkatja prepare himself for flight. Looking upward, he stamps his foot upon the ground and, like a bolt of lightning, soars into the air, keeping watch on the travelers below. — tjarijos

(Five sharp raps; the gamelan plays Sampak Sanga as GATUTKATJA *flies off the screen left. The melody changes to Gandrung Mangungkung as the* KAJON *briefly is placed upright in the center of the screen.)*

Scene 5 — djedjer Pandawa

(As Gandrung Mangungkung continues, the KAJON *moves to the right again, signifying the start of the next scene. Enter from the right* JUDISTIRA, *who stands quietly as his brothers enter. Following the king on from the right,* NAKULA *and* SADEWA *make the sembah, and sit to his rear.* BIMA *strides on from the left, greets* JUDISTIRA *with a gruff pat on the waist, and steps back a few paces, as the dalang raps three times and the music softens.)*

Fig. 44
Nakula, Sadewa,
Judistira, and
Bima

On Thrones of Gold

djanturan   NARRATION *(intoned, following pitch and rhythm of the music)*: Our story now moves to the Kingdom of Amarta, famed throughout the world. Who is the ruler of this Kingdom? It has not one ruler, but five—for it is the Kingdom of the five Pandawa Brothers. He who commands the royal throne is the eldest Pandawa, Judistira. His titles are many and glorious: "Personification of Justice," "Guardian of his Brothers," "Paragon of Virtue," and "Purest of the Pure—the One Whose Blood Flows White." It is said that King Judistira adheres to all that is noble and virtuous. With no thought for worldly things, he would, if asked, willingly sacrifice his life. He is without enemies and though a monarch, the King does not concern himself with affairs of state.

Who is the one who stands forthrightly before the radiant purity of the King? He is Prince Bima, second of the Pandawa Brothers, called: "King of Warriors," "Pillar of the State," "Defender of the Pandawas." A powerfully built warrior is he. A full beard covers his face and from his lip a thick moustache bursts forth. His muscled chest is covered with a mat of curling hair. Pure is Bima's heart, straightforward is his manner. He is loved and respected by all.

Those who sit respectfully behind the King are the twins, Nakula and Sadewa, youngest of the Pandawas, friendly and loyal. And now, seated on his throne in audience with his three brothers, an expression of sorrow clouds the serene countenance of King Judistira, betraying his concern for the welfare of his younger brother, Ardjuna, who is absent.

SONG *(The music Gandrung Mungungkung comes to an end; the dalang sings Sendon Rentjasih)*:

> Birds' sad chirruping
> > Heard from afar,
> Even the breeze ceases
> > Whispering
> > Oooooo . . .
> Echoes of kingly
> > Distress
> Mingle with
> > Unshed tears
> > Oooooo . . . oooooo . . .

JUDISTIRA *(a delicate, almost ethereal voice)*: Brother Bima, welcome. I pray you are well.

The Reincarnation of Rama

BIMA *(gruffly):* Yes, Brother! I salute you! *(Salutes strongly.)*

JUDISTIRA *(accepts salute with a slight gesture):* Thank you, dear Brother, your greeting brings joy to my heart. Nakula, Sadewa, you are well? *(He does not turn to them.)*

NAKULA: Yes, royal Brother. *(Makes the sembah.)*

SADEWA: Through your blessing, Brother. *(Makes the sembah.)*

JUDISTIRA: Brother Bima. Report, I pray you, on the condition of our country.

BIMA: All is well, Brother! *(Salutes.)*

JUDISTIRA: And the army?

BIMA: Ready! *(Salutes.)*

JUDISTIRA: That is fortunate, since our beloved brother Ardjuna is still absent. Brothers, I fear greatly for his safety. It is more than a month now, and it is as though he had disappeared into the earth. What can you report to me, Brothers?

BIMA: Brother, I'm ashamed! My son, Gatutkatja, could easily find him from the air. But . . . he's gone, too. Two missions sent. They report nothing.

JUDISTIRA: If such is the case, Brother, let us firmly grasp our responsibility. This matter concerns our family and it is not for others to resolve. Brother Bima, go seek your brother. Do not return without knowledge of him.

BIMA: Brother, you're too upset. You know Ardjuna. He enjoys running away making us come after him. Besides, if I knew where to search I would. I'd give my life to save him. But to go looking when he might be anywhere! That's foolish, Brother!

JUDISTIRA *(serene as before):* Very well. Do not go. I myself shall search for our lost brother. Rule the Kingdom well while I am gone.

BIMA *(booming):* Brother! Be sensible You're too delicate for such a mission'

JUDISTIRA: If no one else will make the journey, then I, myself, must go. I shall find our brother. I shall go to the ends of the earth. I shall descend into the flaming fires of Hell, where I shall be burned to death. I shall plunge to the depths of the ocean, where I shall be drowned. I shall . . .

BIMA: Enough, Brother, enough! Your story bores me Whenever you say something I don't believe, or order something I don't choose to do, you threaten to burn or drown yourself if I don't obey! Never mind. I'll go. Twins!

NAKULA: Yes, Brother.

SADEWA: Yes, Brother.

BIMA: While I run off to the ends of the earth, help our delicate brother rule properly! Be alert!

NAKULA: Yes, Brother.

SADEWA: We shall do our best.

BIMA (to JUDISTIRA): Noble Brother, will you give your blessing to my journey?

JUDISTIRA: You go with my prayers, Brother Bima.

(The dalang signals for Srepegan Sanga by rapping on the metal plates. BIMA takes leave of his brothers, exiting left; JUDISTIRA turns and goes out right followed by NAKULA and SADEWA. BIMA re-enters from the right, where he stands alone on the screen. The music ends.)

SONG (to steady tapping the dalang sings Ada-ada Gregetsaut Sanga):

> The Prince's soul wishes
> To fulfill its mission,
> Yet confused and doubtful
> Stands he . . . oooooo
> Knowing not which way
> To go . . . oooooo . . .

tjarijos NARRATION (normal speaking voice): Bima stands motionless as a statue, until his troubled thoughts become known to his divine essence, Dewa Rutji, who enlightens him. At once he knows his destination. Quickly, Bima arranges his dress, symbolic of his mystical knowledge: his hair, low in front and high in the back, indicates the union between Man and the Gods; golden fibers in the hair signify Bima's keen perception, a gift of Baju—God of the Wind; ornaments at the temples show he is a bearer of divine wisdom which he humbly conceals; earrings set with sparkling diamonds denote supernatural vision that can see all things; the strength of the Dragon King resides in his necklace of dragon design; armbands shaped like the white cloven fruit of the mangosteen imply Bima speaks without equivocation; his knowledge is as bright as the moon-designs of his bracelets; his royal skirt of the five mystic colors —red for courage, yellow for sensual desire, green for wisdom, white for purity, black for strength—denotes that Bima is expert in controlling, proportioning, and unifying these uni-

The Reincarnation of Rama

versal forces of nature; his silken sash tells of the Prince's ability to distinguish the One True God; Bima's dragon belt says he is wise in the ways of the world. Such is the mystic attire in which Bima travels, alone, accompanied only by the whirlwinds. His path is straight, his stride as broad as the horizon.

(Five sharp raps; the gamelan plays Sampak Manjura, a special melody for BIMA's *journey.* BIMA *leaps three times into the air, walks with three giant strides, then bounds off left. The* KAJON *is placed center, inclined to the left, as the dalang raps and the melody stops.)*

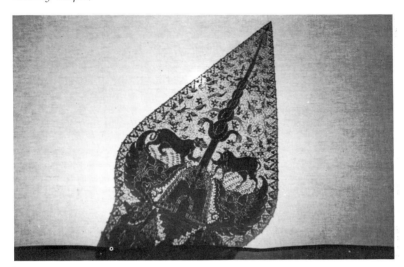

Fig. 45
Kajon

Thinking only of Ardjuna, the great Pandawa Prince plunges through thick forests and over mountains profuse with flowers. The sun rises high, beating down on Bima's iron body. Yet his pace quickens as he strides across the world. Animals flee in panic before his relentless advance. Small creatures fall terror-stricken into ravines, where they lie dying. Ox and buffalo are swept up by the force of the winds which rage outward from Bima's form. Rhinoceroses drown in the swirling waters; bulls are lifted and dashed against the rocks; lions, tigers, and elephants groan and bellow in fear as they rush for shelter in the valleys. Snakes coil tightly to treetrunks, but the trees are uprooted and the serpents slither into the marshes for refuge.

In mountain hermitages, alarmed by the tempest, holy men

and their disciples burn incense. Some pray; others sound bells or cast fresh flowers from the mountaintops. The delicately scented petals fall on the traveler, delighting his surging heart as he rushes through the day and into the night without pause or rest.

PART THREE

SONG (*The dalang sings Patet Manjura Wantah, indicating the start of Part Three of the play, patet manjura*):
> The grey of dawn
>> Turns red,
> The chirruping
>> Of birds
>> Begins
> Oooooo . . .

NARRATION: And now, our story moves to the heavenly abode of the Gods!

Scene 1

(*Three raps on the puppet chest signal the gamelan to play Kawit. The* KAJON *is moved slowly to the right. Into the empty screen moves the four-armed figure of the Heavenly Teacher,* GURU. *From the left enter the gods* NARADA *and* BASUKI. NARADA, *thickset and grotesque brother of* GURU, *stands before him.* BASUKI, *a lesser god, makes the sembah to* GURU, *and sits to the rear. The spirits of* RAMA *and his brother* LEKSMANA *enter and hover in the air. Three raps; music softens.*)

Fig. 46
Guru, Narada,
Rama, Basuki,
and Leksmana

On Thrones of Gold

djanturan NARRATION (*intoned, following pitch and rhythm of Kawit, which continues in the background*): Our story told here is not on earth, but in the realm which is called Suralaja—"The Quiet World" or "The World Between." Situated at the top of the World Mountain—Mahameru—this is the dwelling of the Gods. Infinite is its horizon—like that of Heaven. It has been created through meditation and supernatural powers on the pinnacle of this mountain and, like a straw mat, it may be spread wide or rolled up at the will of its creator. Borrowing neither from the sun, the moon, nor the stars, it is luminous and darkness is unknown. No mortal dares enter its pathway with spirit unprepared.

He who rules this domain is known throughout the world as Guru, "Heavenly Teacher." Despite his authority, the divine Guru is not the Supreme God. Body and soul combine to form the human being; yet they are not the same. So it is with Guru and the Supreme God. In action Guru is paramount. The origin is he and the object of worship, controlling the destiny of all living things. He may punish but he is not, himself, subject to punishment. He may rule but he is not, himself, subject to rule. Humankind and ogres; insects, fish, and animals; spirits, nymphs, and the Gods—all the inhabitants of the Three Worlds —submit to the Heavenly Teacher, Guru, who creates likenesses of Heaven and Hell, complete with the instruments of reward and punishment. His authority is limitless in the world: he sees without eyes, hears without ears, creates without substance. That only which is not subject to the will of Guru is, indeed, the Supreme God himself.

In the great palace of the Gods, the divine Guru sits in audience. Before him is the god Narada, elder cousin of the heavenly Guru, whose grotesque body and humorous ways conceal his great supernatural powers. He is Guru's messenger and intermediary to humans on earth. Behind him sits the god Basuki, powerful beyond measure. The spirits of the late Prince Rama, and his younger brother, Leksmana, also attend, having been summoned by the Gods.

SONG (*The dalang sings Patet Manjura Ngelik, as the melody Kawit ends*):

Far above in the heavens
    Dwell Gods
    And chosen mortals
In divine
    Perfection
    Oooooo . . .

The Reincarnation of Rama

GURU *(a slight gesture):* My divine Brother Narada.

NARADA *(speaking in a tiny, squeaking voice):* Yes, my Brother Guru. What is thy wish?

GURU: I trust you are well in arriving again in Suralaja in our presence?

NARADA: All is well with thy brother. I thank thee.

GURU: And what is your exalted opinion of the worldly condition?

NARADA: Ruled by thy divine self, Brother Guru, all must be well. He, he! Thou need not ask!

GURU: I thank you, Brother, but it is said that no puzzle is solved by he who creates it. Now, tell me directly, I pray, Brother Narada, what is the result of your mission to earth?

NARADA: I wish to inform thee thy portents have been received by the Kings Kresna and Baladewa, and Prince Ardjuna. They prepare to receive thy divine gifts at Gadamadana. Rama and Leksmana have been summoned. They await thy command, divine Brother.

GURU: Rama and Leksmana, my subjects. Despite the good deeds of your lifetimes, your spirits have not yet completed their earthly duties. Be informed: at present the five godly traits of Wisnu are incarnated separately in five mortals.

> Authority is in Rama
> Power is in Kresna
> Truth is in Leksmana
> Excellence is in Ardjuna
> Unity is in Wibisana.

It is proper these divine traits be reunited. As your last duty on earth, I command you, Rama, to reincarnate as King Kresna, thus combining Authority and Power, and you, Leksmana, to reincarnate as Ardjuna, thus combining Truth with Excellence.

RAMA: Divine Guru, I obey thee. Yet, first I beg of thee thy indulgence. *(Makes the sembah.)*

GURU: Speak freely, Rama, my Son.

RAMA: During the great struggle to destroy King Rawana of Alengka, my younger brother, Leksmana, did me service such that I vowed to take the position of younger brother to him in our next reincarnation. Should I reincarnate as King Kresna, and Leksmana as Ardjuna, I should be breaking my vow, divine Ruler. I ask of thee thy divine guidance. *(Makes the sembah.)*

On Thrones of Gold

SONG (*The dalang sings Patet Manjura Djugag*):
>   The moon's pale light
>   On a lake smooth silver
>   Glitters into slivers
>   With a falling stone
>   Oooooo . . .

BASUKI: Heavenly Majesty, may I, too, be allowed a word?

GURU: Of course, Basuki. Please speak frankly.

BASUKI: For years I was cursed with the form of a serpent on earth. It was the father of Kresna who, pitying me, released me from the curse and restored me to my godly shape. I vowed then to reincarnate as his eldest son. I ask thy permission to fulfill my vow. Allow me to reincarnate as King Baladewa, oh divine Majesty.

GURU: Brother Narada, I welcome your advice.

NARADA: Heavenly Brother, Basuki's request poses no problem. Rama's however, conflicts with thy divine command. I urge, oh Brother a heavenly compromise!

GURU: Proceed, I pray, Brother Narada!

NARADA: Consider, divine Brother: Leksmana is endowed with Truth. He is also destined to be celibate. Cannot these two be separated? If, by itself, Leksmana's Truth were bestowed upon Ardjuna, thy holy wish would be fulfilled and Ardjuna would remain the supreme male of the world. Leksmana's Celibacy might then be incarnated into Baladewa along with the spirit of Basuki. Since Baladewa is Kresna's elder brother, Rama's vow would also be fulfilled.

GURU: A perfect solution, Brother Narada. Great is your wisdom!

SONG (*The dalang sings Ada-ada Gregetsaut Manjura to steady tapping*):
>   Serenity returns.
>   Oooooo . . .
>   The Heavenly Teacher
>   Begins meditation.

tjarijos NARRATION: The divine Guru concentrates his mind. As he does so, the spirit of Leksmana divides into Celibacy and Truth. The former combines with the god Basuki; the latter remains separate, shining with the light of Truth.

(*Five sharp raps; Sampak Manjura is played as the figure of*

The Reincarnation of Rama

LEKSMANA *divides into two. One figure of* LEKSMANA *overlaps with* BASUKI *and disappears; the other remains in its former position. The music ends.)*

GURU: Now, Brother Narada, go with Rama, Leksmana, and Basuki. Inform the chosen virtuous mortals of the nature of the divine gifts they are about to receive.

NARADA: I do thy divine bidding, Brother Guru.

GURU: Rama, Basuki! I have complied with your requests. Do not linger, but descend to earth and carry out your duties.

(Five quick raps; the gamelan plays Sampak Manjura as all exit. The KAJON *flutters across the screen from right to left, then is placed to the right of the screen.)*

<table>
<tr><td></td><td style="text-align:center">Scene 2</td><td style="text-align:right">adegan wana</td></tr>
</table>

(A single rap signals the melody to change to Ajak-ajakan Manjura. Enter from the left the aged white monkey, ANOMAN, *who bows before the god* BAJU *entering from the right at the same time. The music ends.)*

ANOMAN: Reverent Deity, allow me to present my humble greetings. *(Makes the sembah.)*

BAJU: Accept my blessing, noble Anoman. I trust you are well.

ANOMAN *(sadly):* Oh, divine Protector, my foster father! I am tired of life. Since Rama, my master, has died, my life is purposeless.

*Fig. 47
Baju and
Anoman*

BAJU: Take heart, brave monkey Friend. The divine will of Guru is at work. This very day the spirit of Rama will be reincarnated as King Kresna.

ANOMAN (*suddenly alert*): Tell me, divine Baju, where may I find this Kresna that I may serve him as I did Rama? (*Makes the sembah.*)

BAJU: Patience, Anoman. Listen: the one who explains to you the riddle of the five colors, the five forces, and the five brothers, will lead you to King Kresna.

ANOMAN: How may I know this man, oh Deity?

BAJU: You will meet him by chance. That is all I can say. Blessings on you, Anoman.

(*Five quick raps; Sampak Manjura is played as* BAJU, *God of Wind, flies up and off.* ANOMAN *is watching his departure when, without warning,* BIMA *leaps in from the right, knocking* ANOMAN *unconscious.* BIMA *continues off left without slackening his speed.* ANOMAN *rises, groggily, as Sampak Manjura ends.*)

SONG (*The dalang sings Ada-ada Gregetsaut Manjura Djugag to steady tapping*):
> Like a bolt of lightning
>> Striking in the clear sky
> Oooooo . . .
>> Oooooo . . .

ANOMAN (*holding his head*): Great God! What was that? (*Shouting off and gesturing.*) Ho! You filthy creature! Where are your eyes? I'll teach you some manners!

(*Five quick raps; Sampak Manjura accompanies the battle between* ANOMAN *and* BIMA. ANOMAN *exits left, flying through the air.* BIMA *appears from the right and* ANOMAN *swoops down from above and bites his thigh.*

Fig. 48
Bima and Anoman

The Reincarnation of Rama

The old ANOMAN *is not as strong as* BIMA, *but he clings to him ferociously, hampering his movements. Music stops.)*

SONG *(the dalang sings Ada-ada Gregetsaut Manjura to steady tapping):*

> Like a snake coiled tightly
>> Around a bull . . . oooooo
> The two struggle
>> Oooooo . . .

BIMA: Hey! Mangy old ape! Let go! What do you want?

ANOMAN: Inconsiderate bull! You stormed past me and knocked me unconscious! Apologize!

BIMA: If you stand in my path you get hit, Ape! Get up in the trees where you belong!

ANOMAN: You have no sense at all! I'm a monkey and I know more about behavior than you! Brute!

BIMA: Out of my way, Ape!

ANOMAN: Do you think I fear your threats?

BIMA: Whether you fear me or not is your problem. But if you care to live, move aside.

ANOMAN: Ha! Then fight, if you want! Announce yourself!

BIMA: I am the warrior, Bima.

SONG *(the dalang sings Patet Manjura Djugag):*

> Clouds dispersed by the wind
>> Oooooo . . .
> Like the troubled heart
>> Made clear . . . oooooo

ANOMAN *(releasing his grip on* BIMA, *steps back dumbfounded):* The Pandawa warrior? And, like myself, the spiritual child of the god Baju? Don't you know me, Brother?

BIMA: I've never set eyes on your ugly face, Ape.

ANOMAN: It was I who led you to Kuwera's divine water lily when we were both younger. Do you remember?

BIMA: Anoman! Is it you?

ANOMAN: It is. I was a skinny young monkey then. Brother Bima, help me! Tell me where I can find King Kresna! Do you know him?

BIMA: Hah! Do I know him! He is adviser to the Pandawas. But I have business first. Judistira has sent me to find Ardjuna. Join me. When we have found the vagabond, I'll take you straight to King Kresna.

ANOMAN: Thank you, Brother! That will give me time to ask you of Baju's words.

BIMA: Ask away, Brother.

ANOMAN: Noble Bima, the God spoke of five colors, five forces, and five brothers. What does this riddle mean?

BIMA: Ha, ha! You ask such easy questions, old Ape! Listen: the five brothers are those under Baju's care. Each is symbolized by a color and one of the five human forces. White is purity; that is you, old Anoman. Red is courage; that is our brother, Djadjagwreka, King of Giants. Green is wisdom; that is our brother, the elephant, Situbanda. Yellow is sensual desire; that is the mountain, Maenaka. Black is strength. And that is . . .

ANOMAN: Yourself, Brother Bima?

BIMA: Yes, old Ape! But listen. We five brothers symbolize the five forces, yet in every complete human being all five forces must reside. Is that clear enough?

ANOMAN: No, no, Brother! Explain everything!

BIMA: I have not all day, Anoman! Most important, these symbols guide us as we strive to attain freedom from worldly desires. Through spiritual exercise we must learn to harmonize and control the five forces. When you are happy or sad, passive or passionate, the five forces are at work. Aaah, you see, old Ape?

ANOMAN (elated): I, Anoman, a beast, am part of a logical, symbolic pattern woven by the Gods! It is wonderful! (Dejected again.) Yet, I do not know the meaning of my life. Can you explain it, Brother?

BIMA: Hah, hah! Anoman, that shows your ignorance! Ask questions, but don't ask another the meaning of *your* life. You are lost because Rama is not here to guide you. Your life is a cloak, but your world is devoid of hooks on which to hang it!

ANOMAN: Ooooh, you are right, Brother Bima! If I understand you right.

BIMA: Only you can answer the puzzle of your existence. Through your own striving. Your search for guidance indicates at least a beginning! And now, friend Anoman, I've stopped too long. Come, we must go!

(*Five sharp raps; the gamelan plays Sampak Manjura as* BIMA *and* ANOMAN *exit left together.*)

The Reincarnation of Rama

Scene 3

(A single rap signals the melody to change to Ajak-ajakan Manjura. The KAJON *is brought across the screen and planted just left of center, where it represents the main crypt of the Pandawa ancestors.* ARDJUNA *enters, followed by* GATUTKATJA, SEMAR, GARENG, *and* PETRUK *who remain behind* ARDJUNA. ARDJUNA *looks at the tomb for a moment, then turns to face the others. The music ends.)*

ARDJUNA: Father Semar, is this the holy ground of Gadamadana?

SEMAR: Yes, my Prince. These are the sacred grounds where the Pandawa ancestors rest. *(Makes the sembah.)*

ARDJUNA: Thank you, Semar. *(Gestures to* GATUTKATJA.*)* Nephew, maintain watch to see I am not disturbed. I wish to enter the crypt alone.

GATUTKATJA: Yes, Uncle. *(Makes the sembah.)*

ARDJUNA: And, Father Semar.

SEMAR: Yes, my Lord? *(Makes the sembah.)*

ARDJUNA: Advise your sons that they should not disturb the quiet of this holy place.

SEMAR: Oh, yes, Master. *(Makes the sembah. Turns.)* Obey your master's words. Contain yourselves while we're here.

GARENG: Sure, Paw, but I don't see anything big enough to hold us all.

PETRUK: Why, Papa, you're the one who's always making speeches. We're not stupid, you know. It's obvious master Ardjuna has come here to meditate and we'll be as quiet as a tomb. Ooops, sorry. Anyway, what cause have we to disturb our master? If he receives a blessing, we might get something too. No noise for me! No sir. I'll sit here just as quiet as I can be. Not one word will escape my lips. Not a single, solitary sound shall I utter. Not . . .

SEMAR: Then be quiet!! *(Makes the sembah to* ARDJUNA.*)* Heh, heh. Go without fear, Master, there will be no disturbance.

ARDJUNA: Thank you, Father Semar.

GATUTKATJA: My prayers go with you, Uncle. *(Makes the sembah.)*

ARDJUNA: Be alert and watchful, all of you.

SONG *(The dalang sings Ada-ada Gregetsaut Manjura):*
> A young Prince's prayers,
>> Flowers of his purity
> Rise to the skies
>> Seeking God's gift
>> Oooooo . . .

(During the song, ARDJUNA *turns and moves left until he is behind the* KAJON, *thereby entering the crypt. The others withdraw to the left. Five spaced raps signal the gamelan to play Ajak-ajakan Manjura. Enter* KRESNA *and* BALADEWA *from the right. They stand gazing at the crypt. The dalang raps; the music stops.)*

*Fig. 49
Baladewa, Kresna,
and Ardjuna
behind Kajon*

KRESNA *(quietly):* Brother Baladewa, note the pure atmosphere of this place. Does it not set your heart at peace?

BALADEWA: Yes, Brother. It augurs well for our mission. Other burial places I visited filled me with fear. Their foul odors were repulsive. Why is that, honored Brother?

KRESNA: The reason is simple, Brother. Other tombs reek with the stench of the deceased's imperfect deeds and carnal impulses. Here there are only tombs of those whose lives were lived purely. Their spirits' perfectness pervades the atmosphere and makes sweet the air. Come, Brother, let us begin our meditation.

BALADEWA: As you say, Brother.

The Reincarnation of Rama

SONG *(The dalang sings Ada-ada Gregetsaut Manjura as they kneel before the* KAJON, *representing the crypt):*
>The two Kings' prayers,
>>Flowers of their purity,
>
>Rise to the skies
>>Seeking God's gift
>>Oooooo . . .

NARRATION: And so it is that the two Kings begin their medita-   tjarijos
tion, unaware of Ardjuna's presence within the tomb. Empty-
ing their minds of all foreign thoughts, they concentrate solely
upon receiving the divine gift. As they pray, the sun sighs and
sinks beneath the purple haze of the mountains, its last rays
bright with golden promises. As the deep blue of the night
swallows the light of the sun, the spirits of Rama and Leksmana,
together with the god Basuki, hover in the sky over Gadamadana. The spirits descend to enter into the corporal bodies
of the three meditating nobles. Stars gleam in the velvet
heavens. The world is still.

(Seven double raps; the gamelan plays Srepegan Manjura. The KAJON *is moved right.* NARADA, KRESNA, ARDJUNA, *and* BALADEWA *take their places. The three spirit figures enter from the left and hover at the top of the screen.* BASUKI *combines with* BALADEWA, *leaving* RAMA *and* LEKSMANA *still visible in the air.*

Fig. 50
Narada, Rama,
Kresna, Leksmana,
Ardjuna, and
Baladewa

On Thrones of Gold

RAMA *combines with* KRESNA *and* LEKSMANA *with* ARDJUNA.
ARDJUNA *returns to the crypt. The two meditating kings are unaware of what has happened. The music stops.)*

NARADA: My subjects. You concentrate too deeply. Awaken! You have received that for which you have striven. Your meditation is complete.

SONG *(The dalang sings Patet Manjura Djugag):*

> From the calm of
>> Meditation
> The Kings are wakened
>> Oooooo . . .

*(*KRESNA *and* BALADEWA *rise and stand before* NARADA.)*

KRESNA: Oh! Blessed Deity! I am amazed to see one so holy at our place of meditation. Accept my greeting, Holiness. *(Makes the sembah.)*

BALADEWA: I honor your feet, oh God Narada. *(Makes the sembah.)*

NARADA: I thank you both, noble Kings. The divine Guru has noted your excellent worldly deeds as representatives of the Gods. Be informed: you are chosen and have received the divine gifts of the Gods! Baladewa, you have received the reincarnation of the god Basuki. The rest have received reincarnations of the god Wisnu. The gift of Authority, in the spirit of Rama, is yours, King Kresna. The gift of Truth, in the spirit of Leksmana, is Prince Ardjuna's.

KRESNA *(surprised):* Forgive me, oh Deity. How can it be that Ardjuna has received the gift together with us when he is not here?

NARADA *(blustering):* Ho, ho! Have you no faith in the Gods, Kresna? *(Calls off.)* Descend from the crypt, Ardjuna. Your doubting brother-in-law thinks we Gods are bunglers!

SONG *(The dalang sings Patet Manjura Djugag):*

> From the calm of
>> Meditation
> Prince Ardjuna is awakened
>> Oooooo . . .

*(*ARDJUNA *comes out of the* KAJON *and faces* NARADA, *bowing low before him.)*

KRESNA *(in good-natured anger):* Well! I should have known you'd be here, Ardjuna! Oh, yes, you're so refined, you never

The Reincarnation of Rama

make a hasty movement, but it's you that always outdistances me. What pains I took, to keep this a secret from you, and when I get here, who's already in the tomb ahead of me? You! Some of us are entitled to use this burial ground! Who gave you permission to enter?

ARDJUNA *(calm and self-possessed):* I seek Your Majesty's pardon, if I have offended you, noble King. Regarding our rights to this sacred ground, however, may I remind you that I, too, am a descendent of the great Kings. Your father was, after all, my uncle.

KRESNA: Enough! It is useless! From the beginning you have always bested me. If we keep arguing, you'll end by ruling my kingdom!

NARADA: Hee, hee, hee! Come, friends, it is the will of the divine Guru that Kresna and Ardjuna shall be inseparable, as the twin pillars that support mankind.

BALADEWA: Forgive me, divine Narada. But may I ask the meaning of *my* gift.

NARADA: Hee, hee! Of course, my Son. The incarnation of the god, Basuki, is an inheritance of the good deeds of your father. But further, from Leksmana you have received, noble and deserving Baladewa, the gift of Celibacy!

BALADEWA *(outraged):* Whaaat? You mean I have meditated and prayed with the greatest fervor and the result is—I've been made *celibate*?

NARADA: Ha, ha, ha! Do not be so quick to despair, my King. You can marry and have children. In this case Celibacy implies holiness. It means you can never be seduced by any woman save your wife! You receive the guidance of the Gods through this gift. You are indeed fortunate, Baladewa!

BALADEWA *(sighs):* I am content, Holiness.

NARADA: Finally, know that you must sustain an ordeal before the receipt of your divine gifts shall be complete. This test of your worthiness will come to you shortly. Now, return to your homes, my subjects. Be alert. My blessings on you.

(Five quick raps signal the gamelan to play Sampak Manjura. All make the sembah honoring NARADA. *He rises in the air, turns, and flies off right.* BALADEWA, KRESNA, *and* ARDJUNA *exit to the left. The* KAJON *moves back to the right side of the screen. A single rap; the melody changes to Ajak-ajakan Manjura.* KRESNA *enters and*

stands right, followed by BALADEWA *and* ARDJUNA. *Enter* BIMA *and* ANOMAN *from the left. The music stops.)*

BIMA *(seeing* ARDJUNA*)*: Ho! Gypsy!! Eldest brother's in a fit! Where have you been? You left without saying goodbye!

ARDJUNA: Why, Brother Bima. I merely followed my royal brothers' precedent, paying respects to our ancestors here.

BIMA: I am sent to bring you home. Come.

ARDJUNA: My mission is done. Shall we depart, Brother? *(To* KRESNA.*)* Have I your permission to leave your presence, my King? *(Makes the sembah.)*

KRESNA *(smiling)*: Ha! You ask my permission in trivial things, Ardjuna. Learn to do so in important matters as well! But wait. Who is that strange creature with you, Bima?

BIMA: This ugly one was Prince Rama's most trusted adviser. He is the white ape, Anoman.

ANOMAN: I beg to serve you, oh, incarnation of Rama! *(Makes deep sembah.)*

KRESNA: I understand. You are welcome here, old Anoman. I know of your past good deeds and would be pleased to have you in my presence.

ANOMAN: Oh, thank you, my King! *(Makes deep sembah.)*

KRESNA: My Friends, let us all depart. The words of the god Narada stay in my mind. I sense a happening of great importance in the Kingdom of Dwarawati. Let us make haste.

(Five quick raps; Sampak Manjura plays as they all exit and the KAJON *is placed center, inclined slightly to the left. Music ends.)*

SONG *(The dalang sings Patet Manjura Wantah)*:
>The grey of dawn
>>Turns red,
>The chirruping
>>Of birds
>>Begins
>Oooooo . . .

tjarijos   NARRATION: So it is that King Kresna and his party depart in haste for the Kingdom of Dwarawati—Gate of the World. Meanwhile, in the palace of that very Kingdom, the wives of King Kresna are seated in the women's chambers, anxiously awaiting the return of their Lord and husband, the King.

The Reincarnation of Rama

Scene 4   djedjer putri

(Three raps; the gamelan plays Perkutut Manggung. The KAJON
moves to the right of the screen. Enter the princess SUMBADRA *from
the right. She crosses the screen and turns back to honor the
entrance of her brother's queens:* DJEMBAWATI, RUKMINI, *and*
SETYABOMA, *with* MAIDSERVANTS *attending. Three raps; music
softens.)*

NARRATION *(intoned, following pitch and rhythm of the melody):*   djanturan
The lovely and delicate beauty who sits before the Queens is
the Princess Sumbadra, younger sister of King Kresna. Incarnation of the nymph Widawati and object of the ogre King
Dasasuksma's desire, she is as yet unmarried. Graceful is her
every movement and perfect her appearance. Her waist is tiny,
her finely shaped breasts look like polished marble. Viewed
from afar she appears like a nymph; words alone cannot describe her beauty. Seated in the palace chamber, the ladies are
concerned about the absence of their beloved Lord, King
Kresna.

SONG *(On a signal from the dalang, the melody Perkutut Manggung
ends; the dalang sings Patet Manjura Ngelik):*
> Stars pale with
>> The approaching dawn,
>
> Beautiful faces
>> Cloud in worry
>
> Over their King
>> Oooooo . . .

DJEMBAWATI: I hope you are well, my Sisters?

RUKMINI: Yes, noble Sister.

SETYABOMA: We are well, my Sister.

DJEMBAWATI: And you Sister Sumbadra?

SUMBADRA: Thank you, elder Sister, I lack nothing. It is seven
days since our King Kresna and his brother have been gone.
Each day I pray for their safe return. What is it they seek,
Sister?

DJEMBAWATI: Dear Princess, I myself do not know. But their
absence disturbs me. I fear some untoward event before their
return.

SONG *(The dalang sings Ada-ada Gregetsaut Manjura to tense tapping):*

Danger hovering in the air
   Oooooo . . . oooooo . . .
Innocence and beauty
   Unprotected . . . oooooo
The Prince's heart leaps
   With joy to see it.

(*Enter* BEGASUKSMA, *flying through the air. He hovers, looking down upon the ladies.*)

BEGASUKSMA: Haaa! What luck! The men of Dwarawati sleep like corpses while these delicious ladies sit unprotected! Ooooohh! That one must be the Princess Sumbadra! Father will love her! What a treasure to be left in the open, unguarded!

(*Five sharp raps; the gamelan plays Sampak Manjura as* BEGA-SUKSMA *swoops down, seizes* SUMBADRA, *and flies off left with her. The queens scarcely know what has happened. Music ends.*)

*Fig. 51
Maidservants,
Setyaboma,
Rukmini,
Djembawati,
Sumbadra, and
Begasuksma*

SONG (*The dalang sings Sendon Tlutur*):
   Oh God look
     And have pity
     Oooooo . . .
   The sun's new rays
     Light new sorrow
     Oooooo . . . oooooo . . .

DJEMBAWATI (*calling*): Oh, Sister! Where are you?

RUKMINI (*crying loudly*): Oh, Sister! What has happened? How can it be? She was just here!

The Reincarnation of Rama

SETYABOMA: Sisters, stop this weeping! Hurry! Inform Minister Udawa in the main hall! He will know what to do.

DJEMBAWATI: Yes, Sisters! Come, make haste!

(Five raps; melody Sampak Manjura is played as the queens exit. The KAJON *is fluttered across the screen and is returned to its place on the right.)*

Scene 5

adegan Dwarawati

(A single rap cues the gamelan to change to the melody Ajak-ajakan Manjura. Enter KRESNA *and* ARDJUNA, *who stand at the right, and* BALADEWA, GATUTKATJA, BIMA, *and the clowns who face them from the left. The dalang raps; music stops.)*

*Fig. 52
Ardjuna, Kresna, Gatutkatja, Baladewa, Gareng, Bima, Semar, and Petruk*

KRESNA: Now that we have arrived at Dwarawati, Brother Baladewa, do not be anxious to return to Mandura. Stay awhile that we may savor your presence.

BALADEWA: Ahh! I'll stay, Brother, gladly. Thank you!

KRESNA: Bima. Ardjuna. We desire your presence here as well. *(He hears something.)* What's that? I hear cries in the distance. Yes, anguished cries!

(Five sharp raps; Sampak Manjura accompanies the entrance of the three queens from the left. They sink to their knees before KRESNA, *weeping, as the music ends.)*

KRESNA *(to* DJEMBAWATI*):* What is it, my Love?

DJEMBAWATI: Ohh! My Lord . . . *(Weeps distractedly.)*

KRESNA: Calm yourself. Tell me the cause of this furor, I pray you.

DJEMBAWATI *(still weeping):* Oh, my Lord! A calamity! Sister Sumbadra has disappeared, without a trace!

(Five raps; as Sampak Manjura plays, ARDJUNA *rises and slips away, unnoticed by the others. The music stops.)*

KRESNA: Disappeared? How could that be? Calmly tell me all that happened, I beg you, Dearest.

DJEMBAWATI *(controlling her tears):* We were all seated in the women's chamber, my Lord, when, for no apparent reason, Princess Sumbadra soared up into the air and out of sight. All that remained was the echo of her voice, crying out in despair.

BALADEWA: Brother, this cannot be!

KRESNA: Remember the words of His Holiness, Narada! "There will be an ordeal," he said. That time has come.

BALADEWA: You are right! What should we do, Brother?

KRESNA: First, let us speak to Prince Ardjuna. *(Notices he is gone.)* What? Gone already? *(Chuckles to himself.)* In fact, I am not surprised. Anoman!

ANOMAN *(entering):* Yes, Majesty. *(Makes the sembah.)*

KRESNA: I give you your first order. Go after Prince Ardjuna. Assist him.

ANOMAN: Immediately, my Lord. *(Makes the sembah.)*

(Five sharp raps signal the gamelan to play excited Sampak Manjura. ANOMAN *quickly exits left; the others go off, leaving the screen empty.)*

**adegan perang
sampak manjura**

Scene 6

(The KAJON *passes quickly across the screen, indicating a change of scene.* BEGASUKSMA *is seen flying across the screen carrying* SUMBADRA *in his arms.* ARDJUNA *follows in close pursuit.* ARDJUNA *passes* BEGASUKSMA *and blocks his way. The music softens.)*

*Fig. 53
Ardjuna,
Begasuksma, and
Sumbadra*

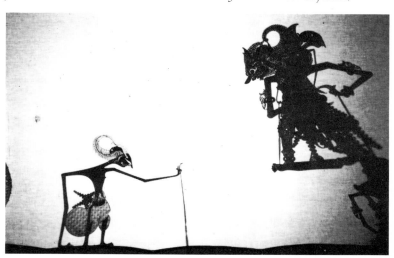

The Reincarnation of Rama

SUMBADRA: Brother Kresna! Brother Baladewa! Do you not know of my fate? Oh, help me, my Brothers!

ARDJUNA: You cry out in distress, Princess, yet presume to choose your savior?

SUMBADRA: Help, Brothers!

ARDJUNA: Do not shun the aid of one who is near, Princess.

SUMBADRA: I do not want to be saved by the one who is near. Why have you come? I did not call you!

ARDJUNA: Shall I turn back then, gentle Princess, because you failed to mention my name?

SUMBADRA: Turn back. No one prevents you. Certainly not I!

ARDJUNA: I do not require your orders, Princess! I shall return according to my wish, and that is to return with you! Name yourself, Ogre!

BEGASUKSMA: Begasuksma, son of King Dasasuksma! And you?

ARDJUNA: Ardjuna of Amarta!

(Sampak Manjura plays loudly. ARDJUNA *attacks* BEGASUKSMA, *knocking him unconscious.* BEGASUKSMA *drops* SUMBADRA; ARDJUNA *dashes forward and catches her in midair.* BEGASUKSMA *revives and snatches* SUMBADRA *from* ARDJUNA. *Using supernatural powers, the ogre prince reduces* SUMBADRA *in size and locks her inside his hairpin.* ARDJUNA *pursues* BEGASUKSMA, *attacks, and knocks him to the ground unconscious. As* ARDJUNA *retrieves* SUMBADRA, *she resumes her normal size.* ANOMAN *enters. At a nod from* ARDJUNA, *he shrinks and takes* SUMBADRA'S *place within* BEGASUKSMA'S *hairpin.* ARDJUNA *exits right, carrying* SUMBADRA. BEGASUKSMA *revives and flees left.)*

Scene 7

adegan Dwarawati

(Music continues as KRESNA *and* BALADEWA *enter from the right meeting* BIMA *and* GATUTKATJA *entering from the left.* ARDJUNA *hastens in from the left carrying* SUMBADRA. *He drops her at the feet of* KRESNA *and* BALADEWA. *Music ends.)*

Fig. 54
Baladewa, Kresna,
Sumbadra,
Ardjuna, Bima,
and Gatutkatja

KRESNA (*suppressing a smile*): Why, noble Ardjuna! You treat my sister as though she were a broken dustpan!

ARDJUNA: She is very heavy, my Lord.

BALADEWA: Heh, Ardjuna! If she was so heavy, you could have asked her to walk! Admit it, Nephew, she was a nice weight to jog along with, wasn't she! Hah, hah!

SUMBADRA (*rising, indignant*): You, Brothers, have nothing to say! For a whole week you abandoned your wives and sisters. And when I was cruelly abducted, neither of you helped me! A stranger had to come to the rescue!

KRESNA: Stranger, Sister? Hm!

BALADEWA: Sister, mind your manners. Don't scold us. Instead, thank this handsome young knight for saving you.

BIMA: Haahh! Brothers! Now, I know why Ardjuna dallies so much at Dwarawati! So! My kingly elders conspire to make a match for my vagabond brother! Haaahh! You too, little Sister! You all have the same idea. Admit it. And stop blaming each other!

KRESNA (*smiling*): For one so straightforward, Brother Bima, you seem to know a great deal. Now, Ardjuna, who was the abductor who dared enter Dwarawati?

ARDJUNA: It was Prince Begasuksma, son of King Dasasuksma.

KRESNA: He is a powerful spirit; no wonder he was successful. And how did you manage to rescue my delicate sister from him, Ardjuna?

ARDJUNA: He had hidden her in his hairpin, oh King. I had Anoman replace her.

BALADEWA: Ho, ho! Old Dasasuksma will go raging mad when he finds his old foe Anoman instead of a bride!

KRESNA: We must not let poor Anoman face Dasasuksma's wrath alone, Brothers. Bima, Gatutkatja, follow him and lend your support.

(*Five sharp raps; fast Sampak Manjura is played. All the characters exit. The* KAJON *is placed in the center, inclined slightly to the left. The music stops.*)

djedjer
Tawanggantungan

Scene 8

tjarijos   NARRATION: And now our story returns to the palace of the Kingdom of Tawanggantungan, where King Dasasuksma sits,

The Reincarnation of Rama

waiting impatiently for news that the bride of his desire has been obtained.

(Three raps; the gamelan plays Liwung. The KAJON is placed to the right. DASASUKSMA enters from the right. BEGASUKSMA rushes in from the left, and falls at his father's feet. Music ends.)

DASASUKSMA: Aaahh, at last! My Son, you've returned! Tell me . . .

BEGASUKSMA: Yes, Father, I met with no danger on the way. Allow me to present my humble greetings, noble Majesty.

DASASUKSMA: Yes, yes! Tell me, where is the Princess Sumbadra? Did you find her and bring her to me?

BEGASUKSMA: Yes, kingly Father, I did.

DASASUKSMA: You did, my Son? My Kingdom is yours. Where is she? Show me her!

SONG *(The dalang sings Ada-ada Gregetsaut Manjura):*
> Like a bolt of lightning
>> Striking in the clear sky,
> An old foe . . . oooooo
>> Anoman . . . oooooo

(ANOMAN emerges from BEGASUKSMA's hairpin, kicking at BEGA-SUKSMA's head and shrieking. The ape confronts his old enemy, DASASUKSMA, who stands aghast.)

DASASUKSMA: Begasuksma! I send you to fetch a wife, and you bring back this filthy old ape? What's the meaning of this?

BEGASUKSMA: Oh, Majesty Father! I don't know. I put the Princess in my hairpin.

ANOMAN: And I took her place. She's safely back in Dwarawati, my King.

DASASUKSMA: Anoman, I shall grind you to pulp for this! You plagued me in the past! You won't plague me now! I'll strip the flesh from your bones!

ANOMAN: King Rawana! That's the name I know best! Eternal troublemaker! It's time I tore you to shreds!

Scene 9

adegan perang
amuk-amukan

(Five quick raps; the gamelan plays very fast Sampak Manjura, accompanying the final battle of the play. ANOMAN bites DASA-SUKSMA's shoulder.

On Thrones of Gold

Fig. 55
Dasasuksma and
Anoman

They fight back and forth. DASASUKSMA *flees;* ANOMAN *pursues.*
BIMA *and* GATUTKATJA *appear, engaging* BEGASUKSMA *and the*
ogre army. GATUTKATJA *fights* BEGASUKSMA.

Fig. 56
Gatutkatja and
Begasuksma

The Reincarnation of Rama

BIMA *battles the ogre* SAKSADEWA. *Finally,* DASASUKSMA, *and the other ogres flee.* BIMA, *alone on the stage, performs the "victory dance."*

Fig. 57
Bima

Then he backs off right. The screen is empty for a moment.)

Scene 10

djedjer tantjeb
kajon

(The melody changes to Ajak-ajakan Manjura. Enter KRESNA *and* ARDJUNA *from the right.* BALADEWA, BIMA, GATUTKATJA, ANOMAN, *and the clowns enter from the left. Music stops.)*

KRESNA: Brother Bima, I congratulate you. Your ferocity in battle inspires fear and terror.

BIMA: The ogres have fled, Brother.

KRESNA: I am relieved and congratulate you all. Now let us remain alert, for though King Dasasuksma has fled his kingdom, he is in reality the spirit of Rawana, killed in battle by Prince Rama. Free from spiritual death for eternity, he will never cease spreading evil throughout the world. Anoman!

ANOMAN: Yes, your Majesty. How may I serve you? *(Makes the sembah.)*

KRESNA: Dasasuksma's evil deeds must not go unchecked. I can trust no one but you to thwart his destructive actions. Therefore, I assign you, faithful and noble Anoman, to practice

On Thrones of Gold

asceticism on Mount Kendalisada. There you must guard forever the spirit of Dasasuksma, and use your spiritual powers to
prevent him from harming the world.

ANOMAN: Yes, Your Majesty. I obey your command. *(Makes
the sembah and exits.)*

KRESNA: And now Brothers, Friends! We have completed our
assigned duties. Let us say our prayers of thanksgiving to the
almighty Gods, and I ask that you join me in celebrating the
just victory of this day!

tjarijos NARRATION: And so Kings, Princes, and warriors exult in the
success of their actions this day.

*(The gamelan strikes up loud and joyous Gangsaran. The KAJON is
brought from its place on the right of the screen and is planted in
the center of the tableau, signifying the conclusion of the play.*

*Fig. 58
Ardjuna, Kresna,
Kajon, Gatutkatja,
Baladewa, Bima,
Gareng, Semar,
and Petruk*

The music changes to Rudjak Djeruk as the audience departs.)

Irawan's Wedding   Irawan Rabi

Translated by Stephen R. Alkire
and Pandam Guritno Siswoharsojo

English version by James R. Brandon

Cast of Characters

KINGDOM OF DWARAWATI

King Kresna, ally of the Pandawas
Prince Samba, Kresna's son, crown prince of Dwarawati
Prince Setyaki, Kresna's brother-in-law
Udawa, chief minister of Dwarawati
Queen Djembawati, Kresna's first wife
Queen Rukmini, Kresna's second wife
Queen Setyaboma, Kresna's youngest wife
Princess Titisari, Kresna's daughter
Maidservants

KINGDOM OF MANDURA

King Baladewa, Kresna's elder brother
Pragota, chief minister of Mandura

KINGDOM OF DJONGBIRADJI

King Barandjana, an ogre
Lajarmega, female ogress, chief minister of Djongbiradji
Mingkalpa, ogre minister of Djongbiradji
Togog, clown-servant of Barandjana, brother of Semar
Saraita, clown-servant of Barandjana
Bantjuring, ogre official of Djongbiradji (portrayed by puppet of Tjakil)
Montrokendo, ogre warrior (portrayed by puppet of Terong)
Pragalba, ogre warrior

HERMITAGE OF JASARATA

Kanwa, religious ascetic
Disciple

PRINCEDOM OF MADUKARA

Princess Sumbadra, Ardjuna's first wife
Princess Srikandi, Ardjuna's second wife
Prince Abimanju, Ardjuna's eldest son
Princess Siti Sendari, Abimanju's wife, daughter of Kresna
Prince Irawan, Ardjuna's son
Maidservants

KINGDOM OF ASTINA

King Durjudana, eldest Kurawa brother
Prince Dursasana, second-eldest Kurawa brother
Prince Lesmana Mandrakumara, Durjudana's son, crown prince of Astina
Durna, adviser to Durjudana
Sangkuni, chief minister of Astina

KINGDOM OF AMARTA

King Judistira, eldest Pandawa brother
Prince Bima, second Pandawa brother
Prince Ardjuna, third Pandawa brother
Prince Nakula and Prince Sadewa, fourth and fifth Pandawa brothers, twins
Prince Gatutkatja, Bima's son
Semar, clown-servant to the Pandawas, in reality the god Ismaja
Gareng, eldest son of Semar
Petruk, second son of Semar

Irawan's Wedding

Before leaving home the dalang begins to concentrate his senses upon the evening's performance. He prays, "Om. May nothing give hindrance, O Spirits of this house, flying over the earth, Mother of Generations. Allah, assist me, fulfill my wish, gratify my intentions. Creatures, male and female, look at my work, be pleased, and love by God's will. Oh, Allah! Oh, Allah! Oh, Allah!" Holding his breath, he stamps three times with his right foot.

On arriving at his host's home the dalang repeats the same prayer, requesting the help of the spirits of the host's dwelling. At about eight-thirty the fifteen to twenty musicians who make up the gamelan begin to play the Talu, or introductory music. As the Talu draws to a close, the dalang takes his place before the center of the screen praying, "O Great Serpent who supports the earth, O Spirits all hear, I ask your help. Let not the onlookers disperse before I have finished performing my art."

The dalang inspects the performance equipment which is set up on the veranda of the host's home. He checks to see that the screen has been fastened tightly, that the banana-log "stage" which holds the puppets is properly installed, that the puppets not being used for this performance have been set up on either side of the screen or put away in the big puppet chest on his left, that those which will first appear in the evening's drama are beside him, within easy reach, and that the KAJON, the "Tree of Life," is firmly planted in the center of the screen.

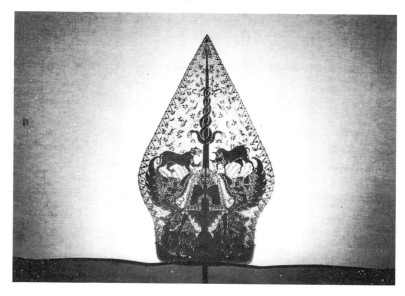

Fig. 59
Kajon

On Thrones of Gold

Most of the audience has gathered. The host and his guests are seated on chairs set up on either side of the screen. Casual passersby sit on the ground or stand crowding around the performance area. Spectators on the dalang's side of the screen will see a "puppet" performance; those on the opposite side will see a "shadow" performance. It is now nine o'clock. As the introductory music concludes, the dalang raps sharply five times against the puppet chest on his left to signal the gamelan ensemble to play Ajak-ajakan Nem, the opening melody of the play, quietly saying as he does, "The hills and mountains are my abode, may the strength of the wind and storm be mine." He reaches above his head to the coconut-oil lamp which casts the shadows on the screen. Adjusting its flaming wick, he prays silently, saying, "Om. O God of the Soul, Essence of the One, O God of Light, may the flame of the lamp shine over the world. May those who come be silent, show pity and love, and may they stay to look at me." The dalang reaches for the KAJON, raises it carefully out of the banana trunk, then slowly lowers it.

He holds the KAJON in his lap so that the tip rests on the puppet chest. Gently, with his left hand, he bends its tip several times, quietly speaking his final prayer before the performance begins: "May my body be large and strong like the mountains. May those who come be silent. May they show pity and love as is God's will." The dalang moves the KAJON from the lower left to the upper right corner of the screen, twirls it three times, and places it at the right of the screen, indicating that the play is about to begin.

PART ONE

Scene 1

(The dalang takes up the puppets of the two MAIDSERVANTS. *One in each hand, he presses them against the screen to make a clear shadow. They enter right and move gracefully to the center of the screen. They look about and see the king, their master, approaching from the right. They sit cross-legged on the floor, their faces cast down, honoring the king with the sembah—the traditional gesture of obeisance in which the hands, palms pressed together, are brought before the face. The imperious figure of* KRESNA *enters from the right.*

Fig. 60
*Kresna and
Maidservants*

KRESNA *acknowledges their sembah and they rise and move deferentially to assigned places to the rear of the king. The two chief members of the king's retinue enter from the left, greet their lord, and take their traditional places in audience before the king. First to enter is* SAMBA, *the king's son. His figure is delicate, refined. He enters crawling, honors* KRESNA *with the sembah, and sits respectfully before him.* SETYAKI, *the king's brother-in-law and commander of the kingdom's armies, enters crawling, makes the sembah, and moves behind* SAMBA.

*Fig. 61
Maidservants,
Kresna, Samba,
and Setyaki*

*The characters remain in tableau as the dalang, by a steady tap-
ping on the side of the puppet chest, signals the gamelan to end
the melody Ajak-ajaken Nem and begin Krawitan. The tapping
speeds up, ending with three loud raps; Krawitan softens and the
dalang begins the story of the kingdom.)*

djanturan   NARRATION *(intoned, following pitch and rhythmic patterns of
Krawitan):* May silence prevail. Numerous are God's creatures
that roam the earth, fly in the sky, and swim the seas. Countless
are the world's beautiful women. Yet none can equal those to
be found in the Kingdom of Dwarawati—Gate of the World.
Search one hundred countries, you will not find two, nor among
a thousand, ten, to match it. Thus, do I introduce this Kingdom
as our story's beginning!

Long, high, sands, mountains, fertile, prosperous, trade,
peace, foreigners. Long is Dwarawati's reputation and the
telling of it. High is its prestige. Ocean's sands border it;
mountains guard its rear. On its right lie fields of rice, to the
left a great river leading to a harbor on its shore. Fertile is its
soil; prosperity abounds. Merchants trade by day and night,
unceasingly in perfect safety, while peasants' flocks and herds
freely roam. Never has rebellion stirred the peacefulness of
this land. Foreigners throng to make Dwarawati their home.
The roofs of their dwellings touch in friendship, crowding the
largest places and making them seem small. All state officials
are united in a single aim—to increase the glory of the Kingdom
of Dwarawati. The Kingdom stands firm over the earth. Its
torch is high, illuminating all the world with its radiance.

Irawan's Wedding

Many are its colonies. Not only on Java do countries submit themselves to its rule, but kings from afar proffer allegiance, so great is their love for the perfection of the Kingdom of Dwarawati. Near, they bow to the earth before its perfectness; farther afield, they incline to show their respect. Annual tribute of maidens and precious gifts is offered by all as token of their submission.

Who is the King who rules this Kingdom? He is King Kresna —"Kresna the Black," whose skin, blood, and bones are black as the color of ebony. Many are his titles: "Guardian of the Pandawas," for he loves and advises these five virtuous brothers, "Bridge Between Man and God," "Giver of Life," "Kresna the Charitable," "Kresna the Seer," "Deterrent to Disaster," and "Incarnation of Wisnu." Among the god Wisnu's several incarnations, it is said that two are King Kresna and the Pandawa Prince, Ardjuna. As a flower and its scent or a fire and its flame, the flower is Kresna, the scent Ardjuna, the fire is Kresna, the flame Ardjuna. Like the front and the back sides of a leaf, their appearance is different, their taste the same. The King of Dwarawati is endowed with the characteristics of sage, judge, warrior, and noble. The most excellent of kings, he is powerful yet humble, wise yet shares his wisdom. He cares for his subjects: he clothes the naked and feeds the hungry, aids the infirm and offers shelter from the sun and rain, cheers the mournful and heals the sick. To recount all the King's virtues and the greatness of his Kingdom would consume the long night. What has been said must be sufficient.

It is on a Thursday that the King appears in the audience hall. He seats himself upon his throne of gold and precious jewels. A lush carpet, strewn with fresh-cut flowers and fragrant with the scent of exotic perfumes cushions his feet. Maidservants, dancers, and concubines in elegant costume attend the King. They bear golden, gem-incrusted figures of state—swan, serpent, cock, and elephant. Servants on either side of the King stir cooling breezes with fans of peacock plumes until the fragrance of the King reaches to the outermost quarters of the palace. In the midst of such spectacle, the King appears no longer human, but the image of the god Wisnu descended to earth and accompanied by heavenly nymphs. In reverence to the King even the breeze ceases to whisper. Still are the leaves on the trees. Only the soft music of the gamelan, the tinkling rhythm of the goldsmith's hammer, and the call of the kolik bird perched in the banyan tree in the square are heard from afar, enhancing the dignity of the occasion.

Who are those who sit respectfully before the King? Directly in front of the King is his son, Crown Prince Samba. He is a handsome young man of great virtue and integrity. Considerate of others before himself, his understanding of human nature is both wise and compassionate. The Prince's energetic actions always accord with his father's desires. Behind the Prince sits the King's cousin and brother-in-law, the warrior Setyaki, adviser to the King and commander of Dwarawati's armies. To the rear, the great audience hall is filled to overflowing with Dwarawati ministers and officials of all ranks, seeking places even in the outer courtyard to attend the King.

SONG (*The dalang raps once on the gong beat; Krawitan is played at full volume for several gong phrases, then ends. Accompaniment for the song Patet Nem Ageng begins, and the dalang sings*):

>Oh Ruler of the Universe
>>My prayers to thee.
>
>On your favor
>>We depend for our well-being
>>In this world and after.
>
>Oh I pray have pity on me
>>And my followers,
>>Night and day worshiping thee.
>
>Shower your blessings on Dwarawati
>>Oooooo . . . oooooo . . .
>
>So the King prays in his heart.

SONG (*The dalang continues with the song Ada-ada Girisa, his singing accompanied by gentle tapping and the soft sound of a xylophone*):

>Silent is all in the great hall,
>>Even the wind ceases blowing
>>In reverence to the King.
>
>Throughout the Kingdom
>>Anticipation
>>Oooooo . . .
>
>The King's daughter
>>Will marry
>>Oooooo . . .
>
>With joy-filled heart
>>The King begins speaking.

Irawan's Wedding

(Since the king and his court have taken their places there has been no movement before the screen. Now the dalang raises KRESNA'S *forearm and the king speaks.)*

KRESNA *(in a tense, strong voice of medium-pitch):* Welcome in my presence, Samba, my Son.

(A triple rap on the side of the puppet chest punctuates the end of KRESNA'S *speech.)*

SAMBA *(strong, but light voice):* Majesty, my Father, I accept your welcome with both hands. Allow me to present my reverent greetings.

(The dalang makes a triple rap on the chest as SAMBA *bows deeply before his father, raising his hands before his face and making the sembah of respect.)*

KRESNA: Your greetings delight me, my Son. I extend to you my blessings. *(Triple rap.)*

SAMBA: I accept them in the warmth of my heart, kingly Father. *(Makes sembah.)*

KRESNA *(gesturing to* SETYAKI*):* Cousin Setyaki, I hope you arrive well? *(Triple rap.)*

SETYAKI: In the presence of Your Majesty, I lack nothing. Please accept my homage, oh King. *(Triple rap as* SETYAKI *makes sembah of respect.)*

KRESNA: Thank you, Cousin. Accept my blessings. Rest comfortably while I speak with my son. *(Triple rap.)*

SETYAKI: Thank you, Your Majesty. *(Triple rap while he makes the sembah.)*

KRESNA *(gesturing to* SAMBA *with forearm):* Samba, were you not surprised when you received the summons of your King?

SAMBA: Majesty, when I received the royal command, I felt as though my spirit had been shattered, crushed against a rock, as though lightning bolts had struck me, but, as if by a miracle, I was unhurt. My heart trembled like grass blown by the wind in the great square; it fluttered like a leaf caught in the eye of a storm. But, when I arrived in Your Majesty's presence, my heart grew peaceful again, as if cooled and cleansed of fear by the sprinkling of holy water. *(Makes deep sembah of obeisance.)*

KRESNA: How is it, my Son, that your anxiety so quickly passed? *(Triple rap.)*

SAMBA: Seeing Your Majesty, I realized that if I were guilty of some sin, it would be Your Majesty who would punish me, that were I to be condemned to death, it would be Your Majesty who would command it. My only wish is to do Your Majesty's will, though it mean my life. Remembering this, I felt content, my King. (*Makes the sembah.*)

KRESNA: My Son, your loyalty greatly pleases me, but you allow imagination to overcome you. There is a saying that, however fierce the tiger, he will not devour his own young. Should he be judged guilty and sentenced to death, the King's forgiveness is always there. He who sits upon the throne of Dwarawati may cut the grass where it blocks the light and give solace to the suffering as he chooses. But do not misinterpret my meaning. Expect neither reward nor punishment. Gifts are as far from my mind as a star in the sky, my Son. (*Three raps.*)

SAMBA: My Father, gifts are not in my thoughts, nor even in my dreams. Your generosity flows like the surge of a mighty river, so that being near you your kindness overwhelms me. I expect nothing, but live only to fulfill your commands. Your smallest word I shall obey. (*Makes the sembah.*)

SONG (*The dalang sings Patet Nem Djugag*):
> The fragrance of flowers
>> Strewn by the breeze,
> The Prince's reply sets
>> A King's heart at ease.

KRESNA: Your esteem pleases me, my Son. Now, let us set aside affairs of state and discuss the matter which is now closest to my heart: the wedding of your sister Titisari. Tell me, Samba, are the preparations proceeding apace?

SAMBA: Majesty-Father, I beg to report that . . .

KRESNA: On this occasion let us dispense with the usual formalities, my Son, and all of you in my presence, as well. Speak plainly and frankly of the wedding plans. This occasion gives me great joy.

SAMBA (*a bit uncertain at first, then becoming excited*): Yes, my . . . Father. There are exactly twenty-three days remaining before the wedding.

KRESNA (*smilingly*): Samba, I know that!

SAMBA: But, Father, I mean there is still plenty of time to finish the preparations. The pavilions for visiting officials and ministers . . .

KRESNA: And kings!

Irawan's Wedding

SAMBA: Yes, Father, and kings, of course . . . are done. The palace has been swept and whitewashed. The women are sewing new garments . . . (*Embarrassed.*) . . . so I have been told. Everywhere in the city the talk is of nothing but the wedding, and the splendid festivities which will accompany it, Father! It is the chief concern of all the people . . .

KRESNA: And kings.

SAMBA: Of course, Father. Every king in Java will be here!

KRESNA: Ah, yes. Yes, yes, yes! How could I have forgotten?

SAMBA (*stopping*): What is it, Father?

KRESNA: In all the excitement, I have forgotten to invite my elder brother, King Baladewa!

SONG (*The dalang sings Ada-ada Mataraman Djugag*):
> Mouths fall agape,
>> Hearts beat loudly,
> As the King speaks
>> Unimagined words.

SETYAKI: Oh, my King, this is a most grievous breach of etiquette. (*Makes the sembah.*)

KRESNA: Indeed, I know it! I have committed a royal blunder. We must do something to assuage his fearful temper.

SETYAKI: Oh, my Lord, I urge you send him a message immediately. Allow me to go, my King, I will describe some accident along the way which has delayed me. (*Makes the sembah.*)

KRESNA: Oh, excellent! Prepare to depart at once. Samba, go with your uncle! Assist him!

SAMBA: Yes, Father.

(*Five raps signal the gamelan to play the melody Ajak-ajakan Nem; the music immediately softens.*)

NARRATION: The emissaries have no sooner begun to leave the presence of the King, when Chief Minister Udawa bursts into the audience hall. The others stop and wait for him to speak.   tjarijos kadjantur

(*Single rap and the music plays at full level as* UDAWA *quickly enters from the left and sits before the king, making a swift sembah. Music stops.*)

KRESNA: Udawa, what is the cause of this uproar? You disturb our audience!

UDAWA: I beg Your Majesty's pardon, but I thought you should know immediately. Your royal brother, King Baladewa of

Mandura, has just been sighted, speeding on his elephant. He will arrive at any moment. *(Makes the sembah.)*

KRESNA: My brother! Here? *(Gestures to* SETYAKI.*)* Our plan is too late.

SAMBA: I would give my life, for my Majesty! *(Makes deep sembah.)*

KRESNA *(dryly):* That is not a solution, Samba. *(Sighs and composes himself.)* Well, there is nothing to do but make the best of it. Help me, my friends. *(To* UDAWA.*)* Show my royal brother into the audience hall, Udawa.

UDAWA: Yes, Majesty.

(Five spaced raps signal the gamelan to play Ajak-ajakan Nem as UDAWA *makes the sembah and backs off left. The music stops.)*

tjarijos NARRATION: Before the high walls of the palace of Dwarawati, raging with the force of an elephant on the rampage, there appears the figure of the King of Mandura riding his huge speeding mount. Called King Baladewa, he is famous for his blunt and forceful ways. With great strides, looking neither left nor right, he mounts the palace stairs and enters the presence of the King of Dwarawati.

(The dalang raps three times, signaling the gamelan to play the melody Diradameta for BALADEWA'S *entrance.* BALADEWA *enters from the left, his rear arm pugnaciously set on his hip. He approaches* KRESNA *and the two kings bow to each other in greeting. As they stand in tableau the melody Diradameta ends.)*

KRESNA: Welcome, my royal Brother.

BALADEWA *(jovial, forceful):* Thank you, kingly Brother! I journey to bring you my greetings!

*Fig. 62
Maidservants,
Kresna, Samba,
Baladewa,
Setyaki, and
Udawa*

Irawan's Wedding

KRESNA *(being as polite as possible)*: May they adorn my throne, my chamber, this palace, and extend throughout the Kingdom, most honored and noble elder Brother.

BALADEWA *(very pleased)*: Hooo!

SAMBA: Revered royal Uncle! I offer you my life! *(Bows to the floor and makes deep sembah.)*

BALADEWA *(surprised)*: Ehh? What's this all about, Brother?

KRESNA: Why, Brother, we are carried away, ah, seeing you arrive so suddenly, unescorted, and unannounced.

BALADEWA *(expansively)*: As my kingdom is yours, and your kingdom is mine, brothers should not stand on formality! Good brothers act directly, out of mutual regard and in good will! Ho, ho! And so I stand before you, Brother!

KRESNA: As you are my elder brother, your desires are mine, as my desires are, I am sure, yours.

BALADEWA: Of course, of course! But tell me, Brother, what would you have done had you known of my intention to visit you?

KRESNA: I would have commanded the royal chariot be sent for you and a guard of honor accompany you, my Brother.

BALADEWA *(laughing delightedly)*: Hooo! Why, Brother, that would swell my pride to the mountain tops! It is good to have kings for brothers! Is it not, Brother?

KRESNA *(wryly)*: Indeed, is it not, Brother!

BALADEWA: Do not despair, there will be other opportunities for honoring me! Ha, ha!

KRESNA *(seizing the opportunity)*: Ah, dear Brother, you have reminded me! We are planning a festivity within the month. Honor us, oh King, with your royal presence. It is a small family affair, but we shall be inconsolate if you are not with us.

BALADEWA: Which reminds me, Brother! While you are planning small family affairs in Dwarawati, the Kingdom of Astina arranges a wedding of gigantic proportions, to which the whole world will be invited. This is the mission on which I have come, oh Brother.

KRESNA *(worried)*: Brother, allow me, I pray, to tell you what is planned in Dwarawati . . .

BALADEWA *(good-naturedly)*: Ho, ho! Who has traveled three days and nights, Brother? You or me? Who has left his own kingdom to carry out a weighty mission, Brother? You or me? Is this your vaunted hospitality, Brother? Ho, ho! Allow me to speak first.

KRESNA (*outmaneuvered*): Yes, elder Brother. Speak.

BALADEWA: I come with joyful news! My good friend, King Durjudana of Astina, was greatly dejected when his son Lesmana Mandrakumara was unable to marry your daughter Princess Siti Sendari. That she was given to Ardjuna's son, Abimanju, depressed him still more. Unable to give up his plan to marry into our family, he has hit upon the idea of Lesmana now marrying your daughter Titisari. Ah, ha! It is a splendid idea, is it not, Brother! (KRESNA *cannot speak for a moment,* BALADEWA *notices the hesitation.*) Well?

KRESNA: Ah, Brother . . .

BALADEWA: You do agree, don't you?

KRESNA: There is a slight complication, Brother.

BALADEWA: Nonsense! Whatever the problem, large or small, I shall sweep it aside for the sake of you, my Brother, and my friend Durjudana! Arrange the wedding any way you want— King Durdjudana will accede to your every wish, Brother.

KRESNA (*becoming alarmed*): Brother, no more of this, please . . .

BALADEWA: I understand. You are overcome with joy! Do not thank me!

KRESNA: Brother, I fear Titisari is not the girl for Prince Lesmana. She . . .

BALADEWA: You are modest, Brother. She is a lovely young thing! Just the bride for an Astina Prince!

KRESNA: But, Brother, I'm trying to tell you . . .

BALADEWA (*misinterpreting* KRESNA'S *protestations as continued modesty*): Say no more! It is settled. (*Magnanimously.*) Hah, hah! As the eldest of our family, I have decided it and it shall be so! Now, what were you telling me before, Brother, about some small celebration? Is that what all the bustle is about in the city? Ha, at first, I thought your people were in a state of rebellion, Brother! Everywhere people are milling about, music pounds the air, young couples are dancing in the streets. What is it, Brother?

KRESNA: Brother, the preparations are for a wedding.

BALADEWA: A wedding! Wonderful!

Irawan's Wedding

KRESNA: To which you are cordially invited, dear Brother.

BALADEWA: It is the season for love! Who're you marrying off this time, eh? Who's the groom?

KRESNA: The son of Ardjuna, Irawan.

BALADEWA: And the bride?

KRESNA: Elder Brother, be informed, I am giving my daughter Titisari in marriage to Irawan.

SONG (*The dalang sings Ada-ada Mataraman Djugag to the accompaniment of tense and steady tapping*):
> The King's ruddy face turns livid,
>> His body turns to flame
> In anger . . . oooooo
>> Oooooo . . . oooooo

NARRATION: Upon hearing the words of his younger brother, *tjarijos* King Baladewa is struck dumb. He stands rooted to the ground. His eyes glare; his ears burn. His nostrils flare and his lips twitch. Then shock gives way to anger and he grinds his teeth in rage.

BALADEWA (*shaking his hand under* KRESNA's *nose*): What does this mean, Brother! How dare you arrange a marriage in our family without my consent? I am the elder. It is for me to make suitable matches for our kin! I was not consulted! (*He almost explodes.*) I was not even *informed*!!

KRESNA: Brother, I pray do not be upset. The wedding is still . . . a month away. Scarcely anyone has been informed as yet.

BALADEWA (*outraged at* KRESNA's *effrontry*): The people are dancing in the streets, Brother!

KRESNA: Have you forgotten you gave your consent to this marriage when the two were engaged last year?

BALADEWA: I cannot be expected to remember everything! That was a year ago. Much has happened since then. Titisari shall be married to Crown Prince Lesmana Mandrakumara, and that is my final word.

KRESNA: But, Brother, Majesty . . .

BALADEWA: *I* will even pay for the wedding! If our Pandawa cousins object, send them to me. I will deal with them.

KRESNA: Oh, Brother Baladewa . . .

BALADEWA: Your *elder* brother has spoken! A King does not speak twice!

KRESNA (*sighs*): Yes, Brother. I, after all, am only father of the girl. I accede to your wish.

tjarijos NARRATION: Oppose the will of the King of Mandura, and one encounters an enraged dragon, snapping left and right, and spitting out angry words in a torrent. Submit to his will, and one discovers a person as calm and pleasant as a child.

BALADEWA: Ha, Brother, you are not renowned for wisdom to no purpose. You see I am right after all. Ho, ho! What are the five Pandawas against the ninety-nine Kurawa brothers? In any case, it is all among friends and cousins. Who should object to a happy marriage like this? And now, dear Brother, allow me to dispatch my minister to Astina to fetch the new bridegroom!

KRESNA (*one last chance*): Brother, pray accompany me into the palace! Your sisters anxiously wait to greet you!

BALADEWA (*jovial again*): Later, Brother.

KRESNA: Join us at the table. Let us drink and recall pleasant times past (*Deprecatingly.*) Your message can wait a few moments.

BALADEWA: Ho, ho! I do not know how you remain a king, Brother! Duty first! Remember that, younger Brother!

SONG (*The dalang sings Ada-ada Girisa to steady tapping as* BALADEWA *exits to the left.* KRESNA *accompanies him partway, then resumes his seat.* SAMBA *takes* BALADEWA'S *place before his father*):

> King Baladewa
>> Departs from the hall
>> Rushing . . . oooooo
> Even divine words
>> Of a divine King
>> Cannot prevent
> The stream of events
>> From flowing
>> Oooooo . . . oooooo

KRESNA: Well, Samba, let this be a lesson to us both, on how not to conduct statecraft. Listen to me carefully, my Son: it is imperative that we inform your uncle, Ardjuna, as delicately as possible of this . . . change in wedding plans.

SAMBA: Allow me to go, Father! (*Makes deep sembah.*)

KRESNA (*weighing the matter*): It will require the utmost tact

Irawan's Wedding

for he has set his heart upon his son Irawan marrying your sister.

SAMBA *(fervently):* Entrust this holy mission to me, Father! I shall not fail!

KRESNA: Yes. Well, it would be good experience for you. *(Deciding.)* Go to Madukara. Convey to your uncle this message: all the Pandawas are invited to attend a new wedding, that of Titisari and Prince Lesmana Mandrakumara, according to the wish of the King of Mandura, my brother. Ask that noble Ardjuna understand the difficulties of this . . . er, matter, and that he give his blessing to . . . the affair. Can you do that, Son?

SAMBA: With your blessing, I go, royal Father!

NARRATION: And so the divine King Kresna gives the signal that he wishes to retire. Escorted by dancing girls and concubines, the King strides from the audience hall appearing to be a likeness of the god Wisnu himself. — tjarijos

(The dalang raps five times signaling the gamelan to play Ajak-ajakan Nem. KRESNA *waves distractedly to dismiss* SAMBA. *The* MAIDSERVANTS *move in front of* KRESNA *and make the sembah. He rises, turns, and crosses off right, followed by the* MAIDSERVANTS. *The others make the sembah to the departing king and exit left. For a moment the screen is empty, then* KRESNA *passes from left to right, going into the palace. The* KAJON *is planted center, inclined to the right. The music ends.)*

NARRATION: The King enters the inner chambers of the palace, where he meets his three Queens. He informs them of the visit of their brother, King Baladewa of Mandura, of the cancellation of the planned wedding, and of Titisari's new husband-to-be. Dismayed by this news, the Queens gently protest to their Lord. Advising them to remain silent, the King leaves their presence and retires to the palace temple where he may meditate undisturbed. — tjarijos / pagedongan

SONG *(The dalang sings Ada-ada Mataraman Djugag to steady tapping and the accompaniment of a xylophone):*

> Fire and incense
>   Reach to the sky,
> Carrying prayers
>   To the heavens
>   Oooooo . . .

**adegan paseban
djawi**

Scene 2

(The dalang strikes the puppet chest sharply three times; the gamelan plays Kadaton Bentar as the KAJON *is moved from the center to the right side of the screen, marking the beginning of a new scene.* BALADEWA *enters from the right, strokes his moustache, turns, and waves on* SAMBA *and* SETYAKI. *They enter from the right and sit beside the king.* UDAWA *and* PRAGOTA *follow them on and make the sembah. They all sit facing the king. Three raps; the music softens.)*

*Fig. 63
Baladewa, Samba,
Setyaki, Udawa,
and Pragota*

djanturan

NARRATION *(intoned, following pitch and rhythm of Kadaton Bentar, which continues to play in the background):* Meanwhile, in the outer audience hall are gathered King Baladewa, Prince Samba, and Prince Setyaki, along with Minister Udawa of Dwarawati and Minister Pragota of Mandura and officials and warriors of both Kingdoms so numerous they seem to crush the pillars of the buildings. Flags wave in the wind, like the waves of the ocean, ebbing and flowing. Ministers Udawa and Pragota, seeing King Baladewa, think, "Oh, God, what is the King's message?" Respectfully they face him.

(One sharp rap; Kadaton Bentar is played at normal level for a gong phrase, then ends.)

Irawan's Wedding

PRAGOTA *(to* BALADEWA*):* I am at your service, Your Majesty. *(Makes the sembah.)*

BALADEWA *(full of energy and high spirits):* Hah, Uncle Pragota I hope you are well.

PRAGOTA: I am, Your Majesty. *(Makes the sembah.)*

BALADEWA: Pragota, you are to go to Astina. Take this message to King Durjudana: say, I send my greetings and it is arranged that Prince Lesmana will marry the Princess Titisari! The Prince should be escorted to Dwarawati to meet King Kresna, his new father-in-law, without delay! Go immediately!

PRAGOTA: I obey, Your Majesty. *(He makes the sembah.)*

BALADEWA *(enjoying this):* Now, Nephew, what have you to say?

SAMBA: I offer my reverent greeting, kingly Uncle. *(Makes the sembah.)*

BALADEWA: Ho, ho! Not to me, to your ministers and officials!

SAMBA *(uncomfortable):* Father Udawa, be informed the wedding of Irawan to my sister is canceled. I leave to visit Uncle Ardjuna in Madukara today. Order my troops prepared to escort me. You may accompany me as far as the border, then return to help our kingly Father with . . . the other wedding preparations.

UDAWA: Yes, my Prince, immediately. *(Makes the sembah.)*

BALADEWA: Excellent, Nephew You may make a king someday!

SONG (UDAWA *makes a sembah and backs off left as the dalang sings the song Ada-ada Astakuswala Alit to steady tapping, underscoring the excitement of the offstage scene):*
> Thunderous is the sound
> > Of trumpet and drum
> > And beating gong.
> Flags and banners wave
> > Like the ocean's tide,
> Beautiful is the sight
> > Oooooo . . .

UDAWA *(off):* Attention Soldiers of Dwarawati! In the name of King Kresna, Giver of Life, hear my orders! Assemble in three divisions: the first will guard the capital city, the second defend our borders, and the third accompany Prince Samba to Madukara

SOLDIERS *(off):* Yes, Sir! We obey, Minister Udawa

UDAWA *(off):* Arm yourselves and assemble in the great square at the sound of the first gong Ready on the second! We march on the third!

SOLDIERS (*off*): Yes, Sir!

SONG (UDAWA *re-enters and takes his place before* SAMBA *during the singing of Ada-ada Astakuswala Ageng, which the dalang accompanies by steady tapping*):

Horses wildly whinny
  As their riders mount.
Sharp bits cut their mouths
  And springs of blood gush forth.
Clamorous signals mix with their cries
  As horses plunge and rear
  Oooooo . . . warrior's strong hands guide them.

UDAWA: The troops stand ready, my Prince. (*Makes the sembah.*)

SAMBA: Sound the gong, Uncle!

UDAWA: Yes, my Prince.

SAMBA: I hope you will enjoy your stay, kingly Uncle.

BALADEWA: Oh, I shall! My blessings, Nephew!

SONG (*The dalang sings Ada-ada Budalan Mataraman to steady tapping as* UDAWA, *followed by* PRAGOTA, *make the sembah and exit left*):

Numerous are the troops
  Their uniforms bright,
Like the sun rising
  From the horizon
To cast its golden
  Rays on the world
Partly visible behind the mountain,
  Illuminating the clouds
  Oooooo . . .

tjarijos   NARRATION: Minister Udawa strikes the gong as if to break it. Three times its booming voice pierces the air. Drums, trumpets, flutes, and bells thunder in response as the mighty Dwarawati army marches from the city.

(*Three raps on the puppet chest by the dalang and the marching music Wrahatbala is played.* BALADEWA *exits right, the others exit left.* UDAWA *re-enters from the right, turns and gestures to the massed troops off-right to pass in review. The* MARCHING ARMY *enters, halts before the prime minister. The army receives his salute, moves past* UDAWA, *and marches off left.* SAMBA *and then*

Irawan's Wedding

*Fig. 64
Udawa, Horse,
and Marching
Army*

SETYAKI *mount horses and ride across the screen.* UDAWA, *on horseback, rides past the* MARCHING ARMY, *his steed prancing and leaping with energy. The* MARCHING ARMY *follows* UDAWA *off. The* KAJON *is placed left of the center of the screen, representing trees in the forest. The* MARCHING ARMY *enters from the right and stops facing the* KAJON. *The music ends.)*

Scene 3

**adegan perang
ampjak**

FIRST SOLDIER: Heh up there, what's up? What are we stopping for?

ginem wadya

SECOND SOLDIER: Yiii! Halt back there! Put those damned spears down!

THIRD SOLDIER: At ease, there! The road's overgrown up ahead. The Prince must pass this way to Madukara! You with the swords and axes, to the front. Cut down the trees. Clean out the underbrush.

SECOND SOLDIER: Say, I'll be glad to see Madukara again. I've got a cousin who lives there. Haven't seen her in years.

FIRST SOLDIER: I'll bet she's your cousin!

THIRD SOLDIER: Let's go, friend. Make way up front!

(The gamelan plays Srepegan Nem. In time to the music, the

MARCHING ARMY *strikes the* KAJON *several times as if cutting a tree. The* KAJON *topples forward and the* MARCHING ARMY *triumphantly tramps up and over the "fallen trees" and on its way.*

Fig. 65
Marching Army
and Kajon

The KAJON *flutters across the screen from right to left, symbolizing the cleared forest, and, after several passes, is planted in the center of the screen, inclined to the right.)*

tjarijos

NARRATION *(The dalang raps; Srepegan Nem stops):* Dwarawati's marching soldiers travel far, escorting young Prince Samba to his uncle's Kingdom of Madukara. So much for the army of Dwarawati. Now our story moves to the ogre Kingdom of Djongbiradji.

djedjer sabrangan

Scene 4

(Three raps; the gamelan plays Madjemuk. The KAJON *moves to the right side of the screen. Enter from the right the ogre king,* BARANDJANA. *He lifts his hand to shade his eyes as he looks intently about. The ogress* LAJARMEGA *and the old giant* MINGKALPA *enter from the left and sit respectfully before the king. Three raps; the music softens.)*

Irawan's Wedding

*Fig. 66
Barandjana,
Lajarmega, and
Mingkalpa*

NARRATION *(intoned, following pitch and rhythm of music):* The **djanturan** ruler of this distant ogre Kingdom is the mighty King Barandjana. Impressive is his appearance: tall as a mountain; his eyebrows are black forests; his eyes twin suns; his nose the prow of a ship; his mouth, a cave edged with fangs and thornlike teeth. Thick hair falls over his heavy shoulders, and bristly tufts mat his chest and arms. His laugh roars like thunder. His scream strikes like lightning. Powerful in battle is he. Indeed, few can match his strength and skill, and other giant kings respect and fear him. Viewed from afar the magnificence of the King is such that he resembles the terrifying god Kala. It is on a Thursday that the King appears in the audience hall, clothed in royal garments and adorned with golden ornaments and jewels. Seated before him is his trusted friend and adviser, the ogress Lajarmega. This strapping female warrior is capable as a man. And so it has come to pass that she has become Chief Minister of the Kingdom. Filling the audience hall are ministers and officials of the ogre Kingdom, wearing poisonous snakes as belts. Warriors playfully toss great boulders in the air.

Now it is said that this great ogre King is uncontrollably in love with the Princess Titisari. Seeing her in a dream one night, instantly his huge heart began to beat with passionate longing. Night after night the King tosses about on his bed, moaning and babbling, as he dreams again and again of ravishing her budding female body. Waking in the morning, the King weeps with raging desire, finding his longings un-

On Thrones of Gold

satisfied by the flowers of sleep called dreams. As he has every morning for weeks on end, the great King enters the audience hall weeping incoherently, as he imagines the tantalizing Princess to be with him in the chamber.

(The music continues softly under the dialogue.)

BARANDJANA *(weeping and moaning)*: Ohhh! Ohhh! Little Titisari! Let me caress you—tiny, trembling, tantalizing Titisari! Boo, hoo! *(Accidentally touching* LAJARMEGA, *he cries on her shoulder.)*

LAJARMEGA *(gruffly)*: Majesty, it is not proper that you should love this human princess. Deities marry nymphs, princes marry princesses, and ogres marry . . . ogresses. *(Realizing what she has said, suddenly embarrassed.)* Oh, Majesty.

BARANDJANA *(clinging to* LAJARMEGA*)*: Boo, hoo! Ohh, let me possess you! I shall die of my desire! Love me! *(He sobs on her shoulder.)*

LAJARMEGA: What is yours is mine, what is mine is yours, Majesty, still . . .

BARANDJANA *(holding* LAJARMEGA *tightly)*: Every night in my dreams you come to my chamber. Like a seductive nymph you say, "I am Princess Titisari, daughter of King Kresna of Dwarawati. I adore you, great King, and have come to serve you. Oh, handsome Barandjana, do what you will with me." I take you in my arms, hold you close, stroke your soft, silky skin, feel your delectable little body quivering with pleasure, and then . . . *(He bursts into tears and buries his head on* LAJAR-MEGA'S *shoulder.)*

SONG *(The dalang sings "Oooooo . . ." as a signal for the gending to end; the dalang sings Ada-ada Girisa)*:

His heart explodes
With grief,
His eyes with
Tears . . . oooooo
Tiny Titisari
Oooooo . . . oooooo

BARANDJANA *(thrusting* LAJARMEGA *from him)*: Just as I am about to have my way with you, I wake to find in my arms a rutting old sow!

LAJARMEGA *(hurt)*: Majesty!

BARANDJANA *(alternating between anger and tears)*: I mean, in my chamber last night! Ohhh, I can't bear it! When I find who put that pig in my room, I'll have the swine stoned! Filthy beast! *(He breaks down and cries again.)* Boo, hoo!

LAJARMEGA: Please, Your Majesty, a King must never cry!

BARANDJANA *(stopping immediately):* Every teardrop erodes a grain of sand in the desert of my reputation! An excellent saying!

LAJARMEGA: From tears grow the flowers of forgetfulness, whose five dark blossoms mark the loss of bravery, health, joy, strength, and position. Tears from a King bear him to his grave.

BARANDJANA: Damn! What, Mother Lajarmega, shall I do?

LAJARMEGA: You must forget her.

BARANDJANA *(petulant):* I can't. *(Furious.)* I won't! *(Weeps.)* I want her! Wait! I know what I'll do! I'll marry her! Ha, ha! A perfect solution. Why didn't I think of that before? Mother Lajarmega, call the troops, I'm going to Dwarawati to ask for Titisari.

LAJARMEGA: Noble King of our race, it is not fitting that one so powerful, rich, feared . . .

BARANDJANA *(very pleased with himself now):* . . . and lovable . . .

LAJARMEGA: . . . should visit this insignificant human kingdom. Send a letter couched in sweet words, with a gift of jewels and golden ornaments.

BARANDJANA: How could she say no? Do it, wise Mother! Summon an officer to deliver the letter. We must not keep my father-in-law waiting!

LAJARMEGA: I obey, exalted Majesty.

SONG *(The dalang sings Ada-ada Mataraman Djugag as* LAJARMEGA *makes the sembah and backs off left):*
> The Minister leaves
> > To obey the King's order.
> She descends the stairs
> > And summons Pragalba
> > Oooooo . . .

NARRATION: The Minister summons Pragalba, the giant officer from the border regions, and orders him to present himself before the King.　　　　tjarijos

(Three raps; the gamelan plays Bedat as LAJARMEGA *returns followed by the enormous ogre* PRAGALBA. PRAGALBA *sits before the king. The music ends.)*

On Thrones of Gold

tjarijos NARRATION *(strong and rhythmic, but in normal voice):* And so the ogre Pragalba presents himself before his revered King, his head bowed low as if to touch the floor. Indeed, excellent is this choice as the King's messenger. Imposing is his appearance; his prestige soars to the mountaintops. The audience stirs at the sight of this high official of the King. In his heart Pragalba wonders at the noble mission for which he has been summoned.

BARANDJANA: Ho! Pragalba! Did your heart beat when you received my summons?

PRAGALBA: Oh King! I heard lightning strike and saw the thunder flash, as if I had been hit but was not. I shook like a leaf. Now, I am at peace, my King. *(Salutes.)*

BARANDJANA *(pleased):* And, tell me, why did your anxiety pass so quickly?

PRAGALBA: Oh, King! I thought I might have committed a crime. Then I thought, if it were so you would kill me. So I was happy, oh King.

BARANDJANA: You do not misunderstand my summons?

PRAGALBA: I expect neither reward nor punishment.

BARANDJANA: My generosity?

PRAGALBA: Flows like the surge of a mighty river. I give my life for my King. *(Salutes.)*

BARANDJANA *(pleased):* Excellent! You have been chosen, Pragalba, to deliver a letter to King Kresna of Dwarawati. Take troops to accompany you.

PRAGALBA *(bowing low):* I honor this trust with my life, oh King! *(Salutes.)*

BARANDJANA: Go! Immediately!

PRAGALBA: Yes, oh King. *(Pause.)* Oh King, where is Dwawa . . . Dwarawati?

BARANDJANA: In Java, blockhead! My servants Togog and Saraita are from Java. Take them as guides. But go and bring back my bride instantly!

PRAGALBA: Ah . . . bride, oh King?

BARANDJANA: Go! *(Begins to weep.)* Oh, I shall die without her! *(To PRAGALBA, who stands totally confused.)* Go, you fool, and don't come back without her!

PRAGALBA: I leave at once, oh King. *(Salutes.)*

BARANDJANA (*waving feebly*): Go with my blessings.

(*Five double raps cue the melody Srepegan Nem.* PRAGALBA *takes a letter from the king, salutes, and backs off left.* BARANDJANA *looks after him, thinking of* TITISARI. *He trembles in anticipation, and slowly backs off right.* LAJARMEGA *and* MINGKALPA *make the sembah and exit to the left. The screen is empty a moment.*)

Scene 5

adegan paseban
djawi denawa

(*Srepegan Nem continues, as* PRAGALBA *enters from the right, crosses the screen, re-enters, stands on the right side of the screen, and waves on his fellow officers. Enter from the left* BANTJURING, *whose nickname is Tjakil, or "Fang," and* MONTROKENDO, *nicknamed Terong, or "Eggplant-nose" ogre. They shake hands with* PRAGALBA, *and stand to his left. The dalang raps; the music stops.*)

BANTJURING (*excitably*): Heh, Brother, what news from the King? Eh? Tell me, tell me!

MONTROKENDO (*speaks slowly, as he moves slowly*): Will we have a feast? With drinking and . . . dancing?

PRAGALBA (*proudly*): Brothers, know that I am ordered on a special mission to go to the distant Kingdom of Dwarawati to find a bride for His Majesty! I want you to come with me. But there is a problem. I don't know where Dwarawati is. Do you, Brother Bantjuring?

BANTJURING: Dwarawati? Heh, heh! Never heard of it!

MONTROKENDO: Nor I, Brother.

PRAGALBA: Togog and Saraita are supposed to know. Call them, Brother.

BANTJURING (*turns and calls off left*): Togog! Saraita! (*Turns back to* PRAGALBA.) Heh, heh! Dwarawati! Crazy name!

SONG (TOGOG *and* SARAITA *enter as Ada-ada Mataraman Djugag is sung*):
> The thunderous summons
>> Hangs in the air,
> Bringing to life
>> The two servants.

TOGOG: Yes, Master, what are your orders? (*Makes the sembah.*)

PRAGALBA: His Majesty orders us to go to Dwarawati in Java. Do you know it?

TOGOG (*happily*): Oh, ho, ho! I know Java like the palm of my

On Thrones of Gold

hand. Name any kingdom—Astina, Amarta, Madukara, Wirata —I know them all.

BANTJURING: You didn't mention Dwarawati!

TOGOG: It's hard to pronounce. Heh!

BANTJURING *(shaking his arms in anger):* You don't know where it is! Do you?

TOGOG: Well, it's been some years since I've been in Java.

PRAGALBA: Enough talk, Brothers. We have our orders. Togog, assemble the troops.

TOGOG: Yes, Master, but what if they don't obey? I'm just a little human and . . .

BANTJURING: You speak His Majesty's word before which all the world trembles! If anyone disobeys, we'll split his skull down to his navel! Heh, heh!

TOGOG: I hope you're right. Let's go.

SARAITA: Let's.

SONG *(As they exit left, the dalang sings Ada-ada Mataraman Djugag):*
  The servants leave
   To give the order
  To prepare
   The army to march
   Oooooo . . .

Irawan's Wedding

NARRATION (*a normal speaking voice*): And now it happens that the soldiers of the ogre army are summoned. Their commanders order them into formation, but they rage about unheeding, like bloodthirsty tigers. Some throw boulders as big as buffalo heads. Some wear live snakes as belts, others ride astride lions, tigers, and rhinoceroses. The ogres roar, the beasts roar. Both eat human flesh. Each ogre demonstrates a new ferocity that makes the others quake. Again and again the commanders call without answer. Then they leap to the towers, striking the enormous alarm gongs whose clamorous tones ring through the air. The ogre warriors gather to receive their orders. Near and far they shout to each other, "Ho-ho, grab your knives and clubs! Bring buckets for blood! We're going to Java!" They are given their King's command, as Togog hurries back to report to his master.

tjarijos

SONG (TOGOG *re-enters and faces* PRAGALBA *as the dalang sings Ada-ada Gregetsaut Mataraman to steady tapping on the side of the puppet chest*):

> The servant returns
>> To make his report
> That the army
>> Is ready to march
>> Oooooo . . .

TOGOG: The troops have received your orders, Master. (*Makes the sembah.*)

PRAGALBA: Let us go, Brothers.

(*Five spaced raps signal the gamelan to play Srepegan Nem. All exit quickly to the right.* BANTJURING *crosses the screen, followed by first* PRAGALBA, *then* MONTROKENDO, TOGOG, *and* SARAITA, *hurrying to Java.*)

Scene 6

adegan perang gagal

(*As Srepegan Nem continues, the* MARCHING ARMY *of the ogres enters from the left, meeting the* MARCHING ARMY *of Dwarawati and Mandura entering from the right. The two* MARCHING ARMIES *fight, rhythmically striking against each other. The ogre* MARCHING ARMY *is defeated and exits left, pursued by the opposing* MARCHING ARMY. BANTJURING *enters from the left,* PRAGOTA *from the right. Suspiciously they eye each other. The music stops.*)

Fig. 68
Pragota and
Bantjuring

SONG *(The dalang sings Ada-ada Gregetsaut Mataraman to steady tapping):*

> Two thundering
>> Hostile armies meet
>> Oooooo . . . oooooo . . .
> As if to beat their foe
>> Into the ground
>> Oooooo . . . oooooo . . .

BANTJURING *(shaking his forearm furiously):* What the hell! What's going on here! We just get to Java and we're jumped from behind! Dog, who are you, heh? Where are you from? Tell me, tell me!

PRAGOTA: You ugly fool, out of here! I am Chief Minister to King Baladewa, brother of the Dwarawati King! Announce yourself!

BANTJURING: I am Bantjuring, official of the renowned Kingdom of Djongbiradji! Dwarawati, eh? Heh, heh, heh! Sorry about those soldiers getting killed just now. Teach them a lesson not to attack us. *(Proudly.)* Be informed, we bear a letter from our King Barandjana to the King of Dwarawati! Step aside and let us pass!

PRAGOTA: You filthy Ogre, back to your cave! A beast like you is not fit to step on Dwarawati soil!

Irawan's Wedding

BANTJURING (*jumping up and down in rage*): Beast? Beast!

PRAGOTA: Turn back before I turn you inside out, Pig!

BANTJURING: Ohhh! Ohhh! You dare fight me? I'm not called the Super-Giant for nothing! I'll cut you to shreds! I'll drink your blood!

PRAGOTA: I'll squeeze you until your bowels explode and your army drowns in a tidal wave of shit!

(*At this insult,* BANTJURING *goes into a near fit. He leaps up and down and roars like an animal in pain. Five sharp raps signal the gamelan to play the fast fighting music, Sampak Nem.* BANTJURING *leaps to attack* PRAGOTA, *but with a single blow old* PRAGOTA *fells* BANTJURING. PRAGOTA *walks calmly off right.* BANTJURING *rises and crawls off left. The clumsy ogre* MONTROKENDO *rushes in from the left, meeting* PRAGOTA *entering from the right.* PRAGOTA *easily knocks down his lumbering opponent.* PRAGOTA *exits right.* BANT-JURING *enters from the left, and helps* MONTROKENDO *escape left. The great ogre* PRAGALBA *enters from the left, meeting* UDAWA *entering from the right.* PRAGALBA *leaps at* UDAWA, *who dodges, then strikes a powerful blow which sends the ogre to his knees.* UDAWA *kicks the ogre in the back of the neck.*

Fig. 69
Udawa and
Pragalba

PRAGALBA *withdraws to the left, beaten.* UDAWA *follows. The melody changes to slower and quieter Ajak-ajakan Nem.* UDAWA *struts on from the right, strikes a pose with his rear arm on his hip, and strokes his moustache. He surveys the scene of the giants' retreat. Three raps; music softens.)*

djanturan NARRATION *(intoned, following pitch and rhythm of music):* Fierce is the clamorous battle among the opposing troops and officers. The ogre troops quail before the lightning attacks of the Dwarawati and Mandura warriors. Their officers are wounded and the whole great army flees into the depths of the forest for safety. The victorious troops encamp for the night. *(Music ends.)*

UDAWA *(strong gesture):* Dwarawati and Mandura men! The ogres have fled. Let us camp here and rest for the night!

SONG (UDAWA *exits to the left and the* KAJON *is planted vertically in the center of the screen, as the dalang sings Patet Lindur, marking the transition between Part One of the play, patet nem, and Part Two, patet sanga):*

Fig. 70
Kajon

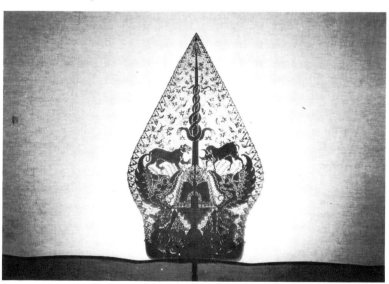

Irawan's Wedding

Commanders and soldiers
  Take their rest
   Oooooo . . .
Weapons glint
  In the light of the moon,
To soldiers on guard
  Serene and beautiful
  Is the night
Oooooo . . .

patet sanga   PART TWO

SONG *(The dalang sings Patet Sanga Wantah):*
    Late at night
        Stars light the sky
        Oooooo . . .
    The scent of flowers
        Supports the seers' prayers
        Like the murmur of bees.

tjarijos   NARRATION: In the morning the Dwarawati and Mandura warriors continue on their separate journeys. Prince Samba, officers, and men of Dwarawati go to the Kingdom of Prince Ardjuna, Madukara. Pragota and his followers go to the Kurawa Kingdom of Astina. Meanwhile, the intended bridegroom, Irawan, has been dispatched by his father to the holy hermitage of Jasarata to seek God's blessing for the match of Irawan and Titisari. Accompanying Irawan are the three faithful servants of the Pandawas, Semar, and his sons, Gareng and Petruk.

djedjer pandita   Scene 1

(Three raps signal the gamelan to play the melody Sumar. The KAJON *flutters across the screen and is placed to the right. A* DISCIPLE *crosses from right to left, turns, and looks off right, bowing low. The holy seer* KANWA *enters and stands at the right. The* DISCIPLE *bows deeply and takes his place to the rear of his teacher.* IRAWAN *enters from the left. He makes the sembah, resting his face on* KANWA'S *knees, then sits respectfully before him.* SEMAR *enters left, makes the sembah, and sits behind* IRAWAN. GARENG *and* PETRUK *enter and do the same, as the dalang raps three times and the music softens.)*

Fig. 71
Disciple, Kanwa,
Irawan, Semar,
Gareng, and
Petruk

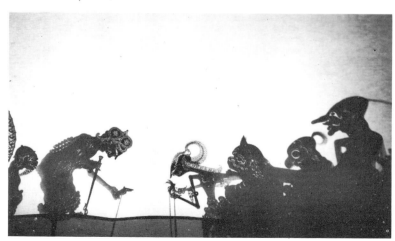

Irawan's Wedding

NARRATION *(intoned, following pitch and rhythm of the music):*   **djanturan**
This is the sacred hermitage Jasarata where the holy Kanwa
practices asceticism. Perfect are his prayers, free from blemish
is his mind; clairvoyant, he speaks solely the truth. This learned
seer is seen in audience with a disciple, imparting to him the
depth of his wisdom, when the holy man's grandson, Irawan,
appears. He halts his instruction and invites the modest Irawan
to approach. He looks upon his young grandson warmly and
wonders, "Oh, Heavens, what can my Grandson's arrival
mean?"

*(A single rap; music returns to normal level for one gong phrase,
then stops.)*

SONG *(The dalang sings Patet Sanga Ngelik):*
>Oh my teacher
>>Reveal to me
>
>The will of the Almighty,
>Why colors spread
>>All over the earth
>>Oooooo . . .
>
>The holy seer's enlightening words
>>Are interrupted
>>Oooooo . . .

KANWA *(serenely):* Irawan, my Grandson. You are welcome here.

IRAWAN: Your words, honored Grandfather, overflow my heart
with joy. I offer my reverent greeting, Holiness. *(Makes the
sembah.)*

KANWA: I accept them, my Child. Brother Semar, welcome. I
pray your journey finds you well?

SEMAR *(smiling contentedly):* Oh, yes, all is well. May your holy
blessing plug up the holes in my faulty character. *(Chuckles,
makes the sembah.)*

GARENG *(over his shoulder to* PETRUK, *but loud enough for the
others to hear):* He, he! Pa's an old fool. *(To* SEMAR, *importantly.)*
Paw, you're getting like a worn-out lopsided old broom. All
these years you've served our Pandawa masters you'd think
you'd have learned something about proper etiquette. Holes
in my character!

PETRUK *(laughing naughtily):* Papa is living proof that the
theories of heredity are a bunch of trash, Gareng. The best thing
to do with the old good-for-nothing is drop him in a well and
seal the lid on tight! Heh, heh!

SEMAR (*chuckling*): Respect your elders, Sons. That includes your dear Papa! Now behave!

KANWA (*smiling tolerantly*): Gareng, do you arrive well in my presence?

GARENG (*caught off-guard*): Ahh, me? (*He thinks.*) Ah . . . ah . . . (*He can't think of anything to say and laughs embarrassedly.*) Heeee, heeee! (*Makes the sembah.*)

PETRUK (*guffaws*): Haw, haw! Papa, you mistook a monkey for a son!

GARENG (*miffed*): That's not nice, 'Truk.

PETRUK (*imitating a monkey*): Heee, heee!

GARENG: Careful, 'Truk. You'll get a curse from His Holiness.

PETRUK (*mock horror*): Eeeeeh.

GARENG: Or a kick in the butt from me.

SEMAR: Boys, boys!

KANWA (*smiling*): Ah, Petruk, it is you. Are you, too, well?

PETRUK (*foolishly*): Yes, I like cookies, Grandpa. (*Makes the sembah.*)

GARENG: Haw, haw, haw! Did you hear that, Pa? (*Over his shoulder.*) 'Truk, that was a dumb thing to say.

PETRUK: I was remembering the cookies His Worshipfulness used to give us. My tongue slipped.

SEMAR (*laughing*): Or your head did, Son. Ho, ho! Such terrible boys, Your Holiness! (*Makes the sembah.*)

KANWA: You are all welcome here. And now, my Grandson, you are sent by your father?

IRAWAN: It is as you say, holy Grandfather. (*Makes the sembah.*)

KANWA (*smiling at* IRAWAN's *modesty*): Then perhaps you have a message from him?

IRAWAN: Indeed, Your Holiness knows all things. (*Makes the sembah.*) My father wishes me to convey to you his respects and to say that your son-in-law is to celebrate the wedding of his son and that he asks your blessing of this event. (*Makes the sembah.*)

SONG (*The dalang sings Patet Sanga Djugag*):
Nature's fragrance
    Scents the breezes,
Settling the heart
    Like joyful news.

Irawan's Wedding

KANWA: I am filled with joy to hear this news, but, Irawan, your father has many wives and more children. What is the son's name and who is his mother? (IRAWAN *is silent, his eyes riveted to the ground.*) Do tell me, Irawan.

SEMAR: Heh! Holiness, it is our young master himself who is to wed. In just three weeks he marries the Princess Titisari of Dwarawati.

KANWA: So, our young visitor is a groom-to-be! My Child, I pray the Almighty will bless this marriage.

IRAWAN: I thank you, honored Grandfather. (*Makes the sembah.*)

PETRUK: Psst! What's Papa talking about, 'Reng?

GARENG: You have ears.

PETRUK: 'Reng, are they talking about the theft of that brass cooking pot last week? If they are, I'm in trouble.

GARENG: What's the matter with you? (*Pokes him in the ribs with his elbow.*) Are you deaf?

PETRUK (*laughing*): Why, 'Reng, now that you mention it, I am having trouble.

GARENG: With your ears, 'Truk?

PETRUK: All last week my head was pounding. My wife said, "My dear, you've got ants in your ears." So I said, "Ants like fried meat," so my wife stuffed my ears with meat.

GARENG (*taking it seriously*): Did it work?

PETRUK: The pounding stopped. But then I couldn't hear.

GARENG: Why?

PETRUK: Because we couldn't get the meat out. So I said, "Wife, mice eat fried meat." So my wife . . .

GARENG (*dumfounded*): Put mice in your ears?

PETRUK: The pain is something fierce, 'Reng! I think they're setting up housekeeping in my brain! So yesterday I said to my wife, "Wife, cats eat mice," and now my wife is looking for a cat to put . . .

GARENG: You! You! You . . . (*Shakes with anger, turns, and tries to hit* PETRUK, *who avoids the blow.*)

PETRUK: Ohhh, don't get so excited, elder Brother. You look even more foolish when your face turns red!

SEMAR: Now, now, Petruk, behave! Where do you think you are?

PETRUK: In a criminal court!

SEMAR (*bemused*): A criminal court? My, my! (*Indicating* KANWA.)

Then who is this noble gentleman facing us?

PETRUK: The prosecutor.

SEMAR: Ahhh! And the one sitting before us? *(Indicating the* DISCIPLE.*)*

PETRUK: The bailiff.

SEMAR: Ahhh!! And what am I then?

PETRUK: Guilty! *(Waves his arms in laughter.)* Haw, haw!

SEMAR: Forgive my foolish sons, Your Holiness. *(Makes the sembah.)*

SONG *(The dalang sings Patet Sanga Djugag):*
> Nature's fragrance
>> Scents the breezes,
> All men's hearts are
>> Settled here . . . oooooo

KANWA: Irawan, be aware of your good fortune. You are to wed the daughter of Kresna, the King who is, indeed, a reincarnation of the god Wisnu. Tell your father, Prince Ardjuna, I am pleased and fully approve of this match. Until the wedding day I shall fast and pray both day and night for your happiness. Be considerate of your wife; act toward your father-in-law as you would toward your own father and a king. Do these two things and your rewards will be double.

IRAWAN: Thank you, Grandfather, for your holy counsel. *(Makes the sembah.)*

KANWA: I imagine there is much for you to do, my Child. Return now to your father with my blessing. May the Gods guide you safely home.

SONG *(The dalang sings Patet Sanga Djugag as* IRAWAN *makes the sembah, resting his face on* KANWA'S *knees, then backs off left):*
> Peace in his heart
>> The Prince takes his leave,
> The blessings of the holy one
>> Protecting him . . . oooooo

KANWA: Advise your young master well in these last days of his bachelorhood. I entrust him to your care during his journey, Brother Semar.

SEMAR: Rely on me and my sons, Excellence. I await only your blessing. *(Makes the sembah.)*

KANWA: Go your way untroubled, Brother Semar.

SEMAR: Sons, come follow our master.

GARENG: But, Pa, His Holiness didn't say I could go yet.

PETRUK: If you want to go, dopey, hold up one finger!

SEMAR: Hush!

KANWA: I give you my blessing, too, Gareng and Petruk, both.

GARENG: Thank you, noble Holiness. (*Makes the sembah.*)

PETRUK: Thank you, noly Hobleness. (*Snickers; makes the sembah.*)

(*Five spaced raps cue the gamelan to play Ajak-ajakan Sanga.* SEMAR *exits left, followed by* GARENG *and* PETRUK. KANWA *and the* DISCIPLE *go off right.* IRAWAN *turns and crosses the screen from right to left several times. One at a time, the three servants cross the screen in the same direction.* IRAWAN *appears alone in the center of the screen, facing left.*)

Scene 2

adegan wana

NARRATION (*music softens on a signal of three raps, and continues softly in the background*): Prince Irawan then descends from the mountains, where lay the hermitage of Jasarata, attended by the three faithful servants. The radiant young Prince enters the lush plains. He passes villages and fields. Everywhere the news of his coming brings forth young maidens, flushed widows, married mothers, and even old grandmothers to his path to gaze upon his matchless beauty. Many are the entreaties that he rest and refresh himself in their company. Seductive smiles and bold motions convey to him their meaning. But the handsome Prince looks neither left nor right, his mind filled only with love for the Princess Titisari.

tjarijos kadjantur

(*Music becomes louder and slower;* IRAWAN *exits left. The* KAJON *is placed left, where it represents the forest.* IRAWAN *re-enters and stands right of the center of the screen, facing the "forest." The three servants enter from the right and sit respectfully around their master.*

*Fig. 72
Petruk, Semar,
Irawan, Gareng,
and Kajon*

Three raps; the music softens.)

Passing now into the dark forest, animals take care not to disturb him. Had they the gift of speech, they would say, "Take care. Do not dare hinder the passage of the one who walks swiftly here." As Irawan plunges deep into the forest, wild animals flee from his path in panic: rhinoceroses, tigers, lions, snakes, monkeys, and deer.

(The KAJON *is planted and its trembling stops.)*

Several birds drop delicious fruit at his feet, but even this does not gain the Prince's attention.

(Three raps; music resumes its normal level for one gong phrase, then stops.)

IRAWAN: Father Semar, are we not lost? I do not know this forest.

PETRUK: I've never seen it before, Master.

GARENG: Nor I. Pa, you're chief forester. Where are we?

SEMAR *(chuckling):* Heh, heh. Why, Master, this is known as the Forest of Non-a-meat-all. Everybody knows it.

PETRUK: Non-a-meat-all? Papa, you're crazy! We've never been here.

SEMAR *(making the sembah):* Forgive my little joke, Master. Heh, heh! People call this the No-name-at-all Forest, because no one comes here, no one lives here. It's a blank on the maps.

IRAWAN: Yet, it is a beautiful forest.

SEMAR: It is, but it is the home of ogres from time to time. We must not linger, my Prince. *(Makes the sembah.)*

SONG *(The dalang sings Ada-ada Gregetsaut Sanga to steady tapping):*

    The trembling earth
      Whispers a warning
    To the Prince
      Beware . . . oooooo

*(*IRAWAN *passes the* KAJON *and goes off left, indicating that he is going deeper into the forest.* SEMAR, GARENG, *and* PETRUK *follow. The* KAJON *is placed center.)*

**adegan perang
kembang
tjarijos**

Scene 3

NARRATION *(accompanied by steady, tense rapping):* And now the Prince enters the very wood where the routed ogre army of

Irawan's Wedding

Djongbiradji is reassembling its ranks.

(Three raps; the gamelan plays Djangkrik Genggong. KAJON *moves to the right. Enter from the left the ogres* PRAGALBA, BANTJURING, *and* MONTROKENDO. *The music ends.)*

PRAGALBA: Well, Brothers, did you find out where Dwarawati is? We have delayed here too long already.

BANTJURING: Haw, haw! The natives aren't friendly, Brother!

MONTROKENDO: The forest's so dark I can't tell south from north.

BANTJURING: No one speaks on Java! Haw!

PRAGALBA: Of course not! You scare speechless every stray villager we meet. But we've got to find Dwarawati. Our King waits impatiently for his blushing bride. Brother Bantjuring, your carousing night and day brings discredit to our Kingdom!

BANTJURING *(waving his arms):* There's nothing else to do in this godforsaken forest! Haw, haw! I'll bash out anybody's brains that tells the King!

SONG (TOGOG *and* SARAITA *enter from the left, and sit before* BANTJURING *as the dalang sings Ada-ada Gregetsaut Sanga):*
> Alert servants
>> Hurriedly enter,
> Eager to impart
>> Their news.

BANTJURING: Haw! 'Gog and 'Raita! You come without being called! A miracle!

TOGOG *(out of breath, his body undulates against the screen):* Oh, Master! A young knight is headed straight for us!

BANTJURING: He may know Dwarawati! *(To* PRAGALBA.*)* Shall we capture him, Brother?

PRAGALBA: Treat him easy if he helps us. Otherwise, destroy him.

BANTJURING *(excitedly):* A young knight! Haw, haw! *(Stops.)* Just one, 'Gog?

TOGOG: Just one, Master. But his servants are terrible! I know them, Master. They're like a plague. You won't believe what one of them did to 'Raita.

SARAITA: Boo, hoo. He was mean to me.

BANTJURING *(shaking his arms in anger and excitement):* What did he do? Tell me, tell me! I'll rip his guts out!

TOGOG: It was the youngest, Petruk. By the way, Masters, watch out for him. He's the worst thief in the world.

BANTJURING: Never mind! What did he do? Tell me what he did!

TOGOG: Well, 'Raita ran across them on patrol. Petruk invited 'Raita to their camp to "share their meal."

SARAITA: I was starved.

TOGOG: "Have some magic porridge of King Solomon!," Petruk said.

BANTJURING: Haw, haw!

TOGOG: Petruk took the lid off a big pot filled with thick, steaming, green-brown stuff . . .

SARAITA (*weeping*): . . . he shoved a big spoon of it down my throat . . .

TOGOG: . . . but it wasn't King Solomon's porridge. It was hot water-buffalo dung!

SARAITA (*wailing*): I'll have bad breath the rest of my life! Boo, hoo!

BANTJURING (*waving his arms*): Haw, haw, haw! Serves you right for being stupid, 'Raita! Haw! Come on, 'Gog! Show me this knight! I'll devour him! Heh, heh! If he isn't nice!

(Seven double raps cue the gamelan to play lively Srepegan Sanga. TOGOG *and* SARAITA *go off right, followed by* BANTJURING, PRAGALBA, *and* MONTROKENDO. *They all cross the screen from left to right.* IRAWAN *enters from the right and stands quietly.* BANTJURING *enters from the left, sees* IRAWAN, *and leaps with fright. Fearfully, he inspects the immobile* IRAWAN *from the front, sides, and back. Getting no response, he jumps up and down, waves his arms, and growls and roars to intimidate* IRAWAN. *Thinking* IRAWAN *frightened, he becomes bolder. He snarls before* IRAWAN'S *face, then sneaks behind* IRAWAN *and is about to attack from the rear when* IRAWAN *calmly puts his hand on the handle of his dagger, scaring* BANTJURING *off.* BANTJURING *crosses left, and waves on* TOGOG *and* SARAITA. *They enter and sit beside* BANTJURING; *the music stops.)*

SONG (*The dalang sings Ada-ada Gregetsaut Sanga to steady tapping and the accompaniment of a single xylophone*):
>   As if struck by lightning
>   Filled with fear and fury,
>   Eager to start the fighting
>   Is the brave Ogre.

BANTJURING: Haw, haw! What the hell, is *this* the knight, 'Gog?

TOGOG: That's him, Master.

Irawan's Wedding

BANTJURING: Weakling! Bean sprout! I'll crush you with my little finger!

TOGOG: He's delicate, but don't think he's harmless, Master.

BANTJURING: Haw! Watch me handle him. (To IRAWAN.) Hey, little Knight! Where's Dwarawati? (Waves his arms.) Tell me, dammit! Don't stand there like a dummy! (Turns to TOGOG.) You didn't tell me he couldn't talk!

TOGOG: Master, you shout. You're rude. He's a knight. You've got to speak politely if you want him to speak to you.

BANTJURING: I'll shout all I please! (To IRAWAN.) Hey, you! I'll ask you nicely just once more! Tell me where is Dwarawati, or I'll chop you up for stew! (Furious that IRAWAN ignores him.) Tell me, tell me, tell me!

(IRAWAN silently backs off right. GARENG enters.)

GARENG (pointing with his forehead as he talks): What's all this ranting? (Walks unconcernedly over to BANTJURING.) Hi, Ogre. You must be rich, wearing both a sword and a dagger. Look at that fancy sash. Want to sell it?

BANTJURING (taken by surprise): What! What!

TOGOG: That's the older brother, Master. Watch out for him.

BANTJURING: Why, 'Gog, what is it? Its arms are bent, it's pigeon-toed, it's cross-eyed, and it points at everything! Yet it almost looks like a human being! Heh, Creature, what are you!

GARENG: Imbecile! I seem like a human being because I am one.

BANTJURING: Haw, haw!

GARENG: Which is more than you can say, Fang.

BANTJURING: Fang? Fang!!

GARENG (calmly): Your teeth hang out of your mouth. Or haven't you noticed, stupid?

BANTJURING (shaking his arms in excitement): Ohhh! Grrh!

GARENG: But then I don't suppose you have mirrors in Ogreland. You'd frighten yourselves to death.

TOGOG: I warned you, Master.

BANTJURING (more carefully this time): Hey, you! What's your name?

GARENG: Gareng.

BANTJURING: Gareng? Haw, haw! You're too big to be a "Gareng."

GARENG: What are you talking about, Ogre. Have you ever seen a smaller Gareng?

BANTJURING: Sure. Everybody has. You eat them. They're salty. They swim in the ocean and they're about so big. (*Hands indicate a few inches long.*) Haw, haw, haw!

GARENG: Blockhead! That's "herring," a fish. I'm Gareng, a wajang puppet. You've no manners. You're an ogre. All your friends are ogres. I haven't time for trash like you.

BANTJURING: Haw! This little rabbit's as conceited as a bear, 'Gog!

TOGOG: Wait till you meet his younger brother!

BANTJURING: Haw, haw! I'll fix him, just like I did this one!

(PETRUK *enters from the right, dancing and singing to the melody Tjao Gletak, which the gamelan plays on a signal of three raps from the dalang. He dances playfully up to* BANTJURING. *With his long arms,* PETRUK *hits* BANTJURING *rhythmically in time to the music, ending with a terrific wallop over the head as the music ends.*)

Fig. 73
Petruk, Gareng,
Saraita,
Bantjuring,
Togog, Pragalba,
and Montrokendo

PETRUK: I "crown" you King of the Play, Ogre!

BANTJURING (*dazed, but happy*): Ohhh! Ohhh! How wonderful! You've made me so happy!

PETRUK: Exactly. I didn't want you to get homesick, Friend. Thought you'd like the same kind of loving care you get at home.

BANTJURING (*sighing happily*): How did you know, Friend, this is what I've been pining for? You must be part ogre yourself.

PETRUK: Oh, no. Just play-acting. It's hard work, too, Ogre.

BANTJURING *(still marveling):* Just imagine. In time to the music, too! Bam! Pow! Whack! Boooom! Oh, I miss my wife so!

PETRUK: I have to make a living, Ogre. This ought to be worth a hundred rupiah to you.

BANTJURING: Fifty.

PETRUK: You're a hard man, Ogre. I'll take fifty. *(Taking a bill.)* I may turn professional, 'Reng.

TOGOG: He, he! I knew this would happen.

PETRUK: Hello, Uncle Togog. I offer you my respects, Uncle. *(Makes deep sembah.)*

TOGOG *(guardedly):* Thank you, Nephew. My blessings on you.

PETRUK: Dearest Uncle, they warm and nourish me. *(Sniffles.)* We need your prayers so much now, dear old Uncle Togog.

TOGOG *(still suspicious):* Why?

PETRUK: It's Father, Uncle. *(Wipes his eyes with handkerchief.)*

TOGOG: Where is Brother Semar?

PETRUK: You haven't heard? For shame, Uncle! Your brother, that you should honor and cherish . . . and help.

TOGOG *(concerned):* Well, what is it, 'Truk?

PETRUK: Papa's at death's door! He's sinking fast. *(Wails.)* Awwww!

TOGOG: Poor old Semar! What are you doing for him?

PETRUK: Everything we can, but the doctor can't help him. His only hope is the Chinese medicine man. *(Sobs.)* And we've got no money to pay him!

TOGOG: Really?

PETRUK: Really.

TOGOG: Poor, poor Brother! To be taken in the prime of life. We must help him. *(Sniffs.)* Here, 'Truk. I have two hundred rupiah. *(Sobs.)* Take it. Save your father!

PETRUK *(taking the money):* Thank you, Uncle. The Gods will bless you.

TOGOG *(wailing):* Poor, dear old Semar!

SEMAR *(waddling on cheerfully):* Do I hear my name mentioned?

TOGOG: Aaugh! Petruk, you tricked me! The old fool's not dying!

PETRUK *(laughing):* Then be happy the old fool's looking so well, Uncle! Heh, heh!

BANTJURING: Haw, haw! After all your warnings, he got you too, 'Gog! Come on, 'Gog, help me bring this statue back to life! *(To* IRAWAN *who enters from the right.)* Heh, you! Tell me your name, or die! *(Leaping about waving his arms.)* Tell me, tell me!

IRAWAN *(calmly):* This ogre begins again. Ogre, what is it others call you? I presume you have a name. Animals do.

BANTJURING: You're rude! I asked you first!

IRAWAN: And where is your home? I presume you have a cave somewhere. Snakes and bats do.

BANTJURING *(beside himself with rage):* Grrrrh! I may be an ogre, but I am an officer of a great King!

IRAWAN: You are still an ogre. A beast of the jungle.

BANTJURING: I am from the great Kingdom of Djongbiradji; my king is the great King Barandjana, renowned and feared through the whole world! Haw, haw! Do you fear me now, puny Knight? Tell me your name while you still can speak!

IRAWAN: I am Irawan, son of the Pandawa Prince, Ardjuna. I shall be speaking long after you are silent forever.

BANTJURING: For the last time, will you tell me where Dwarawati is?

IRAWAN: What use could a jungle beast like you have for this civilized land?

BANTJURING: The insignificant Princess of that country is to be honored by becoming King Barandjana's bride! Titisari, I think, is her name. Lucky little thing!

IRAWAN *(trembling with suppressed rage):* Beast, would you die now?

BANTJURING *(hopping with excitement):* Haw, haw! Not me, little Knight! But I'll slice you up! I'll mangle you! Fight! Fight! Fight!

(Seven double sharp raps cue the gamelan to play Srepegan Sanga, which accompanies the battle between IRAWAN *and the ogre.* BANTJURING'S *companions withdraw left;* SEMAR, GARENG, *and* PETRUK *go off right.* BANTJURING *roars and bellows at* IRAWAN *to frighten him, then repeatedly rushes at* IRAWAN *attempting to strike him from the front and from the back. Each time* IRAWAN *effortlessly evades or wards off the intended blow.* IRAWAN *attacks, and strikes* BANTJURING *to the ground.* IRAWAN *backs serenely away, right.* BANTJURING *rushes off and returns with a dagger. He*

attempts to stab IRAWAN *repeatedly with no success. Then, with one deft motion,* IRAWAN *twists the dagger in the ogre's grip and plunges it into his opponent's chest.* IRAWAN *serenely retires right as* PRAGALBA *rushes on from the left and sees the dead* BANTJURING. *Music stops.)*

SONG *(The dalang sings Ada-ada Gregetsaut Sanga to tense and continuous tapping):*

> As if struck by lightning,
> > Filled with fury
> Oooooo . . .
> > Is the ogre warrior.

PRAGALBA: What has this skinny knight done to you, Brother!

(Five raps signal Sampak Sanga, loud and quick battle music. PRAGALBA *carries off* BANTJURING *and returns to meet* IRAWAN *entering from the right. Music softens.)*

PRAGALBA: Speak! Who is it I am about to butcher?

IRAWAN: Irawan. And you, Ogre?

PRAGALBA: Pragalba! I'll drink your blood! I'll eat your flesh raw! Grrrh!

(Music comes up. PRAGALBA *falls on his back, trying to bite* IRAWAN *from below. He rages about, roaring and screaming to frighten his composed foe. He throws rocks and eats dirt. Recklessly,* PRAGALBA *throws himself at his lighter opponent, who easily evades, then strikes the huge ogre to the ground without looking.*

Fig. 74
Irawan and
Pragalba

On Thrones of Gold

PRAGALBA *rises, grapples with* IRAWAN, *and then blows him off the screen right. He exits in pursuit.* IRAWAN *flies across the screen and, re-entering, falls to earth. He rises, takes out an arrow, looses it, and pursues it off left.* PRAGALBA, *entering from the left, is struck, the arrow piercing his chest.* PRAGALBA *dies. The clumsy ogre* MONTROKENDO *enters from the right. Finding* PRAGALBA *slain, he weeps.*

Fig. 75
Montrokendo and
Pragalba

Tenderly, he lifts his dead companion and carries him off left.

Fig. 76
Montrokendo and
Pragalba

Irawan's Wedding

He quickly returns, alternately growling and weeping, and rushes off right in pursuit of IRAWAN. IRAWAN *enters from the right and is met by the inept but furious ogre who manages to hurl his small opponent off right.* MONTROKENDO *awkwardly runs off in pursuit. Music ends.)*

SONG *(The dalang sings Ada-ada Gregetsaut Gatutkatja, for the appearance of* GATUTKATJA*):*

> From the sky
> > Gatutkatja
> Spies the rising
> > Cloud of battle dust
> Oooooo . . . eager is he
> > To play his part.

*(*GATUTKATJA *flies in from the right, hovering in the sky.)*

GATUTKATJA: Haa! What is the dust billowing below! *(Moves downward.)* Someone is fighting an ogre! What? Irawan! Don't kill him, Cousin! Wait for me!

(Sampak Sanga again, loud and quick. GATUTKATJA *flies off left.* MONTROKENDO, *entering from the left, is intercepted by* GATUTKATJA, *who swoops down from the top of the screen right.*

Fig. 77
Gatutkatja and
Montrokendo

GATUTKATJA *seizes the ogre's head with his bare hands, and snaps his neck.*

*Fig. 78
Gatutkatja and
Montrokendo*

GATUTKATJA *backs off right, as* TOGOG *and* SARAITA *enter from the left. Sampak Sanga stops.)*

TOGOG *(shouting off right):* You may have killed a few Djong-biradji warriors, but don't think you've won yet! The King will sink Java under the sea with the weight of his invading army! Heh, heh! You'll see!

(Five spaced raps. Ajak-ajakan Sanga is played as TOGOG *and* SARAITA *exit left, carrying the corpse of* MONTROKENDO. GATUT-KATJA, *the three servants, and* IRAWAN *enter. The music stops.)*

IRAWAN: I greet you with joy and respect, Cousin Gatutkatja.

GATUTKATJA: Don't be angry because I deprived you of your opponent. I saw a good battle, and couldn't keep out of it.

IRAWAN: Your help was welcome, Cousin. But tell me, why are you far from home?

GATUTKATJA: Father became angry when he learned you had been sent alone to Jasarata. He sent me to find you. The wedding is not far off, Cousin Irawan. Come, let us return.

IRAWAN: Yes, Cousin, let us hurry.

SONG *(The dalang sings Patet Djingking):*

Flowers in the field
  Sway in the wind
  Oooooo . . .
Calmness and sweetness
  Follow their way
  Oooooo . . . oooooo . . .
Journeying
  To find their destination.

(Five slow raps cue the gamelan to play Ajak-ajakan Sanga.
GATUTKATJA *soars into the air, turns, and flies off slowly to the left.*
IRAWAN *makes the sembah to thank him, then exits left followed by*
the three servants. The KAJON *is placed center, inclined to the right.*
The music stops.)

SONG *(The dalang sings Patet Sanga Djugag):*
  Journeying homeward,
    Two noble Princes
  Travel swiftly
    Oooooo . . .

NARRATION: Gatutkatja flies swiftly home to report to his father,   tjarijos
Bima. Prince Irawan and the servants travel toward the Princedom of Madukara, ruled by Prince Ardjuna, father of Irawan.

Scene 4   djedjer Madukara

(Three raps; the gamelan plays Gambirsawit. The KAJON *moves*
to the right of the screen. ARDJUNA *and his wife,* SUMBADRA,
enter from the right. SRIKANDI *enters from the left, makes the*
sembah, and sits behind them. The dalang raps three times as a
cue for the music to soften.)

NARRATION *(intoned, following pitch and rhythm of Gambirsawit):*   djanturan
The story now moves to the Kingdom of Madukara. Though
actually a Princedom, its palace square is shaded by banyan
trees, symbols of a sovereign king. Prince Ardjuna, famed
Pandawa brother, is the country's ruler. Like a king, his names
are many and imposing; he is called: "Third Among Five,"
for he is the third of the five Pandawa brothers; "Ardjuna the
Sinless"; "Invincible Warrior"; "Son of Kunti"; "Raveler of
Riddles"; and "Manifestation of Wisnu," for in him, and in
King Kresna, the spirit of the god Wisnu is incarnate. The two
incarnations of Wisnu are as a flower and its scent, as a fire
and its flame: the flower is Kresna, the scent Ardjuna—Kresna

the fire, Ardjuna the flame. Like the front and back sides of a leaf, their appearance is different, their taste the same. The Prince's hair style is patterned after a lobster claw, his ear-jewels after water lilies, and his belt and sashes are of varied design. The Prince is sitting in the inner chambers of his palace, with two of his wives. Words alone cannot describe the fragile beauty of the Princess Sumbadra, the Prince's elder wife. Viewed from afar she appears like a nymph descended from heaven. Ardjuna's second wife, the Princess Srikandi, sits respectfully to the rear. She is renowned as a warrior, and her face radiates intelligence and resolve. Into their presence comes the serious young Dwarawati heir, Prince Samba, hurrying with his father's message. They all wonder, "Ah, what can be the purpose of this sudden visit"?

SONG (SAMBA *enters from the left and sits respectfully before* ARDJUNA. *The dalang raps; Gambirsawit ends. The dalang sings Patet Sanga Wantah):*

> Oh noble Prince,
>> Reveal to me
>> The will of the Almighty.
> Why do colors spread
>> Over the earth
>> Oooooo . . .
> He hangs upon
>> The Prince's words
>> Of enlightenment.

ARDJUNA: Welcome, dear Nephew. This is a surprise.

SUMBADRA: Greetings, Nephew Samba.

SRIKANDI: Yes, welcome.

SAMBA: I most humbly accept your welcome and think it a talisman for my future life. I offer you my prayers. (*Makes the sembah.*)

Fig. 79
Srikandi, Ardjuna,
Sumbadra, and
Samba

Irawan's Wedding

ARDJUNA: Thank you, Samba. Rest in comfort and tell us the purpose of your sudden visit.

SAMBA *(unsure how to proceed):* Thank you, revered Uncle. I come to pay my respects. *(Makes the sembah.)*

ARDJUNA: I accept them with pleasure.

SAMBA *(filling time):* Long have I been denied the pleasure and honor of meeting you. *(Makes the sembah.)*

ARDJUNA: Thank you.

SAMBA *(pause):* May my presence always please you, my revered Uncle. *(Makes the sembah.)*

ARDJUNA: I trust it always shall, Nephew.

SAMBA: Your reply brightens my day like the rising sun, oh noble Uncle. *(Makes the sembah.)*

ARDJUNA: Samba, it should be clear that your visit pleases us. But is this the extent of your mission? Do you not bring word from your kingly father as well?

SAMBA: Ah, how perceptive you are, my Uncle! It is true; my father asks that I convey a message of . . . some importance.

ARDJUNA: Samba, you may speak freely. Stand on ceremony no further, my Son.

SAMBA *(determining to brazen it out):* You are so warmhearted, Uncle! I shall! I do hope you are well!

ARDJUNA: We are, Samba.

SAMBA: Now that the rainy monsoon has passed, the weather is clear, is it not?

ARDJUNA: Indeed. As every year.

SAMBA: And are affairs in your palace going well?

ARDJUNA: As usual, Nephew.

SAMBA: Oh, Uncle, that's splendid! It is relaxing, is it not, to enjoy the pleasures of palace life! Dancers, servants, the best food, deciding the fate of the world! That is what Father always says.

ARDJUNA: Your father is a wise man, Samba. We are now waiting for you to impart to us some of his wisdom.

SAMBA: I cannot tell you how happy it makes me to see you all so well!

ARDJUNA: Yes, Nephew, we are well. Tell us more of your father's words, I pray.

SAMBA: His message?

ARDJUNA (*smiling*): Yes, Nephew.

SAMBA: Since you are all feeling so well the trifle of family news I bring surely will not disturb you.

ARDJUNA: I am sure it will not, Samba, if only you will inform us.

SAMBA: You recall the wedding, no doubt? Well, Prince Lesmana Mandrakumara will replace Irawan as Titisari's groom, at the order of Uncle Baladewa. (*Pleased he has carried it off so well.*) Well! That's what Father said.

tjarijos NARRATION: And, so, Prince Ardjuna, upon hearing the words of his nephew, dares not speak lest he betray the fury which rages inside him. A long moment passes. Great noble that he is, Ardjuna controls his anger and finally he speaks, in a voice that is clear and sweet.

ARDJUNA: I thank you, princely Nephew, for the trouble of your visit. Though it was my fondest wish to be your sister's father-in-law, I have known in my heart that I did not deserve such an honor.

SAMBA: Uncle, please do not be disheartened. You still may come to the wedding. Father invites all the Pandawas to attend the new wedding. Won't it be wonderful all meeting together again!

ARDJUNA (*smiling all the while*): Tell your father, Samba, that my only wish is to obey the will of the divine King Kresna, in this as in all matters. We now have two happy marriages which unite our families. Still, were he to command it, I should gladly break the marital vow between myself and your aunt, Sumbadra. At your father's word, I would separate his daughter, Siti Sendari, from my son, Abimanju. The wedding between Irawan and Titisari, which both our families have looked forward to, has not yet taken place. If they are not to be united, now is the time to say so. Convey my words to your father, Samba, and tell him that I submit myself to his divine authority.

SAMBA: Well, yes! Thank you, Uncle! Allow me to go tell Father you are content.

ARDJUNA: Go with my blessing, Samba.

SONG (SAMBA *makes the sembah and backs off left as the dalang sings Patet Sanga Djugag*):
> The young Prince
>> Departs elated,
> His difficult
>> Mission completed.

(*A* MAIDSERVANT *enters from the left and makes the sembah.*)

Irawan's Wedding

ARDJUNA: Girl. Find your master Abimanju and his bride. Bid them come before me at once.

MAIDSERVANT: Yes, Highness.

SONG (*She makes the sembah and exits left as the dalang sings Patet Sanga Djugag*):
> The maidservant hurries
>> At her Lord's
> Command
>> Oooooo . . .

(*Three raps signal the gamelan to play Kembang Tandjung.* ABIMANJU *and* SITI SENDARI *enter from the left.*)

NARRATION (*intoned, following pitch and rhythm of music, which softens when the dalang raps three times*): The loving young couple enter the audience hall and sit respectfully before their Lord, Prince Ardjuna. Abimanju is the Prince's favorite son. Siti Sendari is one of King Kresna's most beautiful daughters. So in love are they, not a glimmer of light separates the two youthful bodies. Those in attendance wink and nudge one another with tolerant amusement. The elderly nod happily, remembering their own youth; inexperienced servants gape in astonishment, their jaws hanging loosely, at the perfect beauty and happiness of the princely young groom and his captivating bride. Seen from afar, they are like two long-stemmed flowers, gently swaying in the soft breezes. Silent is all, as Prince Ardjuna looks upon the tranquil joy of his son and daughter-in-law. "Why," Abimanju thinks, "does Father not speak? What has happened that we are summoned suddenly?" At length their Lord speaks. — djanturan

(*Music ends.*)

SONG (*The dalang sings Patet Sanga Djugag*):
> Love's fragrance
>> Scents the breezes,
> Filling every heart
>> With joy.

ARDJUNA: Abimanju, my Son, it is late in the day and I have not seen you about.

ABIMANJU (*embarrassed*): We have been . . . asleep, Father. (*Makes the sembah.*)

ARDJUNA: That is a pleasant luxury of the young. Tell me, my Son, how long is this perpetual honeymoon of yours to endure?

ABIMANJU (*feelingly*): Until the end of time, Father! Or, so I wish it.

ARDJUNA: Is this not the flame of passion that soon dies?

ABIMANJU *(protesting)*: My love for Siti Sendari stands as firm as a mountain! It transcends the highest peak!

ARDJUNA: Mountains may erupt. And you, Princess, do you, indeed, love your husband?

SITI SENDARI: I love him as the hair on my head, long and composed of a thousand strands.

ARDJUNA: Hair can be cut.

SITI SENDARI: Yet it does not cease growing.

ARDJUNA: A good reply, Princess. *(To* ABIMANJU.*)* My Son, we have spoken of love. Now tell me, what of the duty a son owes his father?

ABIMANJU: Deep is my love and respect for you. You are my teacher and my Lord. I shall always do as you command!

ARDJUNA: Would you leap onto a burning pyre, or throw yourself from a cliff?

ABIMANJU: If it were your wish, my Father!

ARDJUNA: Your words please me. Remember them. Now, Princess, what have you to say about this? Are you not concerned that your husband's love for you may, sometime, conflict with his sense of duty toward me?

SITI SENDARI: No, dear Father. I am your son's wife. A wife gladly shares all that befalls her husband. I am a leaf fallen into a stream. Your son is the stream. I go as the stream flows.

ARDJUNA: I see. Now you both may prove the sincerity of your words. My Son, I order you to divorce your wife. Return to Dwarawati, Princess. You are the daughter of a king and your marriage to my son is beneath you.

SONG *(The dalang sings the plaintive Sendon Tlutur):*

    Oh God look
      And have pity
      Oooooo . . .
    The sudden crushing
      Weight of
      Sorrow . . . oooooo
    More terrible
      Than death
      To bear
    Oooooo . . .

Irawan's Wedding

NARRATION: Prince Abimanju lowers his head, hiding from his father the tears which flood his eyes. The young couple sit benumbed at the harshness of Prince Ardjuna's command, wondering in confusion at his reason. Tightly clings Siti Sendari to her husband.

tjarijos

Fig. 80
Srikandi, Ardjuna,
Sumbadra, Siti
Sendari, and
Abimanju

ARDJUNA: Why the silence? You have heard my command. Abimanju! Enter the palace; let your wife return to Dwarawati!

SONG *(The dalang sings Sendon Tlutur):*

> Oh God look
> > And have pity
> > Oooooo . . .
> What sin
> > Have we
> > Committed
> We know not
> > Oooooo . . .
> > Have pity.

NARRATION: Shocked with grief, Princess Siti Sendari clings tightly to Abimanju's belt. Abimanju sits silent a long while, then, remembering the duty he owes his King and father, he unsheaths his dagger and severs the belt his wife desperately holds. Overcome with emotion, the young Prince falls to the floor. Without a word, Princess Siti Sendari rises and, covering her tear-streaked face with her handkerchief, departs for her

tjarijos

distant destination. Prince Ardjuna beckons his servants to care for the unconscious Abimanju.

(Five spaced raps signal the gamelan to play Ajak-ajakan Tlutur. After ABIMANJU *cuts his belt and falls to the floor,* SITI SENDARI *goes slowly off left.* MAIDSERVANTS *carry* ABIMANJU *off right, followed by* SRIKANDI. *Three raps and the melody softens.)*

SUMBADRA *(weeping):* Oh, my beloved Husband! What have they done? Why have you divorced them so cruelly?

ARDJUNA: Your place is in the kitchen, woman. Leave this to me.

(Music comes up to normal level as SUMBADRA *goes off right, crying, and the* MAIDSERVANTS *return. Music softens again.)*

ARDJUNA: Do not leave your young master unattended, and take care he does not harm himself.

(Music comes up again. The MAIDSERVANTS *bow low and go off right. Music stops.)*

SONG *(The dalang sings Patet Sanga Djugag):*
> The maidservants hurry
>> At their Lord's
>> Command,
> Weeping
>> Silently . . . oooooo

(During the song IRAWAN, SEMAR, GARENG, *and* PETRUK *enter from the left, make the sembah, and sit respectfully before* ARDJUNA.)*

IRAWAN: Father, I have returned. *(Makes the sembah. Deep in thought,* ARDJUNA *does not notice* IRAWAN.) Honored Father, I have returned. *(Makes the sembah. Still no response.)* Dearest and most revered Father. Ruler of Madukara, I have returned. *(Makes the sembah.)*

Fig. 81
Ardjuna, Irawan,
Semar, Gareng,
and Petruk

Irawan's Wedding

ARDJUNA *(noticing* IRAWAN*)*: Hm? Oh, it's you, Irawan.

PETRUK: I knew that last one would get him. He, he!

IRAWAN: I return from Jasarata, Father.

SEMAR: We have accompanied Prince Irawan as you ordered, Master. *(Makes the sembah.)*

PETRUK: We hurried back so we wouldn't miss the wedding!

GARENG: Especially Master Irawan's! Hee, hee!

IRAWAN: As you ordered, Father, we brought your greetings to my grandfather. He was pleased and . . . approves of my wedding, Father. *(Makes the sembah.)*

ARDJUNA: Yes, yes, the wedding.

PETRUK: For us there'll be dancing in the streets and drinking and feasting. And for our master, Irawan, heh-heh-heh, there'll be that and more! Ho, ho! I wouldn't miss this wedding for anything.

ARDJUNA: Petruk, enough. *(He considers how to proceed.)* My Son, I know you are tired from your long journey, yet there are many things which must be done. There is no time for you to dally here. I have sent your sister-in-law, Siti Sendari, to Dwarawati to . . . help with the wedding preparation. Now, I want you to give her a message. It is very important.

IRAWAN: Yes, Father, what am I to say?

ARDJUNA: She is to tell King Kresna that he is in possession of something I have great need of. I have a dagger . . . made of choice steel, and of princely design. He knows this dagger and has admired it. But it now lies useless, for it has no sheath. She is to tell the King there is only one sheath in the world which I will allow my dagger to enter. It belongs to him. This sheath is exquisitely shaped, made of fragrant materials, and is of kingly design. What is mine goes with what is his. Each will be of use to the other. Let King Kresna allow my dagger to enter his sheath and both our families will derive great pleasure in the years to come. Repeat to the Princess this message exactly, Irawan.

IRAWAN: I shall, Father. *(Makes the sembah.)*

ARDJUNA: Go then. Accompany Siti Sendari and do anything she may bid you—except for two things.

IRAWAN: Yes, Father?

ARDJUNA: Do not speak of this mission to anyone else, and in Dwarawati under no circumstances are you to meet your . . .

father-in-law-to-be. Semar, Gareng, Petruk. Go with your master, Irawan.

SEMAR: Yes, Master.

PETRUK: Papa, my feet hurt. And I'm coming down with a cold.

SEMAR: Rubbish!

PETRUK: I estimate my cold's arrival time at approximately three in the morning, next Tuesday, so you see I can't possibly leave the palace grounds now.

SEMAR: Your master says for you to go! Now, go before I wallop you!

ARDJUNA: No need to bully the sick boy, Semar. If Petruk has a cold let him stay with me. I shall cure it. There is nothing like a red-hot coal, placed in each nostril, to dry up a cold.

PETRUK: Eeeee! I feel better already! A trip is just what I need! Let's go!

IRAWAN: With your blessing, I take my leave now, Father.

(*Five spaced raps signal the gamelan to play Ajak-ajakan Sanga.* IRAWAN *makes the sembah and goes off left, followed by* SEMAR, GARENG, *and* PETRUK. ARDJUNA *exits right.*)

<table>
<tr><td>adegan putri</td><td>Scene 5</td></tr>
</table>

(*The dalang sings, "Oooooo . . ." as a signal for the gamelan to change to Ajak-ajakan Tlutur.* SITI SENDARI *and* MAIDSERVANTS *cross from right to left, re-enter, and stop,* SITI SENDARI *on the right, the* MAIDSERVANTS *on the left. The metal plates are struck three times to signal the melody to soften.*)

tjarijos kadjantur NARRATION: Long and far has the lovely Princess traveled. Guided by her faithful nurse, she walks, so dazed and numb from grief she knows not where she is going. Tears course down her cheeks, and she covers her face in her anguish. Her nurse has told her of her brother Samba's sudden arrival and how Prince Ardjuna, after hearing the news that Irawan's wedding to Titisari was to be canceled, immediately summoned Siti Sendari and Abimanju and sundered their marriage. The distracted Princess does not understand the meaning of these events, but in her heart there grows the faint hope that all will be well. Now, as they stop in the shade of a wayside tree to escape the sun's rays, Irawan and the three servants are seen approaching.

Irawan's Wedding

*(A single rap cues the gamelan to play at normal level; one gong
phrase later the music ends. During the music,* SITI SENDARI *shades
her eyes and looks off left. The* MAIDSERVANTS *move behind her.
In a moment* IRAWAN *enters, followed by* SEMAR, GARENG, *and*
PETRUK.)

*Fig. 82
Maidservants,
Siti Sendari,
Irawan, Gareng,
Semar, and Petruk*

SONG *(The dalang sings Patet Sanga Djugag):*
>   Nature's fragrance
>   Scents the breezes,
>   Drying the resting
>   Princess' tears.

SITI SENDARI *(overjoyed to see him):* Dear Brother Irawan! The
sight of you is most welcome to my eyes.

IRAWAN: Thank you, Sister-Princess. I am blessed by the
warmth of your greeting.

SITI SENDARI: I had thought you were in Jasarata, dear Brother.
You have not yet spoken to your father, I suppose?

IRAWAN *(happily):* On the contrary, Sister-Princess. I have just
come from him.

SITI SENDARI *(fearful):* Then he has told you the . . . plans about
your wedding?

IRAWAN *(cheerfully):* Oh, yes. It is a pity. But Father is always
right!

SITI SENDARI *(amazed):* You think so?

IRAWAN: Yes, of course. A young man should not think too much about his coming nuptials. It does tend to excite one—if you will excuse my saying so, Sister-Princess—to think of one's wedding night.

SITI SENDARI: Wedding night?

IRAWAN (*suddenly overcome with shame*): Oh, forgive me, revered elder Sister-Princess! I have spoken indelicately before a Princess of noble family! (*He bows his head, continuing more confidentially.*) I thought that . . . as you had just married, I might . . . I mean . . . that you would understand my feelings . . . as I approach my wedding night . . .

MAIDSERVANT: He couldn't have seen His Lordship, my Lady. He's still talking about his wedding night.

IRAWAN (*brightening*): Well, it is my wedding!

MAIDSERVANT: There isn't going to be a wedding night . . .

IRAWAN: What? What are you talking about old woman?

SITI SENDARI (*quickly*): Brother! She means the ceremony was to be in the afternoon.

IRAWAN: But . . .

SITI SENDARI: She's a little deaf. (*Changing the subject.*) But tell me, Brother, why are you here?

IRAWAN: Father sent me to accompany you to a Dwarawati, so that I may help you with the wedding preparations.

SITI SENDARI: He said that?

IRAWAN: Yes. And he sends a message he wishes you to give your father, the King.

SITI SENDARI (*beginning to hope*): Tell me, Irawan! What did he say?

IRAWAN: You are to tell King Kresna these words: I have a dagger made of choice steel, and of princely design. But it lies useless, for it has no sheath. There is only one sheath in the world I will allow my dagger to enter, and it belongs to King Kresna. This sheath is exquisitely shaped, made of fragrant materials, and is of kingly design. Let King Kresna allow my dagger to enter his sheath and both our families will derive great pleasure in the years to come. So saying, my father asked that I deliver this message to you, go with you to Dwarawati, and do all that you might bid me do.

SONG (*The dalang sings Patet Sanga Wantah*):

Sun pierces clouds
  Following the storm,
All becomes bright
  With knowledge
Oooooo . . . oooooo . . .

NARRATION: And so, upon hearing the message, the intelligent Princess grasps its meaning, and her sadness and confusion disappear. To herself she thinks, "Had I but known this before. What pain would I have been spared. My noble father-in-law is a clever man. He wishes me to play the dalang, and manipulate the figures in this little love-show he has devised! I shall do anything to return to my beloved Abimanju!"   tjarijos

IRAWAN: Do you understand any of this, Sister-Princess?

SITI SENDARI: Oh yes, perfectly!

IRAWAN: I don't understand a word of it.

SITI SENDARI: Perhaps when you are married you will, dear Brother. One thing, when we arrive in Dwarawati . . . let's not tell anyone you are with me. I'll tell you what! I'll hide you in the women's quarters!

IRAWAN *(protesting):* But Sister-Princess, a prince can't . . .

SITI SENDARI *(enjoying this):* You will do as I say. Now, whatever happens, don't show your face to my father, the king!

IRAWAN *(in wonderment):* That's exactly what my father said!

SITI SENDARI *(brightly):* Then let us be off, Brother Irawan!

IRAWAN: Whatever you say, Sister-Princess.

SITI SENDARI: You may stop calling me Sister-Princess. "Sister" will do very nicely!

(Five spaced raps signal the gamelan to play Ajak-ajakan Sanga. SITI SENDARI *rises and goes off left, followed by* IRAWAN, *the* MAID-SERVANTS, SEMAR, GARENG, *and* PETRUK. *The* KAJON *is placed center inclined to the right, signaling the melody to stop.)*

Scene 6   djedjer Djongbiradji

NARRATION: And now our story moves once again to the ogre   tjarijos
Kingdom of Djongbiradji, where King Barandjana impatiently awaits the return of his envoys to Dwarawati.

(Three raps; the gamelan plays Galagotang. The KAJON *is moved to the side. Enter from the right* BARANDJANA. LAJARMEGA *and*

MINGKALPA *enter from the left, honor the king, and sit before him. The music softens on a signal of three raps.)*

djanturan NARRATION *(intoned, following pitch and rhythm of Galagotang):* Seated upon his throne is the lovesick King Barandjana. Day and night he is tormented by his desire to possess the delicate Princess Titisari. No one can distract his mind from his erotic obsession, not even his trusted minister, Lajarmega. Silent is all, for none dare speak lest the King's anger be inflamed. Suddenly the King's envoys, Togog and Saraita, rush into the audience hall.

(TOGOG *and* SARAITA *enter. A single rap cues the music to play at normal volume; one gong phrase later the music ends.)*

SONG *(The dalang sings Ada-ada Manggalan to steady tapping and the accompaniment of a xylophone):*
>The raging of the King
>>Is fearful . . . oooooo
>Lightning crashes
>>The world trembles,
>So he seems
>>To those about him.

*Fig. 83
Saraita,
Barandjana,
Togog, Lajarmega,
and Mingkalpa*

BARANDJANA: You've returned! Where is she? Where is my dearest, my beloved? *(Shouting.)* Fix the bedchamber! Lay out my things! 'Gog bring her in! I want to touch her!

TOGOG: Majesty, I regret to inform you we have failed. (*Makes the sembah.*)

BARANDJANA: What? Did King Kresna refuse my request?

TOGOG: We didn't see the King, Majesty. We didn't even get to his capital.

BARANDJANA: Those stupid envoys of mine! I'll have them killed!

TOGOG: They are, Your Majesty. (*Makes deep sembah.*)

BARANDJANA: Killed? (*Begins to weep.*) Ohhh, no! My favorite officers! Who could want to kill them, the sweetest ogres I ever knew?

TOGOG: Majesty, in the forest we met two Pandawa nobles, Irawan and Gatutkatja. Just as nicely as you please we told them you planned to marry Princess Titisari . . .

BARANDJANA (*reminded of his desire*): Titisari!! I love you!

TOGOG (*continuing without interruption*): and they got terribly upset. I can't imagine why. They attacked without warning, and from behind, too. Your noble officers didn't have a chance, Majesty. It was terrible to see them cut down in cold blood. But we couldn't help. We knew we had to report to you.

SARAITA: Did we ever run, Your Majesty!

BARANDJANA: Grrrrh! How maddening! Get out of my sight, both of you!

TOGOG (*glad to be getting off so easily*): Oh, yes, Majesty!

SONG (*The dalang sings Ada-ada Gregetsaut Sanga Djugag*):
>Lightning crashes
>>The world trembles,
>The sky blazes
>>With the King's rage
>>Oooooo . . .

(*During the song,* TOGOG *and* SARAITA *go off left.*)

BARANDJANA: I shall go to Dwarawati myself! When King Kresna sees who he's getting as a son-in-law, he can't refuse! (*Rages.*) And if he does, I'll burn his palace to the ground! I'll plow his kingdom under! Ohhhh! I must have my teensy-weensy Titisari!

LAJARMEGA: Oh, honored King, I beg you! Do not leave your Kingdom! Allow me to fulfill your wishes.

BARANDJANA: How, Mother Lajarmega?

LAJARMEGA: I shall abduct Princess Titisari by stealth! I myself shall bring you your bride!

BARANDJANA: Can you do it? I mean, at your advanced age, Mother?

LAJARMEGA: I vow I shall, Your Majesty. (*Makes the sembah.*)

BARANDJANA: Then go! Take Mingkalpa with you! Do everything she tells you, ruffian!

MINGKALPA: Yes, Your Majesty.

(*Five quick taps and striking metal plates signal the gamelan to play Sampak Sanga.* MINGKALPA *makes the sembah and goes off left, followed by* LAJARMEGA. BARANDJANA *goes off right.* LAJARMEGA *and* MINGKALPA *are seen to soar across the screen and off right. The* KAJON *is placed center, inclined to the left, signaling Sampak Sanga to stop.*)

Fig. 84
Kajon

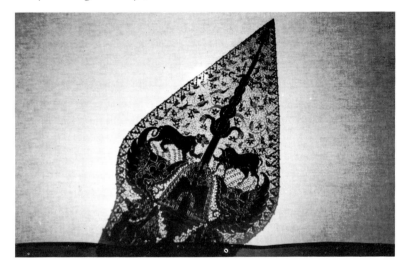

tjarijos NARRATION: Using their magic powers, Lajarmega and Mingkalpa soar swiftly over the ocean and, seeing the coastline of Java beneath them, descend to earth. It does not take them long to find the road to Dwarawati, and soon they stand before the magnificent gate of this peerless Kingdom. Stealthily they creep about, unseen and unheard, for the cunning ogress Lajarmega enters the palace while darkness conceals their shape and sound.

PART THREE

SONG (*The dalang sings Patet Manjura Wantah, indicating the start of Part Three of the play, patet manjura*):

> The gray of dawn
> > Turns red,
> The chirruping
> > Of birds
> > Begins
> Oooooo . . .

NARRATION: And with the coming of dawn our story now moves to the jeweled Kingdom of Astina. King Durjudana waits the return of King Baladewa from Dwarawati, a troubled expression clouding his face.

Scene 1

(*The word cue "troubled" signals the gamelan to play the melody Glijung. The* KAJON *moves to the right of the screen. Then King* DURJUDANA *enters from the right, his rear arm defiantly planted on his hip. The brahman priest* DURNA *and chief minister* SANGKUNI *enter from the left, honor the king, and sit before him, as the dalang raps three times signaling Glijung to soften.*)

NARRATION (*intoned, pitch and rhythm following music*): This is the Kingdom of Astina, a great, powerful, and prosperous country, whose lowest subjects are happy and healthy. Its ruler is known for his wealth and his many brothers, numbering ninety-eight. The King is world-renowned as: "Ruler of the House of Kuru," "Vigorous in His Prayers," and "He Who Inspires Allegiance." He is dressed in magnificent clothes ornamented with gold and jewels of many designs. Seen from afar he resembles no mortal, but the God Baju himself descended from heaven. He is seated on his throne in audience with the Holy Brahman Durna, preceptor of the Kingdom and knowledgeable in secret arts and Chief Minister Sangkuni. All in the great hall wait expectantly for word of King Baladewa's mission to Dwarawati. The King's thoughts range anxiously, "By all the Gods in Heaven! How many times have I tried to gain a bride for my son and failed because of the Pandawas? Should this time fail as well?"

(*The dalang sings "Oooooo . . ." as a signal for the melody to come up to normal level. Two gong phrases later the music ends.*)

DURJUDANA: I feel concerned, Father Durna, that King Baladewa may not be successful.

DURNA: Heh, heh! The King is the elder brother of the girl's father, and his demand cannot be refused. Rest assured, Your Majesty, that King Baladewa has the power and the desire to consummate the match you desire.

DURJUDANA: Your words reassure me, Father.

tjarijos   NARRATION: Their conversation is interrupted by the arrival of Minister Pragota, bearing the report of King Baladewa.

(Five spaced raps signal the gamelan to play Ajak-ajakan Manjura, as PRAGOTA *enters from the left and sits before the king. Music stops.)*

SONG *(The dalang sings Patet Manjura Djugag):*
> The hot sun's rays
>> Beat on the earth,
> Clouds rise towering
>> In the air
>> Oooooo . . .

*Fig. 85
Durjudana,
Pragota, Sangkuni
and Durna*

DURJUDANA: Welcome, Pragota, what news do you bring from your King?

PRAGOTA: I accept your welcome with joy, Majesty. *(Makes the sembah.)* His Majesty, King of Mandura, wishes conveyed to you the information that his mission is successful. Though

Irawan's Wedding

Titisari was already pledged to Irawan and the wedding date set, His Highness insisted that she wed Prince Lesmana Mandrakumara.

DURJUDANA: And what was the King of Dwarawati's reply?

PRAGOTA: Our King is the elder brother. King Kresna was pleased to agree. (*Makes the sembah.*) The King of Mandura insists that he shall pay all expenses of the blessed occasion.

DURJUDANA (*gestures*): Uncle Durna, what is your opinion of the matter? Speak freely, I pray.

DURNA (*speaks meaningless phrase*): Heavenly terrestial sun-moon sea. Incandescent darknesses. All aspects of the situation are satisfactory, Your Majesty. As His Highness wishes to accept full responsibility for the marriage, every difficulty will be swept away. Accept his offer, Majesty. And may I humbly advise that the army prepare to accompany our Prince to Dwarawati.

DURJUDANA: Excellent! Father Sangkuni, does your advice agree?

SANGKUNI: May it please Your Majesty, it is my opinion that every word spoken by the wise seer Durna is correct. The marriage will be most useful.

DURJUDANA: I am overjoyed! (*To* DURNA.) Uncle, you have my permission. When should Prince Lesmana Mandrakumara depart?

DURNA: Today, Your Majesty, according to mystical calculations. Tomorrow is a day of humiliation and the next of danger to travelers. This day is fruitful, this very hour mystically auspicious for the journey.

DURJUDANA: Uncle Pragota, summon Prince Lesmana into my presence.

PRAGOTA: Yes, my Lord.

SONG (*The dalang sings Patet Manjura Wantah as he exits to the left and shortly returns with* LESMANA):

> The gray of dawn
> > Turned red,
> The chirruping
> > Of birds
> > Brightly
> Cheers the
> > Prince . . . oooooo
> As he arrives.

DURJUDANA (*jovial and forceful*): Well, my Son, at last your wedding day has been chosen. You go this afternoon to Dwarawati, to wed the daughter of King Kresna, Princess Titisari. Do everything King Baladewa tells you to, and nothing else!

LESMANA (*without spirit*): Honored am I always to do my father's will. (*Makes a halfhearted gesture.*)

*Fig. 86
Durjudana,
Lesmana
Mandrakumara,
Sangkuni, Durna,
and Pragota*

DURJUDANA (*annoyed at his dull son*): You're getting married! Show some life, Son!

DURNA (*in a dry cackle*): Heh, heh! You are a handsome boy, my Prince. Have you fasted and been abstinent of sleep? Have you avoided, as I instructed, garlic, onions, and other foul-smelling herbs you are addicted to?

LESMANA (*weakly*): Holy Father, I have eaten nothing for a week. I haven't slept a bit.

DURNA: Conserve your strength, my Son. And now, here are your final instructions. You are going to live in the house of a king. Control your natural sentiments, and do not extol your Kurawa relatives. Do not brag of the greatness of the Kingdom of Astina. For you must not embarrass your new father-in-law by making him feel inferior right off. Heh, heh! At least in the beginning show some modesty.

DURJUDANA: Go, my Son. May your marriage be as happy for you as it is for me.

LESMANA: Well, thank you, Majesty-Father. That is more than my wish.

(Five quick raps signal the gamelan to play Sampak Manjura. PRAGOTA rises, honors the king with the sembah, and exits left. He is followed by LESMANA and SANGKUNI. The king turns and exits right, followed by DURNA. The KAJON is placed center, inclined to the right; the music stops.)

NARRATION: And so the Prince Lesmana Mandrakumara marches toward the Kingdom of Dwarawati, escorted by columns of Astina troops. The royal procession makes a colorful sight and people throng to see the carriages and warriors pass by. Leaving the hastening procession, our story moves forward to the Kingdom of Dwarawati, their destination.

tjarijos

Scene 2

djedjer Dwarawati

(Three raps cue the gamelan to play Ramjang. The KAJON moves to the right side of the screen. KRESNA enters from the right, followed by two MAIDSERVANTS, who make the sembah and sit behind him. SAMBA enters from the left, followed by SETYAKI. They make the sembah and sit before the king, as three raps signal the music to soften.)

NARRATION *(intoned, following rhythm and pitch of Ramjang):* The King of Dwarawati sits waiting the return of his son. Seeing the young Prince arrive, Kresna eagerly waves him into his presence. Prince Samba approaches the King, sitting close to make his report.

djanturan

(The dalang sings, "Oooooo . . ." as a signal for the gamelan to resume normal level. After several phrases the music ends.)

SONG *(The dalang sings Patet Manjura Wantah):*
>The gray of dawn
>>Turned red,
>The chirruping
>>Of birds
>>Reminds
>The King of
>>His dilemma
>>Oooooo . . .

KRESNA: Samba, my Son. You have returned. Take your ease and tell me without delay of your uncle's reactions.

SAMBA *(elated):* Yes, Father. I pray you will be pleased. You have taught me well. Not only was I tactful with my uncle, but very clever, indeed.

KRESNA: Ah? Do go on.

SAMBA: First, I placed everything on a friendly family basis. Rather than blurting out my message, we made small talk for a while. In this way I led Uncle to believe I had a message from you.

KRESNA: And then?

SAMBA: I made certain he was in a good mood, and he promised not to be angry if only I would tell him quickly!

KRESNA: A bad sign.

SAMBA (*earnestly*): Oh, no, Father! He sat quietly for a while, and then said that since the wedding had not yet taken place, now was the proper time to cancel it. He said also he would bow to your divine authority in any matter, even if it meant divorcing my aunt or separating Siti Sendari from his son.

KRESNA: He is angry. Very angry.

SAMBA: I am certain he is not, Father. The whole time he never stopped smiling. In fact, I have never seen him smile so broadly. There was nothing in his voice or expression to indicate a trace of anger.

KRESNA: All the years of your life you have known your uncle, and still you do not understand his character, my Son! Let your uncle be consumed with fury, let his heart be torn to pieces—nothing in his manner will betray it. Well, I cannot blame him. Let us pray it all ends well, my Son.

SONG (*The dalang sings Patet Manjura Djugag*):
> The hot sun's rays
> > Scorch the earth,
> Towering clouds
> > Speak of the future
> > Oooooo . . .

tjarijos NARRATION: Suddenly, Princess Siti Sendari enters the hall, interrupting their conversation. She moves directly before the King, sitting at his feet.

(*Five spaced raps; Ajak-ajakan Manjura is played for* SITI SENDARI'S *entrance, then stops.*)

KRESNA (*surprised at seeing her*): Why, Daughter, what is the matter? You leave your new home and husband and come here unannounced?

Irawan's Wedding

SITI SENDARI: Allow me to inform you, Father, that shortly after Brother Samba left Madukara, my marriage was dissolved and I was sent home accompanied only by my old maidservants.

KRESNA: Prince Ardjuna has done this?

SAMBA *(in tears)*: Then uncle *was* angry! Oh, this is all my fault!

KRESNA: Samba, please! Control your tears. They do not become a Prince. And they get on my nerves. *(To* SITI SENDARI.*)* Tell me, my Daughter, did your uncle, by any chance, say anything following his action?

SITI SENDARI *(forthrightly)*: Yes, Father. He sends you a message of importance. Prince Ardjuna owns a dagger made of choice steel and of princely design. It is useless, however, for it has no sheath.

KRESNA: A dagger? A sheath? Go on, Daughter.

SITI SENDARI: There is but one sheath Prince Ardjuna will allow his dagger to enter. Exquisitely shaped, made of fragrant materials, and of kingly design—it belongs to you, does it not, Father?

KRESNA: It does.

SITI SENDARI *(pleading)*: Then make it possible for the dagger to enter the sheath, Father! If you do, Prince Ardjuna promises our families will derive great pleasure in the years to come. And, oh, Father, I am certain of that!

KRESNA: Were it possible I should do so.

SITI SENDARI: Can you not?

KRESNA: I have lent my sheath to my brother, Baladewa. It is no longer mine to bestow.

SITI SENDARI *(sprightly)*: Very well, Father, if that is the best you can do.

(She exits right, pinching her father's arm as she passes.)

SAMBA *(seriously)*: I have several sheaths, Father. My uncle may choose from among them. Perhaps that will smooth the enmity between us.

KRESNA: Oh, Samba! He wants a very special sheath!

SAMBA: Mine are very nice, Father . . .

KRESNA: Never mind, Samba! I'll explain it to you one day. In the meantime keep your sister's presence a secret, as much as you can.

(Five spaced raps; the melody Ajak-ajakan Manjura begins. KRESNA

and the MAIDSERVANTS *go off to the right.* SAMBA *and* SETYAKI *exit left. From the right,* DJEMBAWATI *enters the empty screen, followed by* TITISARI. RUKMINI, SETYABOMA, *and* SITI SENDARI *enter from the left and sit. Three raps; the music softens.)*

<table>
<tr><td>adegan putri</td><td>Scene 3</td></tr>
</table>

djanturan NARRATION *(intoned, following pitch and rhythm of music):* In the inner quarters of the palace of Dwarawati sit the three wives of King Kresna, Djembawati, Rukmini, and Setyaboma, with the King's young daughter, Titisari. Maidservants and ladies-in-waiting attend them. They are all surprised to see the newly married Siti Sendari enter the chamber.

(The dalang raps; music resumes normal level, then stops.)

DJEMBAWATI: Siti Sendari! What a surprise to see you. Are you all right?

SITI SENDARI: I am warmed by your greeting, queenly Mother. With your blessing, I am well. I have just arrived from Madukara, to assist with the wedding plans. *(Brazenly.)* Father ordered me to take charge of the bride.

DJEMBAWATI: If that is our Lord's wish. You look tired, my dear.

SITI SENDARI: It is only lack of sleep, Mother.

SETYABOMA *(smiling):* I can well imagine, dear Sister!

DJEMBAWATI: Very well. Now, Titisari, go bathe with Siti Sendari. It will do you both good. We entrust you to your sister's care. Obey her as you would your father.

TITISARI: Yes, Mother, I will do as you say. *(Makes the sembah.)*

(Five spaced raps; the gamelan plays Ajak-ajakan Manjura. SITI SENDARI *and* TITISARI *make the sembah and go off left.* DJEMBAWATI, RUKMINI, SETYABOMA, *and* MAIDSERVANTS *exit right. After a moment,* TITISARI *enters from the right and stops.* SITI SENDARI *enters and stands behind her. The melody stops.)*

SONG *(The dalang sings Patet Manjura Djugag):*

> The lovely Princesses
> > Leave the radiant
> Queens in the
> > Inner palace.

tjarijos NARRATION: Having bathed themselves, the two beautiful sisters enjoy the cool breeze, seated in the garden in the shade of a banyan tree.

Irawan's Wedding

SITI SENDARI: Dear little Sister, let me brush out your tangled hair. You must act like a young lady, for you are no longer a child you know.

TITISARI: Oh, Sister! I don't want to marry and grow up yet! I just want to play in the sun the rest of my life.

SITI SENDARI: You will find that marriage is often quite like playing games, little Titisari!

TITISARI: But I don't want a husband. Why do they force one on me?

SITI SENDARI: I promise you, once married, you will feel differently. Men perform us a great service. Overnight each man transforms a little girl into a woman. *(Laughing.)* It is something of a miracle, is it not, little one?

(She turns around and signals for IRAWAN *to enter from the left. As he comes on, she withdraws.)*

TITISARI: Perhaps you are right, dear Sister. But I know so little about men. Tell me what to expect. I'm so frightened about my wedding night. Will he be gentle with me, Sister? *(*IRAWAN *puts his trembling hand on* TITISARI'S *arm.)* Sister? Is it so terrible you cannot speak of it? Oh, Sister . . . *(Turns and discovers* IRAWAN, *who stands petrified, unable to speak or move.)* Oh! Irawan! Disaster!

*(*TITISARI *runs off left.* IRAWAN *moves left watching her go off, then turns to face* SITI SENDARI, *who enters from the right.)*

SITI SENDARI *(laughing):* Brother, you look more frightened than she!

IRAWAN: Dearest Sister, it upsets me sneaking about in the women's quarters. What if I am caught? You know men are forbidden to enter here.

SITI SENDARI: You are so unlike your brother. Now, *he* can handle girls.

IRAWAN: I know, but he never taught me anything! Sister, I'm so scared of Titisari.

SITI SENDARI: You are the man, Irawan. She is frightened of you. Be gentle, but strong. Follow her wherever she goes. Smile at her. Speak with her. That is an order! Go!

IRAWAN: Yes, Sister.

(Three raps; the gamelan plays Kinanti Pawukir. SITI SENDARI *and* IRAWAN *exit left.* TITISARI *enters right and stands in em-*

barrassed silence looking left. IRAWAN *enters behind her and sings softly a poem composed in Kinanti form.)*

IRAWAN *(singing):*
> Noble Princess I adore you,
> I your servant always shall be.
> Like a rose you are so fragrant,
> Your jeweled radiance purifies me.
> Dearest beauty bounce on my lap,
> And I shall always cherish thee!

TITISARI *(shocked and titillated, turns to look again at* IRAWAN*):* Oh! It is you again' Why do you torment me? *(Giggles.)* We only met once before—the day we were engaged.

(Melody Kinanti Pawukir is played at full level. TITISARI, *laughing saucily, flees left, pursued by* IRAWAN. SITI SENDARI *and* PETRUK *enter from the right and watch. Music ends.)*

tjarijos NARRATION: Princess Titisari is fleet of foot, Prince Irawan is shy, and so they gambol through the garden, laughing and excited, like children playing hide-and-seek.

SITI SENDARI *(sighs):* They are so young. Act like a ghost, Petruk. Frighten the Princess this way.

PETRUK: Ho, ho! With pleasure! Shall I be a forest ghost or a ghost from the dark pond, Princess?

SITI SENDARI: Be what you wish as long as you frighten her.

PETRUK: Yes, Milady.

*(*PETRUK *rushes off left.* IRAWAN *enters in pursuit of* TITISARI.*)*

SITI SENDARI: Irawan. *(He stops.)* Stay here.

IRAWAN *(protesting):* But . . .

SITI SENDARI: Stand behind me.

IRAWAN: Yes, Sister. *(He does so.)*

PETRUK *(off):* Ooaahh! Hoooooo! Eeeeee! Little girl, I'm a ghost! Down from the trees, out of the pond's dark waters! Fried noodles is my favorite dish! Hoooooo' Hoooooo! With little girl for desert! Oooaaahh! I'm a ghost and here I come'

TITISARI *(off):* Eeeeee! Sister! Help!

(Five quick raps signal the gamelan to play Sampak Manjura. TITISARI *enters from the right, running to her sister for protection. At the last moment,* SITI SENDARI *slips off left.* TITISARI *runs headlong into* IRAWAN'S *arms. Music stops.)*

Irawan's Wedding

TITISARI: Save me, Sister! A ghost is chasing me! I wish it were that handsome . . . (*She realizes it is not her sister.*) Oh! You!

IRAWAN (*holding her firmly, but at arm's length*): Do not cry, Princess Titisari. I shall allow no harm to befall you.

TITISARI: Let me go, you brute!

IRAWAN (*mustering his courage*): You shall not go, Princess!

TITISARI: Ooooh! I want my sister!

IRAWAN: You have me.

TITISARI: I hardly know you, Prince Irawan. It cannot be proper.

IRAWAN: It cannot be improper. A young man and a young woman in each other's arms is the way of the world—I believe.

TITISARI: Let me go or I shall scream!

IRAWAN: If you scream I shall stifle it. Like this. (*He puts his arms around her, pressing her face against his breast.*)

TITISARI (*protesting*): No, no! No! Irawan! Oooooooh! (*Melting in his arms.*) If you insist, my Prince.

SONG (*The dalang sings Patet Manjura Djugag*):
> Welcomed by open petals,
>> Bees hum their songs
> Oooooo . . . mingling with
>> Murmurs of love.

(*During the song,* IRAWAN *lifts* TITISARI *in his arms and carries her off right into the garden.*

Fig. 87
Titisari and
Irawan

On Thrones of Gold

As the song concludes, LAJARMEGA *and* MINGKALPA *enter slowly from the left.)*

adegan perang
sampak manjura

Scene 4

tjarijos NARRATION: Having peeped into every room in the palace, the two ogres have still not found their abduction victim, Princess Titisari. They enter the garden, silently gnashing their teeth in frustrated rage. Soon they hear the sweet voices of lovers floating on the still air from the pleasure pavilion near the pond. Peering through the bushes, they discover the Princess Titisari with Prince Irawan.

LAJARMEGA: Haaa! That must be she! She's with a lover. Hmmm! Perhaps we should take him as well. He's a pretty one'

MINGKALPA: Let's watch for a while! *(He watches.)* Ohhh! Now I see why His Majesty wants her!

LAJARMEGA: Never mind! I'll break down the door. You take care of him while I kidnap the Princess.

SONG *(The dalang sings Ada-ada Gregetsaut Gatutkatja to steady and tense tapping):*
        Hovering in the sky,
          Gatutkatja
        Spies two hiding
          Forms . . . oooooo

*(*GATUTKATJA *appears in the air, unnoticed by the two ogres.)*

tjarijos NARRATION: Here, again, appears the flying knight, Gatutkatja, son of Bima. Sent once more to assist his cousin, Irawan, he sees two crouching forms hidden in the darkness of the garden.

GATUTKATJA: Who is it there? Speak!

LAJARMEGA: Brother, we're discovered!

GATUTKATJA: Who are you?

MINGKALPA: None of your business.

GATUTKATJA: Are you a palace guard?

MINGKALPA: Ah . . . yes!

GATUTKATJA: Are you by any chance the warrior Gatutkatja?

MINGKALPA: Why, ah . . . yes, that's my name.

GATUTKATJA: Liar! I am Gatutkatja!

(Five quick raps; the gamelan plays lively fighting music, Sampak Manjura. GATUTKATJA *swoops down. He breaks* MINGKALPA'S *neck with his bare hands,*

Irawan's Wedding

Fig. 88
Gatutkatja and
Mingkalpa

He kicks the corpse away. LAJARMEGA *enters, then flees to the left.* GATUTKATJA *exits right. Music stops.)*

SONG *(The dalang sings Ada-ada Gregetsaut Manjura Djugag to tense tapping):*

>   Like a bolt of lightning
>   Striking in the clear sky
>   Her friend lies dead
>   Oooooo . . . her fury rages.

(At the end of the song, LAJARMEGA *re-enters from the left, arms akimbo in fighting posture.)*

LAJARMEGA *(shouting off right):* Do not think you have won, Gatutkatja! I shall report to my King! He will return and destroy all of Java to get Titisari as his bride! You, I shall dismember personally!

GATUTKATJA *(off):* Tell your King to visit Amarta! I will meet him there!

(Five quick raps; LAJARMEGA *exits, flying, to the left, to Sampak Manjura. Melody changes to Ajak-ajakan Manjura.* SITI SENDARI *enters and stands at the right,* GATUTKATJA *at the left. Music stops.)*

SITI SENDARI: Cousin Gatutkatja! What happened?

GATUTKATJA: Two ogres came to kidnap your sister. I killed one, the other fled.

SITI SENDARI: How fortunate you were here, Cousin. I thank you for your help. Did your father send you?

GATUTKATJA: Yes. Father always seems to know where the trouble is. I am to help you in any way you say. *(Makes the sembah.)*

SITI SENDARI: Hmm. Now that they have met and are . . . becoming acquainted, shall we say, it is dangerous to keep them in the palace. One look at his lovesick daughter in the morning and Father would know everything! *(Thinking.)* Let me see. Ahh! Let us take advantage of this kidnap plot! You conceal Irawan and Titisari inside your magic ring, Gatutkatja. Fly with them to Amarta. I will tell everyone here that Titisari has been kidnaped by the ogres! They won't believe it for long, but it will keep the lovers together a little while, and by then— who knows what may happen!

GATUTKATJA: Cousin, I obey.

SITI SENDARI *(turns and calls off right)*: Brother Irawan, Sister Titisari! Prepare yourselves! You fly to Amarta!

(Five spaced raps; the gamelan plays Ajak-ajakan Manjura. SITI SENDARI and GATUTKATJA go off right. The KAJON is moved across the screen once, then placed to the right.)

djedjer Dwarawati   Scene 5

(Ajak-ajakan Manjura continues, as KRESNA and BALADEWA simultaneously enter from the right and from the left, greet each other, and sit. In the same fashion, SAMBA and LESMANA MANDRAKUMARA simultaneously enter from the right and from the left. They make the sembah, and sit beside the two kings. SANGKUNI enters, makes the sembah, and sits to the left.)

djanturan   NARRATION *(intoned, following pitch and rhythm of music, which softens when the dalang raps three times)*: Once again our story moves to the audience hall of Dwarawati, where King Kresna receives the wedding procession just arriving from Astina. King Kresna ponders the dilemma he is in. King Baladewa smiles with relief, for at last he has delivered the groom. All is silent for a long moment.

(The dalang raps; music resumes its normal level, then ends.)

SONG *(The dalang sings Patet Manjura Djugag):*

Irawan's Wedding

A royally attired
  Wedding procession
Arrives in Dwarawati
  From the Land of Elephants
  Oooooo . . .

BALADEWA: Ho, Brother! Without further formality, I present to you the bridegroom. He is yours, Brother!

Fig. 89
Kresna, Samba,
Lesmana
Mandrakumara,
Sangkuni, and
Baladewa

KRESNA *(feeling his way):* Ah, yes, indeed. First, however, allow me to welcome Uncle Sangkuni to Dwarawati.

SANGKUNI: Majesty, it is my good fortune to be in your presence. *(Makes the sembah.)*

LESMANA: Presents? Do we get wedding presents, Uncle?

SANGKUNI *(under his breath):* Hush! Stupid boy!

KRESNA *(smiling):* In due time, my Prince. Welcome to Dwarawati.

LESMANA *(his manner of speaking is uncouth, in spite of his words):* Oh, thank you, thank you, great King of Kings. Humbly do I accept the honor of your saying welcome to Dwarawati. I worship your words, put them on my head. tie them in my hair, hang them from my clothes, press them to my heart that they may give me strength. A thousand good wishes to Your Majesty, my Great King, and Uncle-Sire-Father-in-law-to-be. *(Makes awkward sembah.)*

KRESNA: Er, thank you, Lesmana.

LESMANA: And to my princely Brother-in-law-to-be. *(Sembah to SAMBA.)* And to my kingly Uncle-in-law-to-be. *(Another sembah to BALADEWA.)*

tjarijos NARRATION: The audience stands aghast at the Prince's foolish words. Prince Samba turns his head and spits in disgust, thinking to himself, "What a stupid dolt! He dresses like a lunatic and speaks like a madman!"

SANGKUNI: Majesty! Prince Lesmana Mandrakumara is still very young. May you never consider your son-in-law to be a Prince, but merely a servant in your house.

KRESNA: Thank you, Uncle. May King Durjudana never consider the Princess to be his daughter-in-law.

BALADEWA: Brother! You mean he should not consider his daughter-in-law to be a Princess!

KRESNA *(blandly)*: Ah! Indeed, Brother!

tjarijos NARRATION: The conversation is suddenly interrupted by the arrival of Princess Siti Sendari, who falls, weeping, at her father's feet.

SONG (SITI SENDARI *enters as the dalang sings Ada-ada Gregetsaut Manjura Djugag)*:
> Even the breeze
>> Ceases whispering,
> Startled by the sobs and moans
>> Of the young Princess
>> Oooooo . . .

KRESNA: Siti Sendari! What is wrong? Why are you weeping?

SITI SENDARI: Oh, Father! Catastrophe! Dear little Titisari has been abducted! *(Feigns sobbing.)*

KRESNA: What? Explain yourself, Daughter!

SITI SENDARI: Calamity! Oh, woe! Titisari and I were quietly sitting in the garden, when two gigantic ogres descended upon us. One was killed by a palace guard, but the other fled, carrying with him our dear little sister! *(Sobs loudly.)*

BALADEWA *(his plans ruined)*: What? On the wedding eve? Ohhhhh! This is too much! *(To SANGKUNI.)* What shall we do, Uncle?

SANGKUNI: With Your Majesty's permission, let us investigate this matter thoroughly, before making any decision. Ahem.

Princess, you say that one of the ogres was killed by a guard? I wish to question that brave guard.

SITI SENDARI *(improvising)*: He was carried off with Titisari, by the second ogre. *(Quickly makes the sembah to hide her face.)*

SANGKUNI *(doubtful)*: Hmmm.

SITI SENDARI: It was a *large* ogre.

SANGKUNI *(his suspicions are aroused)*: Very large, it would seem. Well then, Princess, if the guard is not to be found, presumably the slain ogre is in evidence?

SITI SENDARI: Oh, yes, Uncle!

SANGKUNI: What does he look like? Is he an officer? A soldier? From what country?

SITI SENDARI: It is difficult to remember, Uncle. Everything is confused. It happened so quickly. He is not a forest ogre, I believe, but one of high rank. Oh, it was a conspiracy, I'm sure, Uncle.

SANGKUNI: And how was he killed?

SITI SENDARI: Bare-handed his neck was broken! *(Realizes she has said too much.)* Ohh!

SANGKUNI: Ohh, indeed, Princess! *(To KRESNA.)* There is a conspiracy afoot, Your Majesty, but it concerns your daughter here, and the Pandawa knight Gatutkatja, the only warrior who kills in this fashion.

BALADEWA *(roaring with rage)*: Brother! This is outrageous! What do you intend to do?

KRESNA *(secretly pleased at this turn of events, for it resolves his dilemma, at least temporarily)*: The wedding is your idea, Brother. I leave it to you.

BALADEWA: What? What, Brother? *(Fuming, as he realizes he is trapped.)* Very well, Brother, *I* shall find Princess Titisari!

KRESNA: Whatever you say, elder Brother.

BALADEWA: Look to your daughter, Brother!

KRESNA: As you say, Brother.

BALADEWA *(to the others)*: Come, we go to Amarta! She must be with the Pandawas!

(Five quick raps; fast Sampak Manjura accompanies the hurried exit left of BALADEWA and the others in his party. Music stops.)

KRESNA: Daughter, my brother suggests you have conspired to

abduct Titisari. (*Suppressing a smile.*) Could such a thing be true?

SITI SENDARI: Forgive me, Father, it is. Ogres did attempt to abduct her, but Gatutkatja saved her. I ordered him to take Titisari and Irawan to safety in Amarta.

KRESNA: Irawan? What was he doing here?

SITI SENDARI: He accompanied me, sent by his father.

KRESNA: Why was I not informed? I am the King of Dwarawati, and your father!

SITI SENDARI: Forgive me, dear Father! I cannot live without Abimanju! Perhaps it was disrespectful, but when you—King of Dwarawati—indicated you could do nothing to satisfy Prince Ardjuna's request, I determined that I should, come what may! Please understand, dear Father. (*Makes deep sembah.*)

KRESNA (*touched by her reply, but pretending brusqueness*): Hmph. And I suppose you conspired to arrange a rendezvous for Titisari and Irawan right here in my palace?

SITI SENDARI: Yes, Father. They have fallen deeply in love.

KRESNA: Indeed! Under my roof!

SITI SENDARI: No, Father, they were in the garden. (KRESNA *covers his mouth to hide a smile.*) Do not be angry, Father. They are very happy.

KRESNA: That happiness won't last long, if we don't get to Amarta before my brother and that incredible bridegroom. We shall have to fly to overtake them. Come, enter my magic ring. We shall see what we can do.

SITI SENDARI: Yes, Father. (*Makes the Sembah.*)

SONG (*The dalang sings Ada-ada Gregetsaut Manjura Djugag to steady tapping, as* KRESNA *extends his forehand and* SITI SENDARI *appears to enter it*):

> The breeze seems
> To whisper
> Consoling words
> Oooooo . . . oooooo . . .

(*Five quick raps; the gamelan plays Sampak Manjura.* KRESNA *flies upward, turns to the right, and soars off the screen. The* KAJON *is placed center, inclined to the right; the music stops.*)

tjarijos NARRATION: As King Kresna flies to the Pandawa Kingdom of Amarta, our story returns once more to Djongbiradji, where the ogres are gathered noisily in the palace celebrating the expected return of their Minister Lajarmega with the Princess Titisari.

Scene 6

adegan
Djongbiradji

(Three raps; the gamelan plays Ritjik-ritjik. The KAJON *moves to the right.* KING BARANDJANA *enters from the right, followed by* MAIDSERVANTS. *A giant* OFFICER *enters and faces the king. Three raps and the music softens.)*

NARRATION *(intoned, following pitch and rhythm of music):* A sound like the roaring of the ocean's surge greets the arrival of the ogress minister, Lajarmega. Excitedly the King waves her into the audience hall and bids her sit before him.

djanturan

(One rap; the music comes up to normal volume, as LAJARMEGA *enters and sits, then stops.)*

SONG *(The dalang sings Ada-ada Gregetsaut Manjura Djugag):*
   As if to wreck
      The world for spite,
   The love-incensed King
      Roars . . . oooooo
   To the heavens.

BARANDJANA *(excitedly):* You have my Princess? Where is she? Let me see her! I want to caress her!

LAJARMEGA: Oh, Majesty! I beg to report we did not succeed in capturing Princess Titisari.

BARANDJANA: No, not again! Ohhhhh! I shall die, die, die! *(Suddenly angry.)* What happened? Tell me, Lajarmega!

LAJARMEGA: We were discovered and Mingkalpa was killed, Your Majesty.

BARANDJANA: What? Killed? Ohhhh, my sweet, innocent Mingkalpa! Who did it? *(Trembling.)* Was it Gatutkatja, the same dog who killed dear Montrokendo?

LAJARMEGA: Yes, Majesty, it was. He taunted you, saying he waits at Amarta.

BARANDJANA: Grrrhhh! Aaaggghh! I'll devour him in a single bite! Ogres of Djongbiradji! Assemble! We exterminate the Kingdom of Amarta!

(Five quick raps; the gamelan plays Sampak Manjura, as all the ogres hasten off. The KAJON *is placed center, inclined to the right, marking the end of the scene. The music stops.)*

NARRATION: And so the King of Djongbiradji leads his hordes of

tjarijos

On Thrones of Gold

howling ogres across the water to the island of Java, seeking to find and destroy the Kingdom of Amarta. Our story now moves forward to this very Kingdom, where the five Pandawa Brothers are gathered in council.

djedjer Pandawa | Scene 7

(Three raps; the gamelan plays Bangbangwetan. The KAJON moves to the right of the screen. JUDISTIRA enters from the right and stands quietly, arms hanging straight down. NAKULA and SADEWA enter, make the sembah, and sit to his rear, heads bowed. ARDJUNA enters from the left, makes the sembah, and sits. The metal plates are rapped to accompany the vigorous entrance of BIMA. He greets JUDISTIRA with a gruff pat on the waist, and stands left, as three raps signal the music to soften.)

Fig. 90
Nakula, Sadewa,
Judistira, Bima,
and Ardjuna

djanturan NARRATION *(intoned, following pitch and rhythm of Bangbang-wetan):* The Kingdom of Amarta is famed throughout the world. It has not one, but five rulers—the sons of Pandu, called the Pandawa Brothers. All unite in support of the eldest, Judistira, who sits upon the Kingdom's throne. He is called: "Paragon of Virtue," "Purest of the Pure—the One Whose Blood Flows White," and other titles too numerous to mention. Prince Bima,

Irawan's Wedding

second of the Brothers, is a powerfully built warrior, pure of heart, straightforward of manner, known as: "Defender of the Pandawas," "Pillar of the State," and "King of Warriors." The third Brother is the handsome Prince Ardjuna, ruler of Madukara. His matchless beauty and gentle ways belie his invincible skill in battle. The other Brothers are Nakula and Sadewa, youngest of the Pandawa Brothers, friendly and loyal.

The Pandawa King and Princes await the return of Gatutkatja, Bima's favorite son, dispatched to help young Irawan. In the midst of their silence, Gatutkatja returns, bringing with him the Princess Titisari as well as young Prince Irawan.

(The dalang hums "Oooooo . . . ," signaling the gamelan to play at normal volume, as GATUTKATJA, IRAWAN, *and* TITISARI *enter. Music ends.)*

SONG *(The dalang sings Sendon Sastradatan):*
> Blessed
>> By the Gods,
> A land of
>> Noble heroes
>> Oooooo . . .
> Its ruler the
>> Most just
>> Oooooo . . .
> King Judistira
>> Oooooo . . .

(The three young people make the sembah to JUDISTIRA, *and sit before him.)*

JUDISTIRA *(with serene dignity):* Ah, my Nephew Gatutkatja. We welcome your return.

GATUTKATJA: Thank you, kingly Uncle. *(Makes the sembah.)*

JUDISTIRA: It surprises me, however, to see you not only with Irawan, but the Princess Titisari. Tell us, I pray you, Nephew, what has transpired in your absence?

GATUTKATJA: It is a long story, my Uncle, but in short: after I had prevented two ogres from abducting Princess Titisari, I followed Princess Siti Sendari's orders, and as directed, brought the two lovers here.

JUDISTIRA: And why, my dear Nephew, have you done this? Do you realize you have brought into our palace the Princess pledged to be the bride of the Astina Prince?

GATUTKATJA: Kingly Uncle, they are in love. That is all I know. (*Makes the sembah.*)

JUDISTIRA: Nephew, I cannot approve what you have done. For good or for evil, you have soiled the name of the Pandawas by this dishonest deed!

BIMA: Ha! Brother, you talk like a fool. We didn't start this mess. If you don't understand schemes like this, don't involve yourself. Leave this to me!

SONG (*The dalang sings Patet Manjura Djugag):*
> The King's pure heart
>> Knows no deceit,
> Cannot conceive
>> Of conspiracy
>> Oooooo . . .

(*During the song,* JUDISTIRA, ARDJUNA, NAKULA, *and* SADEWA *go off right.* BIMA *moves to the right side, turns, and stands with his left arm thrust aggressively on his hip.*)

BIMA (*with rough humor):* Now, Son, they'll come soon to cross-examine you. Answer my question! Did you kidnap Princess Titisari?

GATUTKATJA: Yes, Father.

BIMA (*shouting it):* Did you kidnap Princess Titisari?

GATUTKATJA: Yes, Father!

BIMA: No, no! You must answer "No!" Do you understand? If they threaten to put a curse on you, you still answer "No!" To every question they ask the answer is "No!" The same for you Irawan. Now, you two go inside, and keep out of sight. Ha, ha, ha! I'll take care of this!

(*Five spaced raps; the gamelan plays Ajak-ajakan Manjura as the lovers,* TITISARI *and* IRAWAN, *go off left. Melody stops.*)

tjarijos NARRATION (*accompanied by tense and steady tapping):* An angry tumult in the outer audience hall announces the arrival of King Baladewa, Minister Sangkuni, and the Kurawas.

(*Five quick raps signal Sampak Manjura.* GATUTKATJA *moves to the right, before* BIMA; BALADEWA, SANGKUNI, *and* PRAGOTA *rush on from the left. Three raps; the music stops.*)

SONG (*The dalang sings Ada-ada Gregetsaut Manjura Djugag to tense rapping):*
> With flashing eyes
>> And trembling limbs

Irawan's Wedding

Outraged Kurawas shout
  Their protests . . . oooooo
Oooooo . . . oooooo

Fig. 91
Bima, Gatutkatja,
Baladewa,
Sangkuni, and
Pragota

BIMA: Ha, it's Brother Baladewa! Welcome, to our Kingdom!

BALADEWA *(shaking his arm furiously):* Stand aside, Bima! I have come to deal with that rascal, your son! Gatutkatja has kidnaped Titisari away from her lawful bridegroom, covering his crime by killing a giant!

BIMA: Ho! Do you say so? Answer his charges, Gatut!

BALADEWA: Gatutkatja! Do you deny kidnaping Princess Titisari?

GATUTKATJA *(stunned):* N-n-n . . .

BIMA *(roaring):* Wait!! I'll question him! Did you kidnap Princess Titisari?

GATUTKATJA *(snapping it out):* No, Father!

BIMA: I curse your soul if you lie! Did you do it?

GATUTKATJA: No, Father!

BIMA *(to* BALADEWA*):* Ha! You see? *(Calling off right.)* Irawan, come here.

SONG *(*IRAWAN *enters from the right, and sits behind* BIMA, *as the dalang sings Ada-ada Gregetsaut Manjura Djugag):*

> In apprehension
>> The slender Prince
>> Appears
> To answer questions
>> Oooooo . . .

BIMA: Irawan! Did you kidnap Princess Titisari?

IRAWAN (*modestly, as usual*): No, I did not, Uncle.

BIMA: Louder!

IRAWAN: No, Uncle!

BIMA: I curse your soul if you lie! Did you do it?

IRAWAN: No, Uncle!

BIMA: Now, both of you, out of my sight!

SONG (IRAWAN *and* GATUTKATJA *withdraw right as the dalang sings Ada-ada Gregetsaut Manjura Djugag):*
> The two princes
>> Depart elated,
> Parts played
>> Successfully
>> Oooooo . . .

BALADEWA: Brother Bima, that's no way to interrogate thieves. Give them to me. In Mandura we pour molten lead over thieves to make them tell the truth!

BIMA (*shaking his hand in warning*): You are calling the Pandawas thieves, Brother Baladewa! Beware!

BALADEWA: That's what your son is! You know it, Brother!

SANGKUNI: Heh, heh. Handsome Bima, why look so selfishly at things? The Princess belongs to us. Return her peaceably. We do not like to talk of thieves and thievery. You force us to do so.

BIMA: You Kurawas stole Pandawa cattle! Get out of here with your talk of thievery! Get out! Grrrrrrh!

SANGKUNI (*fleeing*): Oh, my poor stomach.

DURSASANA (*following* SANGKUNI): I don't feel well.

(*Five quick raps; the gamelan plays Sampak Manjura. All quickly exit.*)

adegan perang
sampak manjura

Scene 8

(BALADEWA *and* BIMA *re-enter and face each other defiantly. Music softens.*)

Irawan's Wedding

BALADEWA: You do not frighten me, Brother Bima, with your roaring! But before I tear down the palace to find Princess Titisari, admit that she is here and you are helping her.

BIMA: Ha, ha! I won't deny it, Brother.

BALADEWA: Then give her to me, Brother. Lies and deception do not enhance the glory of the House of Pandu. For shame, Brother!

BIMA (*shaking with indignation*): A year ago you agreed to the marriage of Irawan to Titisari. Now, to please yourself and Astina, you break your word, saying "I forgot." It was you, Brother, a royal King, that lied to us! Shame! Shame, Brother!

BALADEWA (*after being silent a moment*): You are a hard man to best, Brother Bima.

BIMA (*with a great laugh*): Of course I am! I'm strong! And I'm right!

BALADEWA: I see I must give in to you. Still you challenged me. Shall we fight?

BIMA: Seriously, Brother?

BALADEWA: As a joke.

BIMA: Ha, ha! Fine, Brother. (BIMA *gets a firm hold on* BALADEWA.) I'll help you on your journey home, Brother. Here you go, all the way to Mandura!

(*As Sampak Manjura plays loudly,* BIMA *lifts* BALADEWA *into the air and throws him off the screen left.*

Fig. 92
Bima and
Baladewa

On Thrones of Gold

KRESNA *appears in the air above* BIMA, *holding a weapon. The music stops.)*

tjarijos   NARRATION: The mighty Bima hurls King Baladewa miles and miles through the sky. Seeing this, the Kurawas flee for their lives. King Kresna, having just arrived in Amarta hoping to settle the dispute between families, is outraged to see his elder brother, King of Mandura, flung head-over-heels through the air. Kindness in his heart is replaced with tempestuous anger. He vows to revenge this dishonor to his family. Seeing it is Bima who is to blame, he descends quickly to earth, takes out a divine weapon and confronts the startled Pandawa Prince.

(The metal plates are rapped five times, signaling the gamelan to play Sampak Manjura, as KRESNA *flies down to* BIMA'S *left and faces him. Music stops.)*

KRESNA *(trembling with rage):* Bima! How dare you treat my elder brother like a rag doll! You think you are invincible? I shall teach you otherwise!

(The metal plates are rapped sharply; fast Sampak Manjura begins again. BIMA *quickly flees right.* KRESNA *stands alone on the screen, holding the divine weapon, Tjakra. Music softens.)*

BIMA *(off):* Ho! Kresna's furious, Ardjuna. Reason with him. You're his brother-in-law; he won't strike you.

ARDJUNA *(off):* Not I, Brother. I have no wish to die before his divine weapon. Abimanju. You are his son-in-law. He will listen to you. Speak kindly to him.

ABIMANJU *(off):* As you say, Father.

(Rapping of metal plates cues music to resume normal level. Entering from the left, ABIMANJU *throws himself at* KRESNA'S *feet. Music stops.)*

KRESNA: Stand aside, Abimanju. It is despicable for them to hide behind a child. It is your father and your uncle I mean to punish.

ABIMANJU: Dearest Father, if you kill my elders, must I witness it?

KRESNA: Close your eyes.

ABIMANJU: I shall hear it.

KRESNA: Stuff your ears, then.

ABIMANJU: My heart will tell me they are dead. Give me the arrow, Father, please.

Irawan's Wedding

Fig. 93
Kresna and
Abimanju

KRESNA: Ehh?

ABIMANJU: Let me stop my heart before you do this deed.

KRESNA *(putting the arrow away):* No, Abimanju.

ABIMANJU *(head bowed, he does not see the danger is past):* With my families quarreling about me, death will be a relief.

KRESNA: Enough. You make your elders feel foolish.

ARDJUNA *(entering with* BIMA *from the right, he embraces* KRESNA *tightly):* Ah, my Brother, are we friends again?

KRESNA: Ardjuna! No, we are not friends again. You divorced your son from my daughter.

ARDJUNA: I, kingly Brother? Where have you heard such scandal?

KRESNA: From Siti Sendari! *(*KRESNA *moves out of* ARDJUNA'S *grip. He extends his forehand.)* Come out, Daughter!

SITI SENDARI *(appearing):* Yes, Father.

KRESNA: Daughter, did you not tell me it was Prince Ardjuna who forced you to return to Dwarawati?

SITI SENDARI *(sweetly):* Father, what ever put that into your head?

KRESNA: You, young lady!

On Thrones of Gold

SITI SENDARI: I came home of my free will, to help Sister Titisari prepare for her wedding to Irawan, dearest and most honored Father. *(Makes the sembah.)*

KRESNA *(sighs):* For love, a daughter turns against her own father. Ah, well, I will not complain. Return to your husband, Daughter.

SITI SENDARI: Oh, thank you, Father. *(Makes the sembah.)*

KRESNA: Now, is Titisari here?

SITI SENDARI: She is safely here, Father, with Prince Irawan.

tjarijos NARRATION: Suddenly shouts are heard from the guards outside. Giants are seen sweeping through the streets of the city, converging on the palace walls. Hoarse cries are heard demanding the Princess Titisari as the bride of the ogre King, and challenging Gatutkatja to battle.

KRESNA: Brother Bima, with your son, destroy these intruders on our happiness.

BIMA: Ho, ho, Brother! With pleasure!

adegan perang
amuk-amukan

Scene 9

(Five sharp raps; the gamelan plays very fast Sampak Manjura accompanying the final battle. BIMA *leaps off left. The others withdraw to the right. Onto the empty screen rush* BARANDJANA *from the left and* GATUTKATJA *from the right.*

Fig. 94
Gatutkatja and
Barandjana

Irawan's Wedding

To loud rapping of the metal plates, the two fight. GATUTKATJA *wrenches* BARANDJANA'S *head from his shoulders with his bare hands. Exulting,* GATUTKATJA *flies off right; the king's corpse is taken off.* BIMA *meets the ogress* LAJARMEGA, *and fights her. Repeatedly, she stabs him with her dagger, but to no avail for he is invulnerable. He seizes her, and rips her body to pieces with his knifelike thumbnail. In turn,* BIMA *is attacked by other ogres; he dismembers their bodies in the same way. Melody changes to Gandjur to accompany* BIMA'S *exultant "victory dance."*

Fig. 95
Bima

BIMA *backs off right, dancing. The music stops.)*

Fig. 96
Bima

tjarijos   NARRATION: And so the battle concludes and the Pandawa Princes and warriors return to the Palace of Amarta to celebrate the sweetness of their victory.

**djedjer tantjeb
kajon**

Scene 10

(The dalang raps three times. Taking their cue from the word "sweetness," the gamelan plays Manis, or "Sweet Melody" for the final scene of the play. JUDISTIRA and KRESNA enter from the right and the left, meet and embrace in the center of the screen. ARDJUNA, NAKULA, SADEWA, BIMA, SEMAR, GARENG, and PETRUK enter and take places.

*Fig. 97
Ardjuna, Kresna,
Judistira, Nakula,
Sadewa, Bima,
Gareng, Semar,
and Petruk*

Three raps; music softens and continues under dialogue.)

JUDISTIRA: Brothers, welcome into my presence. My blessings on you all.

KRESNA: Kingly Brother, your words give us comfort.

JUDISTIRA: Tell me, I pray, what is it that has occurred? I confess, I have not the least idea what has been going on around me.

BIMA: Then it is best, Brother, that you never know. Ha, ha!

JUDISTIRA: Not so, Brother. Inform me, that I may better know the ways of the world.

KRESNA: To put it simply, Brother: Irawan was to marry Titisari, until Brother Baladewa ordered the groom changed to Lesmana Mandrakumara, who arrived before me claiming the bride, except that she had been kidnaped by Gatutkatja, as a ruse planned by Siti Sendari, in revenge for her divorce from Abimanju, which Ardjuna claims he never ordered. Meanwhile, Barandjana, King of the ogre land of Djongbiradji, lusting for Titisari . . .

JUDISTIRA: Enough, I pray, Brother King. I cannot follow this topsy-turvy. Just tell me, I pray, has all turned out as it should?

KRESNA: It has, Brother. After all our turmoil, Irawan and Titisari will be wed. If you agree, Brother King.

JUDISTIRA: But of course.

KRESNA: Ardjuna?

ARDJUNA: The dagger will welcome its sheath, Brother.

KRESNA: Bima?

BIMA: Ho, ho! Why not, after all this trouble! But have you thought, Brothers, what a great trick has been played on us? Not once, through it all, has the bridegroom known his marriage was in danger! Ha, ha, ha!

JUDISTIRA: Since all has turned out well, let us offer our prayers of thanksgiving to the Almighty and together celebrate this felicitous occasion.

(The melody Manis is played at normal level as the KAJON is brought from its place on the right of the screen and is planted center over the final tableau. This is followed by a few phrases of fast Sampak Manjura indicating the performance is over. The tempo of Sampak Manjura slows, and the music continues to play as the audience departs.)

The Death of Karna   Karna Tanding

Javanese version and English translation
by Pandam Guritno Siswoharsojo

English version by James R. Brandon
and Stephen R. Alkire

Cast of Characters

KINGDOM OF ASTINA

King Durjudana, eldest Kurawa brother
Prince Durgandasena, Durjudana's brother
Prince Kartamarma, Durjudana's brother
Prince Tjitraska, Durjudana's brother
Prince Tjitraksi, Durjudana's brother
King Salja, Durjudana's father-in-law and Kurawa ally
Prince Karna, Kurawa ally
Sangkuni, chief minister of Astina
Durna, adviser to Durjudana
Aswatama, Durna's son
Sandjaja, Kurawa cousin who joins the Pandawas

BATTLECAMP OF RANDUGUMBALA

Gagakbengkol, Bima's chief minister
Kendanggumulung, official to Bima
Podangbinorehan, official to Bima

KINGDOM OF AWANGGA

Princess Surtikanti, Karna's wife
Prince Durta, Karna's foster-brother and Kurawa ally
Prince Djajarasa, Karna's foster-brother and Kurawa ally
Adimenggala, chief minister of Awangga
Suwega, official of Awangga

BATTLECAMP OF GLAGAHTINULU

Princess Sumbadra, Ardjuna's first wife
Princess Srikandi, Ardjuna's second wife
Drestaketu, chief minister of Tjempala, ally of the Pandawas
Maidservants

BATTLECAMP OF THE PANDAWAS

King Matswapati, of Wirata, chief Pandawa ally
King Judistira, eldest Pandawa brother
Prince Bima, second Pandawa brother
Prince Ardjuna, third Pandawa brother
Prince Nakula and Prince Sadewa, fourth and fifth Pandawa brothers,
    twins
King Kresna, ally of the Pandawas
Semar, clown-servant to the Pandawas, in reality the god Ismaja
Gareng, eldest son of Semar
Petruk, second son of Semar

KINGDOM OF SURALAJA

Guru, highest manifested god, ruler of the world
Narada, messenger of the gods, Guru's elder cousin
Ardawalika, a serpent

The Death of Karna

Before leaving home the dalang begins to concentrate his senses upon the performance. He prays silently, "Om. May nothing give hindrance, O Spirits of this house, flying over the earth, Mother of Generations. Allah, assist me, fulfill my wish, gratify my intentions. Creatures, male and female, look at my work, be pleased, and love by God's will. Oh, Allah! Oh, Allah! Oh, Allah!" Holding his breath, he stamps three times with his right foot.

If his host is a village group the dalang repeats the same prayer, requesting the help of the spirits residing in that area. At about eight-thirty the fifteen to twenty musicians who make up the gamelan begin to play the Talu, or introductory music. As the Talu draws to a close, the dalang takes his place before the center of the screen praying, "O Great Serpent who supports the earth, O Spirits all here, I ask your help. Let not the onlookers disperse before I have finished performing my art."

The dalang inspects the performance equipment, perhaps set up before the mayor's house or village hall. He checks to see that the screen has been fastened tightly, that the banana-log "stage" which holds the puppets is properly installed, that the puppets not being used for this performance have been set up on either side of the screen or put away in the big puppet chest on his left, that those which will first appear in the evening's drama are beside him, within easy reach, and that the KAJON, the "Tree of Life," is firmly planted in the center of the screen.

Fig. 98
Kajon

On Thrones of Gold

Most of the audience has gathered. Dignitaries of the village are seated on chairs set up on either side of the screen. Other spectators sit on the ground or stand crowding around the performance area. The ones on the dalang's side of the screen will see a "puppet" performance; those on the opposite side will see a "shadow" performance. It is now nine o'clock. As the introductory music concludes, the dalang raps sharply five times against the puppet chest on his left to signal the gamelan ensemble to play Ajak-ajakan Nem, the opening melody of the play, quietly saying as he does, "The hills and mountains are my abode, may the strength of the wind and storm be mine." He reaches above his head to the coconut-oil lamp which casts the shadows on the screen. Adjusting its flaming wick, he prays silently, saying, "Om. O God of the Soul, Essence of the One, O God of Light, may the flame of the lamp shine over the world. May those who come be silent, show pity and love, and may they stay to look at me." The dalang reaches for the KAJON, raises it carefully out of the banana trunk, then slowly lowers it.

He holds the KAJON in his lap so that the tip rests on the puppet chest. Gently, with his left hand, he bends its tip several times, quietly speaking his final prayer before the performance begins: "May my body be large and strong like the mountains. May those who come be silent. May they show pity and love as is God's will." The dalang moves the KAJON from the lower left to the upper right corner of the screen, twirls it three times, and places it at the right of the screen, indicating that the play is about to begin.

Scene 1   djedjer

(The dalang takes up the puppets of the two MAIDSERVANTS. *One in each hand, he presses them against the screen to make a clear shadow. They enter right and move gracefully to the center of the screen. They look about and see the king, their master, approaching from the right. They sit cross-legged on the floor, their faces cast down, honoring the king with the sembah—the traditional gesture of obeisance in which the hands, palms pressed together, are brought before the face. The regal figure of* DURJUDANA *enters from the right. He walks with his hand defiantly on his hip. With a slight gesture he acknowledges the* MAIDSERVANTS, *who sembah again, rise, and move deferentially to assigned places to the rear of their master. Now the king's retinue enters from the left. Each greets the king according to his rank and takes his traditional place in audience*

Fig. 99
Maidservants,
Durjudana,
and Salja

before him. First to enter is SALJA, DURJUDANA'S *father-in-law, king, and esteemed guest in the palace of Astina. They gesture in greeting.* DURJUDANA *honors* SALJA, *his elder, by offering him the seat of*

Fig. 100
Maidservants,
Durjudana,
Sangkuni,
and Salja

On Thrones of Gold

honor. The wily SANGKUNI, *chief minister of the kingdom, enters next. He crawls before the king, and greets him with a salute.*

Fig. 101
Maidservants,
Durjudana, Durna
Sangkuni, and
Salja

Last to enter is DURNA, *crafty brahman adviser to the Kurawas. His body is twisted, his countenance disfigured. He greets his ruler with a respectful gesture.* DURNA *moves back and takes a place to the rear of* SALJA. *The characters remain in tableau as the dalang, by a steady tapping on the side of the puppet chest, signals the gamelan to end the melody Ajak-ajakan Nem and begin Krawitan. The tapping speeds up, ending with three loud raps; Krawitan softens and the dalang begins the story of the kingdom.)*

djanturan NARRATION *(intoned, following pitch and rhythmic patterns of Krawitan):* May silence prevail. Numerous are God's creatures that roam the earth, fly in the sky, and swim the seas. Countless are the world's beautiful women. Yet none can equal those to be found in the Kingdom of Astina—Land of Elephants. Search one hundred countries, you will not find two, nor among a thousand, ten, to match it. Thus, I introduce this Kingdom as our story's beginning.

Long, high, sands, mountains, fertile, prosperous, trade, peace, foreigners. Long is Astina's reputation and the telling of it. High is its prestige. Oceans' sands border it; mountains guard its rear. On its right lie fields of rice, to the left a great river leading to a harbor on its shore. Fertile is its soil; prosperity abounds. Merchants trade by day and night, unceasingly in perfect safety, while peasants' flocks and herds freely roam. Never has rebellion stirred the peacefulness of this land.

The Death of Karna

Foreigners throng to make Astina their home. The roofs of their dwellings touch in friendship, crowding the largest places and making them seem small. All state officials are united in a single aim—to increase the glory of the Kingdom of Astina. The Kingdom stands firm over the earth. Its torch is high, illuminating all the world with its radiance. Many are its colonies. Not only on Java do countries submit themselves to its rule, but kings from far proffer allegiance, so great is their love for the perfection of the Kingdom of Astina. Near, they bow to the earth before its perfectness; farther afield they incline to show their respect. Annual tribute of maidens and precious gifts is offered by all as token of their submission.

Who is the King who rules this Kingdom? He is King Durjudana, called: "Ruler of the House of Kuru," "Vigorous in His Prayers," "He Who Inspires Allegiance," and "Son of Queen Anggendari." He has merit as a warrior, judge, and benefactor. He is a King fond of military arts, well-versed in strategy. He is skillful in the use of weapons as befits his stature: tall, broad, with whiskered face and hairy breast. He is stern but fair in administering justice. Above all, he delights in giving presents: he clothes the naked and feeds the hungry, gives water to those who thirst and shelter to those in the sun and rain. To all who befriend him he is most generous. But too great love of his brothers is his weakness. He does not curb them, and their misdeeds cause harm to his Kingdom. To recount all the King's virtues and the greatness of his Kingdom would require the whole night through. What has been said will suffice.

It is on a Monday that the King appears in the audience hall. He seats himself upon his throne of gold and precious jewels. A lush carpet of fresh-cut flowers fragrant with the scent of exotic perfumes cushions his feet. Maidservants, dancers, and concubines in elegant costume attend the King. They bear golden, gem-incrusted figures of state—swan, serpent, cock, and elephant. Servants on either side of the King stir cooling breezes with fans of peacock plumes until the fragrance of the King reaches to the outermost quarters of the palace. In the midst of such spectacle, the King appears no longer human, but the image of the god Baju descended to earth and accompanied by the heavenly nymphs. In reverence to the King even the breeze ceases to whisper. Still are the leaves on the trees.

Only the soft music of the gamelan, the tinkling rhythm of the goldsmith's hammer, and the call of the kolik bird perched in the banyan tree in the square are heard from afar. These distant sounds enhance the solemnity of the occasion as if illustrating the doubts and the fears of the King.

Who are those who respectfully wait upon the King at this Council of War? Seated on a throne before the King is Durjudana's father-in-law, King Salja of Mandraka, a great warrior and ally of Astina in the now-raging Great War. Beside him is the Holy Brahman Durna, former teacher of both Pandawa and Kurawa cousins. Wise is he and vigorous in asceticism. He is endowed with supernatural powers and is master of the tactics of war. But wealth and power have corrupted his spirit. He strives to please the King, often ignoring the Hindu scriptures. He who sits with his head bowed to the floor is the skillful warrior Sangkuni, uncle to the King and Astina's Chief Minister. He has no thought but to please his master the King. Behind them sit those brothers of the King not yet slain in the Great War. To the rear, the great audience hall is filled to overflowing with Astina ministers and officials of all ranks, seeking places even in the outer courtyard to attend the King. It is now the seventh day of the great War between Kurawa and Pandawa cousins for rule of the jeweled Kingdom of Astina. Scores are the nobles and thousands are the warriors slain on both sides. Of King Durjudana's ninety-eight brothers, ninety-four lie dead. Silent is the King. All are attentive, waiting for the King to speak.

SONG (*The dalang raps once as the gamelan ends Krawitan; he begins song Patet Nem Ageng*):

> Oh, Ruler of the Universe,
>   My prayers to thee.
> On your favor
>   We depend for our well-being
>   In this world and after.
> Oh, I pray, have pity on me
>   And my followers,
>   Night and day worshiping thee,
> Shower your blessings on Astina
>   In this war may we be the victors.
> So the king prays in his heart.

SONG (*The dalang sings Ada-ada Girisa, accompanied by one xylophone and steady tapping*):

> Silent is all in the great hall

The Death of Karna

> Even the wind ceases blowing
> In reverence to sorrow.
> The Great War is still raging,
> Many killed and more will follow.
> Oooooo . . . where is the end of suffering?
> The King's heart is filled with sadness,
> With heavy heart he starts speaking.

(Since the king and his court have taken their places there has been no movement before the screen. Now the dalang raises DURJUDANA'S *forearm and the king speaks.)*

DURJUDANA *(deep, powerful voice):* Royal Father-in-law, you are welcome in this chamber. *(A triple rap on the side of the puppet chest punctuates the end of the speech.)*

SALJA *(strong, medium-pitch voice):* Majesty, I thank you. Accept my prayers for your well-being, my Son. *(Triple rap.)*

DURJUDANA: I accept them with gratitude, kingly Father. *(Triple rap. Gestures to* DURNA.*)* Welcome to you, honored Durna. *(Triple rap.)*

DURNA *(salutes):* Ohh, yes, Your Majesty, I thank you. Please accept my blessings, oh King. *(Salutes. Triple rap.)*

DURJUDANA: May it increase my dignity and power, Father Durna. *(Triple rap. Gestures to* SANGKUNI.*)* Uncle Sangkuni, do you arrive well before me? *(Triple rap.)*

SANGKUNI *(speaks ingratiatingly):* Your Majesty, I can lack nothing when in your presence. I offer my humblest greetings, my King. *(Makes deep sembah. Triple rap.)*

DURJUDANA: Your words cause me delight, Uncle. Please rest comfortably Father Salja, Holy Durna. Tell me, Uncle Sangkuni, of the latest reports from the field. Expect neither reward nor punishment but speak frankly of today's battle. *(Triple rap.)*

SANGKUNI *(making a deep sembah):* Oh, Your Majesty, may the Gods curse me if I speak what is not the truth. I have received news that last night your field commander, Prince Karna, engaged the Pandawa field commander, Gatutkatja, in fierce and dreadful combat. I beg to report Prince Karna gained victory. He killed Gatutkatja. But, ohhh, and I implore Your Majesty to forgive me, when Bima, the Pandawa Prince, heard of his son's death, he ran amok. For vengeance he ripped apart the body of Your Majesty's brother Dursasana. *(Face to the floor, he makes a deep sembah. Triple rap.)*

On Thrones of Gold

SONG *(The dalang sings Ada-ada Gregetsaut Nem; tapping steadily to heighten the tension, he ends with a triple rap):*
>The King's heart explodes with grief,
>He strikes his chest,
>>Great is your sacrifice . . . oooooo
>>May your soul be at rest.

tjarijos NARRATION *(spoken rapidly, in a normal tone of voice):* Upon hearing the news of his minister, the King is unable to speak, so deep is his love for his fallen brother. The King's grief affects the others, and they sit motionless as marble in the great hall. Suddenly shouts shatter the stillness, announcing the arrival of Prince Karna, Commander of the Astina army. Troops and officials part like a wave to make way for the victorious Prince. He strides up the stairs into the audience hall.

(Three raps; the lively melody Obah plays for KARNA'S *entrance.* KARNA *radiates self-confidence. He does not sembah nor does he bow before the king. He and* DURJUDANA *clasp hands in greeting. The dalang raps three times; the melody Obah softens as the dalang continues.)*

tjarijos NARRATION: All eyes rest upon the radiant countenance of the victorious Field Commander, Prince Karna of Awangga. *(Music ends.)*

*Fig. 102
Maidservants,
Durjudana,
Karna, Sangkuni,
Salja, and Durna*

DURJUDANA: A thousand welcomes, Brother King.

KARNA *(with great pride, his words shoot out like arrows):* Thank

The Death of Karna

you, Your Majesty. Forgive my arriving without being announced.

DURJUDANA *(slight gesture):* Dear Brother, do not be concerned with formalities. Your arrival is welcomed. We have been expecting you. Rest now.

KARNA: Your Majesty, I lack nothing. *(He salutes)*

DURJUDANA: Father Salja, Prince Karna is here. I wish to ask your advice. Each day more Astina warriors are killed in battle. Our ranks are narrowing and I fear for the fate of the Kurawas.

SALJA: My royal Son, it is true that many have fallen. Yet there is hope for victory still. Rely upon my other son-in-law, Prince Karna.

DURJUDANA: Kingly Father, I accept your advice. Let Prince Karna, our brother king, continue as Commander of Astina's armies.

SALJA: I heartily approve, my son.

DURJUDANA; Brother Karna, my Prince, it is not my wish to overburden you, but I ask you to command Astina's army on the battlefield again.

KARNA: Brother King, I shall do what you wish. *(Salutes.)*

DURJUDANA: Have you a suggestion, Father, for the office of Deputy Commander?

SALJA: I am of the opinion that Your Majesty's younger brother, Prince Durgandasena, is the very person to fill the post.

DURJUDANA: Thank you, Father. That is precisely my wish. *(Gestures.)* Uncle Sangkuni!

SANGKUNI *(crawls before the king, makes the sembah):* Yes, Majesty. I am at your service.

DURJUDANA: Summon my brother Durgandasena, Uncle.

SANGKUNI: At once, Your Majesty.

SONG (SANGKUNI *makes the sembah and backs out of the audience hall as the dalang sings Patet Nem Djugag):*

> The Minister leaves
> > To obey the King's order,
> He descends the stairs   .
> > And summons the King's brother
> > Oooooo . . .

SANGKUNI *(off):* Durgandasena, my Son. Come. Your kingly brother summons you to attend him at once.

On Thrones of Gold

DURGANDASENA (*off; in a rough voice*): Ohhhh! Yes, Uncle. I follow.

tjarijos NARRATION: Durgandasena, the King's younger brother quickly straightens his clothes and hurries after the Chief Minister. He enters the audience hall and apprehensively approaches the King who looks like the sun covered by clouds.

(This is a word cue for the gamelan to play the melody Remeng or "Overcast." SANGKUNI *makes the sembah to the king, then retires to his usual position.* DURGANDASENA *crawls before the king, head low, and makes a vigorous sembah. The dalang raps three times as Remeng ends.)*

DURJUDANA: Welcome, Brother Durgandasena.

DURGANDASENA: Ohh, Brother! I give you my reverent greetings! *(Makes the sembah.)*

DURJUDANA: I accept them with pleasure, Brother. Tell me, why do you look concerned?

DURGANDASENA: Ohh, my elder Brother! When I received the royal command, I thought lightning would flash and strike me. I thought the bolts had hit me, but somehow, by a miracle, I was unhurt. My heart whirled, like a leaf caught up in a storm. But now, honored Brother, in Your Majesty's presence my heart grows peaceful again. *(Makes sembah.)*

DURJUDANA: Dear Brother, how can it be your anxiety has passed so quickly?

DURGANDASENA: I . . . I . . . kingly Brother, I felt that even though I might be guilty of some sin, it would be Your Majesty who would punish me, that were I to be condemned to death it would be Your Majesty who would order it. Since I wish only to do what Your Majesty wishes, even if it means my life, I felt content, Your Majesty. *(Makes the sembah.)*

DURJUDANA: My Brother, your great loyalty pleases me. But do not misunderstand my summons. You are to receive neither punishment nor reward. Be informed that the council has decided to retain Prince Karna as Commander of the Astina forces and that you, Brother, have been appointed his Deputy. Accept your new responsibilities with spirit and integrity, Brother.

DURGANDASENA (*looking up*): Ah! Ha-ha! I am a lucky man, Brother! I thank Your Majesty for this honor! *(Makes the sembah.)*

KARNA (*salutes*): Your noble Majesty, my King.

The Death of Karna

DURJUDANA: Yes, Brother Karna?

KARNA *(strongly):* Forgive this interruption, but it is well-known that my greatest adversary in this war is the Pandawa prince Ardjuna. Today we will meet in personal combat. Ardjuna's chariot is to be driven by the godlike King Kresna. Majesty, I ask to have as my charioteer a king as great and skillful as he —our honored father-in-law, King Salja.

SONG *(The dalang sings Ada-ada Mataraman, accompanied by one xylophone and steady tapping, describing* SALJA'S *anger):*
> King Salja's face turns livid,
>> His body turns to fire,
> His breath comes heavy,
>> His limbs tremble
> Oooooo . . .

NARRATION: The presumptuous request of his son-in-law   tjarijos
enrages the King of Mandraka. His face flushes and his chest heaves. His mouth twitches as if in agony. "Oh, God," he thinks, "for a son to humiliate his father thus! Before all present to force me to be a charioteer! Insufferable pride!" But, being a great King, the royal Salja masks his anger in silence. King Durjudana notes his father-in-law's fury and tactfully pleads with him.

DURJUDANA *(placating gesture):* Oh, most noble Father and King, Astina's honor would rise to dizzying heights should you deign to fulfill Prince Karna's request. You alone are Kresna's equal. May the Gods agree, I ask Your Majesty be generous of heart.

SALJA *(controlling his anger):* My Son, I can refuse nothing which benefits your Kingdom. For Astina and you, my King, I shall guide Prince Karna's chariot.

DURJUDANA: Noble Sire, I am pleased. *(Gestures to* KARNA.*)* Your request is granted, my Prince. Have you any further request?

KARNA: Majesty, I wish to return briefly to Awangga. I feel concern for my wife, Surtikanti. Before meeting Ardjuna I wish to see her once more.

DURJUDANA: You go with my blessing. (KARNA *salutes; the king gestures acceptance.)* Brother Durgandasena, lead the troops into battle formation. Make certain all is in order. Then wait for the return of Prince Karna.

DURGANDASENA: With your blessing, Majesty, it shall be done.

DURJUDANA: Go with the Gods, dear Brother.

(Five spaced raps; the gamelan plays the spirited melody Ajak-ajakan Nem. DURGANDASENA *makes a sembah and quickly backs out left. Music stops.)*

Father Salja, let us retire to the inner court. Holy Durna, accompany us if you will.

SALJA: Yes, Majesty. I shall follow.

tjarijos

NARRATION: The courtiers rise and people in the audience hall begin to mill about, but like a giant wave the throng parts at the approach of the King and closes again behind him.

(The dalang again raps five times signaling the gamelan to play Ajak-ajakan Nem. The two kings exit right, side-by-side, followed by MAIDSERVANTS *and* DURNA. SANGKUNI *makes the sembah, exits left.* KARNA *follows. For a moment the screen is empty.* DURJUDANA *and* SALJA *cross the screen from left to right. As the* KAJON *is slanted right in the center of the screen to represent the palace interior, the music stops.)*

Fig. 103
Kajon

tjarijos
pagedongan

NARRATION: The King and his guests enter the inner chambers where they meet the Queen. The King informs her of the decisions of the council and the two Kings and the holy Brahman Durna enter the palace temple to meditate for guidance in the Great War. Durjudana strives to concentrate his mind, to empty his heart, to control his five senses, but he cannot. Repeatedly

The Death of Karna

his mind wanders aimlessly. The King becomes angered and reproaches the Gods for his failure. The Gods indicate their disapproval of the King's actions: they fill the temple with a foul odor which drives the King and his guests to abandon their prayers and hastily return to the inner court.

Scene 2

(The outer audience hall of the Palace of Astina. Melody Kembang-tiba is played as the KAJON *is moved from the center of screen and placed at the right.* SANGKUNI *enters from the right. He waves on* KARTAMARMA, TJITRAKSA, *and* TJITRAKSI, *who enter one at a time from the left, greet* SANGKUNI *with a quick sembah, and face him from the left.*

Fig. 104
Sangkuni,
Kartamarma,
Tjitraksi, and
Tjitraksa

The dalang raps three times; the music softens.)

NARRATION *(intoned, following pitch and rhythm of music):* Our story now moves to the outer audience hall, where Astina nobles and warriors are impatient to know the outcome of the King's Council of War. Who are they that eagerly stand before Sangkuni, their Prime Minister? Foremost is Prince Karta-marma, one of the last remaining brothers of King Durjudana. Behind him stands the Princes Tjitraksa and Tjitraksi. Eagerly they ply him with questions.

SONG *(The melody Kembangtiba ends; the dalang sings Ada-ada Mataraman Djugag, accompanied by one xylophone and steady tapping):*

On Thrones of Gold

> Thunderous is the sound
> > Of trumpets and drums,
> Gongs of bronze are struck
> > As if to break them,
> Signaling Astina's troops to rally.

KARTAMARMA: Uncle Sangkuni, tell us quickly. What is the news? *(Makes strong sembah.)*

TJITRAKSA: Y-y-y-es, please, Uncle. Tell us th-th-the news! *(Hurried sembah.)*

TJITRAKSI: The news, U-u-u-uncle, please. Tell us what has happened! *(Hurried sembah.)*

SANGKUNI *(quiets them with a gesture)*: Patience, my Children. Be informed the Council has retained Prince Karna as Commander of the armies and Prince Durgandasena is his Deputy. Prince Karna leaves for Awangga to greet his consort before the battle; Prince Durgandasena will lead the armies into the field. Kartamarma, make certain all is prepared. Order the troops to ready themselves for battle.

KARTAMARMA *(makes sembah)*: I shall, Uncle. Immediately.

SONG *(The song Ada-ada Astakuswala Alit with steady tapping underscores* KARTAMARMA's *vigorous exit):*

> Thunderous is the sound
> > Of trumpet, drum, and gong,
> Flags and banners wave
> > Like the ocean's tide,
> Beautiful is the sight.

KARTAMARMA *(off)*: Attention, soldiers of Astina and its allies!

VOICES *(off)*: Yes, my Prince! We await your order, my Prince!

KARTAMARMA *(off)*: By the King's order, Prince Karna remains Commander of all Astina armies. Prince Durgandasena, his Deputy, takes command while Prince Karna travels to Awangga. You Awangga men!

VOICES *(off)*: Yesssss!

KARTAMARMA *(off)*: You will escort your Prince to his Kingdom. Go prepare his carriage.

VOICES *(off)*: His carriage waits in readiness, my Prince! We are prepared to leave at once!

KARTAMARMA *(off)*: Warriors of Astina! Prince Durgandasena will lead you to the battlefield. Prepare yourselves, take up your spears, swords, and lances. Saddle the mounts of your commanders. We leave instantly!

The Death of Karna

VOICES *(off):* We're going! Pack up! Do you hear, we leave! Hurry! Hurry!

VOICE *(off):* We're ready. Tell the Prince.

VOICE *(off):* My Prince, the troops are ready! We wait your order to march!

KARTAMARMA *(off):* Excellent! Assemble in columns at the sound of the first gong! Ready on the second! We march on the third!

VOICES *(off):* Yessss, my Prince!

SONG (KARTAMARMA *enters and takes his place before* SANGKUNI *during the singing of Ada-ada Astakuswala Ageng accompanied by steady tapping):*

> Horses wildly whinny
>> As their riders mount,
> Sharp bits cut their mouths
>> And springs of blood gush forth.
> Clamorous signals mix with their cries,
>> As horses plunge and rear
>> Oooooo . . . Warrior's strong hands guide them.

KARTAMARMA *(making the sembah):* The armies stand ready, Uncle.

SANGKUNI: Then sound the gong, my Prince.

KARTAMARMA *(makes the sembah):* Yes, Uncle.

SONG (*Ada-ada Budalan Mataraman is sung accompanied by steady tapping, as* KARTAMARMA *exits left):*

> Numerous are the troops,
>> Their uniforms bright
> Like the sun rising
>> From the horizon
> To cast its golden
>> Rays on the world
> Partly visible behind the mountain
>> Illuminating the clouds
>> Oooooo . . .

NARRATION: Prince Kartamarma strikes the gong as if to break   tjarijos
it. Three times its booming voice pierces the air. Drums, trumpets, flutes, and bells thunder in response as the mighty Astina army storms out of the city.

(Three raps; the marching music Kebogiro is played. All exit left. KARTAMARMA *re-enters from the right, sword in hand, turns, and gestures to the massed troops off-right and gestures for them to pass*

in review. The MARCHING ARMY *enters, halts before the prince, and receives his salute.*

*Fig. 105
Marching Army
and Kartamarma*

The army marches past the prince and off left. KARTAMARMA *turns and follows. Now* SANGKUNI *enters, reviews the* MARCHING ARMY, *and exits.* TJITRAKSA *and* TJITRAKSI *do the same.* DURGANDA-SENA *mounts his horse and marches across the screen.* SANGKUNI *follows on a prancing white steed. Then* KARTAMARMA. *The Astina armies have departed.* KARNA'S *carriage enters from the right, followed by him. The music ends.)*

adegan kereta   Scene 3

SONG (*Ada-ada Mataraman is sung, to steady tapping, as* KARNA *considers the coming journey):*
    Soon the magic carriage
      Will take Astina's Commander
    Speeding like the lightning
      To distant Awangga
      Oooooo . . .

tjarijos   NARRATION: The Prince's carriage is covered with precious gems, its roof composed of tinted seashells. Four golden eagles,

The Death of Karna

their tails joined with a steel band, protect it. From above they seem to swoop and strike when the carriage is in motion. The doors are made of fragrant wood into which are carved delicate designs painted with gold. Yellow silk curtains bordered with lace cover the windows; the wheels are of gold and crimson. The carriage is drawn by four matched horses with hoofs of

*Fig. 106
Karna and
Carriage*

ivory commanded by drivers dressed as Gods. Prince Karna enters the carriage and the carriage leaps forward. The wheels spin, striking sparks in every direction. The carriage speeds so swiftly, indeed, its wheels seem not to touch the ground at all.

(Seven double raps signal the gamelan musicians to play the lively melody Srepegan Nem. The dalang executes the action he has just described: KARNA *enters the carriage, it moves off briskly to the right, turns, and crosses the screen twice from right to left.)*

Scene 4

adegan perang
ampjak

(The KAJON *is placed left of the center of the screen, where it signifies the forest-covered slopes of a mountain. The* MARCHING ARMY *enters from the right and stops facing the forest. Music stops.)*

ginem wadya FIRST SOLDIER; Hey up there, what's going on? Why are we stopped?

SECOND SOLDIER: Slow down, friends. The road peters out ahead. We're going into the mountains.

THIRD SOLDIER: Heh, you in back! Get those damned spears down! What're you trying to do? Be a hero before we even see the enemy? Say, where are we going?

FIRST SOLDIER: Jackass! Where were you when they gave the orders?

THIRD SOLDIER: In the middle of a big business deal. When I heard the gongs and then the trumpets and drums, I dropped everything, grabbed my spear, and fell in.

FIRST SOLDIER: That's great. Here you are armed to the teeth marching along and you don't even know where to!

THIRD SOLDIER: I dressed on the way. Damn it, man, I lost that deal.

FIRST SOLDIER: There's a businessman for you. His country's in danger and he thinks of profit.

THIRD SOLDIER. Don't you ridicule me! I'm as loyal as the next man. I'm here. But who can live on a volunteer's pay? You've got to turn a profit some way to stay alive.

SECOND SOLDIER: Stop arguing, you two. There's work to be done. Clear a road through this forest so the Prince can pass. There's just a trail here. Clear it out!

FIRST SOLDIER: Okay, let's go. Heh, little volunteer! Let's see if you can work with your hands as well as your brains! Pretend this is one of your business deals.

THIRD SOLDIER: Use your brains before you break your back. What if we smash up somebody's fence or cut their trees? We'd better ask the commanders first.

FIRST SOLDIER: Bah! That's the trouble with you merchants. Be a soldier, act with authority. At a time like this who cares if we break up a little private property? The fate of the Kingdom's at stake.

THIRD SOLDIER: Hmm. Well, if we have to disturb anyone, at least we can give him a voucher certifying the damage was done on government business. He can apply for reimbursement.

SECOND SOLDIER: Now there's an idea! Let's get started. Everyone with axe and sword to the front. Clear the brush, cut the trees!

The Death of Karna

SOLDIERS: Make room! Make room! Come on, let's move!
(Seven double raps; the gamelan plays Srepegan Nem. In time to the music, the MARCHING ARMY *strikes the* KAJON *several times as if cutting a tree. The* KAJON *is knocked down.*

*Fig. 107
Marching Army
and Kajon*

The KAJON *is thrown off left and the* MARCHING ARMY *exits after it. This happens three times. The army crosses the screen unhindered, marching away. The* KAJON *flutters across the screen from right to left, symbolizing the cleared forest, and, after several passes, is planted in the center of the screen, inclined to the right. Music stops.)*

NARRATION: Astina's marching soldiers travel far. Column after column passes by. A unit dressed all in black looks like a flock of ravens; a green one, like parrots swooping to feed on grain. One in red is a blazing forest; one in white, herons on the marsh. The sun glints from thousands of burnished and bobbing weapons, so they look like the gleaming scales of fish darting in a pool. The thudding of footsteps, the sounds of drums and gongs, and the whinny of stamping horses blend into a muffled roar, like the fall of rain on a teakwood forest. Thunderclouds of dust rise in the skies. So do the troops of Astina march, arriving, with the last rays of the sun, at the battlefield Kurusetra. Quickly they erect their tents to rest for the night.

tjarijos

On Thrones of Gold

SONG *(The dalang sings Patet Kedu):*
> Looking at the countryside
>> Dimly lit by stars,
> Like fireflies
>> Pale in the sky,
> Paler than the full moon
>> Whose rising beauty
>> Fills men's hearts
> And casts a glow upon the forest's trees.

tjarijos NARRATION: So much for the troops of Astina. Our story now moves to the battle camp Randugumbala, where the Pandawa Prince is holding council. Before their mighty lord, warriors and officials bow low like marsh grass flattened by the storm.

djedjer sabrangan Scene 5

(Three raps; the gamelan plays the melody Gendu. The KAJON *is moved to the right of the screen. The powerful figure of* BIMA *strides on from the right, rear arm akimbo. He gestures off left.* GAGAK-BENGKOL, KENDANGGUMULUNG, *and* PODANGBINOREHAN *enter separately, make the sembah, and sit respectfully before* BIMA.

*Fig. 108
Bima,
Gagakbengkol,
Podangbinorehan,
and
Kendanggumulung*

The dalang raps three times; the music softens.)

djanturan NARRATION *(intoned, following pitch and rhythm of Gendu):* Prince Bima, the second Pandawa Brother, stands before his officers.

The Death of Karna

A powerfully built warrior is he. A full beard covers his face, and from his lip a thick moustache bursts forth. His muscled chest is covered with a mat of curling hair. Beneath his fair skin the veins stand forth. Like thunder is his booming voice. His piercing eyes cause opponents to shrink with fear. But, if one gazes long enough, the Prince's rugged handsomeness attracts like a magnet, his body radiates light like the sun. Though not a King, like a King he has many names: "Born of an Elephant" because at birth an elephant freed him of his placenta, "Persistent Seeker," "Bima-the-Wise," "Commander," "King of Warriors," "Flower of Battle," "Constant Victor," "Strength of the Wind," and "Son of the Wind God Baju." Of the four brothers of King Judistira, Bima stands as the pillar of the Kingdom, destroyer of its enemies, guardian of its virtue. Were the Pandawa Kingdom to shrink to the size of an umbrella's shadow, its soldiers would still fight as long as Bima were to stand among them. Pure is Bima's heart, straightforward is his behavior. He is loved and respected by all his subjects. Seated before the Prince, his face touching the floor in reverence, is his trusted Minister, Gagakbengkol. He is brave and honest, like his master. Behind the Minister, Kendanggumulung and Podangbinorehan sit with other officers. Not a sound is heard. All are aware of the Prince's deep grief. No sooner had Bima's son, Gatutkatja, died at the hands of Prince Karna than Bima's wife, the Princess Arimbi, hearing of her son's death, mounted the pyre and was consumed in flames. But Prince Bima is a noble and a warrior; from his mind he banishes his double grief. His full attention he turns upon the duties at hand.

(The dalang raps; the melody Gendu is played at normal level until it ends.)

SONG *(The dalang sings Patet Lasem):*

> Oh, so noble is the King,
>> Generous and honest
>> And pure is his heart.
> Endlessly to his subjects
>> His gifts pour forth
>> Honoring his word
> Oooooo . . .

BIMA *(speaking brusquely, in a deep voice):* Gagakbengkol, are you well?

GAGAKBENGKOL: Yes, my Lord. I thank you. *(Makes the sembah.)* Accept my reverent greetings.

BIMA: Yes, gladly. Welcome, Kendanggumulung.

KENDANGGUMULUNG: Thank you, my Lord *(Makes the sembah.)* I am honored to be in your presence.

BIMA: Thank you. Podangbinorehan, welcome.

PODANGBINOREHAN: My Lord, I thank you. *(Makes the sembah.)* Accept my humble greetings.

BIMA: Gladly, 'Podang. My blessings to you all. *(Gestures strongly.)* Now, Gagakbengkol, report on the state of our army.

GAGAKBENGKOL: All appears well, my Lord. The troops are in excellent condition. They stand ready for your orders. *(Makes the sembah.)*

BIMA *(gesturing strongly)*: Good. Never relax. The enemy will attack at any time.

tjarijos   NARRATION: In the midst of their discussion, shouts and cries are heard outside. Quickly Bima orders Gagakbengkol to investigate their cause.

BIMA: Gagakbengkol, see what that is!

GAGAKBENGKOL: At once, my Lord. *(Exits to beating of metal plates.)*

GAGAKBENGKOL *(off)*: Hey, out there. What's all this shouting?

VOICE *(off)*: Sir, the Astina army is attacking! Our advance guard is already in the thick of it.

GAGAKBENGKOL *(off)*: Assemble the troops! We wait Prince Bima's command.

VOICE *(off)*: Yes, Sir.

SONG *(The dalang sings Ada-ada Mataraman Djugag to steady tapping as GAGAKBENGKOL returns to his place before the prince)*:
Thunderous is the sound
    Of trumpets and drums,
Gongs are struck
As if to break them
    Oooooo . . .

BIMA: Yes, Gagakbengkol, what is it?

GAGAKBENGKOL *(makes the sembah)*: Astina troops are beginning the attack. They've engaged our advance guard. We wait your orders, my Prince.

The Death of Karna

BIMA *(gestures strongly)*: Signal the army to march! Follow me to the battlefield!

GAGAKBENGKOL: Yes, my Lord.

(Seven double raps signal the gamelan to play quick-tempoed Srepegan Nem. GAGAKBENGKOL *makes the sembah and rushes out left.* BIMA *and the others exit. One by one,* PODANGBINOREHAN, KENDANGGUMULUNG, GAGAKBENGKOL, *and* BIMA *cross the screen from right to left, hurrying to the battlefield.* PODANGBINOREHAN *encounters* TJITRAKSI *entering from the left. They survey each other warily. Music stops.)*

Scene 6

adegan perang gagal

TJITRAKSI *(gesticulating)*: Is this a P-p-p-p-andawa warrior s-s-standing before me?

PODANGBINOREHAN *(gesturing strongly)*: Indeed, your vision is excellent.

TJITRAKSI: D-d-don't die wi-without a name! Announce y-y-yourself.

PODANGBINOREHAN: My name is Podangbinorehan. Who are you?

TJITRAKSI: P-p-prince Tj-tj-tj-tj-tj-tjitraski!!!! You are not w-worth killing. Stand aside.

PODANGBINOREHAN: For whom? All I see before me is a big mouth and a loose tongue.

TJITRAKSI: C-c-come closer, and feel my fists!

(Seven double raps signal the gamelan to play Srepegan Nem. The two fight, their blows and sorties punctuated by the percussive sound of metal plates striking together. TJITRAKSI *is beaten and flung away.* PODANGBINOREHAN *follows. Enter* TJITRAKSA *from the left and* KENDANGGUMULUNG *from the right. They look each other over carefully. Three raps; the music softens.)*

TJITRAKSA *(gesticulating)*: Is this a P-p-p-p-pandawa warrior s-s-standing before me?

KENDANGGUMULUNG *(gesturing strongly)*: Your eyesight is fine.

TJITRAKSA: D-d-don't die wi-without a name! Announce y-y-yourself.

KENDANGGUMULUNG: My name is Kendanggumulung. Who are you?

TJITRAKSA: P-p-pprince Tj-tj-tj-tj-tj-tjitraksa!!!! You're not w-worth killing. Stand aside.

KENDANGGUMULUNG: What for? All I hear are empty boasts.

TJITRAKSA: C-c-come closer, and you'll feel my fists!

(*Music up full. They fight.* TJITRAKSA *is beaten and thrown off screen.* KENDANGGUMULUNG *follows.* KARTAMARMA *enters from the left and encounters* GAGAKBENGKOL. *They stare at each other fiercely. Music stops.*)

KARTAMARMA: Who is it that is brave enough to face me in combat?

GAGAKBENGKOL: Gagakbengkol is my name, Chief Minister of the noble Prince Bima! Who are you, Soldier?

KARTAMARMA: There is but one Prince Kartamarma of Astina and I am he! Move aside for me to pass, while I pity you!

GAGAKBENGKOL: Don't waste your pity on me, Soldier! You boast, but can you fight?

(*Seven double raps; loud and violent Srepegan Nem. Furiously* KARTAMARMA *strikes at* GAGAKBENGKOL, *who evades. They battle first with fists, then clubs.* GAGAKBENGKOL *lands a solid blow and* KARTAMARMA *staggers away. Seeming to appear from nowhere,* DURGANDASENA *leaps on* GAGAKBENGKOL, *knocking him to the ground almost senseless.*)

SONG (*The melody Srepegan Nem ends; the dalang sings Ada-ada Mataraman to steady tapping as* GAGAKBENGKOL *recovers*):

>The warrior's spirit
>>Is angered,
>>Despicable attacker
>Ooooo . . .oooooo

GAGAKBENGKOL (*rising*): Ohh! What a treacherous attack! Who strikes without warning?

DURGANDASENA: Fool, open your eyes! I am Durgandasena, Astina's Deputy Commander, brother of King Durjudana! Now out of the way before I finish you!

GAGAKBENGKOL: Ho-ho! You're a brave commander, sneaking up from behind! Now prove the worth of the rank you flaunt!

(*Five quick raps; the gamelan strikes up Sampak Nem. The two rush forward and grapple with each each other.* DURGANDASENA *proves the stronger. Suddenly* BIMA *appears. The two face each other and* BIMA *remorselessly attacks. He strikes* DURGANDASENA *to the ground, throws him through the air, hits him with fists and feet.*

The Death of Karna

BIMA *lifts* DURGANDASENA *high in the air, and carries his foe off left. The* KAJON *is placed left, symbolizing a rock.)*

NARRATION: Prince Bima holds his foe aloft. With tremendous power he hurls him against a rock. So great is the impact, the body of Durgandasena is crushed to pulp. The rock shatters into fragments, and in its place a spring gushes forth.

tjarijos

(BIMA *re-enters and hurls* DURGANDASENA *against the "rock."*

Fig. 109
Bima,
Durgandasena,
and Kajon

The KAJON *and* DURGANDASENA *are whisked off.* BIMA *is left alone. Enter* GAGAKBENGKOL, KENDANGGUMULUNG, *and* PODANG-BINOREHAN *who make the sembah and take their places before* BIMA. *The music stops.)*

BIMA: What of the battle, Gagakbengkol?

GAGAKBENGKOL: Seeing the death of their deputy commander the Astina forces have fled in panic, my Prince. What are your orders, my Lord?

BIMA: Stand guard while I go to our King's main camp. Be alert. The enemy may still attack again.

GAGAKBENGKOL: My Lord, your orders shall be obeyed. *(Makes the sembah.)*

(Five spaced raps; the gamelan plays Ajak-ajakan Nem. BIMA *exits right, the others left. As the* KAJON *is planted in the center of the screen, inclined to the right, the music stops.)*

SONG *(The dalang sings Patet Nem Djugag):*
    The striken Astina troops

On Thrones of Gold

> Retire to their fortress,
> Fleeing in disorder
> Oooooo . . . oooooo

tjarijos NARRATION: So ends the battle. Terror-stricken, the routed troops seek the protection of Astina's fortress walls. Bima begins his journey to the main Pandawa camp to wait upon his brother, King Judistira. Now our story moves to the Kingdom of Awangga, where Princess Surtikanti anxiously awaits through the afternoon for the return of her royal husband, Prince Karna, her eyes damp with tears.

djedjer sabrang   Scene 7
rangkep

(Three raps; taking their cue from the narration, the gamelan plays Udan Sore or "Afternoon Rain." The KAJON *moves to the right. Slowly* SURTIKANTI *enters from the right, her front arm on her rear shoulder in an attitude of distress. Two* MAIDSERVANTS *greet her with the sembah, then take their places behind their mistress.* DURTA, DJAJARASA, *and* ADIMENGGALA *enter from the left, make the sembah, and sit respectfully before* SURTIKANTI. *Three raps; the music softens.)*

djanturan NARRATION *(intoned, following pitch and rhythm of Udan Sore):* Sitting sorrowfully in audience is the beautiful Princess Surtikanti, daughter of King Salja, and Prince Karna's wife. A gentle and delicate creature is she, faithful and sincere in religious devotion. She is greatly loved by her consort: her only wish is to please him. Her sons have died in the Great War and daily her husband's life is in danger. Anxiously she waits his return. Her attendants are the Princes Durta and Djajarasa and the Kingdom's old Prime Minister, Adimenggala. They sit silently waiting for their Princess to speak.

(The dalang raps three times; the music resumes normal volume until it ends.)

SONG *(The dalang sings Patet Lasem):*
> Oh, noble is her Prince,
> > So generous and brave
> > Is her Lord.
> Gifts pour forth
> > To the needy
> > Honoring his word
> Oooooo . . .

The Death of Karna

SURTIKANTI *(in a small, tender voice):* Brothers Durta and Djajarasa, are you well?

DURTA: Yes, Noble Sister. May I present my greetings. *(Makes the sembah.)*

DJAJARASA: I am well, my Sister. I offer my greetings. *(Makes the sembah.)*

SURTIKANTI: Yes . . . thank you. And you, dear Uncle, are most welcome.

ADIMENGGALA: Oh, thank you Milady, thank you. With both hands I present my homage. *(Makes the sembah.)*

SURTIKANTI: Blessings . . . Uncle.

ADIMENGGALA: Are you well, Milady?

SURTIKANTI: Please. Forgive my silence, dear friends. You well know my mind is distraught. My sons are dead and I fear my beloved husband will follow.

ADIMENGGALA: Noble Lady, free your heart from concern. His Highness is unchallenged as a warrior. Rest assured, no harm can befall him. *(Makes the sembah.)*

SURTIKANTI: Your words comfort me, Uncle, but ill omens disturb me. Night after night the same terrifying dream haunts me.

ADIMENGGALA: I am an old man, Milady, and have tasted much of life's salt. Allow me to say that dreams mean nothing.

SURTIKANTI: I am sure you are right, Uncle. Yet, I fear these omens. Oh! My sheltered life is improper while my Lord is in danger. We have lived as one. If he is to die in battle let me be with him! I shall follow him into the field!

ADIMENGGALA *(raising both hands in shocked protest):* Oh! No, my Princess! What fury would His Highness shower upon this old frame were you to expose yourself to danger. And too, think how his peril would increase. Were he concerned with your safety, he could not care for his. Rest assured our Lord will soon return and safely. *(Makes the sembah.)*

DURTA: Noble Sister, I agree. It is here our Prince wishes you to be. *(Makes the sembah.)*

SONG *(The dalang sings Patet Nem Djugag):*
> Nature's fragrance
>> Scents the breezes,
> Fragrant flowers
>> Soothe the senses
>> Oooooo . . .

tjarijos

NARRATION: Despite their arguments Surtikanti insists upon going to her husband when great cries are heard from outside the palace. The Awangga people, seeing their Lord, excitedly welcome him. Quickly Karna steps down from his carriage and enters the palace. Surtikanti goes to greet her husband and master. Joyfully she takes his hand and leads him to the inner court.

(The dalang raps five times; melody Ajak-ajakan Nem begins. SURTIKANTI *shades her eyes to see* KARNA, *crosses left to meet him. She reaches out her hand; he takes it.*

Fig. 110
Surtikanti
and Karna

Hand-in-hand they move to the center of the screen. SURTIKANTI *embraces* KARNA'S *feet. Music softens.)*

SURTIKANTI: Oh my Lord, my husband. Long have I awaited your return. How unlucky I am to have been forgotten. How sorrow has tortured me in your absence.

KARNA *(touching her gently):* Dearest, do not cry. Please sit and calm your heart.

SURTIKANTI: Yes, my Prince. Please forgive my tears.

(Music plays at normal level as SURTIKANTI *sits, facing* KARNA. *Music ends.)*

SURTIKANTI: My dearest Prince and Lord, I welcome your return from Astina.

KARNA: I return safely because of your prayers, my dearest. May the Gods give you their blessings.

SURTIKANTI: My Lord! *(She bows almost in tears.)*

The Death of Karna

DURTA: May I also present my humble greetings, princely Brother..(*Makes the sembah.*)

KARNA: Yes, Durta. Thank you.

DJAJARASA: Many thousand welcomes, Brother. (*Makes the sembah.*)

KARNA: Thank you, Brother.

ADIMENGGALA: Ah, my Lord. Excellency. I welcome you home with all my heart. (*Makes a deep sembah.*)

KARNA: Uncle Adimenggala, I hope you are well. My blessing, old Friend.

ADIMENGGALA: Thank you, Master. May it increase the well-being of this wrinkled servant and his family.

KARNA (*touching* SURTIKANTI's *shoulder lightly*): My dearest, my worshiped beloved. Pale and melancholy is your face, and how thin you appear. Tell me, what is the matter? Are there difficulties in the palace?

SURTIKANTI (*overwhelmed he does not know that he is the cause of her grief*): Oh, my Prince! Do you not know? My Beloved, is it possible you cannot tell . . .? (SURTIKANTI *falls at his feet weeping.*)

SONG (*The dalang sings the pathetic Sendon Tlutur*):
> My Lord, revered Prince,
>> Pity me
>> My tortured heart,
> Extend your strong and loving hands,
>> Save me from my well of sorrow
>> Oooooo . . .

KARNA (*taking her by the shoulders, raises her to her feet*): My beloved jewel, stop your weeping. Tell me the reason for your sorrow. Am I lacking in devotion, my Love? Tell me frankly. How am I to console you?

SURTIKANTI: My revered Prince, nothing causes sadness but my concern for your well-being. Many were the nights I was tormented by evil omens appearing in my dreams.

KARNA: Dreams are but the flowers of sleep, my Love.

SURTIKANTI: Yet they appear before me with the same clarity as visions of my waking hours. In them I see you, my Prince, with our fallen sons, caught on a vessel in the turbulent seas. Struck by giant waves your vessel sinks and I am unable to help. Again and again this dream affrights your wife awake.

My heart is filled with terror by this omen, my Lord, lest I lose you as well as my sons, oh, my beloved Prince!

SONG (*The dalang sings Ada-ada Mataraman Djugag to steady tapping*):

> The Prince's heart is sundered
>> Struck by grief,
> Knowing of
>> His consort's fear
>> He speaks with words of love
> Oooooo . . .

tjarijos
NARRATION: Upon hearing his wife's story, Prince Karna's mind fills with memories of his just slain sons and for a moment he cannot speak. When he does his voice is soft, to allay the fears of his gentle wife.

KARNA: My Dearest, my jewel, I beg you not to drown in sorrow. Our sons have fallen as honored warriors in pursuit of their duties, and Heaven is their reward. The living all must die. Yet death is but a transition in life as the spirit contained in the body lives forever. It is by performing our duty well that the spirit reaches perfection. Thus, it is out of place to feel sorrow for those who have died well. Pray instead for the spiritual perfection of their departed souls, unseemly grief will only hamper their spiritual journey. (*Touching her gently.*) My dearest Consort, as the wife of a Prince you should be an example to other women. I pray you, have peace of mind.

SURTIKANTI: Oh, my Lord, true are your words. Allow me then to share your hardship in the coming days. Do not be angry with me, I pray, but allow me to follow you into battle that I may tend you there. (*She kneels before him.*)

*Fig. 111
Karna and
Surtikanti*

The Death of Karna

SONG *(The dalang sings Ada-ada Mataraman Djugag to steady tapping):*

> The Prince's heart is sundered
> > Oooooo . . . oooooo
>
> He speaks with tender
> > Words of love
> > Ooooo

KARNA *(tenderly holding her):* Great is your love, my Dear! But love has its place and its time. I am the commander of an army and it is not fit that you should join me in the field. I too must set an example, to the troops I command. Softness on the battle-field would be unseemly. Do not fill your heart with fear and doubt, submit yourself instead to the will of the Supreme Deity.

SURTIKANTI: I shall obey, my Lord, with heavy heart. No longer can I bear this endless waiting to know of your safety after battle. Send me word, my Lord, of your welfare, that I may sleep through the long night.

KARNA: I shall do so, my beloved, at every opportunity.

SURTIKANTI: Long and far have you traveled, Dearest, I invite you now to rest.

KARNA: Uncle, Brothers, alert all Awangga troops. Then wait in the outer audience hall. We march to meet Ardjuna and the Pandawa forces today.

DURTA: Yes, my Brother. All will be ready. *(Makes the sembah.)*

KARNA: My Beloved. *(KARNA takes SURTIKANTI's hand.)*

(The dalang raps five times; the gamelan plays Ajak-ajakan Nem. KARNA and SURTIKANTI turn and move off right.

Fig. 112
Maidservants,
Surtikanti,
Karna, Durta,
Djajarasa, and
Adimenggala

The others make the sembah in the direction of the departed KARNA
and cross off left. The KAJON *is placed right of center, representing
the inner quarters of the Palace of Awangga; the music stops.)*

SONG *(The dalang sings Patet Nem Djugag):*

> Nature's fragrance
> > Scents the breezes,
> Filling lovers' hearts
> > Oooooo . . .
> All worry ceases.

tjarijos pagedongan NARRATION: The Prince and his lovely consort retire to their
private chamber. Gently he soothes her with affectionate words,
drowning her in a bliss of love. Not mentioned are their actions,
but the Queen's sorrow finally abates. As the moon rises Prince
Karna prepares to leave. He thoroughly purifies himself, dresses
all in white, and enters the temple to meditate. Seeing his
attire, Surtikanti is struck dumb with terror, for white is the
color of death. Quickly the Prince assures her his white uniform
merely symbolizes the purity of a commander's heart. Though
his words do not convince her, she keeps her silence so as not
to hinder the performance of his duty. So it is that Prince Karna
disappears from his trembling wife's gaze, and strides away
to the outer audience hall where his Awangga commanders
await him.

*(The dalang raps five times; the gamelan plays Ajak-ajakan Nem
as the* KAJON *is moved to the right of the screen.* KARNA *enters from
the right and takes his place. He motions* DURTA, DJAJARASA, *and*
ADIMENGGALA, *left, to enter. Making the sembah, they sit respectfully before him. Ajak-ajakan Nem stops when they are seated.)*

SONG *(The dalang sings Patet Nem):*

> Silent is all in the audience hall;
> > Even the wind ceases blowing
> > In reverence to sorrow.
> The Great War is still raging
> > Many killed and more will follow
> > Oooooo . . . where is the end of suffering?

KARNA: Uncle Menggala, are the troops assembled?

ADIMENGGALA: Yes, my Lord. They stand waiting for your
command. *(Makes the sembah.)*

KARNA: I am pleased, Uncle.

The Death of Karna

DURTA: Oh, princely Brother, pardon my presumption, but I request to be allowed to assist you in the coming battle. (*Makes the sembah.*)

DJAJARASA: Noble Brother, I too wish to help you lead the troops. (*Makes the sembah.*)

KARNA: Loyal Brothers, a Deputy Commander of the army has been appointed. But you, Durta, shall command our right flank and Djajarasa our left.

DURTA: I accept the honor, Brother! (*Deep sembah.*)

DJAJARASA: And I, my Prince, with excitement in my heart! (*Deep sembah.*)

SONG (*The dalang sings Patet Nem*):
> Silent is the Prince in the audience hall,
>> Doubts trouble his spirit
>> Oooooo . . .
> In the Great War now raging
>> He has a duty
>> To kill his brother
>> Oooooo . . . where is the end of suffering?

NARRATION: Having issued the order, Prince Karna pauses. The enemy troops are commanded by Ardjuna, his half-brother. Still fresh in his mind are the pleas of his and Ardjuna's mother, Kunti, to support the Pandawas and not to fight his own kin. He thinks, too, of the loving aid received from Ardjuna in the past. Doubt clouds his face and this is noticed by his attentive old Minister.

tjarijos

ADIMENGGALA (*making the sembah*): Forgive me, oh my Lord, but are you not troubled? Tell me, I beg, the cause of your concern.

KARNA (*turns to him*): Ah, you are wise to notice, old Uncle. It is just this: in the morning I meet Ardjuna in personal combat. The pleas of my mother still ring in my ears not to shed my brother's blood. Yet, as a warrior I am bound to a warrior's oath to serve the King of Astina. I do not know what I should do.

ADIMENGGALA (*making the sembah*): My Lord, you need not be concerned. I suggest, my Prince, that any Awangga noble will gladly kill Prince Ardjuna. This way you can remain loyal to the state and no fratricidal blood will touch your hands.

KARNA: That is an excellent suggestion, Uncle. Summon Suwega before me.

On Thrones of Gold

ADIMENGGALA: I will, my Lord.

SONG (ADIMENGGALA *exits to Ada-ada Mataraman Djugag melody sung to steady tapping):*

Oooooo . . .oooooo . . .

Ooooo . . . oooooo

(ADIMENGGALA *returns with* SUWEGA. *They make the sembah before* KARNA *and sit facing him.)*

KARNA: You are welcome in my presence, Suwega.

SUWEGA: Thank you, my Lord, allow me to present my reverent greetings. *(Makes the sembah.)*

KARNA: Yes, Suwega, I accept them with delight. Accept my blessing.

SUWEGA: May it be my talisman, my Lord.

KARNA: Were you not surprised to receive my summons, Suwega?

SUWEGA *(makes the sembah):* Yes, my Lord, I was startled—as if I were struck by lightning. But in your presence I find sudden peace of mind. Whatever danger there may be, I will gladly face it, for having enjoyed your generosity, my King, I will give even my life at your command. *(Makes the sembah.)*

KARNA: It pleases me to hear of your devotion, Suwega. Indeed, I have a task for you to accomplish. *(Holds out dagger.)* Take this dagger and with it kill Prince Ardjuna. Though I could myself, I have not the spirit to do so.

Fig. 113
Karna and
Suwega

The Death of Karna

SUWEGA *(taking dagger):* I shall do as you request, my Lord. At once with your permission.

KARNA: Go with my blessing, Suwega.

SONG *(The dalang sings Ada-ada Mataraman Djugag to steady tapping as* SUWEGA *makes a deep sembah and exits left):*
> Full of devotion
>> He takes his leave
>> Oooooo . . .
> Prepared to offer his life
>> To carry out
>> His Lord's order.

KARNA: Uncle Adimenggala, let us depart at once. Give the troops the command.

ADIMENGGALA: Yes, my Lord. *(Makes the sembah.)*

SONG *(The dalang sings Ada-ada Mataraman Djugag to steady tapping as* ADIMENGGALA *makes the sembah and backs off left):*
> Full of devotion
>> He takes his leave
>> Oooooo . . .
> Prepared to offer his life
>> To carry out
>> His Lord's order.

(Seven double spaced raps; Srepegan Nem is played as KARNA, DURTA, *and* DJAJARASA *exit to the left. When the* KAJON *is placed center the music stops.)*

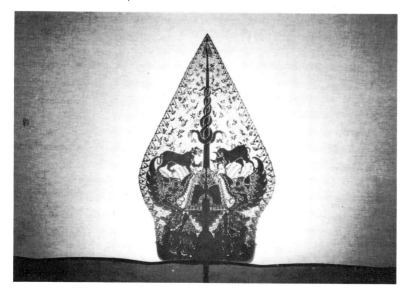

Fig. 114
Kajon

On Thrones of Gold

tjarijos NARRATION: Suwega hurries through the night in the direction
of the Pandawa camp, intent upon carrying out his master's
order. Meanwhile, Prince Karna leads the troops of Awangga
toward the battlefield. Once there, they pitch their tents, and
rest till the morning.

SONG (*The dalang sings Patet Lindur, marking the transition
between Part One of the play,* patet nem, *and Part Two,* patet
sanga):

Commanders and soldiers
   Take their rest
   Oooooo . . .
Weapons glint
   In the light of the moon.
To soldiers on guard
   Serene and beautiful
   Is the night
Oooooo . . .

PART TWO

SONG *(The dalang sings Patet Sanga Wantah):*
>   Late at night
>>   Stars light the sky
>>   Oooooo . . .
>   The scent of flowers
>>   Supports the seers' prayers
>>   Like the murmur of bees.

Scene 1

NARRATION *(accompanied by continuous, tense rapping):* One,
two, three, four, five, six, seven, eight, nine, ten! One: the land,
enclosed by water. Two: the rice, planted in the land. Three: the
mountain, the earth's axis. Four: the sea, encircling the land.
Five: the forest, leaves covering all. Six: the plain, where cattle
graze. Seven: the seers, blessed by the Gods. Eight: the sky,
over the earth. Nine: the Gods, model for man. Ten! The King!
Jewel among men! Nature's upheaval affects them all.

The world erupts! The earth shakes and volcanoes spew out
fire. The oceans' waters boil and tidal waves inundate the
land as if to drown the world. Crops cannot grow. Animals
starve. Wild beasts, reptiles, and poisonous insects invade
men's homes. On earth, men flee in panic seeking shelter.
Plague sweeps thousands away. They appeal to their seers but
their seers cannot meditate and are helpless. They turn to their
kings but their Kings have no power. The world is dark as dust-
clouded night. Lightning streaks and dragons roar. The violence
reaches as high as the chambers of the Gods themselves, breaking the horns of the sacred cow Andini, fluttering Anantaboga's
dragon-tail, and cracking the gates of Heaven askew. Boiling
mud and molten lava vomit from the cauldron of Hell. The
nymphs take flight, seeking the protection of the Supreme One.
In the midst of nature's upheaval there appear two funny
creatures, seemingly unconcerned, the followers of the Prince
Ardjuna. One is Gareng; one is Petruk. The two begin to
quarrel, thereby intensifying the natural chaos.

*(The dalang raps five times in quick succession; medium tempo
Sampak Sanga is played by the gamelan. To indicate the violence
of the scene, the dalang raps steadily against the side of the puppet
chest with his wooden tapper and beats time against hanging metal*

plates with his right foot. The KAJON *trembles furiously, symbolizing the quaking world; it flutters and twirls first to one side of the screen, then to the other. It comes to rest at the left.* PETRUK *dances across the screen, shouting "Ooy, ooy, ooy!" while pointing with his forehand.* GARENG *dances across the screen in the same direction. They re-enter and meet center; Sampak stops.)*

PETRUK (*poking and jabbing with a long, ungainly arm*): Well, look at this would you! I'm the god Endra just down from the heavens and what an odd creature I see. His arms are bent (*poking* GARENG's *twisted arm*), he's pigeon-toed (*pokes* GARENG's *broken foot*), he walks like he's on hot coals (*imitates* GARENG's *skittering walk*), and, heh-heh-heh, he's cross-eyed to boot. Hey, you! Creature! Did you cause this mess?

GARENG (*speaks laconically, in contrast to* PETRUK): My, my. I've got just one brother and he turns out to be mad.

*Fig. 115
Gareng and
Petruk*

PETRUK (*haughtily*): I am the god Endra!

GARENG: No, you're not. I know you. You're my kid-brother.

PETRUK: Oh, hell. You're no fun. Here I am, acting with great artistry and you ruin it.

GARENG: I thought you'd gone loony.

PETRUK: Come on, 'Reng, you be our master, Prince Ardjuna, and I'll be the god Endra come down to earth on disaster call.

GARENG: Well . . .

PETRUK: Let's go.

The Death of Karna

GARENG: Well . . .

PETRUK: You're getting the good part, 'Reng.

GARENG: All right, 'Truk, if that's what you want.

PETRUK: Get ready. *(They turn their backs on each other, walk to the edges of the screen, turn back to face each other, and begin.)* Go. Greetings to you, handsome Noble.

GARENG *(doubling over with laughter):* Handsome Noble. Heh-heh. That's me.

PETRUK: Stop interrupting. *(They repeat routine of getting ready.)* Greetings, handsome Noble. Are you the one to cause this uproar on earth with your prayers?

GARENG: My name is Ardjuna, Your Majesty-Deity-Sire-Uncle-Brother-Cousin-King.

PETRUK: What is the favor you pray for, my Prince?

GARENG: I want, ah, I want . . . a plate of rice.

PETRUK: Cut! Stupid! A noble Prince like Ardjuna doesn't spend a month in a hermitage just to pray for a plateful of rice.

GARENG: I would.

PETRUK: But you're not Ardjuna.

GARENG: I never said I was, 'Truk. You did. Heh-heh.

PETRUK *(For a moment he doesn't know whether to cuff GARENG or laugh. Then he laughs):* Ha-ha!

GARENG and PETRUK *(alternately):* Ha-ha! Heh-heh! Ho-ho!

GARENG: I can't play-act without a script 'Truk.

PETRUK: What do you want to play?

GARENG: An easy one. You be Fang, the ogre. I'll be Ardjuna. Let's do the scene where I kill you. I know that one by heart.

PETRUK: Good! *(Repeat routine of moving away and getting set.)* Ready? Here I come. Fang, stalking through the forest.˙ *(They move toward each other.)* Hi-hi-hi! Hey there, handsome Prince! What's your name? Where are you from? Where do you think you're going? Heh? *(Jumping up and down.)* Tell me, tell me, tell me!

GARENG: Ah. I see an ogre before me. Hey, Ogre, what do other fools call you?

PETRUK: Fools? Ohhhh! Brazen, brazen, brazen! Answer *my* question first.

GARENG: It is common to exchange questions on the battlefield. Where is the hut you call your home?

PETRUK: How dare you call my home a hut!

GARENG: Nobles have their palaces and ogres have their huts.

PETRUK: I may be an ogre but I'm a high-ranking one.

GARENG: What do I care for that? You are an ogre and you are dirt in my eyes.

PETRUK (*hopping about in anger*): Oh, oh, oh! Nasty, nasty! You want the last word, eh? All right, I'll tell you who I am. I am the Super-Giant, Tjakil, an officer of the King of the Ogres!

GARENG: And I am the royal Prince Ardjuna.

PETRUK: Swell, now get out of here. Scat! Go! Shoo!

GARENG: You will be the one to move aside, Ogre.

PETRUK: Stubborn. Stubborn, stubborn, stubborn! Nasty. (*Pause.*) Aren't you scared of me?

GARENG: No.

PETRUK: Not even a tiny bit?

GARENG: A noble knows no fear.

PETRUK: I'm taller than you, Prince Ardjuna.

GARENG: I shall delight in reducing your size.

PETRUK: I have magic powers!

GARENG: So have I.

PETRUK: Brave are your words, Prince, now feel the power of my hands! (GARENG *slips under* PETRUK's *guard and pokes his brother in the stomach.* PETRUK *drops out of character.*) Ohh! Put 'em up 'Reng! (*He takes a boxing stance.*)

GARENG: Careful, younger Brother, I'll fold you in two!

PETRUK: I'll smash you, Pumpkin Nose!

GARENG: I'll bash you, Bean Pole!

(*Five quick raps; the gamelan plays* Sampak Sanga. *The two brothers fight, their actions punctuated by the metal plates.* GARENG *butts* PETRUK *in the stomach.* PETRUK *falls gasping for breath.* GARENG *bites his brother's toe and is kicked off. With his long arms,* PETRUK *pushes the flailing* GARENG *off the screen.* GARENG *returns with a rush and butts* PETRUK *up into the air.* PETRUK *bounces like a ball on* GARENG's *head, driving him into the ground until only the small tuft of hair on* GARENG's *head can be seen.*)

PETRUK (*looks off right*): Gaaaaareng! Where are you? (*Looks off left.*) Gaaareng! Where do you suppose the little shrimp went? (*Sees the tuft of hair sticking up.*) What are you doing down there? Stand up and fight like a dwarf.

The Death of Karna

(PETRUK *pulls* GARENG *out of the ground, then drops him in a heap.* GARENG *rushes at* PETRUK *knocking him over. He dances on* PETRUK'S *stomach, happily humming to himself. Suddenly they hear their father,* SEMAR, *approaching. They leap up, crash into each other trying to run off, and fall in a tangle. They dash off left.* SEMAR *enters. Sampak Sanga stops.*)

Fig. 116
Semar

SONG *(The dalang sings Patet Sanga Djugag):*
> Nature's turmoil quiets
>> Oooooo . . .
> In the east appears
>> An odd creature
>> In tears
> Oooooo . . .

NARRATION: As nature's turmoil subsides, a bright shaft of light pierces the sky in the east and, just as swiftly as it appears, it vanishes. In its place we see one of God's funnier creatures. Plump as a pumpkin he sits quietly like a mound of earth. He is called Clown Semar and people think of him as the father of the two quarreling brothers. One can hardly call him a man for his breasts are long, but one can't call him a woman for he is, in fact, a man. Though extremely ugly, he is in reality the ancient god Ismaja, protector of Java, descended to earth. He acts as servant to the Prince Ardjuna. But in truth he could rule the world if he so desired and the highest Gods could not prevent it. Just now Semar is in a fretful mood and he mumbles to himself . . .

tjarijos

On Thrones of Gold

SEMAR: Ahh! Of all the miracles! Where could my handsome sons have gone? I just heard their merry tumbling about but the minute the old man appears, there's a sudden silence. *(Calling them.)* Hi, Gareng! Hi, Petruk! Come to your old daddy! *(Seeing someone off left.)* You, Child. Have you seen my two darling sons?

CHILD *(off)*: I saw them, Father Semar. Just a minute ago. They were wearing beautiful clothes and they had an escort. *(Giggles.)*

SEMAR *(surprised)*: What beautiful clothes? What escort?

CHILD *(off)*: All the village elders carrying spears and swords were their escort and your handsome sons wore pretty iron bracelets fastened with a chain! *(Giggles.)*

SEMAR: Naughty Child! You make them sound like captured criminals. Stop teasing an old man. *(Gesturing.)* Off with you! Ahh! This shouting doesn't become my age. Hm, hm, hmmmmm. If I sing a song, they may show up. Let's see, what should I sing? They always liked Sendon Kagok Ketanon. Hem, hem. *(He finds his key.)*

> A newly married groom
> In bed with his bride,
> Desperately all a-fumble
> In a hurry to get a . . .

GARENG: Papaaaa! *(Rushing on from left.)*

SEMAR *(delighted his ruse worked)*: Ha-ha-ha!

GARENG: Really, Papa! Early in the morning here you are dancing around like a berserk turtle! Singing a song that makes me ashamed!

SEMAR: Why, Gareng, what's wrong with the song?

GARENG: Paw, you mean you don't know? What a crazy old man. Well, you see, there's this young fellow just married and, heh-heh, his pretty bride is in bed, waiting, but, ha-ha-ha-ha, he can't get his clothes, oho-ho-ho! He-he-he! Ha-ha-ha! Oh, Paw, that's in very bad taste.

SEMAR: You used to like that song, Gareng.

GARENG: Yes, but I never went to school so I understood it.

SEMAR: What a burden a father has. I sing without pay, an innocent little song, and when my son arrives all he can do is be angry and offensive. Where is Petruk?

GARENG: I don't know. We're not speaking.

The Death of Karna

SEMAR: You mustn't enjoy quarreling with your brother.

GARENG: He went too far this time, Paw. He embarrassed me.

SEMAR: Well, well. Tell me all about it.

GARENG: It was like this, Paw, we were fooling around . . .

SEMAR: Yes, I heard.

GARENG: play-acting, and then we got hungry so 'Truk said, "Let's eat, my treat." So we went to the square and had something.

SEMAR: That was nice of your brother.

GARENG: I haven't finished, Paw. You know 'Truk. He ate like a horse, drank like a fish. I didn't care because he was paying. I went to get cigarettes and when I came back he was gone. I didn't have enough with me to pay the bill so they took my sarong for security. I had to walk through the middle of town in my underpants. I was so embarrassed.

SEMAR: My, my, that is too bad.

GARENG: I'm never going to speak to him again.

SEMAR: Call your younger brother and we'll see what he has to say.

GARENG (mumbling): I'll never speak to him. (Calls off.) Hey, Schnozzle-nozzle!

PETRUK (off): Yes, Balloon Nose!

GARENG (turns back to SEMAR): Paw, do you hear that? He speaks disrespectfully to his elder brother. He knows I'm sensitive about my big nose and he's always rubbing it in.

SEMAR: Call him nicely. He'll answer in a like manner.

GARENG: I'll never . . .

SEMAR: It's for you, the elder brother, to forgive him.

GARENG: I'll . . .

SEMAR: Now, now, call him and don't quarrel.

GARENG (moves left and calls off): Attention, if you please, younger Brother. Our honored Father requests your shining presence.

PETRUK (off): Oh, attention, esteemed elder Brother. I speed to obey your reverend Father's command. I come! (PETRUK enters. The two brothers bow elaborately to each other. PETRUK whacks his brother on the head; GARENG turns his back and pokes PETRUK in the stomach.)

On Thrones of Gold

SEMAR: Ah, my charming Son. Gareng tells me you tricked him.

Fig. 117
Semar, Gareng,
and Petruk

PETRUK: Tattle-tale. *(Whacks GARENG again.)* Papa, it was like this. I drank too much and had to go. There wasn't a men's room on the square so I went down to the river. When I got back Gareng had gone. It seems he forgot his sarong. Heh-heh!

GARENG: It was a dirty trick.

PETRUK: Anyhow, I got it out of hock for you.

GARENG: Where . . . ?

PETRUK: I took it home.

SEMAR: Then it's all settled. You know our Pandawa masters are waging a war and we shouldn't be here absorbed in mirth. Our master, Ardjuna, needs our help, especially now that his favorite son, Abimanju, has been killed as well as his beloved son Irawan. I want to go immediately to his camp at Glagah-tinulu. Our mistresses need our help. Come along now.

GARENG: Yes, Paw.

PETRUK: Ok, Papa. Let's go.

(Gamelan plays modern melody "My Beloved Java" as SEMAR, followed by GARENG and PETRUK, dance off right. The KAJON is placed center, inclined to the right; the music stops.)

SONG *(The dalang sings Patet Sanga Djugag):*
On their way to their master

The Death of Karna

Oooooo . . .
Powerful yet humble,
 They can
  Avoid disaster
Oooooo . . .

NARRATION: And so the three odd but faithful companions to   **tjarijos**
the Pandawas journey to the battlecamp Glagahtinulu that
they may be of service to Ardjuna's two favorite wives, the
Princesses Sumbadra and Srikandi.

Scene 2   **djedjer putri**

(Three raps; the gamelan plays Lara-lara. The KAJON *is lowered
and moved to the right.* SUMBADRA *and* SRIKANDI *enter from the
right.* MAIDSERVANTS *follow and sit behind them. Minister*
DRESTAKETU *enters from the left, makes the sembah, and kneels
before them.* SEMAR, GARENG, *and* PETRUK *come in from the left,
make the sembah, and take places behind* DRESTAKETU. *Three raps;
the music softens.)*

NARRATION *(intoned to pitch and rhythm of Lara-lara):* Our story   **djanturan**
now moves to the quarters of Prince Ardjuna, where matchless
Princess Sumbadra and Princess Srikandi sit in audience. The
lovely and delicate Sumbadra inspires peace of mind. Graceful
is her every movement and perfect her appearance. Her waist
is tiny, her finely shaped breasts look like polished marble.
Viewed from afar she appears like a nymph among men.
Words alone cannot describe the fragile beauty of Prince
Ardjuna's elder wife. Behind her sits her husband's second
wife, the Princess Srikandi. A skilled archer, she is renowned
as a warrior few men can defeat. Her face radiates intelligence
and resolve. Her movements are brisk, yet not at all mannish.
Such is her courage that, in his absence, Prince Ardjuna en-
trusts to her the safety of his house. Seated before the Princesses
is Chief Minister Drestaketu of Tjempala, an allied kingdom. A
powerful warrior and trusted friend of the Pandawas is he.
Behind him sit the three loyal servants Semar, Gareng, and
Petruk. Maidservants attend. All is quiet, for their ladies are
steeped in sorrow. Sumbadra mourns for her only son,
Abimanju, killed on the fourth day of the Great War. Sharing
her grief, Srikandi does all she can to console her, offering
strength and understanding.

On Thrones of Gold

(Three raps; Lara-lara plays at normal volume until it ends.)

SONG *(The dalang sings Patet Sanga Ngelik):*
> She turns her soul's
>> Eyes to heaven.
>
> Oh divine God
>> Reveal thy wisdom
>> Oooooo . . .
>
> What is the purpose of life,
>> Its worth,
>> The meaning of our strife
>> Oooooo . . .

SRIKANDI: Elder Sister, do not entertain these sad thoughts.

DRESTAKETU: Yes, Milady, excuse my suggestion but I must agree. We wait for Milady's commands. *(Makes the sembah.)*

SUMBADRA: Thank you, you are right I know. Please forgive the lack of courtesy I show you in my silence. Uncle, I trust you are well.

DRESTAKETU: Yes, Milady, through your kindness I am well. I offer my humble prayers for your well-being. *(Makes the sembah.)*

SUMBADRA: I accept them with gratitude, Uncle. Semar, Gareng, Petruk, you are welcome.

SEMAR: Thank you, Milady. *(Makes the sembah.)*

GARENG: Thank you, thank you, Milady. *(Makes the sembah.)*

PETRUK: Thank you, thank you, thank you, Milady. *(Makes the sembah.)*

SUMBADRA: Uncle, what news of the war do you bring? Speak frankly, for I wish to know the truth whatever it is.

DRESTAKETU: I shall, Milady. *(Makes the sembah.)* Prince Bima has slain Durjudana's brother Dursasana and, just yesterday, Durgandasena.

SUMBADRA: Uncle! Are there casualties on our side?

DRESTAKETU: Milady, I beg your forgiveness for bearing this unhappy news. *(Makes the sembah.)*

SUMBADRA: Tell me, Uncle.

DRESTAKETU: Your nephew, Prince Gatutkatja, has been killed by Prince Karna. And oh, Milady, when Princess Arimbi heard of her son's death, she mounted the pyre in self-sacrifice. *(Makes the sembah.)*

The Death of Karna

SONG *(The dalang sings Sendon Tlutur as the princesses touch their breasts in grief):*
>Oh God look
>>And have pity
>>Oooooo . . .
>A thousand sorrows
>>Upon me,
>To end this life
>>Will set my soul
>>At peace
>Oooooo . . .

SUMBADRA: Oh, Gods, will this war not end! Will our tears never dry?

SRIKANDI: What a loss! What grief to the Pandawas!

DRESTAKETU: Miladies, please. Calm yourselves. The Gods have decreed it. The young have died but their sacrifices assure the Pandawas' future. *(Makes the sembah.)*

SONG *(The dalang sings Patet Sanga Djugag):*
>Like the sun after rain
>>Oooooo . . .
>Their tears are dried
>>And anguish disappears
>>Oooooo . . .

NARRATION: Suddenly, unannounced, Ardjuna's cousin, Sandjaja, arrives breathless from the enemy camp. tjarijos

(Five spaced raps; the gamelan plays Ajak-ajakan Sanga. The slight-figured, modest SANDJAJA *enters from the left, sits respectfully, and makes the sembah. The music stops.)*

Fig. 118
Maidservants,
Srikandi,
Sumbadra,
Sandjaja,
Drestaketu,
Gareng, Semar,
and Petruk

On Thrones of Gold

SUMBADRA: Cousin Sandjaja! You are unexpected, but you are welcome here.

SRIKANDI *(sharply)*: Indeed, Cousin, welcome!

SANDJAJA: Oh, my Cousins, your greetings warm me. Accept my unworthy thanks. *(Makes the sembah.)*

SUMBADRA: Tell me, Cousin, why do you do us the honor of this unusual visit? Please, rest comfortably and inform us.

SANDJAJA: Noble Princess, I come, of course, to offer you my heartfelt respects. But, more than that, I come to beg that I may be allowed to serve you in the Great War. *(Makes deep sembah.)*

SUMBADRA: Why, Sandjaja! All your life you have lived among the Kurawas. Why this sudden decision to leave them?

SANDJAJA: Oh, honored Sister, it is not that I wish to leave them, but that I wish to be with you. I see that virtue and justice are at stake in this war. In this final test I find my heart lies with the Pandawas! *(Makes deep sembah.)*

SONG *(The dalang sings Ada-ada Gregetsaut Sanga to steady tapping)*:
>Oooooo
>The alert Princess
>   Is stirred
>   To suspicion
>Oooooo . . .

SRIKANDI *(speaks sharply, moving forward to confront SANDJAJA)*: Cousin Sandjaja, do you forget you are a warrior? And that a warrior's duty lies in service to the King who protects him? You have enjoyed the favor and hospitality of the Kurawas at Astina all your life. Be loyal to them. We do not need your loyalty now. *(She pauses.)* Or do you come with some other purpose in mind?

SANDJAJA *(making the sembah)*: My noble Sister Srikandi, you are wrong to suggest it!

SRIKANDI: You turn against your lifelong protectors, Cousin. Why should we trust you more than they?

SANDJAJA: I turn toward virtue and honor. Is that wrong? All who are not blind now know they rest with the Pandawas. I swear I wish to fight on the Pandawa side in this war! *(Makes deep sembah.)*

SRIKANDI: Dear Cousin, what you say may be true. But how strong is your resolve? Stronger I hope than your vow to King

The Death of Karna

Durjudana. I should like to see you prove what you so easily say.

SANDJAJA: Princess Srikandi, I am determined. To aid the Pandawas I am prepared to face any test.

SRIKANDI: Your words reassure me, Cousin. Seek out Prince Karna then and slay him.

SANDJAJA *(slight pause):* My Princess, I will do as you say. Permit me to leave for the battlefield at once.

SRIKANDI: You go with my blessing, Cousin.

SUMBADRA: Cousin. *(Instinctively she reaches to comfort him, then withdraws her hand.)* Take care. My prayers go with you.

SONG *(The dalang sings Patet Sanga Djugag as* SANDJAJA *makes a respectful sembah, rises, and quickly goes from the hall):*
> His will is steadfast
>> To defend
> The virtuous
> In this Great War
>> Oooooo . . .

SUMBADRA *(moves left to watch* SANDJAJA *depart, then speaks to her minister):* Uncle, follow our cousin. Protect him if you can. I am afraid for him.

DRESTAKETU: Yes, Milady.

SONG *(*DRESTAKETU *makes the sembah and exits left as the dalang sings Patet Sanga Djugag):*
> His will is steadfast
>> Oooooo . . . oooooo
> In this Great War
>> Oooooo . . . oooooo

SUMBADRA *(facing* SRIKANDI*):* Honest Sister, I think we have done a great wrong to our guileless cousin. You doubted his loyalty and I allowed him to leave.

SRIKANDI *(chastened):* Standing here watching him go I feel you are right, noble Sister. In the past he has shown his love for the Pandawas. Wartime makes us suspicious of all.

SUMBADRA: Sandjaja is no match for Prince Karna. We have sent him to his death, I fear.

SRIKANDI *(animated again):* Oh, Sister, you are right. Allow me to undo this wrong. I shall follow Sandjaja and ask him to return.

SUMBADRA: If that is your wish. You have my blessing, Sister

Srikandi. Semar, Gareng, Petruk. Wait upon Princess Srikandi.
See that no harm comes to her.

SEMAR: Yes, Milady. *(Makes the sembah.)*

GARENG: Yes, Milady. *(Makes the sembah.)*

PETRUK: To the battlefield? Yes, Milady. *(Makes the sembah.)*

*(Five spaced raps signal the gamelan to play Ajak-ajakan Sanga.
When the music starts, SRIKANDI quickly goes off left followed by
the three servants. The two MAIDSERVANTS come in front of their
mistress, honor her with the sembah, and wait to attend her.
SUMBADRA gracefully rises and crosses off right with the MAID-
SERVANTS following her. The KAJON is placed center, inclined to
the right; the music stops.)*

SONG *(The dalang sings Ada-ada Gregetsaut Sanga to steady tapping):*

> All play their parts
> With devotion
> Oooooo . . . oooooo

adegan perang
sampak sanga

tjarijos Scene 3

NARRATION: Many are the travelers in our story whose paths
are crossed by destiny. As Srikandi and the three faithful servants begin their journey, Prince Sandjaja already has gone far,
rushing to confront his former ally and friend, Prince Karna.
Drestaketu chooses a shortcut through the Forest of Surengbaja
in the hope of overtaking Sandjaja.

Meanwhile, Suwega, on his mission to assassinate Ardjuna,
has entered the same forest. And so Drestaketu and Suwega
hurry along, unaware that their paths must inevitably meet,
soon and without warning.

*(Five quick raps; the gamelan plays Sampak Sanga. The KAJON
moves from the center of the screen to the far right. SUWEGA crosses
the screen from the left and moves on. From the right, DRESTAKETU
crosses in the opposite direction. They reappear and meet center,
stop, and survey one another intently. Music stops.)*

SONG *(The dalang sings Ada-ada Gregetsaut Sanga to steady
tapping):*

> The alert soldier's mind
> Is sharpened with suspicion,
> The body strains
> To fulfill its mission.

The Death of Karna

SUWEGA: What's this? A Pandawa officer in my path?

DRESTAKETU: And you're from Astina? You're on Pandawa territory, Fellow! What do you want? Who are you?

SUWEGA: Scum! Who are you to put questions to me?

DRESTAKETU: You are facing Drestaketu, guardian of Prince Ardjuna's estates! Announce yourself.

SUWEGA: I am Suwega, officer of Prince Karna! It is your master I am looking for! Where is he?

DRESTAKETU: Ha! I'll take you to him. Trussed like a goose. How can a piece of trash like you think of meeting a royal Prince? You're a fool or a madman.

SUWEGA: Then die with knowledge, old Man: I am sent to kill your precious Prince! Now take me to him or die.

DRESTAKETU: You'll never meet my Master. I'll crush you to dust first.

(Five quick raps; the gamelan plays Sampak Sanga fast and loud, the metal plates crashing in time to the battle's action. DRESTAKETU *and* SUWEGA *leap at each other, grappling for a hold. They strike, parry, kick, and evade. First one is thrown, then the other. They rise, draw daggers, and continue. At the same instant each leaps at the other with dagger drawn.*

Fig. 119
Drestaketu
and Suwega

They seem to embrace. They stand trembling, then motionless, in the center of the screen. Music stops.)

tjarijos   NARRATION: Fierce is the battle between Drestaketu and Suwega. Trees fall in the wake of their struggle. Dust billows and clouds the arena. They are evenly matched and the conflict rages first one way then the other. Then, as if guided by the same impulse, each plunges his dagger into his opponent. They cling to each other in a grip of death as blood mingles with blood and flows to the earth.

(GARENG *and* PETRUK *enter.)*

GARENG *(looking warily from one side):* Heh, 'Truk. Look. What do you think? Two brothers who haven't seen each other for years? That's a touching scene.

PETRUK *(looking on from the other side):* Stupid. Put on your glasses. Look at their torn clothes and the mess around here. Obviously it's a debtor and a creditor settling accounts.

SEMAR *(entering):* Heh! What in creation are you two doing? Come away from that wrestling match. We've got to help our Lady.

PETRUK: Paw, if there was a contest for the greatest fool in the world you'd win hands down. They're fighting over there. *(Ad-libbing.)* We're, ah, going to stop it.

SEMAR: Then do it. Don't just stand here and gawk at them. Go on.

GARENG: You pull from that side, 'Truk. I'll pull from here.

SONG (GARENG *and* PETRUK *separate the corpses which fall to the ground as the dalang sings Ada-ada Gregetsaut Sanga):*

> Like a bolt of lightning
> > Gorged with horror
> > Oooooo . . .
> Their hearts
> > Skip a beat
> > In terror
> Oooooo . . .

PETRUK: Gagh! Look at the blood. They're dead!

GARENG: Beneath the dirt and blood, it's . . . it's Master Drestaketu!

SEMAR: Oh, oh, Master! Look, his enemy was an Awangga officer. I must tell our Princess. *(Turns and calls off right.)* Milady! Milady!

The Death of Karna

SONG (SEMAR *rushes off right to find* SRIKANDI *as the dalang sings Ada-ada Gregetsaut Sanga to steady tapping):*
> Like a bolt of lightning
>> Oooooo . . .
> Their hearts
>> Skip a beat
>> In terror
> Oooooo . . .

SRIKANDI *(moves on quickly from the right):* What's that, Father Semar? Drestaketu has been killed and by an Awangga officer? *(Sees the bodies.* SEMAR *enters and sits behind her, right.* PETRUK *and* GARENG *sit left, facing her.)* It is my fault that he has been killed. He would not lie here now, had I not been so rashly suspicious of sandjaja.

SEMAR: Milady, please. Don't blame yourself. What has happened is the will of the Gods.

SRIKANDI *(stands silent a moment):* Gareng, Petruk: care for their bodies. Father Semar, let us hurry on ahead. I must go myself to the battlefield. It is for me to save Sandjaja now.

(Seven double raps; the gamelan plays Srepegan Sanga as SRIKANDI *and* SEMAR *exit left.* GARENG *and* PETRUK *carry off the bodies of* SUWEGA *and* DRESTAKETU. *The* KAJON *flutters across the screen and back again.* KARNA *crosses from the left.* SANDJAJA *crosses from the right. They enter together and face one another center. Music stops.)*

SONG *(The dalang sings Ada-ada Gregetsaut Sanga to steady tapping):*
> The warrior's soul
>> Steadfast in devotion,
> Eager to play its role
>> To fulfill its mission.

SANDJAJA *(sharply):* Prince Karna!

KARNA *(surprised):* Why, Cousin Sandjaja. It is a surprise to see you here. My blessings on you, Brother. I hope you are well.

SANDJAJA: I am.

KARNA: That is a cold greeting, Brother. And you come from the direction of the Pandawa camp. Is something wrong, Cousin Sandjaja?

SANDJAJA *(straining to maintain his composure):* What was wrong has been righted, Prince Karna! I have joined with my Pandawa cousins!

SONG (KARNA *stiffens with anger, his arm trembles, as the dalang sings Ada-ada Gregetsaut Sanga to steady tapping):*
>The Prince of Awangga's body
>>Turns to fire,
>>Rage floods his heart,
>His eyes flash,
>>His voice is thunder
>>Oooooo . . .

KARNA: Does fear that your protector is about to lose his throne prompt your treachery, Cousin? Do you join what you now think will be the winning side? (SANDJAJA *is mortified with shame. He cannot speak.)* What kind of "noble" are you? What of your duty to your King?

SANDJAJA: Prince Karna! Do not speak to me of duty. I know where duty lies! More so than you, I fear.

KARNA (*his body trembles with indignation):* How dare you speak to me this way!

SANDJAJA: Should we be polite to one another, now, Cousin? We are enemies. You call yourself Prince, but what you fight for is your own good life! You ignore the just and war for the wicked. You slaughter your own kin. Tell me, princely Karna, is that your warrior's "duty"?

KARNA: You are a traitor, Cousin!

SANDJAJA: Stand, if you have the courage, and fight!

KARNA: With pleasure. I shall kill you with one blow.

SANDJAJA: Try then, my Prince.

(*Five quick raps; the gamelan plays fast and loud Sampak Sanga.* SANDJAJA *rushes at* KARNA *who barely evades his charge.* SANDJAJA *turns, strikes* KARNA, *and hurls him off left.* SANDJAJA *pursues. Music softens.)*

KARNA (*flies across screen, falls, and rises, very surprised):* You fight well, Sandjaja, but we are not finished yet! (*Draws dagger, calling off left.)* Open your eyes, Cousin, what do you see?

SANDJAJA (*off):* Your blood flowing, my Prince!

KARNA: Not mine, Cousin, but your blood will flow!

(*Sampak Sanga up full. The two fight with daggers. They thrust and parry.* SANDJAJA *fights with righteous fury and even* KARNA'S *great skill cannot cope with his foe's furious attack.* SANDJAJA *strikes the dagger from* KARNA'S *hand.* KARNA *withdraws left, pursued by* SANDJAJA. *Music softens.)*

The Death of Karna

KARNA *(backs on from right, panting with exertion and anger):* You fight like one possessed, Sandjaja. *(Calling off right.)* Do not flee the field, Cousin!

SANDJAJA *(off):* It is not I who have left the field of battle, Prince Karna!

KARNA *taking out arrow):* Prepare for your death!

(Sampak Sanga plays loudly. KARNA *looses his arrow, pursuing it off right. The arrow flies across the screen twice.* SANDJAJA *enters. The arrow strikes* SANDJAJA, *piercing his breast. He trembles and falls dead.* KARNA *enters, looks down at* SANDJAJA'S *body, and exits left. Music ends.)*

SONG *(The dalang sings Sendon Tlutur as* SRIKANDI *and the three servants enter and discover* SANDJAJA'S *body):*

>Oh God look
>   And have pity.
>A thousand sorrows
>   Oooooo . . .
>To end this life
>   Will set my soul
>   At peace
>Oooooo . . .

Fig. 120
Petruk, Gareng,
Sandjaja,
Srikandi, and
Semar

SRIKANDI *(gently touching* SANDJAJA'S *body):* We come too late, dear Cousin Sandjaja. How cruel was my test of your loyalty. *(The three servants wail loudly as, one after the other, they embrace* SANDJAJA.)

SEMAR: Boo, hoo! Master Sandjaja, why did this have to happen?

GARENG: Boo, hoo! My heart is torn to pieces, 'Truk.

PETRUK: Boo, hoo! 'Reng, my eyes will never dry!

SRIKANDI: Father Semar, Gareng, Petruk, please. Go now, care for his remains.

SEMAR: Yes, Milady. (*Makes the sembah and exits right.*)

SONG (*The dalang sings Ada-ada Gregetsaut Tlutur. In time to its sweet-sad music,* GARENG *and* PETRUK *lift* SANDJAJA *tenderly in their arms. They are genuinely affected by his pitiful death. The pathetic little funeral procession moves slowly out of sight*):

> How pitiful
>> His blood-smeared body,
>
> Bright life
>> Has become cloudy
>> Oooooo . . .
>
> Nature weeps a drizzling rain
>> Like Srikandi's tears
>> For her cousin
>> Oooooo . . .

SRIKANDI (*moves center and calls off left*): Prince Karna!

KARNA (*off*): Who calls?

SRIKANDI: Your heart is stone! I have come to avenge Sandjaja's death!

KARNA (*off*): Is it you Princess Srikandi? Go home, Sister, where you belong.

SRIKANDI: You will fight me, Prince!

(*Five quick raps; the gamelan plays Sampak Sanga.* SRIKANDI *rushes off after* KARNA. KARNA *backs on from the right pursued by a furiously attacking* SRIKANDI. *He wards off her blows without striking back. Then he withdraws to the left. She follows. Music softens.*)

KARNA (*backing on from right*): This is embarrassing. I cannot strike a Princess. But to flee goes against the grain. Hmm. (*He withdraws to the left.*)

SRIKANDI (*rushing on from the right*): Are you a coward, Brother? Do you fear me? stand and fight!

KARNA (*off*): Be reasonable, sweet Sister. You know my rank and fame. I would disgrace myself striking a woman.

SRIKANDI: You flee like a woman! That makes us equals! Defend yourself!

The Death of Karna

(Music plays loudly. SRIKANDI *rushes off left.* KARNA *backs on from the right followed immediately by* SRIKANDI. *She leaps to attack. He tries to avoid her as before, but she continues to attack so violently he soon begins to loose patience. He tries to hold her off. Finally, provoked beyond endurance, he seizes her and throws her off right. Music softens.)*

KARNA: What an exasperating woman. It's no credit to me to beat her but how much worse for her to beat me. *(He backs off left.)*

SRIKANDI *(Tumbles on from the left, alone on the screen. She falls to the ground. Picking herself up, she takes out an arrow):* Look, Brother Karna, what do you see?

KARNA *(off):* Put it down, Srikandi. Do you want to hurt yourself?

SRIKANDI: We will see whom it hurts! Prepare to receive my awful vengeance!

KARNA *(off):* Women should not play with dangerous toys. Go home, Srikandi.

(Music plays loudly. SRIKANDI *is enraged by* KARNA'S *refusal to take her seriously. She takes aim and looses her arrow, following in pursuit. The arrow is seen flying across the screen twice.* KARNA *appears from the right and avoids the arrow which sails on past him.* SANGKUNI *enters quietly from the left,* KARNA *does not notice him. Music stops.)*

KARNA *(for the first time during the fight he is angry):* She's a crazy woman! She might have killed me!

SANGKUNI *(touching* KARNA'S *waist):* Oh my Prince, perhaps you should rest a bit.

KARNA *(turns and sees* SANGKUNI*):* Oh, it's you, Uncle. Why do you follow me here with your mirthful face? This is serious.

SANGKUNI: Indeed, my Prince, you seem to be having, er, difficulties.

KARNA: It's exasperating, Uncle. I don't want to fight her, but she almost struck me with that arrow! She's out of her senses.

SANGKUNI *(slyly):* Perhaps. Then again she may be purposely trying to humiliate you.

KARNA: Why, what do you mean, Uncle?

SANGKUNI: See for yourself in the mirror. Her arrow has shaved clean one side of your moustache. *(Smirking, he holds up a small hand-mirror.)*

Fig. 121
Karna, mirror,
and Sangkuni

SONG *(The dalang sings Ada-ada Gregetsaut Sanga to steady tapping):*

> Oooooo . . . his body
>> Turns to fire,
>> Rage floods his heart,
> His eyes flash,
>> His voice is thunder
>> Oooooo . . .

tjarijos NARRATION: Prince Karna's pride is stung. All thoughts of Srikandi's femininity leave his mind. Furious, he determines to return the humiliation.

KARNA (SANGKUNI *exits, saluting.* KARNA *calls off right):* Srikandi! A debt of shame is paid with shame! I shall mortify your pride as you have mine!

(Five raps; the gamelan plays Sampak Sanga. KARNA *takes an arrow, aims, and looses it. He follows in pursuit. The arrow is seen flying twice across the screen.* SRIKANDI *appears from the right and the arrow grazes her; she falls to her knees, hands to her breasts. Music stops.)*

SONG *(The dalang sings Sendon Tlutur):*

> Oh God, look
>> And have pity
>> On my shame,
> Humiliation

The Death of Karna

More terrible
Than death to me
Oooooo . . . have pity!

*Fig. 122
Karna's arrow
and Srikandi*

NARRATION: Prince Karna's arrow unerringly finds its mark. It pierces Srikandi's dress, and the garment falls about her feet. In terrible humiliation, the Princess covers her breasts with both hands. Weeping, she sinks to her knees.   *tjarijos*

SRIKANDI: Oh, shame! Shame! Noble Ardjuna, may you know how Karna has dishonored me!

(Five spaced raps; the gamelan plays Ajak-ajakan Sanga. SRIKANDI rises, turns, and exits right. The KAJON is placed center, inclined to the right; the music ends.)

NARRATION: Weeping pitifully and holding her skirt to cover her naked breasts, Srikandi hurries from the scene of her humiliation. Her hair tumbles over her shoulders and streams out behind her as she hastens to the Pandawa camp, intent upon telling of the dishonor Karna has heaped upon her. Meanwhile, at the Pandawa camp the five Brothers hold a council of war with their allies, King Kresna and King Matswapati.   *tjarijos*

Scene 4   **djedjer Pandawa**

(Three raps; the gamelan plays Laler Mengeng. The KAJON is taken from the center and placed to the right. From opposite sides of the screen enter MATSWAPATI and KRESNA. KRESNA bows to

MATSWAPATI, *his elder, and both take their seats. The Pandawas—*
JUDISTIRA, BIMA, ARDJUNA, NAKULA, *and* SADEWA—*enter and*
honor the kings. Three raps; the music softens.)

Fig. 123
Nakula, Judistira,
Sadewa,
Matswapati,
Ardjuna, Kresna,
and Bima

djanturan NARRATION *(intoned, following pitch and rhythm of Laler*
Mengeng): Presiding over the council of the Pandawas is the
great King Matswapati of Wirata, accorded this honor because
he is the eldest, a divine King, just and wise, and the Pandawas'
strongest ally. His three sons have died in the Great War in
aid of the Pandawas. His daughter, Utari, is married to
Ardjuna's son, Abimanju. Seated opposite him is the divine
King of Dwarawati, Kresna, incarnation of the god Wisnu. On
earth he is guide and counselor to the Pandawas. He knows
the future of the whole world. His advice is carefully followed.
Behind Matswapati stands the eldest of the Pandawa Brothers,
King Judistira. He is called: "Personification of Justice,"
"Paragon of Virtue," "Purest of the Pure—the One Whose
Blood Flows White." The second brother is Prince Bima,
"Defender of the Pandawas," and "Pillar of the State." The
third is Ardjuna, whose handsomeness is unparalleled on earth.
He is invested with supernatural powers and can achieve the
impossible. Reserved of demeanor, his cool skill in battle gives
him the titles "Invincible Warrior," "Star Among the Excellent."
Adored by the nymphs and the Gods is the Prince Ardjuna.
The two remaining brothers are the twins, Nakula and Sadewa,
famous as warriors, friendly, and loyal.

The Death of Karna

Grief fills the air. Prince Ardjuna mourns his son, Abimanju, killed four days before. Two days after, Prince Bima's son, Gatutkatja, was slain as well. The others console the bereaved and remind them of immediate duties.

(A single rap; the music continues for one gong phrase, then ends.)

SONG *(The dalang sings Sendon Rentjasih):*

> The birds' sad chirruping
>> Mourns their sorrow,
> Even the breeze ceases
>> Whispering.
> Many are killed
>> And more will follow
> In the Great War
>> Now raging
> Oooooo . . . oooooo . . .
>> Awaiting the words
>> Of the King.

MATSWAPATI: My grandson, King Kresna, do you arrive well before me?

KRESNA: Yes, Grandsire, I arrive well. I extend my greetings, Majesty.

MATSWAPATI: I accept them with delight. Grandson Judistira, you are well I hope?

JUDISTIRA: Majesty, I am well. Allow this grandson to offer his reverent greetings, Grandsire. *(Makes the sembah honoring his elder relative.)*

MATSWAPATI: With delight I accept them. And you, Bima. Are you in good health, as usual?

BIMA: Ahhh, I am well! Greetings, Grandfather! *(Salutes strongly.)*

MATSWAPATI: Thank you, Bima. Grandson Ardjuna, I trust you are well.

ARDJUNA: Yes, Grandsire, thank you. I am blessed to be in your presence, Majesty. *(Makes the sembah.)*

MATSWAPATI: It fills my heart with joy to see you, Ardjuna. Grandsons Nakula and Sadewa, welcome.

NAKULA: Thank you, Majesty. *(Makes the sembah.)*

SADEWA: Our reverent greetings, Grandsire. *(Makes the sembah.)*

MATSWAPATI: You are all welcome. King Kresna, tell me the news of the Great War.

KRESNA: Majesty, certainly you are informed by the Gods of all that is destined. Allow me, nevertheless, to state that many Astina warriors have been slain. Yesterday Bima killed Durgandasena, the brother of King Durjudana.

MATSWAPATI: Thank you, Grandson. As regards our battle strategy in the future, what advice do you offer?

KRESNA: I have been informed, Your Majesty, that Prince Karna continues as Commander of the Astina army. What with the greater number of their forces, they are certain to use a "pincer" battle formation.

MATSWAPATI: What are your recommendations, my kingly Grandson?

KRESNA: Grandsire, I recommend our troops be formed in the "moon-and-sickle" battle array. The proper Commander for our army is your grandson, Ardjuna.

MATSWAPATI: Yes, I agree. My dear Grandson Ardjuna, you have heard the counsel of King Kresna, our divine mentor. Will you lead the army against Prince Karna and the Astina forces as he suggests? I urge you to do so with all possible zeal.

ARDJUNA: I accept my duties, kingly Grandsire. (*He makes a slow and spiritless sembah.*)

SONG (*The dalang sings Ada-ada Gregetsaut Tlutur to steady tapping*):

> Oooooo . . . remembering
>   His fallen son's body,
>   Pierced with thousands
>   Of arrows.
> Oooooo . . . pitying
>   Clouds darken
>   The sun
>   Oooooo . . .

tjarijos NARRATION: Prince Ardjuna's subdued reply causes first dismay, then sadness, for all know the Prince still grieves the death of this beloved son Abimanju. The tone of Ardjuna's response has reminded the court of the many injuries the war has inflicted upon the entire people. They are drawn to silent contemplation. Suddenly the quiet is broken by the unannounced arrival of the weeping Srikandi. They are astounded by her torn clothes and dirt-streaked face. She presents herself to the King sobbing all the while.

(*Five spaced raps; the gamelan plays Ajak-ajakan Sanga during*

The Death of Karna

her entrance. She sits before MATSWAPATI *and makes the sembah; the music stops.)*

MATSWAPATI: Princess Srikandi! Why are you in such a passionate state?

KRESNA: Sister Srikandi, what has happened? Tell us.

ARDJUNA *(roused by her anguish):* My Beloved, do not weep, but inform me of the cause of your tears so I may dispel them.

SRIKANDI *(gaining control of herself she makes the sembah and straightens up):* Oh, Majesty, Grandfather! So many things have happened! Sister Sumbadra and I were visited by Cousin Sandjaja, who had come from Astina. He expressed a desire to join our cause, Grandsire.

MATSWAPATI: Yes, Sandjaja has been well disposed toward us in the past. I am pleased he has decided to join us. *(She begins weeping again.)* Continue, my child. What happened then?

SRIKANDI: Oh, Your Majesty! It is difficult to tell you. I am filled with remorse. At the time I doubted his sincerity. I challenged him to prove himself by . . . by slaying Prince Karna. He left immediately for the battlefield. Sumbadra sent Drestaketu to help him. Then, I, too, realized how wrong I had been, and I went after Sandjaja as well. Semar, Gareng, and Petruk accompanied me. We had not gone far when we found Drestaketu, his blood still fresh upon the ground, killed by an officer of Awangga. I hurried to find Sandjaja, but too late. I shall never forgive myself. Karna had already slain our cousin. *(She weeps.)*

SONG *(The dalang sings Ada-ada Gregetsaut Sanga to tense tapping;* MATSWAPATI *strikes his chest in grief):*

    As if struck
      By lightning,
    Filled with
      Grief and anger
    Oooooo . . .

MATSWAPATI: May the gods be merciful. Sandjaja's is a pitiful fate.

SRIKANDI: Indeed, Majesty. But his death roused me and I challenged Prince Karna. He sent an arrow through my clothing, tearing the garment from my body. Karna laughed at me and left me alone, naked, in the midst of the battlefield.

SONG *(The dalang sings Ada-ada Gregetsaut Sanga as* ARDJUNA *moves in front of the king and makes a deep sembah):*

> As if struck
>   By lightning,
> Filled with
>   Grief and anger,
> Eager to join in battle.

ARDJUNA (*his voice is trembling*): Grandfather. This shall not go unpunished. Allow me to fight Prince Karna at once.

MATSWAPATI: I understand your fury, my Grandson. But first let us know the advice of King Kresna. It is not wise to act upon anger alone.

KRESNA: Your Majesty, I foresee no reason why Ardjuna should not fulfill his desire. I support his determination. Allow us to leave at once, Your Majesty.

MATSWAPATI: My blessings go with you, my Grandsons.

ARDJUNA: Thank you, Majesty. We shall succeed. (*Makes the sembah.*)

(*Five quick raps; the gamelan plays Sampak Sanga.* SRIKANDI, *then* ARDJUNA, *make the sembah and exit to the left.* KRESNA *and* BIMA *salute* MATSWAPATI *and exit.* JUDISTIRA, NAKULA, *and* SADEWA *come before the king, sembah, and wait.* MATSWAPATI *turns and goes off right, followed by the three. For a moment the screen is empty.*)

adegan perang
sampak sanga

Scene 5

(BIMA *strides from right to left across the screen.* DURTA *and* DJAJARASA *enter from left and challenge* BIMA *center. Music softens.*)

DURTA: Hah! It's Bima.

BIMA: Right, Durta. Stand aside or die.

DJAJARASA: Braggart! All you can do is talk. Your reputation is a myth.

BIMA: Ho! I can kill you both and not work up a sweat.

DURTA: You won't live long, Bima. I'll handle this trash myself, Djajarasa.

DJAJARASA: Fight well, Brother.

(*Loud Sampak Sanga.* DJAJARASA *leaves the field of combat.* DURTA *leaps at* BIMA *who easily throws him off.* DURTA *strikes* BIMA *on the head and chest,* BIMA *absorbs the blows without moving, grasps* DURTA, *and hurls him into the air.* BIMA *pursues off left.*

The Death of Karna

DURTA *flies on from the right, falls to the ground, picks himself up, straightens his garments, and rushes after the barehanded* BIMA *with drawn dagger.* BIMA *and* DURTA *fight center,* BIMA *parrying* DURTA'S *dangerous blows until, seeing* DURTA *tire, he disarms the Astina warrior.* BIMA *raises his adversary high into the air and smashes* DURTA *to bits on the ground. The figure of* DURTA *disappears from the screen.* DJAJARASA *rushes in to take up the fight.* BIMA *absorbs his blows, then hurls him into the air.* DJAJARASA *takes up a huge club against his bare-handed opponent. As with* DURTA, BIMA *overpowers* DJAJARASA. *He raises him aloft and smashes him to pieces on the ground. The figure of* DJAJARASA *disappears from the screen.* BIMA *stands exulting, then rushes off left. From the right* KRESNA *and* ARDJUNA *appear on their war chariot. Music softens.)*

NARRATION: The battle between Kurawa and Pandawa forces rages fiercely. Prince Bima destroys many Astina officers, dispersing the enemy ranks. Ardjuna's chariot, driven by the divine King Kresna, charges through the swarming field of battle, leaving a swath of enemy dead in its wake. It is called the Chariot of True Courage. On it ornaments of gold and jewels flash like lightning in the fury of battle. It is a charmed chariot whose supernatural horses draw it through the air. All the while, Ardjuna looks about for his sworn enemy. The Astina Commander, Prince Karna, is also mounted on his chariot, driven by King Salja. His chariot also flies, and so the two mortal enemies are destined to meet. — tjarijos

(Loud Sampak Sanga. ARDJUNA'S *chariot goes off left.* KARNA'S *chariot crosses from left to right,* ARDJUNA *and* KARNA, *on their chariots, meet center. Music softens.)*

KARNA *(icy contempt):* Ardjuna! You dare meet me in battle? I pity you, Brother. Escape while there still is time.

ARDJUNA *(levelly):* You have shamed the Pandawas, Prince Karna. Do not doubt that I shall stay.

KARNA: So be it, Ardjuna! If you will not retreat, you force your brother to attack!

(Loud and fast Sampak Sanga. The chariots race at one another, pass, turn, and fly off in opposite directions. One then the other flash across the screen, rising higher and higher in the air. Music softens.)

The color photographs following were taken in daylight to show better coloring and detail of the puppets. The lamp which normally hangs above the dalang's head has been removed.

KARNA *(chariot appears):* Brother Ardjuna! You take advantage of your chariot's magic power to fly above me. Descend! Fight on equal terms, if you dare!

ARDJUNA *(chariot appears, above* KARNA'S*):* Whatever the terms, Brother Karna, you cannot win.

KARNA: We shall see, Brother!

(Medium tempo Sampak Sanga. Chariots exit in opposite directions. KARNA *and* ARDJUNA *enter on foot, stand measuring one another.* KARNA *leaps to attack* ARDJUNA, *who serenely steps aside. Again* KARNA *attacks and again* ARDJUNA *imperturbably evades. They leap past each other and, almost quicker than the eye can follow,* ARDJUNA *throws* KARNA *to the ground and strikes him, lifts him in the air, and throws him off left.* ARDJUNA *pursues left;* KARNA *falls on from the right, rises, and straightens his dress. Music softens.)*

KARNA: Hah! You are skillful, Ardjuna. You caught me unaware.

ARDJUNA *(off):* Do not flee so soon from the field of battle, Brother Karna.

KARNA: You have not come close to defeating me! *(Draws dagger.)* Come, Ardjuna! Feel this steel in your body! *(Rushes off.)*

(Music speeds up. ARDJUNA *and* KARNA *meet center with drawn daggers.*

Fig. 128
Ardjuna
and Karna

Fig. 124   Ardjuna and Karna: leaping past

Fig. 125   Karna and Ardjuna: striking

Fig. 126   Karna and Ardjuna: lifting

Fig. 127   Karna and Ardjuna: throwing off

The Death of Karna

Initially KARNA *forces* ARDJUNA *back, then* ARDJUNA *strikes and knocks* KARNA'S *dagger from his hand.* KARNA *quickly withdraws to the left. Music softens.)*

ARDJUNA: Come, come, Brother! Feel my steel, you said. Do not flee. Show your courage as befits a prince. *(ARDJUNA pursues.)*

KARNA *(re-entering):* Enough of this fighting on foot, Ardjuna! Match me on horseback if you can!

ARDJUNA *(off):* I shall match you in everything, Brother Karna.

(Fast tempo Sampak Sanga. KARNA *runs off and reappears on horse-back galloping across the screen toward* ARDJUNA. ARDJUNA, *on horseback, appears and crosses the screen in the direction of* KARNA. *Twice the mounted warriors charge past each other, wheel, and charge again.* KARNA *appears alone on the screen, still mounted. He takes an arrow, aims, and looses it. He charges after it in pursuit of* ARDJUNA. *The arrow is seen flying twice across the screen.* ARDJUNA, *on horseback, appears at the right. With his forearm he plucks the flying arrow from the air, sends it back at* KARNA, *and exits in pursuit.* KARNA *reappears in time to catch, in great surprise, the returned arrow. Music softens.)*

KARNA: God of the worlds! Ardjuna is skillful!

ARDJUNA *(off):* Well, Brother, what now?

KARNA: Let us see if that was luck or skill. Once again, Brother!

NARRATION *(music continues, softly):* Prince Karna, this time, takes careful aim, intending to humiliate his foe. So quick and skillful is he that Ardjuna misses the arrow. It strikes his ear lobe, tearing loose the warrior's ear ornament he so proudly wears. Flushing with shame, Ardjuna dismounts and with-draws.

(Loud Sampak Sanga. KARNA *shoots an arrow, and pursues.* ARDJUNA *enters in time for the arrow to strike him; he is carried off-screen right by the force of the blow. He reappears on foot from from the right. Music softens.)*

SEMAR *(waddling on from the left):* Tsk, tsk. Don't be distressed, Master. Take heart. It's nothing.

ARDJUNA: I am more angered than distressed, Semar. Karna has violated the code of battle again. Just as he humiliated Srikandi with his marksmanship, he has shamed me. I shall not forgive you, Brother Karna. *(Calling off.)* Brother Karna!

KARNA *(off):* Ha-ha! Where is your self-conceit now, little Brother?

tjarijos kadjantur

On Thrones of Gold

ARDJUNA: I cannot but admire your marksmanship, Brother, but your conduct is unworthy. You are no Prince, Brother. You have said we should fight on equal terms. So be it!

(Loud Sampak Sanga. ARDJUNA *exits followed by* SEMAR. ARDJUNA *re-enters, takes careful aim, looses his arrow, and exits in pursuit. The arrow flies twice across the screen.* KARNA *enters; the arrow strikes his headdress as it passes over his head.*

Fig. 129
Karna and
Ardjuna's arrow

SALJA *enters from the right. Music stops.)*

SALJA: Karna, my Son. Are you wounded?

KARNA: No, Majesty! He strikes my helmet and sends my hair streaming! How foul, to dishonor me!

SALJA: Karna, my Prince, do not cry like a child. Vent your anger on the cause of it. Forget the trifle of your hair. Ardjuna is still on the field.

KARNA: Yes, Majesty!

(Five spaced raps; gamelan plays Ajak-ajakan Sanga. KARNA *kneels*

The Death of Karna

before SALJA, *who arranges his hair to make him look like* ARDJUNA.

Fig. 130
Salja and
Karna

KARNA *and* SALJA *withdraw.* KARNA, *looking like* ARDJUNA, *re-enters and meets* ARDJUNA.

Fig. 131
Ardjuna
and Karna

Surprised, ARDJUNA *withdraws right, and* KARNA *follows.* KARNA
reappears dressed like himself and meets ARDAWALIKA, *a serpent.*
Music stops.)

KARNA: What is this I see standing in my way? What do you
want? Move aside!

ARDAWALIKA: Noble Prince! My parents were killed by the
Prince we both hate. Allow me to help you gain revenge,
Prince Karna. Together we shall kill Ardjuna. *(Bows respect-*
fully.)

KARNA: You are presumptuous. I do not lack the courage to end
his life alone. Besides, I have been painfully reminded of the
warrior's code which permits no help in single combat. Your
vengeance is no concern of mine. Out of my way, Brute!

ARDAWALIKA: Ahhh, noble Prince Karna. Forgive me. I will
trouble you no more.

(Five raps; gamelan plays Sampak Sanga. KARNA *and* ARDAWALIKA
exit in opposite directions. ARDJUNA *enters from the right looking*
for KARNA. *He is about to go off left, when* KRESNA, *entering behind*
him, places his hand on ARDJUNA'S *shoulder and stops him. Music*
softens.)

KRESNA: Ardjuna.

ARDJUNA *(turns and respectfully faces his divine counselor):* Yes,
my King.

KRESNA: Your skill in battle is admirable, Brother Ardjuna. But
I must warn you of two dangers.

ARDJUNA *(makes the sembah):* I respect your words as law, my
King.

KRESNA: Beware of Karna's magic sword. It possesses a life and
a soul of its own. Do not approach it unguarded; do not allow
it to come near unsheathed.

ARDJUNA: Majesty, I understand.

KRESNA: Beware the vaguely visible figure coiling in the sky. It
is Ardawalika, the serpent whose parents you destroyed. In
an unguarded moment he hopes to devour you. Avoid these
dangers, and it is foretold that victory will be yours, Ardjuna.

ARDJUNA: I cherish your words of advice, my King. *(They exit.)*

(Fast Sampak Sanga. Enter KARNA *and* ARDJUNA *on their chariots.*
Their chariots dart at each other, pass, and return, fly off only
to return again from the other side of the screen.)

The Death of Karna

NARRATION (*music continues, softly*): The Astina commander flashes through the skies on the chariot driven by the wise King Salja. Prince Ardjuna, too, sweeps through the heavens on his magic chariot driven by King Kresna. The hot sun's rays glint from their golden chariots and from their weapons of steel. Gods, goddesses, and nymphs watching from above are enchanted by the spectacle and shower the field with flowers. The opposing armies cease their slaughter to cheer on their champions with shouts, applause, and the sound of gongs, trumpets, and drums. Like flashes of lightning, the two shining princes rain showers of arrows upon each other. tjarijos kadjantur

(*Music rises to clangorous intensity.* KARNA *looses an arrow at* ARDJUNA'S *chariot as it crosses the screen.* KRESNA *avoids the arrow as it sails harmlessly past the chariot. Music softens.*)

NARRATION (*music continues, softly*): Fierce is the battle. Both Princes seem invincible, each avoiding the others best-aimed arrows. Ardjuna maintains his even temper, but Karna, annoyed by the failure of his many arrows, flares and aims at his enemy's horses. His arrows shear them clean of their manes. tjarijos kadjantur

(*Loud Sampak Sanga. The chariots fly past each other.* KARNA *re-enters, shoots many arrows, and pursues them.* ARDJUNA *appears, the arrows graze the horses as they fly past. Music softens.*)

ARDJUNA: It is me you are fighting, Brother, not innocent horses. Again you flaunt the warrior's code of honor. Taste the bitterness of dishonor yourself then, Prince Karna.

NARRATION (*music continues, softly*): Ardjuna takes careful aim. Swiftly and surely his arrow flies to its mark. It strikes Karna's umbrella of state, splitting the shaft in two and dropping Karna's royal emblem in the dust. tjarijos kadjantur

(*Music up.* ARDJUNA *looses an arrow and exits after it.* KARNA *enters in time for the arrow to strike the chariot, carrying it off with its force.* KARNA *and* SALJA *re-enter on foot; the music stops.*)

Fig. 132
Salja and
Karna

SALJA (*choosing his words carefully*): Karna, my Son. Your fighting has been splendid, but I suggest the conflict be suspended. The sun is casting its last rays. Let us signal the troops to withdraw from the field. Tomorrow, when the sun rises, the battle can be resumed.

KARNA: Whatever Your Majesty suggests, I agree to.

(*Five spaced raps; the gamelan plays Ajak-ajakan Sanga.* SALJA *and* KARNA *exit.*)

tjarijos kadjantur   NARRATION (*music continues, softly*): And so the day's battle ends inconclusively. King Salja is deeply disturbed. He interprets the shattered emblem as an ominous foreshadowing of defeat. As the sun sets, the opposing troops withdraw to their tents. Prince Karna, in the aftermath of battle, turns his thoughts to his beloved wife, Surtikanti. He recalls her loving embrace, her gentle ways. Her pleading voice echoes in his mind. "Send word of your welfare," she has said. Knowing they are not destined to meet again, he wishes to offer her a last demonstration of his love. Standing alone in the twilight, he summons his Minister, Adimenggala.

(*Ajak-ajakan Sanga plays at normal level.* KARNA *enters from the right and stands alone.* ADIMENGGALA *enters from the left, makes the sembah, and sits respectfully before his master. Music stops.*)

KARNA: Uncle. (*Pause.*) I want you to go to Awangga.

ADIMENGGALA: I am at your service, my Lord. (*Makes the sembah.*)

KARNA: Go to Princess Surtikanti. Tell her I have not yet defeated Ardjuna but that I am alive and have done my utmost. Give to Her Highness this ring she gave me when we were married. (*Raises his hand.*) Tell her I send it as a remembrance of my love for her.

ADIMENGGALA: I shall do as you command, my Prince. (*Makes the sembah.*)

KARNA: Go then. Here is the ring. (*Takes off ring and gives it to* ADIMENGGALA.) Ask what token of her affection I may carry into battle with me tomorrow. Hurry, there is not much time.

ADIMENGGALA: With your permission I depart at once, my Lord.

(*Five spaced raps; the gamelan plays Ajak-ajakan Sanga as* ADIMENGGALA *makes the sembah and hastens out left.* KARNA *stands alone for a moment, turns and exits right. The* KAJON *is placed center, inclined to the left; the music stops.*)

The Death of Karna

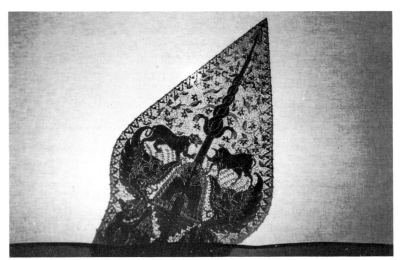

Fig. 133
Kajon

NARRATION: As night approaches, the day's activities cease. But on the road, old Adimenggala rushes through the darkness to Awangga. Heeding his Prince's urgent voice, he pushes his straining legs as fast as they will move. In the palace of Awangga, the lamps burn as Princess Surtikanti sits motionless, praying without ceasing for the safety of her lord. The halls of the palace are silent in deference to Her Highness. And near the battlefield, in his camp, Prince Karna passes the night in an unsettled state of mind, waiting for news from the Princess Surtikanti.

tjarijos

PART THREE

Scene 1

(Three raps; the gamelan plays Perkutut Manggung. The KAJON *moves from the center to the right side of the screen.* SURTIKANTI *enters and sits quietly. Two* MAIDSERVANTS *enter from the opposite side of the screen, kneel before* SURTIKANTI, *and make the sembah. She sits quietly. The dalang raps; the music resumes normal level, then ends, one gong phrase later.)*

SONG *(The dalang sings Patet Manjura Wantah):*

> The grey of dawn
> > Turns red,
>
> The chirruping
> > Of birds
> > Begins
>
> Oooooo . . . oooooo . . .

MAIDSERVANT: Forgive me, oh Milady. You have not eaten since our master has departed, you do not sleep. Have I in some way offended you, noble Princess? *(Makes the sembah.)*

SURTIKANDI *(does not move):* Do not misunderstand. I deny myself for the safety of our Lord. I fast so that my prayers may be better answered.

MAIDSERVANT: Dear Mistress. Please set your mind at ease. Excess passion may ill-affect our master.

SURTIKANTI: Your concern comforts me, but I cannot abandon my vigil for my husband's safety.

SONG *(The dalang sings Ada-ada Gregetsaut Manjura Wantah to steady tapping):*

> Like a bolt of lightning
> > Striking in the clear sky
>
> He arrives unexpected,
> > Hurrying as if
> > His life were threatened.

tjarijos NARRATION: Suddenly the meditation of the Princess is interrupted by the arrival of Minister Adimenggala. He has hurried through the night. His breath comes fast, and perspiration pours down his wrinkled face. His aged legs are limp with fatigue. He enters the room, falling to his knees before his mistress. Noting his appearance, Prince Surtikanti's heart turns cold with dread.

The Death of Karna

(Five spaced raps; the gamelan plays Ajak-ajakan Manjura. Seeing ADIMENGGALA *enter, the* MAIDSERVANTS *rise and move behind* SURTIKANTI. ADIMENGGALA *kneels before* SURTIKANTI, *making a feeble sembah. Music stops.)*

SURTIKANTI: Uncle Adimenggala! Rest, please, dear Uncle! But, please, tell me, has some disaster befallen?

ADIMENGGALA *(panting for breath):* Oh . . . Milady . . . p-please excuse . . . my appearance. I come . . . from . . . from the battlefield . . .

SURTIKANTI: Then is my fear realized? Tell me, Uncle, what of our Lord Karna?

ADIMENGGALA: Prince . . . Prince K-k-karna . . .

SURTIKANTI: Yes? Has my Lord Karna defeated Ardjuna today?

ADIMENGGALA: Milady . . . no, no . . . (SURTIKANTI *draws back in shock.)* . . . Lord Karna . . . fought his best . . . but . . . Ardjuna still lives . . .

SURTIKANTI *(hands to her cheeks):* Then my dearest lord and husband is . . .

ADIMENGGALA *(This reminds him of the ring):* I am instructed . . . Milady, to return . . . this ring . . . of yours . . .

(He holds out the ring. Seeing it SURTIKANTI *gasps and backs away.)*

NARRATION *(rapid and tense tapping on the side of the puppet chest):* Seeing the ring she had given to bind their love, Surtikanti concludes the worst. Waiting to hear no more, she unsheaths a dagger carried in her sash and slips it into her heart.

tjarijos

Fig. 134
Maidservants,
Surtikanti, and
Adimenggala

She falls into her Maidservant's arms and dies.

SONG *(The dalang sings Sendon Tlutur):*
>Oh God, look
>>And have pity
>>Oooooo . . .
>A thousand sorrows
>>Oooooo . . .
>To end this life
>>Brings the soul
>>Peace . . . oooooo

MAIDSERVANT: Oh, my dear Mistress, why have you done this?

ADIMENGGALA *(makes the sembah, then strikes his chest with his fist):* Oh, oh, my Princess . . . what stupid thing have I done! Forgive me, my Lady! *(He embraces* SURTIKANTI'S *feet. The* MAIDSERVANTS *carry* SURTIKANTI'S *body off. He makes the sembah in the direction she has gone.)* How terrible will be Prince Karna's anger! Forgive me, my Lord, I bring calamitous news!

(Five spaced raps; the gamelan plays Ajak-ajakan Manjura. ADIMENGGALA *exits left. The* KAJON *flutters across the screen, then is placed right.* KARNA *enters and stands alone, looking off left.)*

tjarijos kadjantur

NARRATION *(music continues, softly):* Through the dawn old Adimenggala rushes toward his master's camp. The sun appears and Karna rises, anxious for his minister's return. Dressed for battle with Ardjuna, Karna still tarries, hoping to receive some token from his wife. Suddenly Adimenggala enters his master's presence and instantly falls, clasping Karna's feet in both arms.

SONG *(Ajak-ajakan Manjura ends and the dalang sings Sendon Tlutur):*
>Oh Lord, have mercy
>>So hard has he tried
>>To carry out his order
>For the Prince he dearly loves.
>>His tears flow in sorrow
>Oooooo . . .

KARNA: Uncle, what has happened? Why do you wail like a woman and clasp my feet?

ADIMENGGALA: Oh, my Lord . . . *(Makes the sembah.)* . . . a calamity . . .

The Death of Karna

KARNA (*his anger rising*): Speak, Uncle!

ADIMENGGALA (*sitting up*): I hurried to Awangga, with your message, My Lord. When I arrived before Her Highness, sweating and exhausted, she became alarmed. She asked if Ardjuna were defeated. I said he lived. I was about to give her your ring when . . .Oh, dear Master, it was my fumbling words! (*Makes the sembah.*) Thinking you were killed, she stabbed herself. She is dead, my Lord. (*He prostrates himself at* KARNA's *feet.*)

SONG (*The dalang sings Ada-ada Gregetsaut Tlutur to steady tapping*):

> The world darkens
>> For the Prince of Awangga
>> Oooooo . . .
> Motionless
>> And dumb
>> In solitary pain
>> Oooooo . . .

NARRATION: Prince Karna's soul is numbed with grief. Then grief gives way to mounting anger at the cause of his wife's death. Without a word he draws his dagger and stabs the old man to death. *tjarijos*

(*Five sharp raps; the gamelan plays Sampak Manjura.* KARNA *runs his dagger through* ADIMENGGALA's *body. He trembles, then falls dead.* SANGKUNI *enters, salutes, and strikes his chest with grief. The music stops.*)

SANGKUNI: What is this, my Prince? I am astonished to see you kill your loyal minister. What has he done, my Lord?

KARNA: Oh, Uncle Sangkuni! I sent him with a message to my beloved wife. She thought he was bringing news of my death. She remembered her vow to follow me in death as in life, and slew herself!

SANGKUNI: Oh, my Prince! (*He embraces* KARNA.)

KARNA: All my sons have been slain. Now sweet Surtikanti lies dead, because of this bungling old fool!

SONG (*The dalang sings Ada-ada Gregetsaut Manjura Djugag to steady tapping*):

> Hopeless fury so great
>> It shakes the world,
> No more can he endure
>> Oooooo . . . oooooo

SANGKUNI *(rising):* What cruel fate has befallen you, my Prince. None of this would have happened but for this war. It is all the consequence of the Pandawas' greed—demanding to rule the jeweled Kingdom of Astina, which is not rightfully theirs. It is the Pandawas who have killed your sons and now your wife! Turn your justified fury upon them!

adegan perang
sampak manjura

Scene 2

tjarijos

NARRATION: Sangkuni's cunning words find their mark. Prince Karna trembles with grief and rage. Holding the Pandawas responsible for Surtikanti's death, he turns his full wrath against them.

KARNA: Yes, Uncle! Right are your words! I shall destroy the Pandawas!!

(Five quick raps; the gamelan plays Sampak Manjura. KARNA *rushes off left, followed by* SANGKUNI. KARNA *and* SALJA *enter riding their chariot, which speeds across the screen, re-enters, and stops.* KARNA *takes out an ornamented arrow. Music softens.)*

tjarijos kadjantur

NARRATION: Heartsick and distraught, Prince Karna vents his terrible rage on the Pandawa hosts. Like vengeful lightning, he strikes to earth hundreds upon hundreds of Pandawa warriors. Seeing the shining chariot of Prince Ardjuna he is consumed with a passion to destroy his enemy. He draws forth the supernatural arrow, Widjajandanu, given him by the Gods, reciting the magic spell which will release its power. He rises in the chariot, shouts a command at Salja, and aims the arrow directly at Ardjuna's neck.

KARNA: Take care! Salja, take care!

tjarijos kadjantur

NARRATION: King Salja flushes at the arrogance of Prince Karna's command. The humiliation Karna heaped upon him in the audience hall returns fresh to his mind. He remembers Ardjuna's past services to him and to his family. He sees his son-in-law aim the magic arrow that will surely bring Ardjuna to the ground. He sees Karna's arm draw back, and, sharply jerking on the reins, he causes the horses to rear, jolting the chariot violently. Karna's arrow soars into the air and passes over Ardjuna's head.

(Music increases in intensity and tempo. KARNA'S *chariot crosses the screen, then* ARDJUNA'S. KARNA *shoots as the chariot jerks. The arrow flies high, crosses the screen twice, and passes over* ARDJUNA'S

The Death of Karna

head. The chariots exit. Melody changes to Ajak-ajakan Manjura.
Enter the gods GURU *and* NARADA, *flying; the music softens.)*

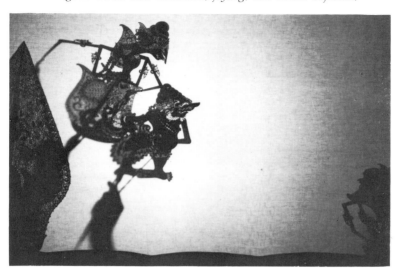

Fig. 135
Guru and
Narada

GURU: Brother Narada.

NARADA: Yes, heavenly Teacher?

GURU: Beautiful is the battle. But take care not to fly overly low.

NARADA: Oh, just a little closer, divine Brother!

GURU: There is danger, Brother. Their weapons are magic.

NARADA: But how elegant they appear. Look, heavenly Brother.
Let us view from a closer place.

(They fly from the upper right corner to the lower left.)

NARRATION *(music continues, softly):* Enraptured by the splendor   tjarijos kadjantur
of the battle, the two deities fly still lower that they might gain
a more enchanting view. Karna's arrow, having missed Ardjuna,
streaks upward, striking Narada who cries out in pain. Even
the Gods are subject to these magical weapons.

(Music up. As the arrow strikes NARADA, *the deities fly up and out*
of sight, then reappear flying backward, high on the screen. Music
softens.)

NARADA: Heavenly Brother, it struck me! Cursed are you,
Karna! May you be struck by an arrow! That is my curse on
you!

GURU: Come, come, Brother Narada. Be not angry. Let us keep a
safer distance and return to watch.

On Thrones of Gold

NARADA: By all means, divine Brother.

(Music up. The two gods fly up and out of sight. KARNA *appears on his chariot. His magic arrow, Widjajandanu, having struck* NARADA, *returns to its owner. Again* KARNA *looses it, and again* SALJA *rocks the chariot. The arrow flies off high on the screen.* KARNA'S *chariot exits right in pursuit.* ARDJUNA *appears from the right.* KARNA'S *arrow streaks across the screen grazing* ARDJUNA'S *headdress.*

*Fig. 136
Karna's arrow
and Ardjuna*

ARDJUNA'S *hair falls loose. Shamed, he sinks to his knees and tries to tie his hair back.* NARADA *appears in the sky, descends, and stands before* ARDJUNA, *who makes a respectful sembah. The music stops.)*

NARADA: My subject, Ardjuna.

ARDJUNA: Worshiped Deity, thy humble servant offers reverent greetings. *(Makes the sembah.)*

NARADA: I accept them with both hands, Ardjuna. My blessings. Do not be startled by my arrival. I have been watching your battle. I see what foul deed your brother has done you. Here, Ardjuna, accept this helmet. Wear it, and you will look exactly like Karna. *(Gives him helmet.)*

*Fig. 137
Ardjuna and
Narada*

The Death of Karna

ARDJUNA: I offer my humble thanks to thee, heavenly God.

NARADA: My blessings, child. I return to the Heavens to watch your battle's conclusion, my noble Son.

ARDJUNA: My prayers accompany thee, Holiness. *(Makes the sembah.)*

(Five fast raps; the gamelan plays Sampak Manjura. NARADA *ascends and disappears.* ARDJUNA, *looking like* KARNA, *crosses the screen, and exits left. Gamelan changes melody to Ajak-ajakan Manjura. The dragon* ARDAWALIKA *appears flying across the upper screen. He passes twice, then looks down intently. Music softens.)*

ARDAWALIKA: Now, where is Ardjuna? I shall avenge myself without Prince Karna's help. Ah! There is Karna. And there is his twin. But I don't see Ardjuna. Wait. Karna has no twin! Has Ardjuna tricked me? Which is he?

(Ajak-ajakan Manjura up. ARDAWALIKA *shakes with rage and flies off right.* ARDJUNA *and* KRESNA *enter from the right on their chariot. Music softens.)*

KRESNA: Ardjuna, take care. Look to the skies. Ardawalika waits to avenge himself. Beware.

ARDJUNA: Kingly Brother, I welcome your advice.

*(*ARDJUNA *and* KRESNA *move off left in their chariot.* ARDAWALIKA *enters from the left flying.)*

ARDAWALIKA: Ho-ho! What luck! So that one is Ardjuna. Your past evil deeds are your undoing, Prince! Prepare to die! Ho-ho-ho!

(Gamelan plays loud Sampak Manjura. ARDAWALIKA *streaks downward and off right.* ARDJUNA *appears from the right on his chariot. He looses an arrow and exits left in pursuit. The arrow flies across the screen.* ARDAWALIKA *strikes down from above, and is hit by the arrow.*

Fig. 138
Ardjuna's arrow and Ardawalika

On Thrones of Gold

ARDAWALIKA *falls dying and is whisked from the screen.* ARDJUNA *appears right on his chariot. Music softens.)*

ARDJUNA: Now, Brother Karna. *(Takes up the magic arrow Pasopati.)* Open your eyes and tell me what you see!

KARNA *(off):* I see the way to eternity, Ardjuna!

ARDJUNA: Indeed it is. And the way is swift. Farewell, Brother Karna!

(Gamelan plays at quickened tempo. ARDJUNA *shoots the arrow. It flies across the screen. Ardjuna exits left in pursuit.* KARNA *appears from the left on his chariot. The arrow strikes* KARNA, *piercing his neck. Melody abruptly changes to Sendon Tlutur, played softly.)*

tjarijos kadjantur NARRATION *(music softly in background):* Standing proudly in his chariot, the radiant Astina Commander, Prince Karna, is slain, his neck severed by Ardjuna's magic arrow Pasopati. Unaware of what has happened, King Salja drives the speeding chariot over the battlefield, urging Prince Karna to loose his arrows. He turns and sees Prince Karna, still standing upright, blood streaming from his throat. Dazed, he reins the horses in and the lifeless body of Prince Karna is spread out on the ground. King Salja departs for the Kurawa camp, leaving the royal corpse unattended.

(Music up. The chariot is taken off. SALJA *places* KARNA *on his back facing right, and exits. The music stops.)*

SONG *(The dalang sings Sendon Tlutur):*

> Oh look
> > And have pity,
> A thousand sorrows
> > Oooooo . . .
> All nature weeps,
> > Rain washing
> > The blood from his wounds.

VOICE *(sad melody Tlutur in the background):* Dear Brother Ardjuna. Come embrace me before I die. You know, do you not, that though my duty lay with the Kurawas, my love was for you and the Pandawa Brothers. Come near me, witness the departure of my soul. Hold me close to you, my dear Brother!

(ARDJUNA enters from the right and moves slowly toward KARNA. KRESNA *enters behind* ARDJUNA.)*

The Death of Karna

*Fig. 139
Kresna, Ardjuna,
Karna, and
Karna's dagger*

KRESNA: Ardjuna! Have you forgotten my warning?

ARDJUNA *(turns to face* KRESNA*):* Noble King, my heart shatters at the voice of my dying brother. Shall I not grant his last wish, to show my respect and love?

KRESNA: Ardjuna. Your brother is dead. His soul has left his body. The voice you hear is that of his magic dagger seeking to avenge his master's death. Unsheath your dagger if you must approach.

ARDJUNA: Kingly Brother, it shall be done. *(Makes the sembah and turns to* KARNA.*)*

(Gamelan plays Sampak Manjura. KRESNA *goes out right.* ARDJUNA *approaches* KARNA, *holding his dagger ready.* KARNA'S *dagger leaps to attack* ARDJUNA. ARDJUNA'S *dagger meets it, they both disappear flying upward to heaven.* ARDJUNA *gazes at* KARNA, *turns, and goes off right. Enter* ASWATAMA *from the left. He falls to his knees, embracing* KARNA'S *body. Music stops.)*

SONG *(The dalang sings Ada-ada Gregetsaut Manjura Djugag to steady tapping):*

> Hopeless fury so great
>> It shakes the world,
> No more can he endure
>> Oooooo . . . oooooo

ASWATAMA: Princely Brother, my heart breaks at this sight. I

On Thrones of Gold

saw how Salja treacherously caused your death. He shall not go unpunished!

(Five quick raps; the gamelan plays Sampak Manjura. ASWATAMA *carries* KARNA *off left, hurriedly re-enters alone, and crosses off left.* SALJA *crosses from right to left.* SALJA *re-enters;* ASWATAMA *stops him from behind. Music stops.)*

ASWATAMA: Stop, Salja! *(Moves in front of* SALJA *and faces him.)*

Fig. 140
Salja and
Aswatama

SALJA: You speak rudely, Aswatama. Do not anger me.

ASWATAMA: You have killed our commander, Salja, more surely than Ardjuna's arrow!

SALJA: You dare speak to me that way? Remember who I am. I am the King's father-in-law. Prince Karna was my own son-in-law. I am entitled to your respect.

ASWATAMA: Oh, Salja, you are vain! But no one has the courage to say it! As a young man you slew your father-in-law to satisfy your vanity. You have betrayed your daughter's husband just now for the same reason!

SONG *(The dalang sings Ada-ada Gregetsaut Manjura to steady tapping):*

> His fury is so great
> > It shakes the world,
> No more can he endure

The Death of Karna

> The insults of his foe
> Oooooo . . .

NARRATION: King Salja's face flushes with anger as he hears ‎ tjarijos
these biting words. His body trembles with rage. Seizing
Aswatama, he hurls him to the ground.

(Five raps; the gamelan plays fast Sampak Manjura. SALJA *attacks
strongly.* ASWATAMA *is unable to ward off the enraged king's
blows for long; he flees.* SANGKUNI *enters from the left, faces* SALJA,
makes a deep sembah. Music stops.)

SANGKUNI: Please, Majesty, curb your anger. Your son, King
Durjudana, anxiously awaits your return. I beg, Sire, compose
yourself, that you may attend His Majesty and inform him of
today's events. *(Makes sembah.)*

SALJA: Thank you, loyal Sangkuni, let us depart together.

(They depart. The KAJON *is placed center, inclined to the right.)*

SONG *(The dalang sings Patet Manjura Djugag):*

> The sun's hot rays
> Scorch the earth mercilessly
> In anticipation of
> The coming slaughter
> Oooooo . . .

NARRATION: Aswatama has fled, intending to return when he ‎ tjarijos
has mustered sufficient power against King Salja. King Salja
and Sangkuni return to the Kurawa camp where King Durjudana has gathered his remaining officers in urgent council.

Scene 3 ‎ djedjer Astina

*(Three raps; the gamelan plays the melancholy melody Glijung.
The* KAJON *is placed right.* DURJUDANA *enters and takes his place
right.* SALJA, SANGKUNI, *and* KARTAMARMA *enter, greet the king,
and take places left. The dalang raps; Glijung plays at normal level
until it ends.)*

SONG *(The dalang sings Patet Manjura Wantah):*

> The darkening sky
> Turns blood red
> Oooooo . . . oooooo
> Gathering clouds
> Rumble
> Oooooo . . .

On Thrones of Gold

DURJUDANA: Royal Father, tell me the news!

SALJA: My Son, disaster has fallen upon the Kurawas. Prince Karna is killed, slain by Ardjuna's arrow.

SONG (*The dalang sings Ada-ada Gregetsaut Manjura Wantah to steady tapping as* DURJUDANA *strikes his chest in rage*):
> Like a bolt of lightning
>> Striking in the sky
>> Oooooo . . .
> Rage strikes his breast
>> Oooooo . . . oooooo . . .

Fig. 141
Maidservant,
Durjudana,
Sangkuni, Salja,
and Kartamarma

DURJUDANA (*gesturing*): Uncle Sangkuni! Go! At once! Sound the alarm! Gather the army! I myself will lead Astina's forces to destroy the Pandawas!

SANGKUNI: At once, Majesty.

(*Quick double raps; the gamelan plays Srepegan Manjura.* SANGKUNI *makes the sembah and exits left, followed by* KARTAMARMA. *Music softens.*)

DURJUDANA: Royal Father. Assist me in this battle, I beg you.

SALJA: As you wish, Majesty.

(*Music up. Both exit right. The* KAJON *quickly flutters across the screen and back, and is placed to the right.* SANGKUNI *enters from the right. Music softens.*)

SANGKUNI: Astina warriors!

The Death of Karna

VOICES *(off)*: Yes, Minister Sangkuni! We await our King's orders!

SANGKUNI: His Majesty leads you into battle himself! Order your ranks! Prepare to march at once!

VOICES *(off)*: Yes, Minister! For our King! We are ready, Master!

SANGKUNI: Your Princes Kartamarma, Tjitraksa, and Tjitraksi will lead your columns, with His Majesty at the head! Do your utmost, Astina men! Destroy the Pandawas!

Scene 4

adegan perang
amuk-amukan

(Gamelan plays clangorous Sampak Manjura. The Astina MARCHING ARMY *is reviewed by* SANGKUNI, KARTAMARMA, TJITRAKSA, *and finally* TJITRAKSI. *The* MARCHING ARMY *of Astina meets the* MARCHING ARMY *of the Pandawas center. They battle, the Astina army withdraws left pursued by the Pandawa army.* BIMA *meets the Astina* MARCHING ARMY. *With a single blow he hurls it from the screen.* BIMA *dances off in pursuit.* ARDJUNA *meets* TJITRAKSA, *lands blows in quick succession, throws him off the screen left.* TJITRAKSI *enters and, like* TJITRAKSA, *is hurled off the screen left.* KARTAMARMA *rushes in, grasps* ARDJUNA *and throws him high into the air and off the screen right.* KARTAMARMA *exits in pursuit.* ARDJUNA *flies across the screen and falls into the arms of* BIMA, *who enters from the right.* ARDJUNA *withdraws as* BIMA *rushes to attack* KARTAMARMA. *The two meet center. A furious battle ensues,* BIMA *fighting barehanded against* KARTAMARMA *using first a sword, then a club.* BIMA *disarms his opponent.* KARTAMARMA *flees for his life.* BIMA *starts to pursue him, but is stopped by* KRESNA *entering from behind. Music stops.)*

KRESNA: Brother Bima, stop.

BIMA: There are Kurawas to kill! Stand aside, Brother!

KRESNA: Bima, calm yourself. There is no need. Your ferocity inspires such terror, the Astina forces have melted away. The sun is low in the sky. Order our troops to withdraw from the field.

BIMA: As you say, Brother.

KRESNA: Arrange for the troops to return to their respective camps. Let them gather the dead and treat the wounded. We shall meet our kingly grandfather, to tell him of this victory.

(Three raps; the gamelan plays Gandjur. KRESNA *goes off right.* BIMA *exultantly performs a "victory dance.")*

Fig. 142
Bima

djedjer tantjeb kajon

Scene 5

(Melody changes to Manis, or "Sweet Melody." MATSWAPATI, KRESNA, JUDISTIRA, BIMA, ARDJUNA, NAKULA, SADEWA, GARENG, PETRUK, *and* SEMAR *enter. Music softens.)*

tjarijos kadjantur

NARRATION: And so the Pandawa Princes and allied Kings gather at the conclusion of the day's battle.

(Single rap on gong beat, music continues for one gong phrase, then ends.)

MATSWAPATI: I eagerly await your news, King Kresna.

KRESNA: With your blessings, Brother King, we have been victorious. Our noble Ardjuna slew Prince Karna in personal combat, and the fearless Bima turned back the Astina general attack with great casualties to their side. Your grandsons are unwounded.

MATSWAPATI: I receive your news with joy, divine King. Let us offer our prayers of thanksgiving. And now Brothers, Grandsons, Friends! I ask that you join me in celebrating your just victory.

tjarijos

NARRATION: And so the Pandawa Princes, Kings, Commanders, and their officers, exult in their triumph of the day.

The Death of Karna

(The vigorous melody Gangsaran begins. The KAJON *is brought from its place on the right of the screen and is planted in the center of the final tableau, thus ending the performance.*

Fig. 143
Judistira,
Sadewa,
Matswapati,
Nakula, Kajon,
Ardjuna, Kresna,
Bima, Gareng,
Semar, and
Petruk

The lively melody Rudjak Djeruk accompanies the audience as it departs.)

Appendix A. Gending and Their Dramatic Function

Ninety-nine gending and their traditional dramatic function in Surakarta-style wajang are listed here. (Ajak-ajakan, Srepegan, and Sampak, discussed in the Introduction, are not included.) They are drawn from the larger list given in Nojo-wirongko, *Serat Tuntunan Padalangan*. Columns indicate the scene in which a gending occurs, its function, name and translations in which it is used (R, *The Reincarnation of Rama;* I, *Irawan's Wedding;* and K, *The Death of Karna*).

SCENE	FUNCTION	GENDING	PLAY
Part One (patet nem)			
First Audience (djedjer)	Under djanturan for King Judistira in Amarta	Kawit	—
	Under djanturan for god Guru in Suralaja	Kawit	—
	Under djanturan for King Durjudana in Astina	Kabor	K
	Under djanturan for ruler of any other kingdom	Krawitan	R, I
Arrival of visitor in First Audience	Entrance of King Baladewa as guest	Diradameta	R, I
		Sobrang	—
		Remeng	K
	Entrance of Prince Karna as visitor	Obah	K
		Peksikuwung	—
	Entrance of King Judistira as guest	Mangu	—
	Entrance of Prince Ardjuna as guest	Srikaton	—
	Entrance of Prince Sadewa as guest	Kembang Pepe	—
	Entrance of Minister Sangkuni reporting	Lere-lere	—

Appendix A

SCENE	FUNCTION	GENDING	PLAY
	Entrance of ogre minister reporting	Sobrang	—
Inner Palace (kedatonan)	Entrance of Queen, Kingdom of Amarta	Gantalwedar	—
		Larasati	—
	Entrance of Queen, Kingdom of Astina	Darmarkeli	—
		Gandrungmangu	—
	Entrance of Queen(s), Kingdom of Dwarawati	Titipati	R
		Kadukmanis	—
	Entrance of Queen, Kingdom of Mandura	Kanjut	—
		Gantalwedar	—
	Entrance of Queen, Kingdom of Mandraka	Laranangis	—
		Gandrungmanis	—
	Entrance of Queen, Kingdom of Tjempala	Maskumambang	—
Outer Audience (paseban djawi)	Entrance of King Baladewa	Tjapang	—
	Entrance of Prince Bima	Dandun	—
		Gendu	—
	Entrance of Prince Samba or Minister Setyaki	Kadaton Bentar	R, I
	Entrance of Prince Karna or Minister Sangkuni	Kembangtiba	K
	Entrance of Prince Dursasana	Semukirang	—
		Prihatin	—
	For reviewing and marching of troops of any kingdom	Kebogiro	K
		Wrahatbala	R, I
		Manjarsewu	—
		Bubarannjutra	—
		Singanebah	—
Foreign Audience (sabrangan)	Entrance of Ogre King Dasasuksma and retinue in Tawanggantungan	Babad	R
		Parianom	—
	Entrance of young ogre King and retinue in any kingdom	Madjemuk	I

Gending

SCENE	FUNCTION	GENDING	PLAY
	Entrance of old ogre King and retinue in any kingdom	Lobaningrat	—
		Guntur	—
	Entrance of King Durjudana and retinue in Astina	Djamba	—
		Budjangga	—
		Lana	—
	Entrance of King Judistira in Amarta or King Baladewa in Mandura with retinue	Budjangga	—
	Entrance of ruler and retinue in any nonogre kingdom	Udan Sore	K
	Entrance of god Narada and retinue	Peksibaja	—
	Entrance of Prince Bima and retinue	Gendu	K
	Entrance of summoned official or minister of an ogre kingdom	Bedat	I
		Muntjer	—
		Alaskobong	—
		Kembang Gadung	—
Part Two (patet sanga)			
Hermitage (pandita)	Entrance of Prince Ardjuna and Seer Abijasa in Saptaarga Hermitage	Lunta	R
		Lara-lara	K
	Entrance of Ardjuna in a forest scene	Lagudempel	—
	Entrance of Ardjuna in a cave scene	Denda Santi	—
	Entrance of Ardjuna in Kingdom of Madukara	Kuwung-kuwung	—
	Entrance of Ardjuna in Ghost Kingdom of Setragandamaji	Lontangkasmaran	—
		Gendreh Kemasan	—
	Entrance of Prince Irawan and Seer Kanwa in Jasarata Hermitage	Sumar	I

Appendix A

SCENE	FUNCTION	GENDING	PLAY
	Entrance of Prince Abimanju and Seer Abijasa in Saptaarga Hermitage	Gandakusuma	—
	Entrance of other refined young Prince and seer	Bondet	—
		Lara-lara	—
	Entrance of young Prince Nagatatmala	Ela-ela	—
		Sumedang	—
Forest (wana)	Journey of refined Prince through fields and woods	Langengita	R
Flower Battle (perang kembang)	Entrance of ogre officers (Tjakil and companions)	Djangkrik Genggong	R, I
		Kagok Madura	—
	Entrance of forest ogres	Babad Kentjeng	—
		Embat-embat Pendjalin	—
		Kagok Madura	—
	Entrance of snake or tiger figures	Babad Kentjeng	—
		Gedrug	—
	For refined Prince aiming arrow at ogre opponent	Srimartana	R
Audience following Flower Battle (djedjer)	Entrance of King Durjudana and retinue in Astina	Kentjeng Barong	—
	Entrance of King Kresna and retinue in Dwarawati	Rondon	—
		Semeru	—
	Entrance of King Judistira and retinue in Amarta	Gandrung Mangungkung	R
	Entrance of King Drupada and retinue in Tjempala	Laler Mengeng	K
	Entrance of god Guru and retinue in Suralaja	Madukotjak	—
	Entrance of ogre King and retinue in any kingdom	Galagotang	I

Gending

SCENE	FUNCTION	GENDING	PLAY
	Entrance of the gods Narada and Endra	Gegersore	—
	Entrance of Prince Gatutkatja in Pringgadani	Kentjeng Barong	—
		Gendjonggoling	—
	Entrance of Prince Bima	Babad Kentjeng	—
		Kagok Madura	—
	Entrance of Seer Kesawa	Djongkang	—
	Entrance of refined noble with palace lady (often lovers)	Kembang Tandjung	I
	Entrance of the disciple Djaladara	Gambirsawit	I
Part Three (patet manjura)			
Any Audience except the last (djedjer)	Entrance of Durjudana and retinue in Astina	Glijung	I, K
	Entrance of King Judistira and retinue in Amarta	Bangbangwetan	I
		Budjangganom	—
		Lagudempel	—
		Ramjang	—
	Entrance of King Baladewa and retinue in Mandura	Tjapang	—
	Entrance of King Kresna and retinue in Dwarawati	Ramjang	I
	Entrance of ogre King and his retinue in any kingdom	Ritjik-ritjik	I
		Liwung	R
	Entrance of the ape Anoman and Prince Gatutkatja	Eling-eling	—
	Entrance of Queens or Princesses in female quarters of any kingdom	Perkutut Manggung	R, K
		Montro	—
		Manis	—
	For pathetic scene (often death)	Tlutur	K

Appendix A

SCENE	FUNCTION	GENDING	PLAY
Great Battle (perang amuk-amukan)	Bima's victory dance	Gandjur	I, K
Final Audience (tantjeb kajon)	Entrance of King and his retinue (of "good" kingdom, usually Amarta, Dwarawati, Wirata, Mandukara)	Manis	I, K
		Lobong	—
		Bojong	—
		Ginondjing	—
	Planting the Kajon over final tableau	Gangsaran	R, K

Appendix B. Suluk and Their Dramatic Function

Thirty-eight suluk are arranged in order of their normal occurrence. The listing follows Surakarta wajang style, and is drawn from Nojowirongko, *Serat Tuntunan Padalangan,* and Probohardjono, *Primbon Langen Swara.* Columns indicate the scene in which a suluk occurs, its function, name, and translations in which it appears (R, *The Reincarnation of Rama;* I, *Irawan's Wedding;* K, *The Death of Karna*). Numbers in parentheses indicate suluk which have the same melody, but different names.

SCENE	FUNCTION	SULUK	PLAY
Part One (patet nem)			
First Audience (djedjer)	After opening djanturan	Patet Nem Ageng	R, I, K
		Patet Nem Wantah	—
	Immediately follows Patet Nem Ageng (or Wantah)	Ada-ada Girisa (1)	R, I, K
	Used to indicate arrival of a guest or sad emotion within dialogue	Sendon Pananggalan (2)	R
Inner Palace (kedatonan)	After opening djanturan (if Queen Banowati of Astina)	Patet Manjura Ageng	—
	For exit at close of scene	Sendon Kloloran	R
Outer Audience (paseban djawi)	For exit of minister to assemble troops	Ada-ada Astakuswala Alit	R, I, K
	For return of minister after assembling troops	Ada-ada Astakuswala Ageng (3)	R, I, K

Appendix B

SCENE	FUNCTION	SULUK	PLAY
	For exit to order troops to march	Ada-ada Budalan Mataraman	I, K
Road-clearing (perang ampjak)	For troops resting after road-clearing	Patet Kedu	R, K
Foreign Audience (sabrangan)	After opening djanturan	Patet Lasem	R, K
	After opening djanturan (if an ogre kingdom)	Ada-ada Girisa (1)	I
Opening Skirmish (perang gagal)	For troops resting at night following victorious battle; bridge to Part Two	Patet Lindur	R, I, K
Any scene in Part One	After any gending with unspecified suluk	Patet Nem	R, K
	Used within dialogue to underscore mild emotion or just before a gending is played	Patet Nem Djugag	R, I, K
	Used within dialogue to underscore tense emotion	Ada-ada Mataraman	R, I, K
		Ada-ada Mataraman Djugag	R, I, K
		Ada-ada Gregetsaut Nem	K
	Used to underscore highly pathetic incident, often death	Sendon Tlutur Manjura (4)	K
Part Two (patet sanga)			
Nature's Turmoil and Clown (gara-gara)	Before first scene, as bridge to religious mood	Patet Sanga Wantah	R, I, K
	Semar's song for calling his sons	Sendon Kagok Ketanon	R, K
Hermitage (pandita)	After opening djanturan	Patet Sanga Ngelik (5)	R, I, K
Flower Battle (perang kembang)	As refined hero takes out arrow with which he kills ogre	Ada-ada Astakuswala Sanga (3)	R

Suluk

SCENE	FUNCTION	SULUK	PLAY
	As ogre weeps after being struck by refined hero	Ada-ada Palaran	—
	For mature Ardjuna's exit after battle; indicates calm elation	Sendon (A)bimanju	—
	For young refined hero's exit after battle; indicates calm elation	Patet Djingking	R, I
Audience following Flower Battle (djedjer)	After opening djanturan, if an ogre kingdom	Ada-ada Manggalan (1)	I
	After opening djanturan, if Pandawa Kingdom of Amarta	Sendon Rentjasih (2)	R, K
Any scene in Part Two	Used to underscore highly pathetic incident, often death	Sendon Tlutur Sanga (4)	R, I, K
	Used to underscore tense emotion, especially anger or exasperation	Ada-ada Gregetsaut Sanga	R, I, K
		Ada-ada Gregetsaut Sanga Djugag	I
	Used to underscore agonized emotion (pathos plus anger)	Ada-ada Gregetsaut Tlutur	K
	Before Bima (Wrekudara) exits leaping	Ada-ada Wrekudara	—
	For entrance of Gatutkatja	Ada-ada Gregetsaut Gatutkatja	R, I
	Can be used wherever needed within any scene	Patet Sanga Wantah	I
		Patet Sanga Djugag	R, I, K
Part Three (patet manjura)			
Audience in Amarta	After opening djanturan	Sendon Sastradatan (2)	I

Appendix B

SCENE	FUNCTION	SULUK	PLAY
Audience in Astina	After opening djanturan	Patet Manjura Ageng	—
		Patet Manjura Ngelik (5)	—
Any scene in Part Three	Used to underscore highly pathetic incident, often death	Sendon Tlutur Manjura (4)	K
	Used to underscore tense emotion, or before Sampak Manjura	Ada-ada Gregetsaut Manjura	R, I, K
		Ada-ada Gregetsaut Manjura Djugag	R, I, K
	Used to underscore agonized emotion (pathos plus anger)	Ada-ada Gregetsaut Tlutur	K
	After gending lacking specific suluk	Patet Manjura Wantah	R, I, K
		Patet Manjura Djugag	R, I, K
	For entrance of Gatutkatja	Ada-ada Gregetsaut Gatutkatja	—
	Before Bima (Wrekudara) exits leaping	Ada-ada Wrekudara	—

Appendix C. Basic Fighting Movements: a Section of the Flower Battle (perang kembang)

This example is given as a student dalang in Jogjakarta would normally record it: movements of the "left" figure are written in the left column, those of the "right" figure in the right column. They are numbered in order. Javanese terminology is terse; some explanatory words, in parentheses, have been added for clarity. The 31 basic movement sequences given here would be greatly elaborated upon in an actual performance.

Flower Battle (perang kembang) Between Terong and Ardjuna

<table>
<tr><td align="center">TERONG</td><td align="center">ARDJUNA</td></tr>
<tr><td>1. ___</td><td>2. Enter and stand</td></tr>
<tr><td>3. Enter, leap at roaring</td><td>4. Back (slowly) off</td></tr>
<tr><td>5. Rush off pursuing</td><td>6. Back on, advance off (in direction entered)</td></tr>
<tr><td colspan="2" align="center">7. Meet center</td></tr>
<tr><td>8. Roar, shake arm, roll on back, eat earth, throw rocks; rush at and past (opponent), return</td><td>9. Avoid, show back (in disdain)</td></tr>
<tr><td>10. Leap at (opponent's) back, miss, return</td><td>11. (Without looking) avoid, turn (to face opponent)</td></tr>
<tr><td>12. Leap past and return, twice</td><td>13. Back off</td></tr>
<tr><td>14. Roar (with joy), rush off pursuing</td><td>15. Back on, advance off</td></tr>
<tr><td colspan="2" align="center">16. Meet center</td></tr>
<tr><td>17. Roar, rush at and past, return</td><td>18. Avoid, show back</td></tr>
<tr><td>19. Rush at (opponent's) back</td><td>20. Catch head with rear hand (without looking), strike head (with forearm)</td></tr>
<tr><td>21. Rise, stagger, roll on back, roar, shake arm, leap on head</td><td>22. Avoid, back off</td></tr>
</table>

Appendix C

23. Roar, pursue

24. Back on, advance off

25. Meet center

26. Leap at roaring

27. Grasp head (with forehand), flick (rear arm in arc), strike (downward blow)

28. Sag, moan, rise, leap and crush (in bear-hug), lift in air

29. Draw dagger, stab (in chest)

30. Fall (on back), die

31. Advance (calmly), inspect corpse, back off

A Note on Sources

Translations of the copper inscriptions referring to performances in early Java can be found in Claire Holt, *Art in Indonesia* (Ithaca, N.Y., 1967), pp. 281–282. Quotations from early Javanese literature are taken from passages quoted in G. A. J. Hazeu, *Bijdrage tot de kennis van het Javaansche tooneel* (Leiden, 1897), pp. 10–11; translation by Pandam Guritno Siswoharsojo. For detailed discussion of the origin of wajang kulit see Hazeu, pp. 18–24, 42–43, 54–57; and excellent English summaries of evidence in W. H. Rassers, *Panji, The Culture Hero* (The Hague, 1959), pp. 95–115; and Holt, pp. 128–131.

The Indian shadow play, *Dutangada,* is mentioned in Chandra Bhan Gupta, *The Indian Theatre* (Banaras, 1954), p. 151, as is *chaya nataka,* p. 11. The two terms in early Indian literature interpreted to mean shadow theater were first noted by R. Pischel, "Das Altindische Schattenspiel," *Sitzungsbericht der Koeniglich Preussischen Akademie der Wissenschaften,* 23 (1906), 482–502; English translations of the relevant passages can be found in Holt, p. 129. The reference to Ceylonese shadow players is in Ananda Coomaraswamy, "The Shadow-Play in Ceylon," *The Journal of the Royal Asiatic Society of Great Britain and Ireland* (1930), p. 627.

The dating of wajang history based on traditional Javanese accounts is found in L. Serrurier, *De wajang poerwa, eene ethnologische studie* (Leiden, 1896), pp. 48–70. Analysis of the Djalatunda reliefs is in F. D. K. Bosch, "The Oldjavanese Bathing-place Jalatunda," in *Selected Studies in Indonesian Archaeology* (The Hague, 1961), pp. 47–107. A number of general descriptions of wajang forms, other than shadow theater, exist; the most convenient English ones are in Holt, pp. 124–128; and James Brandon, *Theatre in Southeast Asia* (Cambridge, Mass., 1967), pp. 42–55, 287–292.

The Plays. The list of 179 wajang kulit plays, referred to many times, can be found in J. Kats, *Het Javaansche tooneel* (Weltevreden, 1923), pp. 87–98; the quote and discussion concerning the Amarta period, p. 277; and the correlation of play type with performance occasion, pp. 108–110. An excellent examination of ruwatan exorcism performance is in Rassers, pp. 44–56. Hazeu's discussion of trunk and branch plays, pp. 122–124, is more complete and useful than Kats's,

A Note on Sources

pp. 85–86. The genealogy of Javanese kings and wajang forms is based on Harsono Hadisoeseno, "Wayang and Education," *Education and Culture*, 8 (October 1955), 9; and Kats, p. 85. Semar's importance is discussed in detail in Kats, pp. 40–41. Some of the many mystical interpretations of wajang can be found in Hadisoeseno, pp. 5–6, 10, and Holt, p. 146.

The use of the terms djedjer and adegan is not adequately described in any written source I am aware of, but a brief statement of Surakarta usage is in M. Ng. Nojowirongko, *Serat Tuntunan Padalangan* (Jogjakarta, 1960), I, 58, and also can be deduced from play scenarios written in Surakarta style; Jogjakarta usage was described to me in conversations with dalang, especially M. B. Radyomardowo, teacher at the Habirando Dalang School, Jogjakarta. Dramatic structure is outlined in Nojowirongko, I, 58. Types of narration, songs, and dialogue are covered briefly in Nojowirongko, I, 12–14, and Hazeu, pp. 103–115; other information is from lessons given by M. B. Radyomardowo.

Wajang in Performance. Types of scenarios are described in Hazeu, pp. 133–135. Terminology for stage equipment and musical instruments can be found in Hazeu, pp. 14–23, and Nojowirongko, I, 65–67, among others. The difficult question of who sits where at a wajang performance is gone into in exhaustive detail by Rassers, pp. 124–140. I believe R. M. Sajid, *Bauwarna Wajang* (Jogjakarta, 1958), pp. 25–29, is the only place the manner of arranging puppets in the banana log is outlined. Identifying physical features of puppets are discussed and illustrated in Sajid, pp. 65–77; throughout R. M. Sulardi, *Gambar Print-jening Ringgit Purwa* (Djakarta, 1953); and Nojowirongko, I, 56–64. The two wanda of Semar illustrated in the text can also be seen in Sajid, p. 35.

The number of gamelan sets in Java is taken from a table in Jaap Kunst, *Music in Java* (The Hague, 1949), II, 570. The discussion of patet draws on Kunst, I, 15–18, and Mantle Hood, *The Nuclear Theme as a Determinant of Patet in Javanese Music* (Groningen, 1954), pp. 127–128. Gending structure is analyzed in Kunst, I, 296–301, and Hood, p. 15. Nojowirongko, I, 34–44, is the most important source for the names and dramatic function of gending; and for suluk and their uses, Nojowirongko, I, 14–28, and R. Ng. S. Probohardjono, *Primbon Langen Swara* (Solo, 1961), pp. 5–14. Music cues and tapping signals are mainly from Nojowirongko, I, 44–45.

Terminology for puppet handling is taken from Nojowirongko, I, 48, and the description of how movements are timed with music, from Nojowirongko, II, 3. The only published description of linked fighting movements is found in the text of *Irawan Rabi,* in Nojowirongko (II, 32–33, for example); the examples given in the book are from the instruction of M. B. Radyomardowo, Habirando Dalang School, Jogjakarta. Rules to guide the dalang in performance are found,

A Note on Sources

with some variation, in Hazeu, pp. 116–118, Kats, pp. 33–34, and Nojowirongko, I, 57–58.

The Translations. An interesting discussion of the ethical values exemplified by wajang characters is found in Benedict Anderson, *Mythology and the Tolerance of the Javanese* (Ithaca, 1965), pp. 8, 15–18.

Bibliography

ENGLISH LANGUAGE

Anderson, Benedict R. O'G. *Mythology and the Tolerance of the Javanese,* Monograph Series, Modern Indonesia Project. Ithaca, N.Y.: Southeast Asia Program, Cornell University, 1965. Character descriptions of major wajang figures (illustrated) and a brief synopsis of nuclear story of Javanese *Mahabarata* and *Ramayana* as well as title subject.

Bosch, F. D. K. "The Oldjavanese bathing-place Jalatunda," in *Selected Studies in Indonesian Archaeology,* Koninklijk Instituut voor Taal-, Land- en Volkenkunde Translation Series 5. The Hague: Martinus Nijhoff, 1961. On the basis of analysis of reliefs of the Pandawa cycle at Djalatunda, Bosch hypothesizes that wajang drama existed as early as the fifth century A.D.

Brandon, James. R. "Indonesia," in *Reader's Encyclopedia of World Drama,* ed. John Gassner. New York: Thomas Crowell, 1969. A summary of the major characteristics of dramatic forms in Indonesia that emphasizes wajang kulit.

_____ "Indonesia's Wajang Kulit," *Asia,* 5 (Spring 1966), 51–61. Discusses the theatrical elements of wajang kulit which make this form so effective in performance.

_____ *Theatre in Southeast Asia.* Cambridge, Mass.: Harvard University Press, 1967. History and characteristics of wajang are described within the context of Southeast Asian performing arts. Gives an account of wajang in contemporary life, economic and social organization, government influence, and wajang as communication.

Hadisoeseno, Harsono. "Wayang and Education," *Education and Culture,* No. 8, Indonesian Ministry of Education and Culture (October 1955), pp. 1–19. A reliable introduction to the various forms of wajang, with emphasis upon the educative function of wajang kulit.

Holt, Claire. *Art in Indonesia: Continuities and Change.* Ithaca: New York: Cornell University Press, 1967. Chapter 5, devoted to wajang, provides a sensitive interpretation of wajang's history, characteristics, and significance. Solid scholarship, thorough bibliography, translations of early records, and synopses of eight wajang plays make this a valuable work (second only to Rassers) in spite of its brevity.

Bibliography

Hood, Mantle. "The Enduring Tradition: Music and Theatre in Java and Bali," in *Indonesia*, ed. Ruth T. McVey. New Haven, Conn.; Human Relations Area Files, 1963. Emphasizes the close interplay between wajang, gamelan music, and dance, and their cultural significance.

—— *The Nuclear Theme as Determinant of Patet in Javanese Music.* Groningen: J. B. Wolters, 1954. Includes an important analysis of how patet functions within wajang performance.

de Kleen, Tyra. *Wayang: Javanese Theatre*, 2nd ed. Stockholm: Gothia, 1947. The brief introduction is not dependable, but the detailed synopsis of the Sundanese wajang golek play *Arayana*, of which Ardjuna is the hero, illustrated with 17 drawings in color, is unique.

Kunst, Jaap. *Music in Java: Its History, Its Theory, and Its Technique,* 2 vols., 2nd ed., trans. Emile van Loo. The Hague: Martinus Nijhoff, 1949. The standard work on Javanese music, with several sections on the music of wajang kulit; also in Dutch.

Mangkunagoro VII of Surakarta. *On the Wayang Kulit (Purwa) and Its Symbolic and Mystical Elements,* trans. Claire Holt. Data Paper No. 27. Ithaca, N.Y.: Southeast Asia Program, Cornell University, 1957. An erudite exposition of some of the more esoteric aspects of wajang kulit drama, by a prince of Surakarta.

Mellema, R. L. *Wayang Puppets: Carving, Colouring, and Symbolism,* trans. Mantle Hood. Amsterdam: Royal Tropical Institute, 1954. The author's speculations on color symbolism of wajang puppets is the most interesting part of this small book. Also contains drawings of some iconographic features of the puppets.

Moebirman. *Wayang Purwa: The Shadow Play of Indonesia.* The Hague: van Deventer-Maasstichting, 1960. A small book (79 pages) with many illustrations in color. Simple, accurate, but sketchy.

Moerdowo. *Reflections on Indonesian Arts and Culture,* 2nd ed. Sourabaya: Permata, 1963. A brief introduction to wajang kulit in chapter 7.

Narasimhan, Chakravarthi V. *The Mahabharata: an English Version Based on Selected Verses.* New York: Columbia University Press, 1965. An excellent condensation of the Indian *Mahabharata* epic.

Rassers, W. H. *Panji, the Culture Hero: a Structural Study of Religion in Java.* Koninklijk Instituut voor Taal-, Land- en Volkenkunde Translation Series 3. The Hague: Martinus Nijhoff, 1959. In spite of a misleading title, most of the book consists of a provocative and exhaustive examination of the meaning and the origin of Javanese drama, with emphasis on wajang kulit.

DUTCH LANGUAGE

Hazeu, G. A. J. *Bijdrage tot de kennis van het Javaansche tooneel* (A study of Javanese theater). Leiden: E. J. Brill, 1897. The case for

Bibliography

Javanese origin of wajang is argued in this early, standard work.

Kats, J. *Het Javaansche toneel, I: Wajang Poerwa* (Javanese drama, vol. I: Wajang Purwa). Weltevreden (Batavia): Volkslectuur, 1923. Includes a comprehensive exposition of the plots and themes of 179 plays. The single most important book on wajang dramatic literature.

Serrurier, L. *De wajang poerwa: eene ethnologische studie* (Wajang Purwa: an ethnological study). Leiden: E. J. Brill, 1896. Important for its detailed chronology of traditional wajang kulit history as drawn from Javanese sources.

Tjan Tjoe Siem. *Hoe Koeroepati zich zijn vrouw verwerft.* (How Kurupati Takes A Bride). Leiden: Drukkerij Luctor et Emergo, 1938. A complete translation of the play *Kurupati Rabi* (Durjudana's Marriage), including suluk lyrics and indications of gending and stage action. The only translation of a wajang play into a European language.

INDONESIAN LANGUAGES

General Works

Hardjowirogo. *Sedjarah Wajang Purwa* (Genealogy of Wajang Purwa). Djakarta: Perpustakaan Perguruan, Kementerian P. P. dan K., 1955. Major figures in wajang plays are described and illustrated; in Indonesian.

Nojowirongko, M. Ng. *Serat Tuntunan Padalangan* (Guide to the art of the dalang), vols. I–IV. Jogjakarta: Djawatan Kebudajaan, Departemen P. P. dan K., 1960. The most comprehensive textbook for wajang kulit performance; in Javanese. Volume I covers music, puppet movements, dramatic structure, and vocal techniques. A script of *Irawan's Wedding (Irawan Rabi)* takes up volumes II through IV.

Poerbatjaraka, R. M. Ng. and Tardjan Hadidjaja. *Kepustakaan Djawa* (Javanese literature). Djakarta: Djambatan, 1952. Brief description of major works of classical Javanese literature; in Indonesian.

Probohardjono, R. Ng. S. *Gending-gending* (Instrumental melodies). Jogjakarta: Sinduniti, 1957. Melodies of 161 slendro mode gending used in Surakarta-style wajang kulit; in Javanese.

———— *Primbon Langen Swara* (Collection of traditional songs). Solo: Ratna, 1961. Traditional suluk lyrics and the use of suluk in wajang performance, in Javanese.

———— *Sulukan Slendro* (Songs in slendro mode). Surakarta: Ratna, 1966. Words and music of suluk used in Surakarta-style wajang; in Javanese.

Sajid, R. M. *Bauwarna Wajang* (Types of wajang). Jogjakarta: Pertjetakan Republik Indonesia, 1958. Lists standard puppets in a 400-piece set, types of facial expression, and Hazeu's chronology of wajang history; in Javanese.

Bibliography

Salmun, M. A. *Padalangan* (Art of the dalang). Djakarta: Balai Pustaka, 1961. A general textbook for the wajang golek performer in west Java, based on performance techniques and dramatic literature of wajang kulit; in Sundanese.

Seno-Sastroamidjojo, A. *Renungan Tentang Pertundjukan Wajang Kulit* (Wajang kulit and its performance). Djakarta: Kinta, 1964. History, characteristics, philosophy, performance techniques, and literature of wajang kulit; in Indonesian.

Sulardi, R. M. *Gambar Printjening Ringgit Purwa* (Detailed illustrations of wajang figures). Djakarta: Balai Pustaka, Kementerian P. P. dan K., 1953. Identifying characteristics of puppet figures—nose, eyes, mouth, body stance, hair, and decoration—are illustrated in line drawings; in Javanese.

Play Scripts and Play Scenarios

Kamadjaja, and U. J. Katidjo. *Lampahan Bratajuda* (The Great War), 3 vols. Jogjakarta: U. P. Indonesia, 1965 (vols. 1 and 2), 1966 (vol. 3). Condensed texts of three plays (*Seta Gugur, Bisma Mukswa,* and *Pedjahipun Angkawidjaja*) of the Great War, in Jogjakarta style; in Javanese.

Kodiron, Ki. *Kresna-gugat* (Kresna and the Great War). Surakarta: Tri-jasa, 1965. Play text and instructions for performance in Surakarta style; in Javanese.

———— *Lampahan Murtjalelana* (Abimanju as King Murtjalelana). Surakarta: Tri-jasa, 1964. Play text and instructions for performance in Surakarta style; in Javanese.

———— *Lampahan Sembadra-Larung* (The killing of Sumbadra). Surakarta: Tri-jasa, 1963 (?). Play text and instructions for performance in Surakarta style; in Javanese.

———— *Wahju Pantjasila* (The gift of the five principles.) Surakarta: Tri-jasa, 1964. Brief play text and instructions for performance in Surakarta style; in Javanese.

Prawirasoedirdja, Ki. *Pakem Wajang Purwa* (Wajang plot synopses), 2 vols. (vol. 2 with R. M. Sulardi). Solo: Sadu-Budi, 1960. Brief outlines of twenty and ten plays in Surakarta style; in Javanese.

Probohardjono, R. S. *Pakem Wajang Purwa* (Wajang plot synopses), 3 vols. Solo: Ratna (vols. 1, 3), Sadu-Budi (vol. 2), 1961–62. Brief plot synopses of fourteen plays in volume 1, sixteen in volume 2, and seventeen in volume 3 in Surakarta style: in Javanese.

———— *Parta Krama* (The marriage of Ardjuna). Surakarta: Mahabarata, 1966. Very complete play text and instructions for performance in Surakarta style; in Javanese.

Radyomardowo, M. B., Soeparman, and Soetomo. *Serat Baratajuda* (The Great War). Jogjakarta: Kedaulatan Rakjat, 1964. Detailed

Bibliography

synopses of the twelve plays which, in Jogjakarta-style wajang, make up the Great War. Based on performances held in the palace of the Sultan of Jogjakarta during 1958; in Javanese.

Reditanaja, Kjai Demang. *Pakem Pangruwatan Murwa Kala* (The exorcism play: the birth of Kala). Surakarta: Tri-jasa, 1967. Brief synopsis of scenes and explanation of prayers and offerings associated with the play; in Javanese.

Siswoharsojo, Ki. *Kresna Madeg Ratu* (Kresna becomes King). Jogjakarta: published by the author, 1961. Play text with instructions for performance in Surakarta style; in Javanese.

———— *Lampahan Ringgit Purwa Warni-warni* (Collection of wajang kulit plays). Jogjakarta: published by the author, 1960. Brief synopses of fifteen plays in Surakarta style; in Javanese.

———— *Makutharama* (The crown of Rama) Jogjakarta: published by the author, 1963. Play text with instructions for performance in Surakarta style; in Javanese.

———— *Pandhawa Mukswa* (Ascension of the Pandawas) Jogjakarta: published by the author, 1955. Play text with instructions to the dalang for performance in Surakarta style; in Javanese.

———— *Wahju Purba Sedjati* (The divine gifts of authority and truth). Jogjakarta: published by author, 1962. Play text with instructions to the dalang for performance in Surakarta style; in Javanese.

Soemantri Soemosapoetro, R. M. *Donorodjo.* Surakarta: Tri-Jasa, 1964 (?). Play text with instructions for performance in Surakarta style; in Javanese.

Soetarsa, Ki Slamet. *Lahiripun Rama–Brubuh Ngalengka* (The birth of Rama to the fall of Alengka). Solo: Keluarga Soebarno, 1964. Synopses of wajang plays based on the eighteen books of the *Ramayana,* without indications of scenes or performance techniques; in Javanese.

Sulardi, R., Kasidi, and Darmatjarita. *Serat Padhalangan Ringgit Purwa* Book of wajang kulit plays). Jogjakarta: U. P. Indonesia, 1965. Brief synopses of twelve plays in the collection of K.G.P.A.A. Mangkunagara VII of Surakarta, first published 1930–1932; in Javanese.

Wignjawirjanta, Ki. *Kartapijoga Tjidra* (Kartapijoga's betrayal). Solo: Keluarga Soebarna, 1961. Play text with instructions to the dalang for performance in Surakarta style; in Javanese.

———— *Kusumalelana.* Solo: Keluarga Soebarno, 1961. Play text with instructions to the dalang for performance in Surakarta style; in Javanese.

———— *Surjandadari (Bima Paksa).* Solo: Keluarga Soebarno, 1964. Play text with instructions to the dalang for performance in Surakarta style; in Javanese.

Glossary

Javanese and other foreign names and words appearing in the Introduction and the three translations are briefly defined here, with the exception of names of musical selections. Orchestral melodies (gending) can be found in Appendix A and mood songs (suluk) in Appendix B.

Abijasa: Ardjuna's grandfather, former king of Astina, holy teacher or seer; lives in Saptaarga hermitage.

Abimanju: Son of Ardjuna and Sumbadra, father of Parikesit; slain in the Great War by a barrage of hundreds of arrows.

ada-ada: One of three types of suluk, sung by dalang to accompaniment of one gender and beating of kepjak (see Appendix B).

adegan: Literally, "standing up," hence a scene; any scene except the first in Surakarta; a minor scene in Jogjakarta.

Adimenggala (Suradimenggala): Chief minister of Karna's kingdom of Awangga.

ageng: Literally, "great"; a suluk with lengthened lyrics.

Airlangga: Eleventh-century king of Java.

Alengka: Island kingdom ruled by ogre king Rawana in the Rama cycle; said to be Ceylon.

Allah: God of Islam.

alus: Refined; a puppet of a refined character.

Amarta (Ngamarta): Kingdom of the Pandawas ruled by Judistira; period of Pandawas' "Golden Age."

Amir Hamzah: Islamic hero of Menak cycle plays.

ampjak (prampogan; rampogan): Marching Army puppet depicting ranks of troops, cannon, battle flags.

Anantaboga: Dragon god, father-in-law of Bima.

Andini: Sacred cow on whom Guru stands.

angganter: Steady, fast tapping on the puppet chest with the tjempala.

Anggendari: Durjudana's mother.

Anoman: Monkey-warrior, serves Rama in Rama cycle and, in Pandawa cycle, Rama's incarnation, Kresna.

antawatjana: Technique of characterizing puppet figures by the pitch of the voice.

Glossary

Ardawalika: Serpent who tries to kill Ardjuna for slaying its parents.

Ardjuna: Middle of the five Pandawa Brothers, handsome, skilled warrior, spiritual son of the god Endra; the chief wajang hero.

Ardjuna Lahir (The Birth of Ardjuna): A play of the pandawa cycle.

Ardjuna Sasra Bau cycle: One of four purwa cycles of plays; takes name from hero who kills Rawana in a former life.

Ardjuna Wiwaha (The Meditation of Ardjuna): Original Javanese epic written in eleventh century.

Arimba: Former king of Pringgadani, ogre brother of Bima's wife Arimbi.

Arimbi: Ogress wife of Bima and mother of Gatutkatja.

Astina (Ngastina): Chief kingdom of Java, ruled by Durjudana of the Kurawas but disputed by the Pandawas.

Aswatama: Son of Durna, Kurawa ally, he survives the Great War.

Awangga: Karna's princedom.

Bagong: Third son of Semar; appears in Jogjakarta-style plays.

Baju: God of Wind, son of god Guru, spiritual father of Bima.

Baladewa: King of Mandura, elder brother of Kresna, ally of the Kurawas in the Great War.

banju tumetes: Literally, "dripping water"; slow, steady tapping on puppet chest with tjempala.

Bantjuring: Name given Tjakil puppet in *Irawan's Wedding*.

banyan: Wide-spreading tree, symbol of kingly authority.

Barandjana: Ogre king who rules Djongbiradji.

Basuki: A minor deity in Suralaja.

bedolan: Technique of removing puppets from the debog.

Begasuksma: Spirit of Indradjit of Rama cycle, reincarnated as crown prince of Tawanggantungan and son of Dasasuksma.

bersih desa: Literally, "village cleansing" ceremony; occasion for performance of play of animistic cycle.

Bhatti-Kavya: A Sanskrit version of the Rama epic; first Indian epic adapted into written Javanese.

Bima: Second of the Pandawa Brothers, spiritual son of god Baju, blunt and powerful warrior; has two or three sons in wajang.

Bima Bungkus (The Birth of Bima): A play of the Pandawa cycle.

blentjong: Oil lamp to cast puppet shadows.

bonang: Tuned set of inverted bronze bowls.

Brama: In wajang the God of Fire.

Bratajuda (The Great War): Concluding portion of the *Mahabarata* epic; dramatized in twelve wajang plays.

Bremani: Ancestor of the Pandawas, son of the god Brama.

budalan kapalan: Movement of puppets across the screen riding on horseback in the Outer Audience scene in patet nem.

camma rupa: Leather puppet; from a Ceylonese work, *Mahavamsa*.

chaya nataka: Shadow play (Sanskrit).

Glossary

dalang: Main performer in a wajang kulit play, who narrates, sings, speaks dialogue, directs musicians, and manipulates puppets.

Damarwulan: *See* wajang klitik.

dapur: *See* pokok.

Dasamuka: Rawana in a former life; antagonist of the Ardjuna Sasra Bau cycle of plays.

Dasasuksma: Spirit of Rawana (king of Alengka in Rama cycle); reincarnated as spirit-king of Tawanggantungan.

debog (gedebog): Banana trunks laid at base of kelir and into which puppets are stuck.

dempak: Large nose shape, thick with a bump at the end.

dero dug: Onomatopoetic name of triple rap on puppet chest with tjempala (like Morse code · – –); has several uses as signal to gamelan musicians.

Dewa Rutji: Personification of Bima's "divine essence."

Dewi Sri: Animistic Goddess of Rice.

Diponegoro: *See* wajang Djawa.

Djadjagwreka: An ogre king, spiritual brother of Bima.

Djajarasa: Foster brother of Karna, Kurawa ally.

Djajavarman II: Khmer king of the ninth century, probably raised in Java.

Djalatunda: Bathing place in east Java; reliefs of Pandawa cycle were carved there in tenth century.

djangkahan: Wide foot stance of large puppets.

djanturan: Narration introducing a major scene; intoned to pitch and rhythm of soft background music.

djedjer: Major audience scene, normally introduced with specific gending and djanturan; lakon djeder, *see* pokok.

Djembawati: Beautiful daughter of the ape-seer Djembawan; first wife of Kresna.

Djongbiradji: Ogre kingdom ruled by king Barandjana.

djugag: Literally, "short"; a suluk with shortened lyrics.

Drestaketu: Chief minister of king Drupada of Tjempala.

dudahan: Literally, "taken out"; wajang puppets taken from puppet chest and laid flat ready for use in performance.

dunuk: One of Semar's gold wanda; literally, "plump," showing him in a smiling mood.

Durga: Ferocious goddess and wife of god Kala.

Durgandasena: One of Durjudana's ninety-eight younger brothers.

Durjudana: Eldest of the ninety-nine Kurawa Brothers, king of Astina, chief antagonist of the Pandawas in pokok plays; is slain by Bima in the Great War.

Durna: Brahman seer and adviser of king Durjudana; teacher of both Kurawas and Pandawas.

Dursasana: second eldest and crudest of the Kurawa brothers.

Glossary

Durta: Foster brother to Karna and Kurawa ally.

Dutangada (Angada the Envoy): An Indian shadow play of the thirteenth century.

Dwarawati: Kresna's kingdom, literally, "Gate of the World."

Endra: A god, son of Guru, spiritual father of Ardjuna.

gabahan: Literally, "rice grain"; the most refined eye shape, long and thin.

Gadamadana: Burial ground of Mandura royal family.

gagah: Muscular; a puppet of the largest human type.

Gagakbengkol: Bima's chief minister.

Galijuk: Third of Tjakil's ogre companions; appears in *The Reincarnation of Rama*.

gambang: Xylophone of wooden keys.

gamelan: Musical ensemble which accompanies performance.

gapit: Main stick of puppet.

gapuran: Literally, "gate"; adegan gapuran is Gate scene, follows first scene of a play.

gara-gara: Literally "nature's turmoil," refers to description of natural calamities plus the clown scene which follows, in the patet sanga part of a play.

Gareng: Slow-thinking eldest son of Semar; serves the Pandawas.

garuda: Eagle.

Gatutkatja: One of Bima's several sons.

gedebog: *See* debog.

gelung keling: Conservative hair style with bun in the back.

gender: Xylophone of bronze keys suspended over resonating tubes.

gender barung: Most important gender; leads gamelan and gives dalang pitch during dialogue and tjarijos narration.

gending: Instrumental gamelan melody; accompanies puppet entrances, exits, and battles, and plays under djanturan (see Appendix A).

gerong: Unison singing of musicians during a gending.

geter: Literally, "heart beat"; music signal of double taps on puppet chest with tjempala.

ginem: Dialogue.

ginem wadya: Literally, "soldiers' dialogue"; in perang ampjak only.

Glagahtinulu: Battlecamp of Ardjuna during the Great War.

gombangan (ombak): Technique of dalang singing "ooo . . . ," or other meaningless syllable, instead of suluk lyrics.

gong: Large hanging gong.

grambjangan: *See* tingtingan.

grebeg: Thrice-yearly animistic festival; often occasion for performance of wajang.

Glossary

greget: Literally, "excitement"; causing audience to be aroused by the play's action.

gunungan: *See* Kajon.

guru: Teacher.

Guru: Heavenly Teacher (Batara Guru), chief god who appears in wajang, ruler of gods' kingdom of Suralaja; equivalent of Siwah (Shiva).

gusen: Literally, "gums"; sneering or foolishly laughing puppet figures with exposed gums.

Indradjit: Crown prince of Alengka and son of Rawana in the Rama cycle; his spirit reincarnates as Dasasuksma's son Begasuksma in *The Reincarnation of Rama.*

Irawan: Son of Ardjuna and Ulupi.

Ismaja: A local, pre-Hindu, Javanese god; is cursed and comes to earth in wajang in form of Semar.

Jadajana: Legendary son of Parikesit, and described as first "historical" king of Java.

Jasarata: Hermitage of the holy ascetic Kanwa.

Jogjakarta: A center of wajang kulit development in central Java.

Judistira: Eldest of the five Pandawa brothers; king of Amarta; so pure "His Blood Flows White"; spiritual son of god Darma.

kabogelan: Cut short; a performance which incorrectly ends before dawn.

Kajon (gunungan): Puppet representing "tree of life" or a mountain; marks the end of a scene or can represent forest, tomb, mountain, palace, or other location.

kaju: Literally, "wood"; possible source of word kajon.

kajun: Literally, "living"; possible source of word kajon.

kakawin: Old-Javanese epic in poetic form.

Kala: The god Kala; bloodthirsty and ferocious son of Guru; exorcised in ruwatan performance.

Kalimasada: Judistira's divine weapon, said to be inscribed with the Islamic profession of faith the Kalimat Sjahadah.

Kanwa: Irawan's grandfather, holy seer, lives in Jasarata hermitage.

karahinan: Daylight; a performance which continues past dawn is not correct.

karma: Religious concept that each human act receives its due punishment or reward, either in this life or future lives.

Karna: Son of the Sun God Surja; elder half-brother of the Pandawas, but allied with the Kurawas.

Kartamarma: One of Durjudana's younger brothers, third of the Kurawas.

Glossary

kasar: Coarse, crude, vulgar.

kaul: Literally, "vow," hence a thanksgiving performance for a favor received from the gods.

Kawi: Old-Javanese; the language used in kakawin epics.

kedatonan: Literally, "of the palace"; adegan kedatonan is the Inner Palace scene in patet nem.

kedelen: Literally, "soy bean"; medium-sized eye shape, of moderate refinement; a character with this type of eye.

kelir: The puppet screen.

kempul: Medium-sized hanging gongs.

Kendalisada: Hermitage where Anoman keeps watch over spirit of Rawana.

kendang: Two-faced drum beat with the fingers.

Kendanggumulung: One of Bima's officers.

kenong: Set of inverted bronze bowls.

kepjak (keprak; ketjrek): Four or five hanging bronze plates struck with foot or tjempala as sound effect.

keraton: Palace.

kereta: Chariot; adegan kereta is the Chariot scene which may occur in patet nem.

ketuk: Single inverted bronze bowl.

Kinanti: One of several poetic forms collectively called tembang matjapat.

kiwa: Left; wajang kiwa are the Pandawas' opponents, those puppets which face them from the left side of the screen.

kolik: Small bird whose melancholy call sounds like "ko-lik."

kotak: Large chest in which puppet set is kept.

krama: High-Javanese language.

Kresna: King of Dwarawati, an incarnation of Wisnu, first cousin and adviser of the Pandawas.

Kumbakarna: Brother of Rawana in the Rama cycle.

Kunti: Wife of Pandu; mother of Karna as well as Judistira, Bima, and Ardjuna.

Kurawa: Literally, "descendents of Kuru," the ninety-nine brothers and one sister who rule Astina, first cousins and enemies of the Pandawas.

Kuru: Ancestor of both Pandawas and Kurawas; in Pandawas' generation, Durjudana is ruler of the House of Kuru.

Kurusetra: Literally, "field of the Kurus," place where the Great War is fought.

Kuwera: God of Wealth; sometimes another name for Guru.

ladjer: *See* pokok.

Lahirpun Lara Ireng (The Birth of Sumbadra): A play of the Pandawa cycle.

Glossary

Lajarmega: Ogress, chief minister of ogre kingdom of Djongbiradji.

lakon: Play; story of a play, often in scenario form.

lampahan: Technique of moving puppets in walking, sitting, and standing.

langak: Up-turned gaze; puppet with an up-turned gaze.

lanjapan: A refined puppet whose head is erect and who looks aggressively forward.

Leksmana (Laksmana; Lesmana): Younger brother of Rama of the Rama cycle.

Lesmana Mandrakumara: Uncouth and foolish son of Durjudana; crown prince of Astina.

lijepan: Most refined puppet type, with modestly downcast face and gaze.

Limbuk: Fat and ugly female servant; appears in scenes set in the women's quarters of the palace.

Lodra: Name given Terong puppet in *The Reincarnation of Rama*.

longok: Intermediate gaze; puppet with an intermediate gaze, neither high nor low.

lugu: *See* pokok.

luruh: Narrow, refined puppet stance; downcast gaze of a puppet.

lutju: Joking of the clowns.

Madukara: Ardjuna's princedom.

Maenaka: Mythical mountain symbolizing one of nature's five powers; one of Bima's spiritual brothers.

Mahabarata: Epic about Pandawas and Kurawas written and told in many versions in Java; originally adapted from Indian epic of same name (Sanskrit, *Mahabharata*).

Mahameru: Great Mountain; home of the gods; often thought to be Mount Semeru on Java.

Mandraka: Kingdom ruled by king Salja.

Mandura: Kingdom ruled by king Baladewa, traditionally held to be the island of Madura.

mantra: Prayer.

Manumajasa: Son of Parikenan; fourth generation in Pandawa cycle.

Maritja: Spirit of ogre in Rama cycle who reincarnates as the ogre puppet Tjakil in *The Reincarnation of Rama*.

Mataram: Kingdom in central Java, established in sixteenth century; also earlier kingdom in east Java.

Matswapati: King of Wirata, ally of the Pandawas.

mawajang: Wajang performance.

mbangir: Most refined nose shape, long and tapering.

mega: Semar in a black wanda; literally, "cloud," meaning he is in a black or angry mood.

Glossary

Menak cycle: Plays dramatizing the exploits of the Islamic hero Amir Hamzah.

Mingkalpa: Minister of the ogre kingdom of Djongbiradji.

Montrokendo: Name given Terong puppet in *Irawan's Wedding*.

Mpu Sedah: Author of twelfth-century Javanese *Bratajuda* epic.

Murwakala (The Birth of Kala): Play in the animistic cycle of purwa plays.

Nakula: The fourth Pandawa Brother; with his twin, Sadewa, is a spiritual son of the twin Aswin gods.

nang sebek: Cambodian shadow puppets and play.

Narada: A god; elder cousin of Guru, and his adviser and emissary to earth.

Natya Sastra: Famous Indian treatise on Sanskrit dramaturgy.

nges: Technique of inducing mood of sadness in audience.

ngoko: Low-Javanese language.

nijaga: Musicians of the gamelan ensemble.

Nilikhanta: Seventeenth-century Indian commentator who described shadow theater in India.

njuluki: Technique of dalang singing meaningless syllable during a gending.

ombak: *See* gombangan.

pakem: Literally, "guide"; written form of a lakon, in a page or two of terse outline (pakem balungan or "bone guide"), an expanded form of scenario (pakem gantjaran or "prose guide"), or in script form including dialogue, narration, and music (pakem padalangan or "guide-for-the-dalang").

Palasara: Father of Abijasa; seventh generation in Pandawa cycle.

Pamade: Ardjuna's name when he is young.

Panataran: Fourteenth-century temple in east Java with reliefs of wajang-like figures.

Pandawa: Literally, "sons of Pandu" (Judistira, Bima, Ardjuna, Nakula, Sadewa), but can include their allies and children as well; the cycle of lakon about the Pandawas.

pandita: Literally, "holy teacher" or "seer"; djedjer pandita is the Hermitage scene in patet sanga or whatever scene occurs in its place (also djedjer pertapan).

Pandji: *See* wajang gedog.

Pandu: Once king of Astina; father of the five Pandawa brothers, uncle of the Kurawa brothers.

Paramajoga: History of Javanese kings written in Surakarta in nineteenth century.

Glossary

Parikenan: Son of Bremani; third generation in Pandawa cycle.

Parikesit: Abimanju's son, Ardjuna's grandson; last Pandawa ruler of Astina.

parva: Sanskrit for "volume" or "book" of an epic; possible source of Javanese word purwa.

pasarean: Graveyard; adegan pasarean is a cemetery scene.

paseban djawi: Literally, "outer audience hall"; adegan paseban djawi is a scene set in the outer audience hall of the first kingdom in the patet nem section of a play.

paseban djawi denawa: Outer Audience scene of a foreign, often ogre, kingdom (denawa means "ogre"), in patet nem.

Pasopati: Ardjuna's supernatural arrow with which Karna is killed.

patet: Literally "mode" or "key" of gamelan music; by extension the part of a play in which gamelan music of a particular patet is played; also an abbreviation of patetan, one type of suluk.

patet(an): One of three types of suluk mood songs, usually abbreviated to patet in suluk title (see Appendix B).

patet manjura: The third part of a wajang play; also indicates key or mode of gamelan music played in the third part of a play.

patet nem: The first part of a wajang play; also indicates key or mode of music played in the first part of a play.

patet sanga: The second part of wajang play; also indicates key or mode of music played in the second part of a play.

pelog: Scale of gamelan tuning in which the octave is divided into seven notes; some pelog melodies may be played in wajang kulit performance.

penjepenging: Technique of grasping the puppet.

perang: Combat or battle.

perang ageng: Jogjakarta term for perang amuk-amukan.

perang ampjak: A battle scene in patet nem of a play, in which the ampjak clears a path through a forest.

perang amuk-amukan (perang ageng): Final pitched battle of a play; literally, "running-amok battle."

perang begal: Jogjakarta term for battle between refined hero and forest ogres in place of Flower Battle in patet sanga, literally, "high-wayman battle."

perang gagal (perang simpangan): Opening skirmish between forces of the first and second kingdoms introduced in a play, which normally ends Part One; literally, "inconclusive battle."

perang gendiran: Jogjakarta term for perang kembang; literally, "flicking-arms battle," referring to hero's fighting movements.

perang kembang (perang gendiran): A combat in patet sanga of re-fined hero versus Tjakil and his companions; literally, Flower Battle.

perang sampak manjura (perang tandang): A battle in patet manjura fought to very loud, fast Sampak Manjura music.

Glossary

perang sampak sanga (perang tanggung): A battle in patet sanga fought to vigorous Sampak Sanga music.

perang simpangan: *See* perang gagal.

perang tandang: Jogjakarta term for perang sampak manjura.

perang tanggung: Literally, "middle battle"; *see* perang sampak sanga.

pertapan: Meditation; djedjer pertapan is Jogjakarta term for djedjer pandita.

pesinden: Female singer.

Petruk: Mischievous second son of Semar; serves the Pandawas.

pideksa: Medium body-build puppet figure.

Podangbinorehan: One of Bima's officers.

pokok: Literally, "trunk"; a trunk play dramatizes events as described in the epics and in Javanese mythology.

praba: Literally, "throne"; thronelike ornament worn on shoulders signifying kingship.

Prabawa: One of two chief ministers of king Baladewa.

Pragalba: Name given ogre figure in *The Reincarnation of Rama* and *Irawan's Wedding.*

Pragota: One of two chief ministers of king Baladewa.

prampogan: *See* ampjak.

Pringgadani: Princedom ruled by Gatutkatja.

punakawan: Clown-servant.

pupak-puser: Birth rite marking falling off of navel cord.

purwa: *See* wajang purwa.

Purwakala: See *Murwakala.*

Purwa Kanda: History of Javanese kingship written in Jogjakarta.

Pustaka Radja Madya: History of Javanese kings; basis of wajang madya.

Pustaka Radja Purwa: History of Javanese kingship written in Surakarta.

putri: Literally, "female"; adegan putri is a scene in which women appear as the main figures.

Rama: Prince and hero of the Rama cycle of plays.

Rama cycle: One of four purwa cycles of plays; based on Javanese Rama epics.

Ramayana: Epic about Rama.

rampogan: *See* ampjak.

Randugumbala: Bima's battle camp in the Great War.

Ranggawarsita: Nineteenth-century court poet; author of *Pustaka Radja Madya.*

raseksa (buta; denawa; rasaksa): Ogre or giant figure.

raseksa hutan: Literally, "forest ogre"; refined hero's opponents in perang begal.

Rawana: King of Alengka and Rama's bitter enemy in Rama cycle.

rebab: Two-stringed fiddle.

Glossary

remben: Hesitation or ragged transition between song, action, or dialogue.

Rukmini: Kresna's second queen.

rupiah: Indonesian currency.

rupopajivana: Term in the Indian *Mahabharata* epic which may refer to shadow theater.

rupparupakam: Term in a first-century B.C. Pali text which may refer to shadow theater in India.

ruwatan: Animistic exorcism; play *Murwakala* is performed as ruwatan.

sabetan: Inclusive term for puppet manipulation of all kinds.

sabrangan: Literally, "overseas," hence non-Javanese or foreign; djedjer sabrangan is scene in patet nem in which a second kingdom, most often a foreign ogre kingdom, is introduced.

sabrang rangkep: Literally, "repeat overseas" scene, that is, a scene introducing a third kingdom in patet nem.

Sadewa: The fifth Pandawa Brother; he and his twin, Nakula, are spiritual sons of the twin Aswin gods.

Sakri: Son of Sakutrem; sixth generation in Pandawa cycle.

Saksadewa: Ogre warrior of kingdom of Tawanggantungan.

Sakutrem: Son of Manumajasa; fifth generation in Pandawa cycle.

Salja: King of Mandraka and father-in-law of Karna, Baladewa, and Durjudana; though an ally of the Kurawas, he sympathizes with the Pandawas.

Samba: Crown prince of Dwarawati; Kresna's son.

Sandjaja: First cousin of both Kurawas and Pandawas; lives in Astina but sides with Pandawas in the Great War.

Sangkuni: Uncle of king Durjudana and chief minister of Astina.

Saptaarga: Hermitage of the holy seer Abijasa.

Saraita (Sarawita; Sarahita): Nicknamed Bilung; one of two clown-servants (with Togog) who serves sabrangan king.

saron: Xylophone of heavy bronze slabs.

sem: Love; technique of arousing romantic emotions in audience.

Semar: God-clown-servant who serves the Pandawas; actually the god Ismaja and elder brother of Guru.

sembada: Nose of medium size.

sembah: Greeting by an inferior to a superior indicating respect; hands, palms pressed together, are brought up to the face until thumbs touch nose.

sempalan: A tjarangan play which is wholly invented.

sendon: One of three types of suluk mood songs, most commonly sung during pathetic moments (see Appendix B).

Setyaboma: Youngest of Kresna's three wives.

Setyaki: Brother of Setyaboma, strong ally of Dwarawati.

Glossary

simpingan: Literally, "tapering ornament"; tapering arrangement of puppets in the debog on either side of the screen going from small near the center to large on the outside edges.

sinden: Singing of female singer(s) during gending.

Sinta: Rama's wife in the Rama cycle.

sirepan: Quiet playing of a gending during djanturan narration.

siti hinggil: Main audience hall of a palace; setting for major audience scenes.

Siti Sendari: Kresna's daughter, wife of Abimanju.

Situbanda: Name of an elephant, Bima's spiritual brother.

Siwah: Javanese for Shiva.

slendang: Scarf worn over one shoulder by religious ascetics and gods.

slendro: Gamelan tuning scale with five notes to the octave; slendro gamelan ensemble accompanies wajang kulit performance.

Srikandi: Second of Ardjuna's wives, an adventuresome female warrior; daughter of king Drupada.

Sri Mantuk: A play of the animistic cycle.

Sri Unon: Daughter of Wisnu; second generation in Pandawa cycle.

Sujudana: Another name for Durjudana; *su* means "good."

Sukasalja: An incarnation of Rawana's beloved nymph Widawati.

suling: Flute.

suluk: Mood songs sung by the dalang; there are three types: patet(an), sendon, and ada-ada (see Appendix B).

Sumbadra: Ardjuna's chief wife, modest and quiet younger sister of Baladewa and Kresna.

Sunan of Giri: Sixteenth-century Islamic Javanese ruler.

Sunan of Kudus: Sixteenth-century Islamic Javanese ruler.

supit urang: Literally, "shrimp's tong"; curling hairdress of Ardjuna, Bima, and other figures.

Surakarta: A major center where wajang kulit developed in central Java.

Suralaja: Kingdom of Guru and other Javanese gods, on Mahameru.

Surengbaja: Forest; site of Suwega-Drestaketu battle.

Surja: Sun God, father of Karna.

Surtikanti: Karna's wife, one of king Salja's three daughters.

Suwega: An Awangga officer, sent by Karna to kill Ardjuna.

tajungan: Bima's victory dance in patet manjura.

Talu: Introductory music played before performance, about thirty minutes long, consists of several melodies (in Surakarta-style: Tjutjurbawuk, Pareanom, Srikaton, Sukmailang, Ajak-ajakan Manjura, Srepegan, and Sampak).

tantjeban: Technique of placing a puppet in the debog.

tantjeb kajon: Literally, "planting the kajon"; djedjer tantjeb kajon is the concluding scene of a play.

Glossary

Tawanggantungan: Ogre kingdom ruled by spirit-king Dasasuksma.

telengan: Round, staring eye shape of the largest human puppets.

tembang matjapat: Poems sung by characters (usually clowns), in various meters and rhyme schemes.

tengen: Right; wajang tengen are the Pandawas and their allies, those puppets which appear on the right side of the screen.

Terong: Literally, "eggplant nose"; name of puppet of clumsy ogre companion of Tjakil; *see also* Lodra; Montrokendo.

tingkeb: Seventh month of pregnancy and occasion for wajang performance.

tingtingan (grambjangan): Quiet improvising on gender barung to give dalang his pitch during dialogue.

Titisari: One of Kresna's daughters, married to Ardjuna's son Irawan.

Tjakil: Literally, "Fang"; name of the puppet figure who is chief ritual antagonist to refined hero in perang kembang, named Maritja in *The Reincarnation of Rama* and Bantjuring in *Irawan's Wedding*.

Tjakra: Kresna's divine, disk-tipped weapon.

Tjangik: Female clown-servant, mother of Limbuk; appears in scenes set in women's quarters of a palace.

tjarangan: Literally, "branch," and hence a play invented or departing from events in epics or mythology.

tjarijos: Narration of action spoken without background gending.

tjarijos kadjantur: Tjarijos, but with gending background.

tjarijos pagedongan: Literally, "in-the-building narration"; description of action within a building without action being shown by puppets.

tjelempung: Plucked zither.

tjempala: Two tapering wooden tappers hit against puppet chest or metal plates for sound effects and music signals.

Tjempala: King Drupada's kingdom.

tjempurit: Collective term for main stick and arm sticks of puppet.

Tjitraksa: One of Durjudana's ninety-eight younger brothers.

Tjitraksi: One of Durjudana's ninety-eight younger brothers.

Tjitrawati: One of four incarnations of the nymph Widawati.

Togog: Javanese clown-servant who serves sabrangan king with Saraita; considered brother of Semar.

trampil: Adroitness in puppet manipulation techniques.

tuding: Arm stick(s) of puppet.

tutuk: Clear presentation of plot during performance.

Udawa: Chief minister and half-brother of Kresna.

Ulupi: One of Ardjuna's wives; mother of Irawan.

unggah-ungguh: Court customs and etiquette dalang must know.

Utari: Daughter of king Matswapati, wife of Abimanju, mother of Parikesit.

Glossary

vidusaka: Stock clown-servant in Indian Sanskrit drama.

wahju: Gift or boon from the gods.

wajang beber: "Paper-scroll play"; dalang narrates story as he shows audience picture scrolls.

wajang Djawa: Shadow play about prince Diponegoro and the Java War (1825–1830); rarely performed.

wajang dupara: Shadow play depicting events of Surakarta history.

wajang gedog: Shadow play dramatizing adventures of mythological Javanese hero prince Pandji; occasionally performed.

wajang golek: Literally, "doll-puppet play"; purwa cycle plays performed in Sunda (west Java) and Islamic Menak cycle plays performed in central Java by three-dimensional doll-puppets; often seen.

wajang klitik (wajang krutjil): Play cycle about Damarwulan of Madjapahit period (c. 1300–1520); puppets are of flat wood; rarely performed.

wajang kulit: Literally, "shadow play," but specifically refers to chief form of shadow play in which purwa cycle plays are performed.

wajang madya: Literally, "middle wajang"; cycle of plays linking early purwa cycle with later Pandji cycle and performed as shadow drama; rarely seen.

wajang Menak (wajang tengul): Islamic Menak cycle plays performed by leather shadow puppets.

wajang orang (or wajang wong): Literally, "human wajang"; purwa plays performed as dance-drama by live cast.

wajang Pantja Sila: Shadow plays in which the five Pandawas are presented symbolically as the five principles of Pantja Sila.

wajang purwa: Purwa literally is "original"; wajang purwa consists of four cycles of mythological plays of which the Pandawa cycle is most important; purwa plays were created in wajang kulit and comprise its repertory.

wajang suluh: Shadow plays dramatizing events of Indonesia's revolutionary struggle, using realistically carved and painted puppets; occasionally performed.

wajang tengul: See wajang Menak.

wajang topeng: Masked dance-play; chief figure is prince Pandji.

wajang wahana: Shadow play of events of the 1920's; rarely performed.

wana: Literally, "forest"; adegan wana is a forest scene.

wanda: Emotion or mood of a character; puppets of a major wajang figure will be carved and painted in several different wanda.

wangsalan: A word cue indicating to gamelan musicians the title of the gending the dalang next wishes them to play.

wantah: Literally, "normal"; a suluk of normal length.

Glossary

Widawati: A heavenly numph loved by Rawana; she reincarnates as Sinta in the Rama cycle and as Sumbadra in the Pandawa cycle.

Widjajadanu: Karna's supernatural arrow.

Wirata: Kingdom ruled by Matswapati, twice the refuge of the Pandawas.

Wisnu: With Siwah (Shiva) and Brama form the trinity of Hindu gods; in wajang is son of Guru, ancestor of the Pandawas, and the source of the virtues reincarnated in Kresna and Ardjuna.

Wrtta Sancaja (Treatise on Poetic Composition): East Javanese court composition of the fifteenth century.

Index

Index

Index

Index

Index

Index

Index

Index